SCOTTISH FOOTBALL
QUOTATIONS
3

I always turn to the sports pages first. They record people's accomplishments; the front page, nothing but a man's failure.

Earl Warren, former Chief Justice,
U.S. Supreme Court and chair
of the Warren Commission, July 1968.

The glory of the sports pages is but the worship of false idols, and tempts him not.

Billy Bragg, 1996.

SCOTTISH FOOTBALL QUOTATIONS 3

Kenny MacDonald

BLACK & WHITE PUBLISHING

First published 2009
by Black & White Publishing Ltd
29 Ocean Drive, Edinburgh EH6 6JL

1 3 5 7 9 10 8 6 4 2   09 10 11 12 13

ISBN: 978 1 84502 276 1

A CIP catalogue record for this book is available from the British Library.

Quotation from 'God's Footballer' copyright BMG Music Publishing Limited.
Used by kind permission of Billy Bragg.

Typeset by Ellipsis Books Ltd, Glasgow
Printed and bound by MPG Books Ltd, Bodmin

Contents

For Cath, Jack and Ben

Acknowledgements

Thanks: Doug Baillie, Bill Bateson, Gareth Davies, Kevin Donnelly, Jim Duffy, Martin Frizell, John Gahagan, Roberto Manservisi, Phil Shaw.

Hello: my mother, Gary Armitage, David Belcher, David Bellew, Gavin Berry, Aleksandr Bobrov, David Brown, Graeme Bryce, Sandy Bryson, Craig Campbell, Graeme Croser, Billy Davies, Andy Devlin, Gordon Dryden, Mike Dunn, Ray Farningham, David Farrell, Alan Ferguson, Jan-Erik Fjeld, Michael Grant, Robert Grieve, Mark Guidi, Davie Irons, Ross Jack, Graeme Kerr, Miodrag Krivokapic, Bill Leckie, David Leslie, Lindsay MacDonald, Colin McAdam, Gary McAllister, Ian McCall, Ally McCoist, Scott McDermott, John McGarry, Jim McInally, Stevie McKenzie, Alex McLeish, Steven McNeil, Fraser Mackie, Danny Marlin, Michael Marra, Steve Morrison, Eric Musgrave, Pat Nevin, Dennis Newall, Alan Pattullo, Barrie Prescott, R.E.M., Stuart Rafferty, Tommy Reilly, Rob Robertson, Ron Scott, Walter Smith, Graham Spiers, Simon Stainrod, Gregor Stevens, Scott Struthers, Rudi Vata, Loudon Wainwright III, Bobby Williamson, Ian Wood.

ADVOCAAT ⚽

He was a wee bulldog of a player, all muscles, with these fat calf-muscles on his legs, who would launch himself with two feet into the tackle. Dick was never a Cruyff but the fans loved him in Holland – Dunfermline manager **Jimmy Calderwood** on Dick Advocaat, August 2001. The pair played and coached in Holland at the same time.

Dick Advocaat turned to me and said, 'Hugh, am I dreaming?' I just smiled and said, 'Naw, Dick, you're having a nightmare' – Referee **Hugh Dallas**, on the 6–2 Celtic victory over Rangers in August 2000, March 2003. Dallas was fourth official in the game.

Sometimes you need to be more friendly with the players who aren't playing – Ex-Rangers defender **Lorenzo Amoruso** on Advocaat, November 2002.

We would never pass in the corridors of Murray Park without him greeting me warmly, and that wasn't true of all the guys in the Rangers side. Dick knew I would play for him whenever called upon, and that wasn't true of every player in the squad either – Former Rangers striker **Billy Dodds**, February 2003.

When big Oz joined Borussia Munchengladbach the first thing Dick said to him was, 'Craig, how is your friend Billy? I always liked him. If not as a player, then certainly as a person.' – **Billy Dodds** recalls Dick Advocaat sending him good wishes – sort of – via defender Craig Moore, May 2008.

Various players served their time on the bench, but (Ronald) de Boer always played. Gabriel Amato – an absolutely superb forward – played only three games, and sat out the rest of his time in Glasgow as a sub. He must have asked himself why be bothered leaving sunny Mallorca – Former Rangers winger **Andrei Kanchelskis** on life under Advocaat at Rangers, August 2003.

Guys like Andrei Kanchelskis always struggled with Advocaat. I used to sit next to Andrei in the mornings and wee Dick would always say, 'Hello Billy, good morning'. But he just blanked poor Andrei – Former Rangers striker **Billy Dodds**, May 2008.

We ended up with no less than ten Dutchmen at Ibrox – six players and the various people behind the scenes. It became more usual to hear Dutch in the dressing room than English and inevitably we ended up with a clan culture – **Andrei Kanchelskis** on life under Advocaat at Rangers, August 2003.

The thing I never liked about Advocaat was that, after 100 years of Rangers history, along he comes and tries to change the rules. He was someone who demanded respect, but wouldn't give it. I can't get on with people like that.

I see respect as a mutual thing. (Walter) Smith and (Graeme) Souness had both done well before him, but he wanted to bring Dutch ways to Scotland. If someone came to coach Milan and tried to bring British club methods, they'd be getting everything wrong – AC Milan's former Rangers midfielder **Rino Gattuso**, March 2003.

To this day, I don't know why Advocaat signed me. Or Allan (Johnston) for that matter. Kenny (Miller) was a bit different because he was younger, but I don't think Advocaat ever had any plans to play either me or Allan. Allan stuck it out and got one or two games, but, for the talent he has, he never got a fair chance either – Former Rangers defender **Paul Ritchie**, January 2004. Ritchie was signed by Advocaat in June 2000 then sold to Manchester City for £500,000 77 days later without playing a competitive game.

I also get criticised for Paul Ritchie and Allan Johnston but they came for free and we ended up making £1.4m on these players. We took a gamble on them but I saw in training that they were not good enough for Rangers so I moved them on. I admit I didn't think about their feelings. I thought about Rangers. Of course people feel sorry for them, especially for Ritchie who is a good person and who has always been very polite. But it's not my job to feel sorry for players. My job is to look after the interests of the club – **Advocaat**'s take on the transfers, September 2002.

I think a big part of being a good manager is man-management and Advocaat was very, very poor – Former Rangers midfielder **Derek McInnes**, April 2004.

I have no peace in my body. Sometimes I see people sitting on balconies. Then I think to myself, 'What is that, sitting on the balcony with a cup of tea?' I've never done it – Holland coach **Dick Advocaat**, May 2004.

We collected the money in just three minutes. All he needs is his passport. He doesn't have to come back to the Netherlands – Dutch fan **Johan de Laat**, June 2004, after arranging a whipround to buy Advocaat a plane ticket out of Portugal at Euro 2004. Advocaat had made a controversial substitution, replacing Arjen Robben against the Czech Republic. 2–1 up at the time, the Dutch lost 3–2 – but still went on to qualify and reach the semi-finals.

Why did it happen? Maybe because some of the substitutions weren't good. (Arjen) Robben played a very good match and, if I was the trainer, that's not a change I would have made. It's always easy to say these things after the match, but I personally think it had to do with the changes – Barcelona striker **Patrick Kluivert**, June 2004, after the 3–2 defeat to the Czech Republic at Euro 2004.

Dick Advocaat should be hung. No, that would be too quick, he should be stoned – Dutch TV host **Jan Mulder**, after the Holland v Czech Republic game, June 2004.

When people talk about stoning and hanging you, I don't find that normal – **Advocaat**'s response, June 2004.

This is outrageous. I don't think this kind of thing should be allowed – you only need one idiot who will actually do something like this – Dutch Prime Minister **Jan Peter Balkenende** steps into the Advocaat debate, June 2004.

From the first day of the season I realised that me and Dick Advocaat couldn't get on together. At the time I had just signed my first boot deal with an Italian brand, 'La Pantofola d'Oro', and I was wearing this brand-new pair of blue boots when Dick Advocaat said to me, 'What do you think you're doing with these shoes? These are made for champions, you're just a youngster, take them off or you won't train today.' That was the start. So after a few weeks I stormed into the dressing room and said to Advocaat that we had 20–25 days to find a solution or it would have not worked for us. During my career I've been very lucky in having an exceptional relationship with all the managers I've worked with – everyone but Advocaat. Credit to my wife Monica, who calmed me down a lot at the time, because every day I woke up determined to go to Ibrox and have a fight with Advocaat – Milan midfielder **Rino Gattuso**, on Italian TV show *Sfide*, March 2008.

Advocaat said that I asked him to come back. I've got a very strange memory; I can't remember. It would have been tongue in cheek. The whole thing with Dick is he doesn't drink, so he might be telling the truth – Rangers chairman **Sir David Murray**, November 2008, on previous reports Advocaat had been asked to return to Rangers.

Do you know Michael Bolton? I know him personally and I went to one of his concerts in Korea. He came with two bodyguards and I came with nine bodyguards. In Korea people were more interested in seeing me than seeing Michael. I had nine months there. That was more than enough, otherwise you will get a really big head – Zenit St Petersburg boss **Dick Advocaat**, on his spell as South Korea national coach, May 2008.

Those who say he is arrogant can't know him at all. Dick isn't arrogant in the slightest – Dunfermline manager **Jimmy Calderwood**, August 2001.

AGE

I'm not scared of growing old, but I'm scared of losing my humour, because once you do I think it's time to depart – Southampton manager **Gordon Strachan**, January 2003.

As long as my Zimmer frame gets oiled weekly then I'm not too bad – Sheffield United's 38-year-old **Stuart McCall** after helping his side to the Division One play-off Final, April 2003.

People have said my legs have gone but they are talking crap. If I have been left out of the team this season it has not been because of fitness – 33-year-old Celtic midfielder **Paul Lambert**, June 2003.

People ask me what I'll do when I retire but I'm happy as a pig in shite when I'm with my pigeons. There's not enough hours in a day for me – Partick Thistle manager **John Lambie** contemplates retirement, in *Fanatical About Football*, ed. Jeff Connor, 2003.

I'm an adolescent about football. I'll quit when I grow up – Preston manager **Craig Brown**, then 63, January 2004.

It's not been a great week. I played my dad at golf yesterday and was beaten after 13 holes by a 68-year-old man with a bad limp – Celtic manager **Gordon Strachan** after the Champions League second qualifying round defeat by Artmedia Bratislava, July 2005.

I have not come up here on an ego trip or to unwind. People think I am 94, not 34. I'm not necessarily in the game to be popular – **Roy Keane** on joining Celtic, December 2005. He played 13 games for the club.

I didn't want to be 40, telling my kids, 'I played in the Nou Camp,' or 'I kicked this guy in the head,' or 'I failed a medical at four clubs'. They'd be saying, 'What's he on about?' – West Brom's **John Hartson**, December 2006.

Whenever the lads took the piss I'd say, 'Boys, I'm the only man who's getting paid to go bald.' – **John Hartson** on his newspaper advert for Advanced Hair Studio, February 2007.

You keep forgetting Evander Sno's only 19. When I was 19, I was trying to get into nightclubs, not the Champions League – Celtic's **Paul Telfer** after the young Dutch midfielder's performance against AC Milan in the San Siro, March 2007.

Age and experience alter your priorities and remind you of what's important in life. Which is? Let's see . . . well, there's love, family, the path towards enlightenment and, of course, football – Actor **Dougray Scott**, February 2008.

Because of the age I'm at you say to yourself, 'If you have too many disappointments, you're not going to get another job'. If I was in my mid-40s I'd have another reasonable opportunity. But I know that's limited – Rangers manager **Walter Smith**, the day before defeating Fiorentina to reach the UEFA Cup Final, April 2008.

The older you get, the last thing you want to identify with is people who are twenty years younger than you. That's a problem for me, especially – they'll only let themselves do it with footballers – KLF main man **Bill Drummond**, June 2008.

The older I get, the more frightened I get of retiring – Manchester United manager **Sir Alex Ferguson**, October 2008.

BAD DAY ⚽

I've tried to erase it from my memory. I had a stinker. It was an absolute nightmare. I was probably back in Edinburgh before the ground had emptied. I've never drunk so much in my life as that night, and in the morning the nightmare was still going on. The papers were full of it. I threw my medal in my bag, and I've never even opened the box to look at it. And I never will – **Gordon Marshall** recalls playing for Celtic against Raith Rovers in the November 1994 League Cup Final, March 2002.

Despite the fact it was just four days before one of the biggest games in the history of the club, I was as drunk as I'd ever been. I couldn't see straight when I walked out of the restaurant. Tosh McKinlay took advantage of my condition and managed to squeeze my head through some railings. It was a great day and exactly what we needed – Former Celtic goalkeeper **Jonathan Gould** on a drunken day out the Tuesday before the title-clinching win over St Johnstone in May 1998, quoted in Mark Guidi, *The Inner Sanctum*, 2008.

People seem surprised when I tell them, but I was never terrified or worried for my safety that day. The truth is that the only time I ever have felt really threatened was when I was refereeing a junior match early in my career. The police were called that day but I don't know if they ever arrived because I was changed and out of there as fast as possible – Referee **Hugh Dallas**, March 2003, on the league-deciding Old Firm game of May 1999, when he was hit by a coin.

I don't care about great entertainment for the fans with a nine-goal game – because that was a complete disgrace from my squad. We have a cup game coming up against Livingston and in the next few days I would really like to go out and sign six new players. Some might say not playing well and winning is okay – not me. To me a 1–0 defeat with the correct attitude through the team is much more acceptable. But a 5–4 win with a defence that was just a total disgrace is just not on – Partick Thistle manager **John Lambie** after a 5–4 Second Division win over Queen of the South, February 2000. (see under 'The Game' for more of the clearly dissatisfied Lambie's views on this game.)

We might have been playing brilliant football for all I know – Kilmarnock boss **Bobby Williamson** after being unable to see the first half of a fog-shrouded game against St Mirren, December 2000. Kilmarnock were 1–0 down at half-time but won 3–1.

When I take all the bullshit I had to contend with into account, it's a wonder we didn't finish fifth in the league, never mind second – Former Celtic coach **John Barnes** on his spell in charge in 1999–2000. Celtic finished 21 points behind champions Rangers.

There was so much shit flying about at Celtic during that time that you didn't know if you were eating your dinner or having a haircut. And sometimes you can get caught up in that – Former Celtic midfielder **Craig Burley** on ex-Parkhead no. two Eric Black, January 2004.

It's almost theft taking money after a performance like that. I'll be using the winter break to make the players' lives as miserable as possible – Hearts manager **Craig Levein** after defeat at Aberdeen, 2001.

When people say to me Celtic had a few bad years I think, 'Yeah, well, your bad year is finishing fourth in the league and not making it to the Scottish Cup Final. Our bad years are getting relegated, going 20 games without beating Hearts or almost going bust.' Nobody who follows the Old Firm has any conception about what it's like to follow a team that does not win – **Charlie Reid**, Proclaimer and Hibs fan, quoted in *Fanatical About Football*, ed. Jeff Connor, 2003.

In 35 years as a professional, I've never been involved in a game of football like that – Newcastle boss **Graeme Souness** after losing 4–1 at home to Fulham, November 2004. Newcastle had 19 corners (to Fulham's none) and 26 shots at goal in the game.

I played with Kenny Dalglish not long ago and he's a cheat – Former Wet Wet Wet singer **Marti Pellow** on his golfing pal, February 2005.

Brian Quinn, who has done gigantic work for the club – he has been unselfish, dedicated, balanced, visionary, respectful. Every good adjective I could use, he has been for the club. When you see someone like that who is embarrassed by a section of the crowd, I would expect the majority who disagree with it to clap and knock down the din. To me that was a black day in my involvement with the club. It was nearly as black as Seville was good – Majority shareholder **Dermot Desmond** to the Celtic Supporters Association, December 2005. Celtic chairman Quinn had been booed at half-time in a game against Hearts in April 2005.

I have been a manager for eight years and a player for 25. This is out and out the worst football night I have ever had – Celtic manager **Gordon Strachan** on the 5–0 Champions League second qualifying round defeat by Artmedia Bratislava, July 2005.

When I die, the inscription on my headstone should read, 'This is much better than Bratislava.' – Celtic manager **Gordon Strachan**, *My Life In Football*. His side lost 5–0 away to Artmedia Bratislava in the Champions League second qualifying round in his first competitive game in charge in July 2005.

They took everything from the groin area and at this moment in time there isn't anything there so I'm clear. That doesn't mean it won't come back. It may come back whenever. – Sadly prophetic words from Celtic coach **Tommy Burns**, July 2006, after his second cancer operation. He died in May 2008.

It had been coming and then it happened. It was the right thing for (Manchester) United, maybe not the right thing for Roy Keane, maybe not for Alex Ferguson, but for the club. I always said when the day came, I'd be ready. Locker cleaned out the evening before: I was ready – **Roy Keane** on leaving Manchester United, September 2006.

Yeah, I wobbled inside. But people forget I'd been there before. When I was a young player at Aberdeen, I used to get booed at first when I went to Pittodrie. I was one of those players who used to get abuse every time the ball was passed to me – you'd hear this loud groan – and when I got the chance to leave Aberdeen to go to Bristol City at that time, I thought, 'Naw, I'm going to stay here another year and really annoy this lot, or prove that I really can play.' – Manager **Gordon Strachan** on early problems at Celtic, June 2007.

Just to get that taken away is like a candle being blown out. It was undoubtedly the most remarkable seven years of my life – Former Gretna manager **Rowan Alexander** as the club folds, June 2008.

With Gretna, it was a matter of when, not if. I have great sympathy for some individuals there, but as a club they weren't very magnanimous. They steam-rollered everyone else by paying astronomical wages – and then every other chairman had his fans shouting at him, asking why we can't spend more money. But I'm afraid Gretna's success was built on nothing. – Airdrie Chairman **Jim Ballantyne**, after Gretna's demise, July 2008.

The terrible memories are coming through those main doors and being sent upstairs to the boss's office and to be told you're no longer part of Rangers. I got released on the back of an injury, smashed my cartilage. They said they'd keep an eye on me but that's just a polite 'f*** off' – TV chef and former Rangers youth player **Gordon Ramsay**, *The F Word* TV show, July 2008.

If there's even a minor disturbance, a bit of trouble in the crowd maybe, it all comes flooding back – Former Nottingham Forest defender **Terry Wilson** on playing at the Hillsborough disaster in 1989, 20 years later, April 2009.

He's one of the most honest players in the game and to miss the final, it's a tragedy – Manchester United manager **Sir Alex Ferguson** after Darren Fletcher's unlucky red card against Arsenal ruled him out of the Champions League Final, 5 May 2009.

I honestly believed the referee made the right decision at the time. From his angle – and from mine – it looked like a penalty. It was only when I saw the replay that I saw that Darren had managed to get his leg round Fabregas and flick the ball away – Manchester United manager **Sir Alex Ferguson** on the Fletcher red card, 8 May 2009.

BERTI ⚽

A team of eleven Berti Vogts would be unbeatable – England striker **Kevin Keegan** after playing against the German defender, 1975.

Some sceptics may claim that he only accepted the position because he lacked options, but that would be unfair. I don't believe for a moment it's true, either. Somebody with his pedigree and reputation would be wanted, all right. But I do know he has always admired British football and it didn't surprise me that he should be keen to go to Scotland – Manchester United manager **Sir Alex Ferguson** on new Scotland manager Berti Vogts, March 2002.

What's the guy's name? Vorti Begts? I don't like Germans. They shot my dad – Former Nottingham Forest manager **Brian Clough** on Vogts, 2003.

One thing I can bring to the job is that I have never been beaten by England as a manager – Newly-appointed Scotland coach **Berti Vogts**, 2002.

I don't understand how you can go and hound him after six games. What do you do? Does he leave, then somebody else comes in and they've got to start again? What if it doesn't go right again, do people say, 'Get him out too'? – Scotland midfielder **Paul Lambert** on Vogts after the 2–2 draw in the Faroes, September 2002.

You could put together the achievements of every player in Scotland and they still won't have done between them what he has done in his career. Germany are expected to win things, not just qualify. That's a massive pressure he's had to deal with in the past, which people tend to overlook – Scotland midfielder **Paul Lambert** on Vogts, after the 2–2 draw in the Faroes, September 2002.

I can't see what Berti is attempting to do. Where are the tactics? Where's the discipline? – **Gunter Netzer**, former Germany teammate, after Vogts' Scotland drew in the Faroes, September 2002.

For years Berti Vogts warned German football experts that there are no small football nations any more. But he was wrong: Berti and his Scotland team are now the tiniest football country – **Bild**, German newspaper, after the Faroes game, 2002.

There's always a problem when a foreign coach comes in. It was the same with Ivano Bonetti when he wanted to put something across to the players. It must be hard for Berti Vogts, but he needs to come up with some sort of interpreter. It's up to him or the SFA to sort it out – Dundee defender **Lee Wilkie**, March 2003.

He needs to explain himself better when he leaves somebody out of the squad. He's obviously got a reason behind it, but he should take players aside so they know what's happening. I didn't know why I had been left out – Dundee defender **Lee Wilkie**, March 2003. He'd been dropped from the Scotland squad by Vogts for a friendly against Ireland the previous month. Later that month he scored the winner for Scotland in a European Championship qualifier against Iceland.

He (Vogts) has come in at probably the worst time, because the quality is not brilliant. But, two to three years down the line, you will see a resurgence – Scotland's English scout **Archie Gemmill**, June 2003.

Berti talked about the 5–0 defeat by France in March 2002 and said what a great learning curve it was for the players but I'm sorry, I don't believe players learn much from getting hammered 5–0 – Former Scotland international **Craig Burley**, November 2003.

Exactly how long are we going to experiment? Berti's been in the job for nearly two years, so are we going to experiment for five years? Are we waiting on a baby boom to produce some new talent? Let's cut the bullshit – Former Scotland international **Craig Burley**, February 2004.

By the amount of players he's picked Berti has shown that he doesn't have a clue what his next 22 is going to be – Former international **Craig Burley** before the 4–0 defeat by Wales, February 2004.

It's shameful what's happening with that guy and I think we should support and encourage him. I've seen mass murderers and rapists not getting the abuse that Berti's getting for being a football manager. It's ridiculous – Hibs boss **Bobby Williamson** defends Vogts after criticism of the Scotland boss following the 4–0 defeat by Wales, February 2004.

I tell you very clearly we will be in Germany in 2006 on the pitch playing, not in the stand drinking Coca-Cola and eating hot dogs – Defiant **Berti Vogts** names his squad for a friendly against Romania, March 2004. Scotland lost 2–1. Vogts resigned eight months later.

It is a fallacy that Vogts can't get his point across because of the language barrier. I've been in the squad and there's no barrier there whatsoever. What we need are different ideas and better ideas. We need fresh impetus and a fresh approach from somebody who puts players in their correct positions – Former international **Craig Burley**'s view on Vogts, after the draw in Moldova in what was Vogts' last game in charge of Scotland, October 2004.

I only worked once with Berti Vogts before he changed it. Vogts came up with some rubbish in the papers that I had told Rab Douglas he was going to play the second half of the game in France. I was disgusted and it was an insult. I never did that. I wrote Vogts a letter but he hasn't had the decency to reply – Former Scotland goalkeeping coach **Alan Hodgkinson**, February 2005.

The nuclear winter of Berti Vogts' reign – Journalist Michael Grant, *Sunday Herald* newspaper, September 2007.

The thing I didn't know was that Berti Vogts was the German coaching the football team and I didn't realise the massive antipathy towards him. It was wrongly placed because it was based on racial grounds and when he left, that got placed on me – Former Scotland rugby coach **Matt Williams**, November 2007. Australian Williams was the first foreign Scotland rugby coach. He won three tests in 17 before his contract was terminated in May 2005.

Jim Sinclair could not understand what the new generation needs. It was old-fashioned thinking, that was Jim Sinclair. Always behind my back. I love when you speak face-to-face and you tell me, 'That's wrong', but when you are always smiling and saying, 'That's a good idea', and then behind my back you say, 'He's a German'. I am not a German, I am a European – Former Scotland manager **Berti Vogts** on SFA Head of Football Development Jimmy Sinclair, November 2007.

I just found that (Vogts' comments) really distasteful and patent nonsense. He made some reference to my ideas being dated, yet never once saw me working. He was invited down to Largs to contribute to courses, to see courses, and he steadfastly refused on a number of occasions. So he didn't even know what was going on, he wasn't speaking from a position of strength or knowledge. It was absolute ignorance – **Jimmy Sinclair**, by then director of Rangers' Youth Academy, responds to Vogts, December 2007.

BOOZEGATE ⚽

I spoke to Glenn Hoddle last year and he said international management is like a volcano. It's quiet, quiet, then all of a sudden it comes to an eruption – **George Burley**, 2 April 2009.

I have no problem with Barry Ferguson, no problem at all – **George Burley** after the 2–1 win over Iceland, 1 April 2009.

Nobody is putting two fingers to anything . . . I could be sitting like that and somebody said this. I am not going to give judgement on one picture, all I am judging is the team. They could easily say whatever. It's your opinion – was it meant? If somebody is sitting like that or that, you cannot say definitely that somebody has got two fingers up or whatever. The trouble is we are speculating again. Do we want to finish this conversation? – Scotland manager **George Burley** refuses to accept Barry Ferguson and Allan McGregor's gestures from the bench during the previous night's game would cause a problem, 2 April 2009.

I fully support George's decision. We will be issuing players with a code of conduct and will be tightening up arrangements within the team hotel. We now consider this matter to be closed – SFA chief executive **Gordon Smith**, 2 April 2009.

The overall conduct of the players during the last week while on Scotland duty has, regrettably, fallen considerably short of the standards expected by Rangers Football Club and our supporters and has brought the Club into disrepute. The management of the Club has taken the view that this has damaged both Rangers and Scotland and is unacceptable – Rangers chief executive **Martin Bain**, 3 April 2009.

These are not actions we have taken lightly because it doesn't help us from a football point of view, but we had to take them. It's not something we'd have wanted but the timing is not in our own control. We have to react to the circumstances. The most disappointing aspect for me was the subsequent reaction on the bench and from the club's point of view I don't think that was a good image – Rangers manager **Walter Smith**, 3 April 2009, as Rangers ban the players for two weeks and fine them two weeks' wages.

In light of the events of the past 48 hours and following further discussions between the National Team Manager and the Chief Executive, it has been decided that Barry Ferguson and Allan McGregor will no longer be considered for international selection by Scotland. This action has been taken in the best interest of the squad, the fans and the country. We are determined to qualify for the World Cup and we must ensure that nothing is allowed to distract us from achieving this goal – **SFA** statement, 3 April 2009.

At that stage, I hadn't really seen any papers or watched the match again. When I did, I realised we (him and Gordon Smith) needed to speak again. The gestures had clearly made a lot of people very angry. We talked again first thing on Friday morning and it was clear that Gordon, George Peat and myself were in agreement about what needed to be done – About-turn from Scotland manager **George Burley**, 3 April 2009, after the SFA had announced neither player would be considered for Scotland selection again.

Strong drink and thick footballers. What a cocktail – News of the World columnist **Davie Provan**, 5 April 2009.

Reputations ruined by schoolboy hand gestures. Even by the standards of witless footballers this was a new one. What next? Lighting their own farts? – Sunday Herald journalist **Michael Grant**, 5 April 2009.

Burley, you sense, is a nice fella but he needs to discover his inner Souness and fast – Scotland on Sunday journalist **Tom English** on Burley, 5 April 2009.

You have been waiting for your shot and here it is. The guy who has nailed down the No. one jersey for Scotland for five years is out of form and out of his club's first team. Keep your head down, do your job and that position is yours for keeps. Or, alternatively, drink until 11am, get caught and then make a childish gesture at newspaper photographers at the national stadium. Nice one, Allan – Former Scotland midfielder **Craig Burley** on Allan McGregor, 5 April 2009.

Banks went bust and didn't get the column inches we've had in the last few days – Rangers manager **Walter Smith**, 5 April 2009, after the 1–0 win over Falkirk.

What happened on Sunday was a yellow card; what happened on Wednesday night was another yellow card. That results in a red card and that's what's happened here – SFA Chief Executive **Gordon Smith** on Ferguson and McGregor, announcing no further action would be taken against any other player in connection with the Boozegate affair, 9 April 2009.

(George) assumed that experienced international players – players at the top level – (would behave). There was food laid on on the advice of the sports scientists. If a player sneaks out his room after going to his bed, is that the manager's fault because he didn't have the window locked? Should players be under guard? – SFA chief executive **Gordon Smith**, 9 April 2009.

It wasn't George's responsibility to take them by the hand and walk them up to their rooms. The lads in question, Allan and Fergie, were senior members of the squad. They shouldn't have to be mollycoddled. With all due respect to George Peat or anyone else who has made statements about it, they weren't there. There have been a lot of people commenting on the situation who weren't involved – Scotland assistant coach **Terry Butcher**, 9 April 2009.

As to whether the players will be picked again, that's an SFA decision. I don't ban them. It's not the Chief Executive, it's not the President. It's the Board (of Directors) – Scotland manager **George Burley**, 9 April 2009.

As a manager I'll try and protect my players all I can. I stuck by the two players in question but when I actually saw the TV on Thursday I couldn't say I wasn't disappointed or hurt by their actions. Especially since the last words on my team talk to them were 'the whole nation's looking at you'. Everyone's looking at your commitment to Scotland and your behaviour, so let's go out there and everybody stick together. So I was very hurt by that and felt it was totally disrespectful – Manager **George Burley**, 10 April 2009.

The SFA have started a new trend in criminality. If you leave the scene of the crime early then you are not guilty – Rangers manager **Walter Smith**, 15 April 2009, as Ferguson and McGregor's two-week ban ended. Smith announced he'd previously briefed the press the pair wouldn't play for Rangers again in anger and said they were now available for selection again.

I think the players were due the courtesy of being allowed to give their side of the story and sit and talk to George Burley, George Peat and Gordon Smith and explain what went on and apologise for their actions. The players can do no more – they have admitted what they did was wrong and apologised unreservedly – PFA Scotland chief executive **Fraser Wishart**, 16 April 2009.

Remember, there's only two people who have caused all this – Scotland manager **George Burley**, 9 April 2009.

CELTIC ⚽

It's the hardest job in Britain because of the expectancy of everyone connected with Celtic – Former Celtic coach **John Barnes**.

We were the champions, we were Inter, it would be enough just to go out there and we would win. We thought we were strong, they weren't, and in football that always comes back to bite you. We'd stayed behind to watch Celtic train at the stadium the night before and it was an error. We'd had our usual day-before routine, really intense and concentrated, then we saw their session and it was total confusion. It wasn't just players out there; there were directors, hangers-on, all sorts. We couldn't figure out what was going on, who was who, who was even a player. It was hard then to create the right level of worry or anxiety – Inter Milan striker **Sandro Mazzola** recalls the day before the 1967 European Cup Final, May 2007.

Big Jock had everybody playing in different positions. We had as much fun watching them as they did watching us. Jock said, 'You play left back, Bobby, Tommy Gemmell will play centre forward and Billy McNeill will go to the sidelines.' In that session nobody actually played where they would have normally. The cat and mouse stuff had started – **Bobby Lennox** recalls the training session watched by Inter Milan before the 1967 European Cup Final, *FourFourTwo* magazine, May 2007.

My relationship with Celtic as a player was hostile. I was scared of this club. I was scared of guys like Roy Aitken, Tommy Burns, Murdo MacLeod and Davie Provan. Basically, anyone that could stop me from winning, I was scared of – Celtic manager **Gordon Strachan**, June 2007.

They had been spending their money signing players – bad ones in those days – instead of getting on with life and death stuff like a new ground. He (Fergus McCann) told me in that case Celtic would retire from Scottish football, retire from the SFA Resign their membership. I said, 'That's up to you but do you mind me asking where you would intend to play your football?' He said they'd play a series of big friendlies: Man U, Real Madrid, Barcelona. I said, 'You'll not kick a ball, no one will be able to play against you because you will become an unauthorised football club. Not one club in the world will be able to set foot in Parkhead if you do that.' I remember telling him, 'You'll be lucky if you get a game against the Harlem Globetrotters,' which didn't endear me to him – Former SFA secretary **Ernie Walker** on Celtic in the early 90s, February 2009.

'There you are,' said Peter. 'For 51 years you have been subjected to generally positive media comment and your image has not been in question. Now you have joined Celtic. You haven't done anything. You haven't made a decision. But you are now portrayed as a joke. Welcome to the club!' – Celtic Public Relations Manager **Peter McLean**, to new General Manager Jock Brown on the morning of his appointment in June 1997, quoted in *Celtic-Minded: 510 Days In Paradise*, 1999. The *Daily Record* headline on it had been '*Joke Brown*'.

When I was on Scotland duty, I'd see Ally McCoist, Stuart McCall, Andy Goram and Gordon Durie always going around together. I wouldn't say that they were a clique; they were more like brothers. We needed some of that spirit – Former Celtic striker **Darren Jackson** recalls a players' meeting after Celtic went bottom of the table in August 1997, quoted in Mark Guidi, *The Inner Sanctum*, 2008.

Celtic reminded me of Feyenoord and this was another example. The internal wrangling. The chaos. Less than two years after we won the title with Feyenoord, we were 14th in the league. The fans went crazy and invaded the pitch several times. Honestly, terrible, terrible times. This felt similar – Former Celtic winger **Regi Blinker** on the shambolic end to Celtic's 1997–98 title-winning season, which saw manager Wim Jansen quit less than 48 hours after clinching the title, quoted in Mark Guidi, *The Inner Sanctum*, 2008.

People who work at Rangers, whether as players, managers or coaches, are seldom heard offering criticism towards the current custodians of the club's fortunes. Quite the contrary afflicts Celtic — Former Celtic general manager **Jock Brown**, quoted in *Celtic-Minded: 510 Days In Paradise*, 1999.

I just find it odd, really, because if you want to build on something, you've got to keep your better players. If you sell them just because a good offer comes in, other players can be disillusioned — Celtic's **Alan Stubbs** as the club prepared to sell Craig Burley to Derby for £3.5m, November 1999.

It came out that the body language of the referee, like patting people on the bottom, really doesn't send very positive signals to the home crowd — Celtic chief executive **Allan MacDonald**, January 2000, after it came to light he had commissioned a behavioural psychologist, London-based Christopher Lewis, to assess the Old Firm game the previous May, when referee Hugh Dallas was felled by a coin thrown from the crowd, three players were sent off, four supporters ran on to the field and 100 arrests were made after Rangers' 3–0 win secured the championship. An SPL Commission of Inquiry into the unrest fined Celtic £45,000 after defender Stephane Mahé had refused to leave the pitch after being sent off.

Are Celtic really claiming a pat on the bum is now a legitimate reason to throw coins? Celtic have got themselves into such a paranoid state that it's questionable if they can give a rational judgment. It's grotesquely unfair that a report with psychobabble is leaked without any consideration of the damage it can cause — SFA referees committee chief **Jim Oliver** on Celtic's comments, January 2000.

It was a bit too intense for me at that stage in my career, but I can respect it. It was unbelievable. It is the greatest supported club in the world, they're amazing supporters and it was a privilege to play for them. They were great — Former striker **Ian Wright** on Celtic, July 2006.

I wanted Burley to sit more. He played the role for Scotland and was happy to do that for his country and for Craig Brown but not for me. You have to question players' agendas when that happens. I know what was really behind it all yet I was always the one made out to be the bad guy — Former coach **John Barnes** on midfielder Craig Burley, July 2000.

You have a nightmare eight months, one of the biggest disaster periods in Celtic's history and then you come out and blast other people who have been top players for Celtic and done a job for the club. He tries to make out that they were part of the factors that made him a failure. Incredible — Burley's agent **Gordon Smith** responds, July 2000.

My experiences at Celtic were unique ones. Things didn't work out. I wouldn't like to say it was because of my colour but I know that black managers here aren't given an opportunity, or longer, because of the stereotypes they have – Former coach **John Barnes** rewrites history, *BBC Four* documentary, October 2003.

I have three words for him. Inverness Caley Thistle – Celtic Supporters Association General Secretary **Eddie Toner**'s considered response to Barnes, October 2003.

A couple of weeks later, having scrambled a victory over Bray Wanderers in Ireland, we went to Leipzig, who were in the third division of the German league, and they beat us quite easily. I was muttering away to myself on the touchline and our club doctor, Roddy McDonald, overheard me saying, 'This is going to be one long, hard season.' – **Martin O'Neill**, March 2003, talking about the start of the 2000–1 season (his first at the club). Celtic won the title by 15 points.

You can never forget Celtic are a very good team. They don't get injured, they reached a UEFA Cup final. It would be crass to say otherwise, but time will tell. Celtic play as a unit, but that unit will break up and we'll come through – Rangers chairman **David Murray**, January 2004.

Whatever you say about Fergus (McCann), whatever fights people had with him, whatever way he wanted to run the show, if this (Celtic Park) is the legacy, then I am absolutely delighted with it – Celtic manager **Martin O'Neill**, February 2004.

McCann was quoted as saying that he wouldn't have the management team that Allan MacDonald brought in anywhere near the place. He used to say, 'The dugout will only end up being the bus stop for all their mates.' – Former player **Craig Burley**, February 2004. MacDonald, who'd joined as McCann's replacement in July 1999, resigned as chief executive in September 2000.

That's from the team that won nothing last year. Listen, a move to England isn't going to happen for the Old Firm – Dundee manager **Jim Duffy**, March 2004, on Celtic chief executive Peter Lawwell's claims that the club would have to quit Scottish football because it wasn't competitive enough.

We always refer to them as 'Celtic' or 'Celtic Football Club', never 'the Celtic', so no one here confuses them with the Boston Celtics – Championsworld director of communications **Rich Schneider** on Celtic's American tour, July 2004.

As a fan, I did take what was going on at Celtic very seriously. I'll be honest, I cringed during the Dalglish era. What the hell was this going on? – Livingston's then-prospective owner **Pearse Flynn**, January 2005. He'd invested £1m in a previous Celtic share issue.

I'm never quite sure when people pull a figure out of thin air, whether the wage bill is attached to a club with regard to every single person that works there or just the players' wages. It's interesting that Jim Hone – a man who left this football club and went to the Premiership – was telling me the wage bill here when he left wouldn't be in the top 12 of the Premiership. There's not a prayer of the players' wages being remotely near the figure that has been quoted – Celtic manager **Martin O'Neill** on chairman Brian Quinn's claim that Celtic spent £40m on wages and that only five Premiership sides' wage bills were higher, April 2005.

I'm trying to head off another storm created by our esteemed manager who has now, I believe, contradicted the numbers I used in the radio interview given this morning. The £40million is total wages and salaries compared to Rangers' £30million, which is total wages and salary. Secondly, the statement that there are only five clubs in the Premier League with a higher wage bill was done after checking with the Celtic finance department, who named the five clubs in England and who got this stuff from benchmark data collected from published sources. I'm not going to be made a liar by Martin O'Neill, so you're going to have to use your skills to try and defuse this thing – Phone message inadvertently left on the phone of 18-year-old Kayley Elkington of Walsall by Celtic chairman **Brian Quinn** in response. He'd intended it to be left on the phone of Celtic's PR chief, April 2005.

I got this strange message but didn't have a clue what it was about. We phoned it back but the guy said he hadn't phoned us – Puzzled **Kayley Elkington** on the message, April 2005.

I don't go through any special process just like I didn't bring a lawyer here or a PR person or I didn't say you can't ask me this question or that. I give you the answers and that's the way I do it. I'm not a prisoner of the Celtic support, I'm not going to act the way they want me to act, I'm going to act in the honest way that Dermot Desmond thinks and believes in and what is in the best interests of Celtic all the time – Majority shareholder **Dermot Desmond** to the Celtic Supporters Association, December 2005.

At our meeting to discuss the move, at Dermot's house in London, I told him, 'I still see you as a central midfielder. But the problem is that Neil Lennon and Stilian Petrov are doing too well in that area to be left out or moved elsewhere. If I had to select a team for the next match, and the three of you were all fit, I'd have to plump for Neil and Stilian.' He was perfectly happy with that, for the simple reason that because of his affection for Celtic he had genuinely set his heart on playing for the club – Celtic manager **Gordon Strachan** on signing Roy Keane, *My Life In Football*, 2006.

When I was at Celtic, some of the players said, 'Can I have your number?' I said, 'No, I don't want you annoying me with banter.' By the time I left there, two guys had my number – Former Celtic midfielder **Roy Keane**, September 2006.

This is the only place in the world where you can be on a tour of the stadium and see the manager bollocking a player. The tour's going by and it's 'This is Mr Strachan over here, bollocking him' – Manager **Gordon Strachan** on Celtic's 'family club' reputation, May 2007.

I just couldn't understand his decision. If you're going to bring me off then surely you bring on an attacking midfield player. Not Gary Caldwell. I don't mean to sound disrespectful to Gary but at the end of the day he's a centre half – Celtic's **Neil Lennon** on being substituted by Gordon Strachan in his last game for the club, the 2007 Scottish Cup Final against Dunfermline, June 2007.

The Scottish League is obviously not as good as the Premiership but Celtic, that team we had, would have done very well in the Premiership. Look at Sutton, Thompson, Lennon, Larsson, Mjallby. It was a team full of internationals, leading figures on international teams – Helsingborgs and ex-Celtic striker **Henrik Larsson**, August 2007.

I have had great sympathy for (Paul) Hartley, who is often the one who suffers for the continued inclusion of Donati. I don't think I could take it if I was him, sitting in my tracksuit watching this guy get overrun by Falkirk's £500-per-week midfielders – and he did. When a player with that pedigree can't deliver in the Premier League, he's not going to deliver at all – Former Celtic midfielder **Craig Burley** on Massimo Donati, March 2008.

Even if they play rubbish for three or four weeks on the bounce, they still get a game. The only ones he really does change are Massimo Donati and Paul Hartley – Celtic striker **Derek Riordan** on manager Gordon Strachan's selection policies, April 2008. He left Celtic four months later.

I came to Celtic three years ago and it's been a fantastic journey. But the best part of it is being able to call Tommy Burns a friend for the last three years – Celtic manager **Gordon Strachan**, after the death of coach Tommy Burns, May 2008.

It's been an incredible night at the end of an incredible season. I have to thank the players for their character, their belief and their ability. This has been the most memorable season of my life and now, if you'll forgive me, I think it's only fair I should go and be with the people who have supported me all season – Celtic manager **Gordon Strachan** chooses his words carefully in a brief press conference after clinching his third title in succession with the 1–0 win over Dundee United, May 2008.

Who is he trying to kid with his after-match comments? 'It is only fair that I go and celebrate with the people who have supported and believed in us the whole way through the season' – that's what he said. In that case he must have gone for a quiet pint by himself. Because let's get this straight, no one on this planet gave them a hope in hell of winning the title six or seven weeks ago. And I mean no one – Former Celtic striker **John Hartson** on Strachan's remarks, May 2008.

I didn't want to explain anything, I didn't want to talk about anything. I just wanted to pack my bags and be with my family. In fact, you might have noticed in the technical area there were two big bags ready to go. As soon as the game was finished I was off. There was nothing sinister to it, I just felt people should go and enjoy it on their own. Everyone had been talking all season anyway so I thought they could just continue talking and I'd go away and play golf. We need to be fresh with each other and I'm sure the press get fed up with some of my sarcastic answers. It wasn't a snub. It was just like, 'Let's have a break.' – Celtic manager **Gordon Strachan** explains his press conference after his side's title win at Tannadice three months before, August 2008.

At Celtic you're a draw away from a crisis – Former Celtic midfielder **Paul Lambert**, in DVD, 'The Official History of Celtic', 2008.

I listened to (Gordon) Strachan saying, after the 3–0 Old Trafford defeat, it was the greatest performance from any team they have played against in Europe. A load of nonsense. United, by their standards, were average – Former Celtic midfielder **Craig Burley** on Celtic's Champions League October 2008 defeat by Manchester United, November 2008.

I think Gordon (Strachan) became a glove-puppet manager because the people who were controlling the funds were controlling the issues. This team has hit a brick wall and it's going to take a lot of financial repair to get them back to a decent level – Former Celtic striker **Charlie Nicholas**, after Celtic missed out on the 2008–09 SPL title, May 2009.

The writing was on the wall because Gordon was hated by the Celtic support – Former Celtic striker **John Hartson**, after Strachan quit, May 2009.

COACHING ⚽

He knows how to push peoples' buttons. His motivational skills were brilliant; you'd want to tear the dressing room door off to get on to the pitch. He would make you feel like a great player even when you knew you weren't. I'd played in the lower leagues all my life but there were days I went out playing for Martin when I thought I was the best player in the world – Wycombe's **Keith Ryan** on Martin O'Neill, in Alex Montgomery, *Martin O'Neill – The Biography*, 2003.

Rieps (Marc Rieper) used to hate the fact that Gouldy (Jonathan Gould) would never come off his line to take a cross ball, and he would scream at him to do so. Gouldy would just laugh. Rieps used to say to Gouldy that the opposition only had one shot but still managed to score two goals. Training was also competitive and we would half each other in two. (Coach) Wim (Jansen) would stop the session and ask us all to calm down. You know, we didn't stop that Rangers team by being talentless pissheads – Former Celtic midfielder **Craig Burley** on 1997–98 season, in Mark Guidi, The Inner Sanctum, 2008.

Seeing a player walk on the training field was one of the few things that made Wim angry – Former Celtic assistant manager **Murdo MacLeod** on 1997–98 title-winning manager Wim Jansen, in Mark Guidi, The Inner Sanctum, 2008. Jansen liked high-tempo training sessions.

People think of me as screaming a lot from the sidelines, but 90 per cent of it is sheer encouragement. Of the rest, half is tactics, half criticism – Coventry City manager **Gordon Strachan**, in Rick Gekoski, 'Staying Up: A Fan Behind The Scenes In The Premiership', 1998.

With the experience I've had, Largs can't show me anything new. That may sound arrogant, but I've been down and watched sessions and, to me, it seems superficial – **Steve Archibald**, then director of football with Benfica, on the SFA coaching courses, June 1999.

If I'd stayed at Rangers all these years I would not be as good a coach as I am today – **Graeme Souness**, then unemployed shortly before being appointed Blackburn manager, February 2000.

I would have changed the system to 4–3–2. Most people would have done. But it was a piece of tactical brilliance, which not one journalist picked up on – Motherwell Chief Executive **Pat Nevin** on a master stroke by manager Billy Davies, March 2000. In a game at Kilmarnock the previous month, Motherwell had switched to a 3–3–3 formation after the sending-off of striker Don Goodman, and scored twice to win 2–0.

I think Dick Advocaat's system is poor. It's wrong. Leaving two at the back marking and pushing his fullbacks on? I wouldn't play that way – St Mirren manager **Tom Hendrie**, March 2000. St Mirren were then in the First Division.

He was stuck in that system of playing (Eyal) Berkovic and (Lubomir) Moravcik when it was obvious it wasn't working – Former Celtic midfielder **Craig Burley** on former coach John Barnes, April 2001.

Supervision through observation. I watch them all the time. Best thing I ever did – Manchester United manager **Sir Alex Ferguson**, 2002.

I made the decision to try and provoke something, which I did. It didn't quite work out the way I had thought, but never mind. I just tried to provoke a reaction because I thought Marko was the one player that could have changed the game for us – Former Celtic assistant manager **Eric Black**, in Graham McColl, *The Head Bhoys*, 2002, about the half-time altercation with Mark Viduka in the Scottish Cup-tie against Inverness Caley.

I have never necessarily wanted players to like me. What a coach needs is respect – Rangers manager **Dick Advocaat**, September 2002.

Coaching is easy – coaching is an absolute doddle. Management is far harder and there's a big difference between a coach and a manager, that's for sure. I love coaching, it's great fun. I don't like being a manager but the only reason I'm a manager is so I get full control of the coaching. There's a huge difference between the two – Southampton manager **Gordon Strachan**, September 2003.

I remember, going back six or seven years ago, a jump test and it was an Italian fitness coach. I never liked him. My results must have been hopeless. I remember him saying to the manager I couldn't jump. He might be right, my results might have been the worst in the team, but it's the desire to get there in a game that matters – Rangers defender **David Weir** recalls coaching matters at Everton, May 2009.

Martin's a very serious chap, deep-thinking, but very likeable with it, and quite humble. He's also very articulate and very, very vibrant. John Robertson once said to me, 'You know, before a game, Martin will come into the dressing room a minute before the match and within that minute he'll really turn them on. It's a gift, a gift of motivation.' – Shepshed Charterhouse Executive Chairman **Maurice Clayton** on Martin O'Neill, in Alex Montgomery, *Martin O'Neill – The Biography*, 2003.

He'd do the team talk and you had to be there, to hear the way he was saying it, the way it came out of his mouth. You were just transfixed. He had a knack, something from within, of finding the right words. He is without doubt the best motivator I've ever known, by far – Everton's **Alan Stubbs** on Martin O'Neill, October 2002.

There's an image of me that's built up of a manager who turns up five minutes before the players go out on match-day, has a bit of a rabble-rouse in the dressing room and isn't seen for the rest of the week. If you could work like that, fantastic, but I'm afraid that kind of genius is well beyond me – Celtic manager **Martin O'Neill**, January 2004.

They have their own ways. Martin never named his team until ten-past two on a Saturday. Then, at the end of training, there'd be a game with the losing team doing a run. There was nothing scientific about it. He'd say, 'You've got

24 seconds to get round that tree and back. Oh, and Gunny, you can have 25.' He'd give the goalie an extra second. I thought that was brilliant – Former Norwich goalkeeper **Bryan Gunn**, on his old boss O'Neill, January 2004.

If somebody has a poor left foot, I am not one for saying, 'Go and work on your left foot.' I'll say, 'Make sure your right is the best it can possibly be.' Practise with your left obviously, but if you work on your weakness too much, you can forget your strength – West Ham assistant manager **Peter Grant**, February 2004.

I take some of the responsibility, not for failing to win the game but for losing it. I could see something was happening and I should have changed it but I didn't – Brighton manager **Mark McGhee**, after a 2–1 defeat to Sheffield Wednesday, March 2004.

I love Steve. He's a very loyal and very nice person with a lot of knowledge about football. I'll always look at him as a great man. I wish him luck and maybe one day he can go out on his own. Like all Scots he is proud. Proud and stubborn – Former Chelsea manager **Ruud Gullit** on Steve Clarke, 2004. The pair worked together at Stamford Bridge and Newcastle.

He was the link between the old and new faces of the club, he knew the dressing room and he had experience, although I don't believe the new man came over from Portugal thinking, 'Great, I'll have that Steve Clarke as my No. two!' Now, though, Steve is even beginning to look like his manager and the two of them have yet to crack a smile between them this season. That will change soon and the bottom line is that Steve will soon be the assistant manager of the first Chelsea side in 50 years to win the Championship and possibly the Champions League too. Not bad for your CV, that – Former Scotland midfielder **Craig Burley** on Chelsea assistant manager Steve Clarke, April 2005.

He knows every player – he knows this player is from the academy, he has 179 centimetres, he is fast, he is slow, he is fat – Chelsea manager **Jose Mourinho** on assistant Steve Clarke, January 2007.

When you become a coach, it's like being a doctor, you take an oath to make people better. You do it to help people and that's what I want to do again – Former Southampton manager **Gordon Strachan**, January 2005.

I've given my coaches full control of the team, full rights, and then the games have been lost. The only question I'm asking of my coaches all the time is, 'Show me the analysis. Show me the rationale.' But never once have I received an answer to those questions. It seemed to me that my driver back in Kaunas could have done a better job than Rix and Duffy – Hearts owner **Vladimir Romanov** on former head coach Graham Rix and his assistant Jim Duffy, May 2006.

I was in charge at Hearts for two months and in that time we only lost one match. I don't think that's too bad but maybe his driver will have a more impressive CV than me and be encouraged to apply for the job – Former Hearts assistant manager **Jim Duffy**'s wry response, May 2006.

Guys like him (Japan goalkeeper Yoshikatsu Kawaguchi) and (Peter) Crouch mean I'll have a bit of interest in the World Cup although Scotland aren't in it. I worked with John Terry and Robert Huth at Chelsea and Kelvin Jack and Brent Sancho at Dundee so it's nice to see these guys playing at the level they'll be at. Most of what these guys have achieved has been down to them and they all deserve great credit for it. But whether it's moving someone like John Terry up from the youths to the reserves at Chelsea or with someone like Crouchy in the first team, it's nice to have a played a small part in their development, to have helped them up a rung of the ladder. I don't know if there are too many Lithuanian taxi drivers who can say the same thing – Former Hearts assistant manager **Jim Duffy**, May 2006.

The question I commonly ask the coaches is, 'Have you forgotten that this is a game of 90 minutes?' The answer they always give is 'no'. So I say, 'Well, why is the team only playing for 45 minutes? Do you know why the team is playing like this?' When the answer comes back 'yes', then I say, 'Well, if you don't put it right for the next game, I'll remove you.' – Hearts owner **Vladimir Romanov**'s leadership techniques, May 2006.

It didn't make any sense for their pundits, players and people in charge to continually insist they were going to come good. Where was the evidence to base this contention on? Eriksson had no formula for changing the pattern within games and between them – Former Dundee and Hibs manager **Jim Duffy** on England during the World Cup, July 2006.

– What is your strangest experience?
– Being stuck in a team meeting with Rowan Alexander and Davie Irons. We seem to have more meetings than AA. We have meetings to plan meetings. We have them every single day and they can last from five minutes to half an hour – Gretna's **Ryan McGuffie**, August 2006.

The fact that you have been excellent as a player is neither here nor there as far as your coaching abilities are concerned, but Berti (Vogts) wanted international players to go straight on to the Pro Licence. It was fast-track, ridiculously fast-track – Former SFA head of football development **Jimmy Sinclair** on Berti Vogts' ideas while he was Scotland manager, December 2007.

He didn't actually take a session – he just came along and watched us training. But at one point while he was standing on the sidelines, in the mud, the ball came to him and he just flicked it up in the air and caught it on the back of his neck, which was something you never saw in those days. It was a great piece of skill. And the fact that he was dressed in his immaculate Italian designer gear made it somehow all the more memorable – Former Scotland manager **Craig Brown** on new England coach Fabio Capello, February 2008. The then 35-year-old Capello had come to Brown's club Clyde in 1982 on a three-week Italian study programme.

I told the team at half-time if they were going to play that kind of shit they should run out of the stadium and go and prepare for Mother's Day. It was a very poor first half but the second half was very sexy. Any team who'd been playing against a team playing the way we did in the first half would have felt confident. If you had seen our dressing room at half-time I wanted to kill some of our people. But if I'd done that I'd have had to go to jail and we wouldn't have got a point – Hearts manager **Csaba Laszlo** after his side came from 2–0 down to draw 2–2 against Rangers, March 2009. (*Mother's Day was the following day.*)

DI STEFANO ⚽

I know a lot about football. It nearly took over my life. I took a Division Four team called Campobasso into the play-off zone. It is based in Molise, a godforsaken place in the south where I was born. I rebuilt the team, spent £1m on it. I blew it, actually. I became president, director, chief executive, the Meester (manager), selector, groundsman, doctor, physiotherapist, dietician, lawyer, secretary, man at the gate, and PR. I became the jack of all trades and master of sweet FA – Dundee director **Giovanni di Stefano** after being appointed to the club's board, August 2003.

The harder you are, the better. I learned that lesson from Batesie – Dundee director **Giovanni di Stefano** on old chum Ken Bates, August 2003.

Nixon was a man who didn't have committees. He made his own decisions, like me. I don't like people making decisions that affect my pocket – Dundee director **Giovanni di Stefano** on the former U.S. president, who he claimed to have met twice, August 2003.

You could wake him at 4.26 in the morning and ask him, 'Shall we drop the bomb or not?' He would make a decision. Straight away. I'm the same. You can call me at any time, day or night, and I'll give you an immediate answer. If I'm wrong, I've got enough time to put it right. If I'm right, I've got more time to enjoy the decision – Dundee director **Giovanni di Stefano** on the former US president Richard Nixon, August 2003.

I'm limited in my knowledge. I mean, I'm not stupid completely, but I'd never ever heard of Mr McFadden – Dundee director **Giovanni di Stefano** after making a £500,000 bid for Motherwell's James McFadden, August 2003.

I'm very much the sceptic, a bit like Casca in Julius Caesar – Dundee director **Giovanni di Stefano**, August 2003. (Publius Servilius Casca was one of the assassins of Julius Caesar in 44 BC.)

People said there was match-rigging and everything. OK, let's just assume we rigged two, three, five or 10 matches, but how the hell do you rig all of them? It's impossible – Dundee director **Giovanni di Stefano** on alleged events at his club in Belgrade, FK Obilic, August 2003.

Saddam Hussein's not going to play for Dundee. I'm not playing for Dundee, either. Look, the job can't be done overnight, but we've come a helluva way already. Let's deal with facts, not conjecture . . . that's for priests – Dundee director **Giovanni di Stefano**, August 2003.

I can only speak as I found him and he was a nice guy. The war was not necessary. The public were lied to – Dundee director **Giovanni di Stefano** on Iraqi president Saddam Hussein, September 2003.

He was a nobody then and it wouldn't have been a bad idea if he had stayed that way. I don't know what he is actually wanted for because I haven't seen any concrete evidence. You can't convict him just because he was celebrating the events of 9/11. You'd need to arrest half of Palestine or the Sudan. I would defend bin Laden under the proper conditions and if I was paid properly – Dundee director **Giovanni di Stefano** on Islamic militant Osama bin Laden, September 2003.

He was a great guy – I just wish there were more like him. Arkan was my friend, he was my client and if people don't like it then they can bugger off – Dundee director **Giovanni di Stefano** on Serbian paramilitary leader Želijko Ražnatović, aka Arkan, September 2003.

If you criticise my ideas, attack my proposals, or claim that I am a dreamer, then that is perfectly okay; that is your prerogative. But if you describe me as a crook, a swindler, or a villain, I will see you in the courts – Dundee director **Giovanni di Stefano**, October 2003.

I have no reverse gear and, as Mrs Thatcher once said, you can turn if you want, but this man's not for turning – Dundee director **Giovanni di Stefano**, October 2003.

We have been in dispute with the Inland Revenue but that's because I refuse to be bullied by these legalised thugs – Dundee director **Giovanni di Stefano** dismissing claims Dundee were about to close down over unpaid tax, November 2003.

The Scottish Football Association are nothing but a bunch of perpendicular ponces . . . they are like a fly around a cow's backside – Dundee director **Giovanni di Stefano**, December 2003. He resigned as a Dundee director the following month.

What he (Giovanni di Stefano) did was give us hope which turned out to be false. We would probably have considered Charles Manson if he had offered to put up £20m. It was the last throw of the dice for the club – Dundee manager **Jim Duffy**, a year after the club went into administration with debts of £20m, November 2004.

DIRECTORS

She said, in front of us, 'Well, I think the chairman's right,' and when he'd gone I just told her, 'Don't you bloody do that again.' – **Alex Ferguson**, on an argument with St Mirren chairman Willie Todd involving office secretary June Sullivan, in Michael Crick, *The Boss: The Many Sides of Alex Ferguson*, 2002.

When Dick came down it was almost eerie, everything was so quiet. He was crying. He hugged me, and he was not the type of person to be demonstrative like that. He was the old school – **Alex Ferguson** on Aberdeen chairman Dick Donald after the club had won the European Cup Winners' Cup in 1983, May 2003.

I think I got the best of him. After that, he started to have an opinion on who was a good footballer, which isn't always the best recipe for a manager – Former Rangers manager **Graeme Souness** on chairman David Murray, November 2008.

The chairman didn't want to talk about my contract, which he'd promised to do if I played well. I'd been voted Player of the Year. But he said I didn't deserve it. Well, I go, it's that easy. I don't play for liars and traitors – Former Celtic striker **Paolo di Canio**, asked by magazine reader why he left the club after one season, December 2006.

When we won the league, I did not receive a handshake or congratulations from Fergus McCann or Jock Brown. I think that tells you what was going on by that stage – Former Celtic assistant manager **Murdo MacLeod** on the title-winning 1997–98 season, in Mark Guidi, *The Inner Sanctum*, 2008.

You could write everything he knows about football on the back of a postage stamp – Defender **Shaun Teale** on Motherwell chairman John Boyle, after being sacked by him, March 2000. Teale claimed Motherwell had gone back on their word over a new contract.

If the only person people can find to have a go at me is Shaun Teale I can't be that unpopular after all – **John Boyle**'s response, March 2001.

I find it very, very interesting and it's rewarding because of that. I'd be a lying git if I said it was enjoyable – Motherwell's **Pat Nevin** on his roles as first chief executive then director of football at the club, May 2001.

Managing the football team is hard enough without going on to the board and deciding whether to sack myself or not – **Martin O'Neill**, declining the chance to become a Celtic director, 2001.

I said to the directors, 'If that had been me, I'd probably have done exactly the same.' They said, 'Don't dare say that, don't *ever* say that. Christ, the press will *slaughter* you.' – Manchester United manager **Sir Alex Ferguson** on Eric Cantona's 1995 kung-fu kick at Crystal Palace, 2002.

He's not a businessman in the long-term sense of planning and prudence, he's more of an impresario . . . Rangers, with Murray, is a one-party state and the man in power has an allergy to any form of personal criticism – Former Rangers director **Hugh Adam** on David Murray, February 2002.

Celtic have been, since Fergus McCann's arrival, much the better-run club. Fergus was the most unjustly-maligned man in the history of the game, when you consider that he took the club from bankruptcy into the mainstream and built that stadium along the way – Former Rangers director **Hugh Adam** on former Celtic chairman and managing director McCann, February 2002.

When I needed to, I could reveal my inner doubts or concerns to David (Murray), at a time when I couldn't with anyone else. In football, whenever you feel weak you must never show it, but I could with David without feeling even weaker. I'd say ours is a relationship to the death – Rangers director of football **Dick Advocaat**, September 2002.

I went mental at the manager, whom I am not prepared to name, when I heard he had signed for Dundee – Former Dundee United manager and chairman **Jim McLean** on defender Lee Wilkie, October 2002.

It seemed so obscene that the first chance I get to become disloyal is when I'm surrounded by good people, rather than the charlatans I was surrounded by in the past – Falkirk manager **Ian McCall**, October 2002. He was being pursued by Dundee United at the time.

I'm always pictured as the bad boy, but my views are 90 per cent similar to the nine other clubs. I'm just a bit more vocal – Dunfermline chairman **John Yorkston**, September 2003.

To get on the Ibrox board is definitely my ambition. I've got a timescale of two years on it – Rangers fan and Glasgow Asian restaurateur, **Satty Singh**, January 2004.

He sought no interaction with the players and, similarly, the players weren't interested in interacting with him. He was that kind of businessman – Former Celtic midfielder **Craig Burley** on former chairman and managing director Fergus McCann, February 2004.

I would go to three games a day sometimes looking for players but he said I wasn't working hard enough at my job and that did annoy me. If he tried the same things with Martin O'Neill he would think it was as ludicrous now as I did then – Former Celtic manager **Lou Macari** on former chairman and managing director Fergus McCann, February 2004.

Allan MacDonald, on the other hand, was airy-fairy in his approach. He was all, 'We'll do a bit of this and a bit of that,' and between him, Kenny Dalglish and John Barnes, they all fell flat on their faces. I would have taken McCann over MacDonald any day. You always knew where you were with Fergus. Most of the time that was nowhere, but at least you knew – Former Celtic player **Craig Burley** on former chief executive Allan MacDonald and former chairman and managing director Fergus McCann, February 2004.

He wasn't a chatty man. He didn't indulge in boardroom banter about football in general the way other people did and that meant he wasn't terribly popular with other directors, although he was always perfectly courteous to me. He was an oddity but I am not exactly a conformist myself and I like people who are what they are and don't give a damn what anybody else thinks – Former Rangers vice-chairman **Donald Findlay** on former Celtic chairman and managing director Fergus McCann, March 2004.

I was at a dinner recently at which I heard the present Rangers chairman talk about the club being 'a family'. This is bollocks. It is patently not the case – Former Rangers vice-chairman **Donald Findlay**, March 2004.

I'm a qualified lawyer and even I cannot get my head round why this has suddenly become acceptable. It is astounding. The SPL can change any rules they like, but they would be expected to do so between seasons, not within them. What do you think the man with the wig in Edinburgh's Court of Session would think about this sudden change of approach? – Partick Thistle chairman **Tom Hughes** on Inverness Caledonian Thistle's bid to get into the SPL at Partick Thistle's expense by ground-sharing, May 2004. Two days later Inverness's bid was rejected but a second vote approved their promotion and Partick Thistle were relegated.

When I started out at 15 or 16 I never thought that I would be dealing with multi-millionaires, media moguls, agents, directors and chairmen. I never got into football because of that and I find it hard to handle these people because they are different from me completely. You have to be a better politician to deal with these people and I'm not very good at that. I only went to one board meeting at Southampton. I told Rupert (Lowe) not to let me come and after one meeting he said, 'You're right Gordon, probably best if you don't come again.' – Former Southampton manager **Gordon Strachan**, January 2005.

Gaining ownership of the club has been like a bad episode of *Eastenders* – Livingston's then prospective owner **Pearse Flynn**, January 2005.

Norwich didn't work out simply because the chairman at the time, Robert Chase, and I were quite incompatible. And what happened there is the reason I never break a contract. When it happened at Norwich, it irritated me for a long time afterwards and I vowed it wouldn't happen again. So, when I arrived at Celtic and signed that first contract I knew that, by hook or by crook, I would see it out – **Martin O'Neill** after leaving as manager of Celtic, June 2005.

He remains the only show in town and whether we like his management style or not we just have to accept it, and pray that it brings success on the park. He is determined and he is fanatical about football. I genuinely think that any suggestion he is going to sell Hearts off and turn the ground into flats or run away is not the case – Former Hearts director **George Foulkes** on club owner Vladimir Romanov after resigning from the board following the sackings of manager George Burley and chief executive Phil Anderton, November 2005.

I don't want to own Celtic. I'm not interested in the ownership of Celtic. I'm not interested in controlling Celtic. It's not on my agenda, it's not my ambition. I am the largest shareholder in Celtic but I don't want Celtic to be a subsidiary of mine – Majority shareholder **Dermot Desmond** to the Celtic Supporters Association, December 2005.

People say we're buying the league. Rubbish. We've got a good manager who finds good players. Our record signing cost £60,000. We've spent a couple of hundred thousand in my whole time here. As for wages, the lower leagues in England and the Conference pay more. Nobody here is even on a four-figure weekly wage – Gretna's chief backer **Brooks Mileson**, February 2006. The club were in Division Two at the time.

Brooks could sack me tomorrow and I'd still walk away very happy to have known the man, happy to have had the chance to work with him. There are remarkable men, and then there's Brooks Mileson – Gretna chief executive **Graeme Muir**, March 2006.

Burley and (Simon) Hunt (chief scout) were wanting players and I was handed a list with hundreds of names on it. I looked at this list and threw a lot of names out straight away but we agreed on players like Michal Pospisil, (Rudi) Skacel, Julien Brellier, (Roman) Bednar and Edgaras Jankauskas. In the case of Ibrahim Tall, they (Burley and Hunt) twice tried to get rid of him.

They wouldn't even let him train. I also made it clear that Pospisil had the potential to bring an awful lot to the team, particularly when he played next to Bednar or Jankauskas. But there was a lot of resistance to that idea from Burley – Hearts owner **Vladimir Romanov**, May 2006.

I'd like to think I'm a reasonably skilful negotiator. Once I get them on the dance floor, I've got a chance, you know. I haven't lost many in business like that, but it's getting them there. Once we got to Paul, I always thought we had a chance – Rangers chairman **David Murray** on new manager Paul le Guen, June 2006.

What has changed dramatically is the public dissection of individuals who run football clubs. It can be quite painful. I have seen it happen to other club chairmen and owners and I've had a bit of it myself. That's the price you pay if you cross that threshold into the football community – Rangers chairman **David Murray**, July 2006.

I've had a few requests to write a book but I think when you start having to justify things in football then, inside, you must have insecurities. And I don't think I need to justify anything – Celtic defender **Steven Pressley**, aiming a dry dig at Hearts owner Vladimir Romanov, March 2007, two months after he'd been released by Hearts.

If somebody said to me, 'Would you want to be the chairman of Glasgow Rangers or even Chelsea?' I'd have no interest whatsoever – Dundee United chairman **Eddie Thompson**, July 2007.

If you are in a position of authority in any company and you never have a fight, then somebody is not doing his job – Celtic chairman **Brian Quinn**, September 2007. Quinn had had a famous disagreement with former boss Martin O'Neill.

Over a five-year period, there was a certain gentleman who kept calling me names and hell would have to freeze over before he'd let me take control. But eventually there was nobody else, so he took the money – Dundee United chairman **Eddie Thompson** on ex-United chairman Jim McLean, February 2008.

He's a good lad. He's also an intellectual, a clever guy, a university student type, different from the rough and the scruff of Billy Davies coming up from Pollok. I mean, he wasn't stealing apples in Ralston the way I was – **Billy Davies** on his former Motherwell chief executive Pat Nevin, February 2008.

From a health point of view, I would like you to portray that we are going in the right direction. I am a very, very resilient person, there's nothing gets me down. Dundee United? They get me down – Dundee United chairman **Eddie Thompson**, who was battling cancer at the time, March 2008. He died in October 2008.

We asked for details of his background and they said they would fax them. The fax machine rolled and rolled. By the end, we added up that Brooks was director, owner or accountant for no fewer than 36 registered companies, and that put our mind at rest a bit – Gretna chairman **Ron McGregor** recalls the club's first contact with financial backer Brooks Mileson, as they went into administration, March 2008.

When we were running it in the past, probably slightly recklessly in a financial sense, I was criticised for not running it more soberly; I'm now trying to balance the books and I'm criticised again. Other than me going on the park and scoring goals, which I'm incapable of doing, I don't actually know what else I can do – Rangers chairman **Sir David Murray**, August 2008.

He likes you or doesn't like you. When he likes you, he will show that – Former Rangers manager **Dick Advocaat** on chairman David Murray, November 2008.

Heaven has just gained a new chairman – Tribute outside Tannadice after the death of Dundee United chairman **Eddie Thompson**, October 2008.

DRINK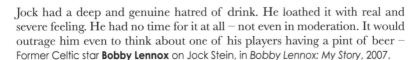

Jock had a deep and genuine hatred of drink. He loathed it with real and severe feeling. He had no time for it at all – not even in moderation. It would outrage him even to think about one of his players having a pint of beer – Former Celtic star **Bobby Lennox** on Jock Stein, in *Bobby Lennox: My Story*, 2007.

Win or lose, have some booze . . . get a draw, have some more – that was our motto – Life at Portsmouth for winger **Peter Marinello**, in *Fallen Idle*, 2007.

I used to drive home from United training along the M56 and there was a left turn for Wilmslow, where I lived, and a right turn for Hale, where Norman Whiteside, Paul McGrath and Bryan Robson lived. I used to say it was left for under three pints a night and right for more than ten – **Gordon Strachan** on his Manchester United days, 2004.

I went out for a Chinese meal with my then wife after the match and got so drunk that I fell asleep at the table – Former Celtic striker **Tony Cascarino**, October 2002, recalling scoring for Celtic against Rangers in a 1–1 draw at Ibrox in November 1991.

It annoyed me when George said I was a bad example to others. Look what (Tony) Adams and (Paul) Merson were doing. He turned a blind eye to them because he was far more bothered about players who disagreed with him than those who drank heavily – Winger **Anders Limpar** on life under George Graham at Arsenal, February 2008.

I can't remember his name but there was a lad at Tranmere. He was with us on trial while we were on tour in Ireland. The kid had a reputation as a bit of a drinker, so they put him in with me, supposedly the sensible one, to keep an eye on him. I woke up at 4am and he was standing on my bed, completely blootered, relieving himself. It was his last day at the club – Former Scotland international **Pat Nevin** recalls his worst room-mate, November 2007.

I have always been against players drinking and I'm always thinking of ways of getting a team that doesn't drink – Manchester United manager **Alex Ferguson**, 1997.

As soon as the words 'night' and 'out' were mentioned, the hands couldn't go up quickly enough . . . Wim (Jansen) knew we liked a night out but he didn't know the half of it. If he had, I think he would have had a seizure . . . we spent a year bevvying our way to the title! – Former Celtic midfielder **Craig Burley** on the title-winning 1997–98 team's bonding sessions, in Mark Guidi, *The Inner Sanctum*, 2008.

If you go to a nightclub, you're fair game. Punters have had a few drinks, get brave, they want a chat with you or maybe give you a bit of stick – Everton's **John Collins**, January 1999.

Scottish players booze, smoke and eat whatever comes to hand – French agent **Jean Luc Wetzel**, 2000.

I don't drink, which is why the pressure was on me from morning till night. If you go to the pub and get pissed I'm sure you wouldn't be worried who you were going to be playing and who you were going to drop – Former Dundee United manager and chairman **Jim McLean**, November 2001.

It becomes a compulsion. I would honestly intend to go for one pint and then go home but I would still be sitting at the bar at midnight – Kilmarnock striker **Andy McLaren** on being an alcoholic, January 2002.

I'd always wanted to be Jimmy as a footballer. I couldn't manage that, so I tried to be the same as him as a drinker. I couldn't do that either – Southampton manager **Gordon Strachan** on Jimmy Johnstone, January 2003.

I don't really drink now. I might have one beer, maximum, on a Saturday night. If you've got problems, there's nothing worse than waking up with problems plus a hangover – Southampton manager **Gordon Strachan**, January 2003.

They are both terrified of flying. You will always see them half-cut at airports before every flight – Former Leicester defender **Gerry Taggart** on Martin O'Neill's Celtic assistants John Robertson and Steve Walford, March 2003.

I expected the sack and I deserved the sack. They chose a more humane way and I don't see a problem with my players either because I have always felt one of my major strengths is my relationship with my players. I am prepared to be open with them. I'll tell them I've got a problem I am going to beat — Aberdeen boss **Steve Paterson** admits to a drink problem, March 2003. He'd missed the match against Dundee three days before because he was hungover.

I don't expect my mates to start drinking f****** soda water and lime when I'm there — Aberdeen manager **Steve Paterson**, May 2003.

Obviously Alex Ferguson will be sending me a bottle of red. I hope it's a crate, but, knowing him, it's a bottle — Leeds manager **Peter Reid**, May 2003, after his side's win at Highbury secured Manchester United's Premiership title.

He's Irish and he has the gift of the gab; with a few glasses of wine he's off and running. He's not a big drinker, a couple of glasses of sweet white wine was his limit, but that's all it took. 'Loquacious', I think you would call it — Wycombe director **Alan Parry** on Martin O'Neill, in Alex Montgomery, *Martin O'Neill – The Biography*, 2003.

There is so much innuendo surrounding me up here it is unbelievable. I couldn't be out drinking as much as some people seem to believe and continue to play football at this level for as long as I have; it just wouldn't be possible — Celtic midfielder **Neil Lennon**, May 2003.

Q: Describe manager Steve Paterson in three words?
A: Off the drink
— Aberdeen defender **Russell Anderson**, newspaper questionnaire, August 2003.

You've never seen a man in such a physical condition. You've only got to look at that advert on the telly — that is him. He doesn't drink. He eats the right food. He just lives for his profession. We had our moments but, you know, he just wanted excellence all the time. He'd get the hump with people who didn't train as well as him. One day Paolo came over and said to me, 'That Neil Ruddock, 'ee talk about what a great night he had last night. He tell me he drunk ten pints of beer. f****** hell, what ees going on?' I just love that man — Portsmouth boss **Harry Redknapp** on former Celt Paolo di Canio, who he'd had at West Ham, September 2003.

I remember what that was like when I was drinking myself, there was always the pain-in-the-arse guy who stays sober and tells everybody what they were like the next day — Dundee United's **Andy McLaren**, a self-confessed alcoholic, October 2003.

Because I had to come out in public I was labelled an alcoholic. I think I had a problem with drink that I've now resolved. I still have a drink at weekends but that's about it – Aberdeen manager **Steve Paterson**, November 2003.

Within two years I was earning over £600 a week and just spending it on booze and gambling. I was addicted to both. I even ended up borrowing thousands from loan sharks and teammates – just to throw away at cards, blackjack or roulette – Doncaster's **Michael McIndoe**, December 2003. He'd been called into the Scotland Future Squad four years after being sent to The Priory by Luton Town for treatment to gambling problems.

I kept going into the ring with drink expecting a different result, and it basically whipped me every time – Wolves midfielder **Alex Rae** after six drink-free years, January 2004.

Terry Hurlock – the only footballer I've ever seen who could play properly while drunk – Boxing promoter **Frank Maloney** on the former Rangers midfielder, 2004.

I think that interview must have been done when Allan was still bevvied – Livingston manager **Davie Hay** after winning the CIS Cup, March 2004. Coach Allan Preston had said he should be involved in/with coaching Scotland.

I went home and got quietly pissed – Dundee's **Lee Wilkie** on the April 2005 injury against Dunfermline which necessitated his second cruciate operation in 15 months, June 2005.

We put a lot of water with the wine but I'm afraid Celtic just wouldn't adjust – Jimmy Floyd Hasselbaink's agent **Humphry Nijman** as transfer talks with Celtic collapse, July 2006.

I don't think the drinks trolley will get anywhere near us with all that lot on board – Celtic manager **Gordon Strachan**, October 2006, on news that the Lisbon Lions would travel on the team flight to the Champions League game against Benfica in Lisbon the following week.

Myself and Maurice Malpas used to get together with John and Stewart Robertson, who works for him at Hamilton Portfolio, for a budget meeting every year. We would go somewhere like the *Ubiquitous Chip*, discuss the budget for about five minutes and spend six hours drinking red wine – Former Motherwell manager **Terry Butcher** on club owner John Boyle, amid reports he was selling out to Tommy Coakley, May 2007.

When you've got the drunkest guy in the place shouting 'Alky' at you it is difficult to deal with. If I have a wee go back people are running to the police. I've had match commanders coming in after games and wanting to arrest me. Football fans can suddenly become the most sensitive wee souls in the world and run to the police saying, 'He stuck his fingers up at me'. Yet I've just taken 90 minutes of abuse – Ayr striker **Andy McLaren**, October 2007, on supporters targetting him after his alcohol and drug problems.

You can go to Firhill on a Friday night and watch the Glasgow Warriors rugby team, take a pint of beer to your seat, and enjoy watching your chosen sport. Twelve hours later when Partick Thistle are playing, you're prohibited from doing any such thing. That's nonsensical. Why should football fans be singled out? – Motherwell chairman **John Boyle**, March 2008.

When I played under Walter at Rangers we had conversations about politics all the time. He, of course, is a staunch socialist and I would ask him whether he could be that and have success and a few bob at the same time. To be fair to Walter, he has stuck to his principles. It's just that he has gone from drinking wine from a box to the very best of stuff – Partick Thistle manager **Ian McCall** on Walter Smith, prior to facing Rangers in the Scottish Cup, April 2008.

Now it's home for a couple of glasses of red. Not the bottle, let's not get carried away. There's 45 games left – Swindon Town manager **Maurice Malpas** after his side's opening-day win against Tranmere, August 2008. He was sacked three months later.

I still speak to her today, but if the roles were reversed I probably wouldn't speak to her. There's no doubt that I humiliated her and humiliated my family – Former Nottingham Forest and Scotland striker **Ian Wallace**, on how his drink problem affected his relationship with ex-wife Carol, February 2009.

I'm teetotal, my mum was too. A teetotal Scotsman draws plenty of laughs but when I went to Manchester it was on the absolute understanding that there could be no going out to all hours. It stuck with me. I took it upon myself to give it everything to become a professional footballer and then, when I made it, I didn't feel the need to start drinking. I do think that played a part. I don't begrudge anyone who does drink but I had three years to make professional and I feel you should dedicate your life in that time. You shouldn't be out every weekend – Manchester United midfielder **Darren Fletcher**, March 2009.

The boys in the nine-in-a-row team often exaggerate things themselves. They wouldn't have won nine in a row if they'd done all the things they said they did. If they were doing that, what were the rest of them (the other clubs) doing at that period of time? I don't think that was a proper reflection of them – Rangers manager **Walter Smith** looks back, in the midst of the Boozegate affair, April 2009.

ENGLAND AND THE ENGLISH

I was also introduced to Emlyn Hughes for the first time – or rather, the future England captain marched over to me before the kick-off and stated quite brazenly, 'If you come anywhere near me, you little Scottish bastard, I shall break both your f****** legs!' Emlyn was a big man who hated losing almost as much as he hated tricky Scottish wingers – Arsenal winger **Peter Marinello** recalls facing Liverpool, in *Fallen Idle*, 2007.

They'd just come down from the old First Division and Teddy Sheringham played for them but when I turned up at the old Den, it was like a knacker's yard. I almost thought, 'Bugger that, I'm back off to Falkirk.' I wondered what I'd let myself in for – Wolves midfielder **Alex Rae**, March 2004, recalling joining Millwall in 1990.

That's why I'm still so popular in Scotland. My brother once went there and all the people bought him drinks – San Marino striker **Davide Gualtieri**, *FourFourTwo* magazine, December 2008. Gualtieri scored against England after 8.3 seconds in the World Cup qualifier in Bologna in November 1993.

I was the regular penalty-taker but McAllister had taken over the role in my absence when I was injured. When we were awarded the penalty, McAllister assumed he was taking it and picked the ball up. I wasn't having any of it though because I was desperate to take it, so I went over to him and started trying to wrestle the ball from his grasp. 'F*** off, you fat c***, I'm on 'em,' he said, resisting my attempts to grab the ball. 'F*** off, you Scotch bastard,' I replied, 'I'm taking it against these cunts, I fucking hate Sheffield United.' We were like two kids, fighting over a ball in a school playground – Former Leeds and Rangers midfielder **Mel Sterland** on a debate with Leeds teammate Gary McAllister in a match in October 1991, quoted in *Boozing, Betting & Brawling: Mel Sterland, A Footballer's Life*, 2008. Sterland won the argument and scored.

They just said, 'Oh, he's signed his mate. Old pal's act.' Wrighty scored goals, you know, but nobody was really interested – Former coach **John Barnes** reflects on his October 1999 signing of Ian Wright for Celtic, March 2003 (*Wright scored three goals in 10 appearances for Celtic*).

What percentage of teams in England can win the league? I'd say that maybe four have the financial clout to do it – which is the same (as Scotland), 20 per cent – Former Scotland international **Pat Nevin**, March 2000.

People think I spend every moment pining to go back but that's rubbish. I'm not saying I wouldn't go back because anybody who turned down a club as big as Celtic or Rangers would be daft. But I'm not sitting there thinking, 'Why isn't the phone ringing?' – Derby midfielder **Craig Burley**, April 2001.

We believe it's more likely than unlikely it will happen in the next three to five years. It's about restructuring British football so we are in a more competitive environment – Then-Celtic chief executive **Ian McLeod** on Celtic playing in England, September 2001.

We had three recounts. But it still came out the same: 86–0. Against – Tartan Army spokesman **Hamish Husband**, asked by the Scottish Tourism Authority whether Scotland fans would support England's World Cup campaign, January 2002.

When people call me an English bastard or harangue me in the street, it just makes me feel even more patriotic, and after talking to the likes of Maurice Malpas and Graeme Souness, I appreciate that they have the same attitude towards Scotland – Motherwell assistant manager **Terry Butcher**, March 2002.

As I say to people in Scotland, it's worse than you being called English – Hibs' Canadian defender **Paul Fenwick**, March 2003, on being mistaken for an American.

Suggestions that Celtic and Rangers will some day play in the English Premiership continue to surface every now and then. Similarly, there is talk occasionally about a British League. Neither of these situations will ever materialise – Former SFA chief executive **Jim Farry**, July 1999.

Until they invite us, their league won't be as good as it would be with Celtic and Rangers – Celtic majority shareholder **Dermot Desmond**, June 2003.

It seems impossible. If we can go to England, why can't Bayern Munich go to Serie A or Ajax and PSV to the Bundesliga? I see it as an impossible dream. I'd rather concentrate on reality – Rangers manager **Alex McLeish** on the Old Firm joining the English Premiership, 2003.

The resistance is in the main from those clubs that feel threatened by Celtic and Rangers, who may get relegated – Celtic majority shareholder **Dermot Desmond**, August 2003.

In every league there are three, four, five teams that dominate but over time these teams change, that's what makes football so intriguing. I can understand there's a problem where you only have two teams. But it is a problem I cannot solve. What would the English clubs make of Celtic and Rangers joining them? Or the other Scottish clubs for that matter? – UEFA president **Lennart Johansson** on speculation the Old Firm would move to England, December 2003.

I have never given up any hopes. I think it is a logical step – Celtic majority shareholder **Dermot Desmond** on the Old Firm moving to England, December 2003. It will not happen in my lifetime. Personally I am not convinced they are drawing the correct conclusions. It is partly the fact that, as in many other parts of society, the grass seems greener on the other side of the fence. But if they are placed between 12th and 18th in the Premiership, I think they would have problems with their fans. I have a question for them: what would they achieve? If you look at the 'rich list' of clubs, Celtic and Rangers are in the top 20 but that doesn't help them in winning the European competitions. So it's not only a question of finance – UEFA chief executive **Lars-Christer Olsson** on the Old Firm joining the Premiership, May 2005.

The way the vote is structured in the English Premiership, with a 16–4 vote required, there is no chance of the Old Firm getting in – Celtic chief executive **Peter Lawwell**, December 2005.

There is no sign of it happening. Why do they need us? Why would they want us? – Rangers chairman **Sir David Murray** on the prospects of an Old Firm move to England, November 2008.

Q: You were picked as Scotland's Player of the Year in 2002 – how do you feel at being chosen for an honour which has previously been won by such legends as Maradona, Van Basten, Pearce, Waddle, Brolin, Koeman, Southgate, Batty, Ince, Beckham and Phil Neville? – David MacLennan, Aberdeen.
A: Was that because I saved a penalty in Euro 96 or because I played when we beat them in the Euro 2000 play-off? It's quite amazing that they can't find a Scottish player, isn't it? Ha, ha. Get a life. Ha, ha – Former England goalkeeper **David Seaman**'s charming response to *FourFourTwo* magazine questionnaire, January 2004.

Reading's Graeme Murty is a strange choice. He's 29 and he's always been a lower-league player. He's not young, he's not a big name down here in England, he's not somebody that's talked about in the context of getting a move to a big club. He was quoted as saying he was absolutely thrilled. Well, with respect, he would be – Former Scotland international **Craig Burley** on Berti Vogts' selection policies before international against Wales, February 2004.

I read a piece in a newspaper a couple of weeks ago which said that if Sir Alex Ferguson has one more season of the kind he's just had, Martin O'Neill can expect a summons to Old Trafford. I thought, 'A summons? A summons to Old Trafford?' Do they think he's working for some tinpot club? – Celtic chairman **Brian Quinn**, May 2004.

Reporter: Do you think James Beattie deserves to be in the England squad?
Strachan: I don't care. I'm Scottish – Exchange from **Gordon Strachan**'s time at Southampton, quoted in *FourFourTwo* magazine, July 2004.

Anyone but England – Scottish tennis player **Andy Murray**, June 2006, after being asked who he'd be supporting in the 2006 World Cup. (*Murray subsequently explained that his comments were said in jest in response to provocation from an English reporter who had asked if Murray would be supporting Scotland in the World Cup. The reporter had asked the question in the knowledge that Scotland hadn't qualified for the tournament.*)

In five matches, Sven-Goran Eriksson's men were mediocre and average. Yesterday, they just happened to lose in painful circumstances to opponents who were also mediocre and average; alongside Ukraine, the weakest of any possible opponents in the quarter-finals. England had been drawn in a kind group and were blessed to meet the poorest last-16 side in the form of Ecuador. The breaks have to even themselves out somewhere along the line – Former Dundee and Hibs manager **Jim Duffy** at the World Cup, July 2006.

I keep trying to tell them that their notion of themselves is unbelievable. The rest of the world hates their guts – SFA president **John McBeth** on the English, preparing to take up his new post as FIFA vice-president, May 2007. He resigned the post a few days later over remarks he'd made about African and Caribbean nations.

All my extended family from England were there although I don't know who they were supporting. But it was a funny experience. The national anthems were a bit awkward. I just kept quiet – Hearts' **Andrew Driver**, October 2007. The English striker had played – and scored – for Scotland Schools against England as a teenager.

If that was a penalty – or even a free kick – I would change my name to Alex McJockstrap and wear a kilt every day – Leicester manager **Ian Holloway** after a decision against his side against Southampton, December 2007.

I am pleased to see with Scotland that international football does mean as much as when I played. I don't think that's necessarily the case with England – Scotland assistant boss **Terry Butcher**, March 2008.

I lost a fortune when Steve Bruce and Bryan Robson were here and we had bets whenever the Scots and English were involved in matches, not just football but rugby as well. I used to get carried away by national loyalty – Manchester United manager **Sir Alex Ferguson**, October 2008.

I still can't watch a football match without wanting whoever it is playing England to win – Edinburgh-born restaurant critic **AA Gill**, December 2008.

I was never one of those Scottish guys who hated the English anyway; my dad did not bring me up like that. We wanted England to do well in the World Cup, still do – Manchester United midfielder **Darren Fletcher**, March 2009.

EUROPE ⚽

You looked around for a man who could take the game by the scruff of the neck, and realised people like Suarez were missing. Normally, when things were going badly, we would look into Suarez's eyes and never see any fear. But in Lisbon he wasn't there. Celtic came out and went for us on the flanks, and there was no one there to calm us down, to tell us everything would still be okay – Inter Milan's **Sandro Mazzola** remembers the loss of injured Luis Suarez in the 1967 European Cup Final against Celtic, May 2007.

We won two European Cups yet we never practised a free kick. 'Just give it to Robbo' was the cry – Former Nottingham Forest midfielder **Martin O'Neill**, in *Clough: The Autobiography*, 1994.

I can remember going for a sleep. It had been overcast, but nice and dry, so when I woke up at about 4.30 and saw that it was pissing down, I thought, 'Oh Christ.' People said it suited us, but it didn't. It didn't suit men like Strachan, McMaster, Black and Weir. We wanted a good pitch for those players – Manchester United manager **Sir Alex Ferguson**, May 2003, recalling Aberdeen's Cup Winners' Cup success in 1983 20 years on.

We had ten minutes to go, as well as time added on, with a midfield who couldn't tackle, and a front three who couldn't defend. But we were hanging on because, in Willie Miller and Alex McLeish, we had the two best centre halves in Britain. The ball was like a magnet to Miller that night – Manchester United manager **Sir Alex Ferguson** on Gothenburg, May 2003.

It was going to be the most embarrassing thing I've ever done. But it was amazing. The streets were lined with people and it underlined to me and to everybody associated with it just how unique that team was. We had a shape and a way of playing and an understanding of what was required of us. Everyone knew the job he had to do – Millwall manager **Mark McGhee**, September 2003, recalling the 20th anniversary celebrations of Aberdeen's Cup-Winners Cup victory.

There were some strong sides in Sweden at that time, it was a good league. The culture was very different though, very quiet. Television stations switching off at 9pm, I remember with total disbelief. People were out in the forest hunting moose – Preston manager **Billy Davies** recalls playing in Sweden for Elfsborg Boras in the mid-80s, November 2004.

Even now, when he rings my mobile, the name comes up as 'God' – Former Norwich goalkeeper **Bryan Gunn**, September 2007, on Jeremy Goss, who'd scored in Norwich's 2–1 UEFA Cup win over Bayern Munich in the Olympic Stadium in March 1993.

In one of my early matches we were winning 4–1 with 10 minutes to go and I pushed up, about five yards into the opposing half. Jurgen Kohler shouted, 'Hey! What are you doing? Get back!' That's how disciplined Dortmund were. You play the same at 0–0 or 4–1 – Celtic's **Paul Lambert** on Bundesliga life, May 1999.

We were thrown to a veritable wild horde. It was a meeting of warriors where neither weakness nor nonchalance had a place. It was a test in the pure British tradition – Monaco goalkeeper **Fabien Barthez**, 2000, on playing at Ibrox in the Champions League for Marseille in 1992.

We were told 10 days ago by the Foreign Office not to travel (to Dagestan). Regrettably, the world hasn't become a safer place in the last 10 days – Rangers chairman **David Murray**, September 16, 2001. Rangers had been drawn against Russians Anzhi Makhachkala from the Soviet Republic of Dagestan, close to the border with Chechnya, in the UEFA Cup. The World Trade Centers were attacked by terrorists on September 11. The match was eventually played on a neutral ground in Warsaw.

The Germans were better organised, better formation, better team and everyone knew what they were doing. But Real had Zidane – Former Southampton manager **Gordon Strachan**, May 2004, on the 2002 Champions League Final between Real Madrid and Bayer Leverkusen at Hampden.

I knew people were saying, he's kidding himself on. I knew that. That was the chance I had to take. But I had nothing – not a thing – here in Scotland. The foreigners gave me a chance that not many people here did – **Paul Lambert**, BBC Footballers' Lives programme, March 2003. Lambert won a European Cup Winners' medal in his first season at Borussia Dortmund.

I laugh off the suggestion that it might be the right time to play Liverpool because they're having such a poor time of it. They're having such a poor time that they've just won the Worthington Cup against one of the best sides in Europe – **Martin O'Neill**, March 2003, before Celtic's UEFA Cup quarter-final meeting with Liverpool, who'd just beaten Manchester United in the Worthington Cup Final.

I know Henrik (Larsson) has said that, at Anfield, he heard from Martin one of the best pre-match speeches of his life, and I know what he means. He was brilliant. The hairs on the back of my head were standing up. He told us we could beat Liverpool, that this was the moment, this was our chance, and that for some of us, maybe it was our last chance for European glory. Before we went out, we knew we could win – Celtic's **Neil Lennon**, May 2003, recalling O'Neill's pre-match talk before the UEFA Cup game against Liverpool in March 2003.

If you work in a Glasgow travel agent, get to bed, you're going to have a busy day tomorrow – *BBC Scotland*'s **Dougie Donnelly**, April 2003, after Celtic had beaten Boavista 1–0 to qualify for the UEFA Cup Final.

He didn't know the half of it. We've got twelve lines here and they haven't stopped all day. By 2pm we'd taken 3,000 calls – **Glasgow travel agent** the next day, quoted in *The Sun*, April 2003

I will probably get into trouble for this, but it was poor sportsmanship. The rolling over, the time-wasting. But they have beaten us, well done to them and it's up to us to learn from this. It's a steep learning curve, but this was a wonderful, wonderful experience – Celtic manager **Martin O'Neill** after losing the UEFA Cup Final to Porto in Seville, May 2003.

I'd prefer to ask whether the behaviour of the Celtic players was normal in your country. What (Bobo) Balde did to Deco in front of me could have ended his career. The referee didn't affect the result, in that there were no doubtful decisions, but I think Balde could have had a direct red for his foul and (Alan) Thompson could also have seen a second yellow card on two occasions. The referee wanted to end the game with 11 against 11 and I think maybe he was a bit afraid to send anyone off. There was a lot of commitment in Celtic's game – commitment, toughness and aggression. I'm tempted to use another word, but I won't – Porto coach **Jose Mourinho** after the same match, May 2003.

I'm in a team sport. Like the UEFA Cup Final, that ended in disaster. We didn't win. We didn't pick up the trophy. In ten years time when I look back I might feel different, but not at this time. I still feel, whenever anybody asks me about it, I just feel, 'Uugh'. I'd rather not have scored two goals, any goal, and we won the trophy. Then you can say that you won, you did it – Celtic's **Henrik Larsson** on the 2003 UEFA Cup Final defeat to Porto, March 2004.

Let's face it, Rangers only won the league because Celtic were so obsessed with winning the UEFA Cup. They arrived at the final game of the season completely shattered while we were well rested with one trophy already in the bag – Rangers striker **Claudio Caniggia** on the title his side had just won, June 2003.

It makes me wonder whether some people are growing scared that Dundee are about to become a really major force in European football. I am genuinely excited at the prospect of Dundee playing in the Champions League in the next two or three years. Why not? – Dundee director **Giovanni di Stefano**, October 2003.

We went on pre-season to Holland and our game against the Turkish team Rizespor was abandoned by the referee because their goalkeeper got in a fight with a streaker who'd run on to the pitch – Former Falkirk defender **Jack Ross** on European experiences, September 2008. The game was in July 2006.

It's incredible. Rangers didn't want to play football. They practised anti-football from the first minute – Barcelona's **Lionel Messi** after the 0–0 Champions League draw at Ibrox, October 2007.

It just seems like the pitch is double the size when they've got the ball, and they condense it right down when we've got it – Celtic defender **Gary Caldwell** reflects on facing Barcelona after the 3–2 defeat at Parkhead in the Champions League, February 2008.

Unless I've missed something and people hide players on pitches in the games that I watch in the Champions League, the vast majority of teams playing in European football play with one striker. But when Rangers or Celtic do it, people ask, 'Why are they doing that?' Well, maybe we do it because everyone else is doing it. Maybe we do it because we think, European-wise, it might give us a better opportunity to win. If people tell me it's the wrong way to play, then fine. I've tried the other way and they told me that was the wrong way as well – Rangers manager **Walter Smith** on critics of his one-man-up-front style after the 2–0 win over Werder Bremen in the UEFA Cup, March 2008.

Our co-efficient is the highest since 1983, and it could be higher yet. We were 26th in Europe when the Premier League started, now we're 11th – SPL executive chairman **Lex Gold**, March 2008.

He actually asked me how we were sitting with the penalties when Nacho went forward and I said to him, 'I've got news for you, if this one goes in, you'll know soon enough how we're sitting.' – Rangers assistant manager **Ally McCoist** reveals boss Walter Smith lost track of the penalty kicks tally during the UEFA Cup semi-final shoot-out against Fiorentina, May 2008. Nacho Novo scored from the penalty to take Rangers through to the final.

Do you really think we were going to stop 100,000-plus Glaswegians wanting to have a drink? – Manchester council leader **Sir Richard Leese** defending his city's decision to sell alcohol at the UEFA Cup Final, May 2008.

The ned's defence – Journalist **Tom English**, *Scotland on Sunday*, May 2008 on claims the trouble at the UEFA Cup Final in Manchester was caused by a screen showing the game breaking down.

The basics of what Barcelona did were very similar to our own, from the warm-ups to the set-piece work and passing drills. The only difference is the Barcelona lads could control the ball – Bradford City manager **Stuart McCall**, July 2008. His side had shared the same training complex as Barcelona at St Andrews.

After reaching a European final last season, it's going from the sublime to the ridiculous – Rangers manager **Walter Smith** after his side went out of the Champions League in the second qualifying round against FK Kaunas of Lithuania, August 2008.

Scottish football is not in a desperately poor situation just because Celtic got beat 3–0 by a team who can probably beat any team in Europe 3–0 – Rangers manager **Walter Smith** after Celtic's Champions League defeat to Manchester United, October 2008. It meant that the five Scottish clubs had played eleven games in the various European competitions that season without winning any.

No one has shown us a table that says we are ahead. It's a bit Kafkaesque – you don't really know what's happening – Motherwell manager **Mark McGhee**, May 2009, amid reports his side stood to pick up an entry spot in the Europa League through a Fair Play table place. They duly did.

EXCUSES ⚽

I remember that incident in Zagreb and I remember the reaction to it. How could I forget? I was labelled a 'shitebag' and also 'the guy who cost Celtic a place in the Champions League group stages' – Former Celtic winger **Regi Blinker** on appearing to pull out of a 50-50 challenge with the Croatia Zagreb goalkeeper in the Champions League qualifying tie in August 1998, in Mark Guidi, *The Inner Sanctum*, 2008. Blinker claimed he was 'feigning going for the ball', hoping his quick movement would allow him to get to it first.

There was just such a tremendous sense of euphoria and the crowd are going and songs are sung and you join in. Because you want people to know that as vice-chairman of Rangers you're not a suit – Former Rangers vice-chairman **Donald Findlay**, October 1999, on being asked to resign his position on the board in June 1999 after being caught singing 'The Sash' and 'The Billy Boys' following the Scottish Cup Final the previous month.

There wasn't the belief in what I was saying, not because they were particularly bad ideas or the players couldn't understand them. It was just the belief in me – Former Celtic coach **John Barnes**, May 2000

The players I had signed were crucified, the players I hadn't signed weren't – Former Celtic coach **John Barnes**, who signed Stephane Bonnes, Eyal Berkovic, Olivier Tebily, and Ian Wright.

I have talked it over with him, and he told me he felt frightened when he went into the crowd. They were not helping him back on to his feet, you know. It was more than a playful tap – Liverpool manager **Gerard Houllier**, March 2003, defending his player El-Hadji Diouf, who spat at Celtic fans during the UEFA Cup game between the clubs.

I remember falling back into the crowd and someone slapping me on the back of the head. I realise now that I took that contact in the wrong way, but at the time it genuinely frightened me because I had no idea what was going on behind me. I've since invited both of the Celtic fans who were taken away by the stewards to be my guests at Anfield on Thursday because I want to shake hands with them and tell them to their face how sorry I am. I sat next to the boss on the coach after the game and he explained to me that although the club would stand by me, I had got it wrong big style, and that sort of behaviour was totally unacceptable for a Liverpool player – **El-Hadji Diouf**, March 2003. He was given a two-match ban by UEFA and fined £5,000 by Glasgow Sheriff Court for the incident.

I think everybody could have virtually predicted the result at Ibrox before kick-off. Well, many people did. It's disappointing from the players who have put the effort in. We knew they (Dunfermline) would lie down, and they have done – Celtic striker **Chris Sutton** accepts losing the league with good grace, May 2003. Rangers' 6–1 win over Dunfermline meant they won the title by one goal. Sutton, who'd been sent off in the tunnel after his side's 4–0 win at Kilmarnock, was subsequently given a one-match ban for his remarks, in addition to the four-game ban he'd received for the two red cards he'd received in the tunnel that day.

It appears there is a culture at Celtic that, if anything goes against them, the conspiracy theory comes out – Dunfermline chairman **John Yorkston**, May 2003.

I apologise sincerely to Dunfermline Athletic Football Club, the players, management team and supporters for any offence which my comments may have caused. As everyone will know, these comments were made in the immediate aftermath of us losing the title and at the end of an extremely disappointing week. I have great respect for the Dunfermline players as fellow professionals and I hope that they will accept this apology in the manner in which it is offered – Celtic's **Chris Sutton**'s apology, May 2003.

An apology of an apology – Dunfermline chairman **John Yorkston**, on Celtic striker Chris Sutton's retraction of his remarks about the club, September 2003.

Davie Provan, the *Sky* pundit, said to me, 'You keep pouring fuel on the fire', but who started that fire? Who had the opportunity of putting the fire out? We needed to stand up for ourselves, because we were in the right. We were hurt by those allegations – the players, the coaches, everybody – Dunfermline chairman **John Yorkston** on the Sutton incident, September 2003.

An agenda in every sentence – Journalist **Bill Leckie**, *The Sun* newspaper, January 2004, on Martin O'Neill, after the Celtic manager had launched a far-fetched defence of striker John Hartson on a charge of elbowing Hearts' Andy Webster the same month. The striker was booked for the second-minute incident.

On January 17 we were four points clear of Arsenal; Rio Ferdinand decides to take his suspension, and from that moment everything changed. I wasn't sure Rio should have done that – Manchester United manager **Sir Alex Ferguson**, May 2004, on Ferdinand missing a drug test in September 2003 and being banned for eight months. Arsenal won the title, finishing 15 points ahead of Manchester United.

It was a moral argument and I defy anyone not to do what I did – Celtic manager **Gordon Strachan**, August 2007, after being sent to the stand following an argument with a steward at Pittodrie. He was banned for four games by the SFA for 'unacceptable conduct', though this was subsequently halved on appeal.

We've had a much better season than Celtic. They didn't get to any cup finals or as far in Europe as us. If it hadn't been for us fighting on all four fronts, we'd not only have won the league, we'd have won it by a considerable number of points – Rangers defender and Scotland's Player of the Year **Carlos Cuellar**, May 2008.

FAMILY ⚽

I wish I'd let him know what I really felt about him. I never once told him I loved him. Never hugged him enough. I kept my distance emotionally. It was such a mistake – Former Celtic manager **Lou Macari**, January 2000, following the April 1999 suicide of his 19-year-old son Jonathan.

Going for £10m, I knew I was going to be judged on goals, but that's not the be-all and end-all. I don't think they ever tried to accommodate me or my style. In many ways, I'm glad to be out of it, especially if it means my wife and kids are not being abused in the streets – Celtic striker **Chris Sutton**, October 2002, on his July 1999 move to Chelsea which saw him score three goals in 39 matches.

If you read the papers, people think Gascoigne and I have a father-and-son relationship. Well, I've got two sons and I have never felt like hitting them, but I have certainly felt like smacking Gascoigne a couple of times – Everton manager **Walter Smith** on Paul Gascoigne, who he'd managed at Rangers and Everton, 2000.

I did this interview in Glasgow and turned up with a Celtic hat and a Rangers scarf and said, 'This ain't no partisan shit, I'm singing for everyone.' That's the two things that Scottish folks love the most; music and football, and they got one representative from each of those from my family – Musician **Gil Scott**

Heron, 2000, on his Jamaican father, who played for Celtic. Giles Heron signed in August 1951 and played five games, scoring two goals, between August and December 1951.

Occasionally we used to take Colin (son) to Tannadice and he would sit there reading a book. That was my fault. When he was young I decided I wasn't going to spend a lot of time teaching him to play football. Wrong – because kids need sport to mix – Former Dundee United manager **Jim McLean**, November 2001.

The most protected species in the world is a son. The most protected. The mother and father don't see anything wrong. They might tell 'em in private, but they'll no' tell the neighbours – Manchester United manager **Sir Alex Ferguson**, 2002.

I was lucky. I had a wife and two boys to go home to. The lad in the bed next to me was paralysed and his wife had left him because she couldn't handle it – Rangers chairman **David Murray** on losing his legs in a car crash in 1976, January 2002.

If they manage to avoid being burdened with the label 'The next Terry Butcher', then so much the better. I would hate to think they were under extra pressure because of their old man – Motherwell assistant manager **Terry Butcher**, March 2002, on sons Edward and Alistair.

I don't think he would have questioned me owning a racehorse. He might have laughed at me now knowing the difference between a thoroughbred and the horse that pulled the coal-cart in Govan – Manchester United manager **Sir Alex Ferguson** on his father, August 2002.

I was a mother's boy. We had a match against Celtic the next day and she was on the phone to me for a long time, maybe about an hour, insisting she tell me this and explain that. I wondered why she was telling me so much, then my brother explained that she was poorly. She died an hour after we spoke, in her chair beside a cup of tea – Rangers director of football **Dick Advocaat**, September 2002, on his 89-year-old mother's death on January 1, 1999 – the day before an Old Firm game.

Neil has been away from home, through football, from when he was 15 years old, and, when the phone rings at half-past two or three in the morning, it's loneliness. So, you sit at the bottom of the stairs freezing, and you talk for an hour and a half. And you still have to do that – **Gerry Lennon**, father of Celtic's Neil, September 2002.

It takes five minutes but it's five minutes more than I ever spent with him when I was a manager – Former Dundee United manager **Jim McLean** on driving son Colin to work as a computer engineer after quitting Dundee United, October 2002.

Three of my kids from my first marriage to Agnes don't even speak to me. There is no contact at all, no cards, no calls, no presents. It was a heartbreak at first, but now it doesn't even bother me. Ironically, those three have been married and divorced themselves. I think if they came back and said we should start from scratch, I wouldn't do it. No, not now – Former Manchester United manager **Tommy Docherty**, November 2002.

You're basically what your parents have instilled in you in terms of your discipline, your manners – Manchester United manager **Sir Alex Ferguson**, 2002.

Paul will escape a fine this time. Season of goodwill and all that nonsense. But no doubt he held the wife on a bit longer so it fell on Christmas Day and the kids only get presents for Christmas or their birthdays – Hibs manager **Bobby Williamson** on defender Paul Fenwick missing training after wife Debbie gave birth to twins on Christmas morning, 2002.

I love being with football people, just love it, but football comes a long way behind the family – Southampton manager **Gordon Strachan**, January 2003.

The reason that I am proud of Scot has nothing to do with football, it's because he is such a nice person. He is polite, he treats people right. Footballers can be a bit you-know-what, but he's not. He's never touched any alcohol, which I'm also delighted about – Scotland scout **Archie Gemmill** on son Scot, June 2003.

I would not be a footballer if my dad hadn't been Archie Gemmill. At 15 or 16, when decisions are made about young footballers becoming professionals, I was physically immature and nowhere near good enough. I was only given the chance as an apprentice at Nottingham Forest because my surname was Gemmill – New Zealand Knights midfielder **Scot Gemmill**, August 2006.

I've got daughters and you would be happy if they came home with him – Blackburn manager **Graeme Souness** on his defender Lucas Neill, September 2003. Neill's tackle had left Liverpool's Jamie Carragher with a broken leg.

I think that I'm perfectly sane and that everybody else around me is mad. But then I see videos of myself, and think, 'God, is that what I look like?' To watch myself on tape brings major embarrassment sometimes and, I've been told, to my daughters too. How embarrassed must they be when they see their father behaving like a lunatic on the sidelines? The worrying thing is that I never truly realise what I'm doing – Celtic manager **Martin O'Neill**, January 2004.

I've got two sons, Mark Walters Singh and Oleg Kuznetsov Singh, named after former players – Rangers fan and Glasgow Asian restaurateur **Satty Singh**, January 2004.

My children even phone me now, which is an improvement. They used to phone their mum and ask if it was worth speaking to Dad. It was a shame. I was listening but I wasn't hearing – Former Southampton manager **Gordon Strachan** on life during his break away from the game, February 2005.

I'm a Celtic supporter from way back. The family team were actually Queen of the South but I had a great-uncle played for Celtic in the early 20s. He was a Thomson without the P – Musician **Richard Thompson** on his family legacy, March 2005.

When I look at the way they have turned out as people, I think, 'I am not sure if you have ever wished you could be like me, but I certainly wish I could be like you.' – Celtic manager **Gordon Strachan** on sons Gavin and Craig, in autobiography, *Strachan: My Life In Football*, 2006.

During his career his surname has been a problem for other people, not him, because it's the only one he has ever had – Former Scotland striker **Kenny Dalglish** on son Paul, *FourFourTwo* magazine interview, May 2006.

In the old days it used to be 'That's Jim Fleeting's daughter', now it has turned round to 'That's Julie Fleeting's dad' – SFA director of football development **Jim Fleeting**, September 2006. Daughter Julie is a successful Scotland international.

My dad used to referee me when I was a kid. I remember him booking me – and asking my name – Coventry striker **Kevin Kyle**, 2006.

I tell him Michael Jackson has his picture on his wall. I don't know if that impresses him much – Gretna manager **Davie Irons**, October 2007, on meeting Jacko in Disney World in Florida in 1994. Jackson asked to take a picture of Irons' year-old son, Lewis.

My family say it to me every week. Walter Smith doesn't know why I do it. He says, 'What are you putting up with this for?' Oh, in the beginning it was ego maybe, a chance to stick out my chest, but I feel huge responsibility to the club. I could just say 'f*** it' and go. I've plenty of things to do. But I won't do that. I'll do my best until somebody comes up with the answers – Rangers chairman **Sir David Murray**, August 2008.

Plenty of people might have imagined my old man prancing up and down the touchline at my under-10s match, making himself heard slaughtering the ref, but nothing could be further from the truth – Notts County midfielder **Gavin Strachan**, son of Gordon, November 2008.

Well it makes a change from Graeme dropping something – Motherwell manager **Mark McGhee** after goalkeeper Graeme Smith became a father to daughter Mia the night before the game against Rangers, November 2008.

When I was playing I enjoyed myself too much at times but now I have Sunday with my boy, and Saturday night – which is traditionally a sociable night for managers – is a quiet time because I don't want to waste the time I have with Edson. I do not want to cheat my own son – Partick Thistle manager **Ian McCall** reflects on his marital break-up, January 2009.

I hammer it into them the work ethic is what got them through the door here in the first place and they must never lose it. I say to them, 'When you're going home to your mother, you make sure she's seeing the same person she sent to me, because if you take all this fame and money the wrong way, your mother will be disappointed with you.' – Manchester United manager **Sir Alex Ferguson**, March 2009.

I always remember when I was about 25 or 26 and my mother came up to me and said, 'Have you voted?' I said, 'I don't know how to vote.' She said, 'What do you mean you don't know how to vote? You get down that bloody school and get your bloody vote! What do you think your father would say?' That was the very last time I ever dared to mention voting. My mother was normally quite a quiet woman but she went mad – Manchester United manager **Sir Alex Ferguson**, May 2009.

FANS ⚽

I went to the traditional Wembley game the year after England won the World Cup in 1967 and we got a special bus from Johnstone, well from a small village called Kilbarchan, actually, and the first stop was the toilets in Johnstone Square – a journey of about four minutes – Scottish League secretary **Peter Donald**, quoted in *Fanatical About Football*, ed. Jeff Connor, 2003.

We hate Jimmy Hill, he's a poof, he's a poof – **Scotland fans**' chant, 1990s. Hill had described David Narey's goal for Scotland against Brazil in the 1982 World Cup as a 'toe-poke'.

I was aware that kids not blessed with footballing ability tended to kick with the toe rather than with their instep. I wasn't accusing David (Narey) of that; I merely believed he couldn't have reached the ball and shot so powerfully in any other way. Crestfallen, disappointed Scots (Brazil won 4–1) wanted to believe otherwise and have never let me forget it – **Jimmy Hill** in *The Jimmy Hill Story: My Autobiography*, 1998.

Why do you think you're so unpopular north of the border? Does it bother you at all? And why do you think Scotland fans questioned your sexuality so relentlessly? – Richard Rush, Glasgow.

I never knew I was unpopular in Scotland and to be honest, there's no country in the world where I get a better reception. As for the sexuality rumours, I can only guess that was from a journalist looking to make up a story, and he must have misfired. I can tell you that I have 13 grandchildren, so I certainly didn't misfire! – **Jimmy Hill**, FourFourTwo magazine questionnaire, January 2006.

I was ex-treasurer of the Episcopal Church in Broughty Ferry. Back in 1982 we played Radnicki Nis, an Eastern bloc team. We'd won at home and so I had a wee prayer the Sunday morning before the return leg. But we lost and I remember the next Sunday going and giving God a wee piece of my mind, saying, 'Jesus Christ, how could you let the bloody communists win?' – Dundee United chairman **Eddie Thompson**, March 2008.

My name was ringing around Ibrox, something I had never heard at Celtic Park – Former Celtic striker **Tony Cascarino** recalls scoring at Ibrox in November 1991 October 2002.

There was no doubt he could be idiosyncratic. He very rarely replied to mail. He got lots of crank letters, and they can be irritating if you let them get to you . . . Martin would just keep those letters, and if they were really having a go at him, he would leave them in a drawer or in a file. I remember we were having chat about the year ahead in the Premiership and as we sat in his office he opened a drawer, took some letters out, and rang the people up. 'Is that John Smith?' 'Yes.' 'Martin O'Neill here.' There would be a silence, and Martin would say, 'You wrote me a letter and you called me this and that and said I couldn't do this job, so I thought I'd ring you and ask what your thoughts are now.' – Former Leicester secretary **Ian Silvester** on Martin O'Neill, in Alex Montgomery, Martin O'Neill – The Biography, 2003.

My main memory of the Dunfermline game is running out wide to collect the ball trackside to take a throw near the end of the match when we were losing. A fan leaned over and shouted, 'Why don't you just f*** off back to Chelsea?' I wished I could have. I'd have gone back in a minute. I didn't want to be at Celtic – Teething problems for **Craig Burley** as a Celtic player, in Mark Guidi, The Inner Sanctum, 2008. Celtic lost 2–1 to Dunfermline in August 1997 in their first home game of the season and went bottom of the SPL.

You're well tempted to say, 'Eff off'. I mean, the postman doesn't have to deal with 'You're having a shocker today, you useless bastard! My ma could deliver letters better than you!' But you learn in this game that you can never please everyone – Everton midfielder **John Collins**, January 1999.

It only takes two or three people to start that in football. There are leaders and sheep, and the sheep just join in — Coventry manager **Gordon Strachan** after midfielder Gary McAllister was jeered by Aberdeen fans during a pre-season friendly, July 1999.

It reached the stage where he really could not be selected for a home match — Former Celtic general manager **Jock Brown** on the Celts fans' treatment of Darren Jackson, in *Celtic-Minded: 510 Days In Paradise*, 1999.

You always have to try to be professional but I was playing in front of bigger crowds at school — Clydebank defender **Joe McLaughlin** after a crowd of 29 turned up to watch his side face East Stirling in a CIS Cup-tie in July 1999.

'Spot the Ball?' We were playing 'Spot the Fan' out there — Clydebank manager **Ian McCall** after the same game.

You don't go to Tynecastle to relax. You go to be gnawed, to feel the acid eating away your stomach — Scots Tory leader (and former Hearts club lawyer) **David McLetchie**, January 2000.

Motherwell is rising like a mighty storm, a force so swift that no power, however great, will be able to hold it back. It will sweep all its rivals like a tornado which tears apart buildings — Letter from **Stephen Mbiriyakare**, Karoi, Zimbabwe, printed in Motherwell v Hearts programme, March 2000. Motherwell lost the game 2–0 – their third consecutive home defeat – and took their total to ten goals conceded in three home games.

It was great to see the people, in the rain, ringed around the barriers who, by the applause and cheers I got, seemed actually pleased to see that I was the manager. To me, that was invigorating and kind of exciting — **Martin O'Neill** recalls being appointed manager of Celtic in June 2000, March 2003.

I was standing in the centre circle when there was a thud and as I looked down there was a steaming hot baked potato. It just so happened that it was Rino Gattuso who was standing nearest me and I looked at him and asked, 'Lunch?' I still don't know how they managed to get it so far onto the pitch. They must have used a rocket launcher — Former ref **Hugh Dallas**, March 2003, recalling handling an October 2000 Champions League game between AC Milan and Barcelona.

The decent fans are in the minority. The other 80 per cent are a waste of time. Half of them wouldn't know a football if it hit them on the head — Motherwell's **Derek Townsley**, quitting the club after taking abuse from fans, May 2001.

For me to be arrogant or obnoxious and not explain myself after a disappointing result isn't what I'm about — Kilmarnock manager **Bobby Williamson** explaining why he held an impromptu inquest among fans at the bar of Stavanger Airport after his side's 2–0 UEFA Cup defeat by Viking, September 2001.

When I arrived I think they put the stocks up but I made sure the bread was soft and the tomatoes had all gone – **Gordon Strachan** on attending a forum for Coventry supporters, 2001.

Martin (O'Neill) has reduced the number of nutters at Celtic because he has given them less to be nuts about – Former Nottingham Forest manager **Brian Clough**, February 2002.

I've been known to attend Parkhead occasionally, more because of the inclinations of my son than mine. I presented the League Cup to Rangers. I did my best to look pleased for them – First Minister **Jack McConnell**, September 2002.

I went there once and got caught at some traffic lights near Elland Road. This bunch of supporters, skinheads, 20 or 30 of them, they see me and go 'Ferguson!' and start running across the road. The lights are still red, I'm almost shitting maself, they're getting nearer, then the light goes to amber and (*impersonation of a tyre-squeal*) I'm away – Manchester United manager **Sir Alex Ferguson** on a visit to Leeds, 2002.

The long walks to the dugout can be a nightmare. At Coventry it was a scary walk. Archie Knox once saved me from a nutcase who tried to jump over the barrier and get me – Southampton manager **Gordon Strachan**, January 2003.

Even now, when I walk up the steps on a Saturday afternoon and see the pitch, the hairs on the back of my neck stand up – Actor and Hibs fan **Dougray Scott**, March 2003.

There I am, a middle-aged man sitting watching at Berwick, a so-called sensible person, and they score and you find yourself on your feet with your arms in the air shouting. I can't explain it. Can anyone? – *Scotsman* newspaper farming editor **Fordyce Maxwell**, quoted in *Fanatical About Football*, ed. Jeff Connor, 2003.

I love Celtic and I love the fans, but this thing has been endemic among them this season. Against Celta Vigo they were on our backs, and against Liverpool they were on our backs as well. To be honest, when I got it, I thought, 'What's this all about?' Like I said at the time, I wobbled for 10 minutes, gave away a foul because I'd let the crowd affect me, and when Boavista won that free kick, I thought, 'If this goes in I'm going to get almighty pelters.' It really f***ing annoyed me, so it did, and I hope Martin O'Neill remembers it. He will, too. He's got a memory like an elephant over things like that – Celtic's **Neil Lennon** on fan criticism, May 2003. Fans had jeered when he passed the ball back to goalkeeper Robert Douglas in the UEFA Cup semi-final against Boavista in April 2003.

I don't have anything against Rangers and Celtic fans but they do like to give me some banter. I try and smile when I pass their buses now so they don't recognise me – Former Dundee United manager **Jim McLean**, June 2003.

I got this letter from somebody suggesting I didn't deserve to be at this club. They called me a gypsy and told me I should head back to where I belonged. 'Gypsy go home', I think that was how it ended. That upset me, but I got over it – Celtic midfielder **Stilian Petrov**, September 2003.

It is their problem. They are not guaranteeing the facilities and the overdraft – Dundee director **Giovanni di Stefano**, September 2003, on Dundee fans' scepticism over his background.

I heard a shout behind me, 'All right, ya effin' fud' shouts this guy, and I knew it must have been a Celtic fan. I just burst out laughing and gave him a wave. Then I realised that I really missed the banter here – Blackburn's **Barry Ferguson**, December 2003. He rejoined Rangers in January 2005.

Our fan base is diminishing – if we lose one fan, who's going to replace that person? – East Stirling director **Les Thomson**, December 2003.

When I was born I was christened Stuart John Francis Cosgrove, so my initials are SJFC, St Johnstone Football Club. I didn't have a lot of choice about who I supported – *Channel 4* Head of Programmes **Stuart Cosgrove**, in *Fanatical About Football*, ed. Jeff Connor, 2003.

I have followed Raith Rovers for a long time. There was one great moment in 1995 when they beat Celtic to win the League Cup. My flight was delayed from London and I had to listen to it on the telephone. The friend on the other end had a radio and held it to the other end of the phone. I keep saying to people in my speeches, when I talk about training and skills, that you would be emphasising training and skills too, if you had to watch Raith Rovers – **Gordon Brown**, MP for Dunfermline East and chancellor of the exchequer, in *Fanatical About Football*, ed. Jeff Connor, 2003.

Something I've developed over the years is watching the game for the game, not my team. I'm quite impassive. I have to be. If I went to a game and started singing for Celtic, people would point out I work for Livingston, but I had no qualms in Seville. You couldn't not get caught up in the whole experience. After being greeted by Celtic fans in the street beforehand, when the game came along, with a few beers in me, there was only one thing to do and that was sing for Celtic – Livingston manager **David Hay**, March 2004.

It's like dismissing Renoir as artist-in-residence and bringing in Rolf Harris. Only worse, far worse – Coventry City fans' website on the club sacking manager **Eric Black** to bring in Peter Reid, June 2004.

Once you have played for either half of the Old Firm they (supporters) automatically think that's the team you support, for some bizarre reason – Queen of the South fan and Dundee United manager **Ian McCall**, February 2005.

We could go straight to 85,000 capacity overnight, with 80,000 season ticket holders, there's no question of that – Former Celtic manager **Martin O'Neill**, June 2005.

Gordon told me that, after returning from the match overnight, the next day he took his wife, Lesley, shopping in Hamilton. After parking his car he found himself being verbally accosted by a passing punter. 'Hi, Strachan, you're a ******* disgrace.' To escape, Gordon tried to do the fastest nonchalant walk in history, only for the irate man to follow. 'You're an embarrassment!' Then, as if that was not bad enough, he signed off with the most damning comment of all. 'And I'm a ******* Rangers supporter!' – Motherwell manager **Mark McGhee** recalls his close friend Gordon Strachan meeting the public after Celtic's defeat to Artmedia Bratislava in his first game in charge, May 2009.

I think I've had one letter of support in my 11 years of being involved at Celtic. I've had plenty of letters of criticism – Majority shareholder **Dermot Desmond** to the Celtic Supporters Association, December 2005.

I was at two World Cups with the Tartan Army. Spain 82 was fantastic, especially the Brazil game. I was in the main stand and I've told Alan Rough I got closer to Eder's chip than he did. I was also at Italia 90 and managed to swap shirts with a Brazilian lady – Ref **Kenny Clark**, The Sun newspaper questionnaire, March 2006.

A lot of the fans know it because they are intelligent people, but there are one or two not intelligent enough to pick it up and they are the ones who cause most bother – Celtic manager **Gordon Strachan**, claiming the club's budget isn't even that of an English Championship club, August 2006.

There's only two clubs on this planet I wouldn't play for, even for £1m a week. That's Rangers and Cardiff – West Brom striker and Swansea fan **John Hartson**, December 2006.

I did have a major credibility hurdle to overcome with the fans. It could be that I still do – Celtic manager **Gordon Strachan**, My Life In Football, 2006.

Perth's not a football place, I don't think anyone would say that it is and it never will be. The one thing that never comes out is there's 41,000 people

Perth, and if you've 5 per cent of that number attending, what other club in the country has that as a ratio? – St Johnstone chairman **Geoff Brown**, April 2007.

If I ever listen to a phone-in, I will pack in football – Celtic manager **Gordon Strachan**, April 2007.

The last time Celtic played Dunfermline in the final, my friend Douglas, who is a big Celtic fan, phoned me up and let me hear 20,000 or so Dunfermline fans singing it. He described it as monumental. It brought the Celtic fans to a standstill. The Dunfermline fans sang every word. I said, 'How did they know the words? No one has ever understood them.' – Skids singer **Richard Jobson** on fans singing 'Into The Valley', before the Dunfermline v Celtic Scottish Cup Final, May 2007.

We had Celtic fans in Seville, and probably three times as many as got into the stadium for the UEFA Cup four years ago, but they stayed in the city and watched on the big screen, had a party and we had no problems. I think everyone should have that mentality – UEFA head of communications **William Gaillard**, May 2007, after Liverpool's crowd and ticket problems in the Champions League Final in Athens.

At Falkirk the other week the police were asked to speak to me about smiling at the crowd. Someone reported me for smiling in his direction. Obviously it's not the best smile in the world. I see a lot better smiles, but I never knew my smile could be offensive – Celtic manager **Gordon Strachan**, August 2007.

Having been victim first-hand to some drunken imbeciles who do nothing but criticise people online, I thought I'd join them. Best, Ian Holland McCall – The Partick Thistle manager kicks off his blog, August 2007.

One of the things that annoys me about Hampden is that if you're behind the goals down at the front, you're miles away from the field. I certainly wouldn't like to sit there – SFA president **George Peat**, October 2007.

There is a fantasy pressure out there which comes from the phone-ins. Three or four people can phone in who might not even be Celtic supporters. They might not even be sober. They might not even know they are on the phone. And I've got to answer questions from these kinds of people – Celtic manager **Gordon Strachan**, December 2007.

Frances Fairweather was in charge of the Scotland Supporters Club. What she knew about football you could write on the back of a stamp in capital letters but when it came to handling Scotland supporters she was in a class of her own. He'd never understood how she got into the job but whoever had appointed her had got extremely lucky. Maybe he should be picking the team — '**J. Craig**', in murder mystery novel about the Tartan Army, *One Team In Tallinn*, 2007. (*Veteran Tartan Army footsoldiers may recognise the pseudonym of the book's author and the real identity of the person he's describing.*)

A lot of people have thought that was one of the worst things that could have happened, they think he's not playing me because of that. He doesn't want to look like he is giving in to people — Celtic striker **Derek Riordan**, April 2008, on manager Gordon Strachan being booed when substituting Riordan in the Scottish Cup semi-final against St Johnstone in April 2007. He left Celtic four months later.

Like a pack of wolves who had not been fed for days — Former soldier **Tom Bardsley**, who helped policeman Mick Regan when he was set upon by Rangers fans after the UEFA Cup Final in Manchester, May 2008.

In my days in the juniors I was running the line at Cumnock. They were winning 3–0 so although the crowd were close enough to breathe down my neck, they were breathing in a friendly way. This guy shouted to me, 'What size are your boots, nee'bour? I'm playing fitba tomorrow and I quite fancy them'. Like a fool, I said, 'You need to catch me first.' At which point he just grabbed me by the shirt collar. I was like a cartoon character — my legs were moving but I wasn't going anywhere. As play raged on he looked me in the eye and said, 'You're not so smart now, young 'un.' I basically had to beg him to let me go — Former referee **Kenny Clark** recalls fun in the juniors, August 2008.

Make sure you beat those Scumdee b******* next time you play — Plymouth manager **Paul Sturrock** addresses travelling fans at a pre-season friendly against former club Dundee United, August 2008. He was fined £250 for his remarks by the English FA in October 2008.

I don't think within our club we help ourselves. We have people involved with this club who put bile — that's the word for it — on websites every day. Half of our problems, I believe, are self-inflicted. Some people who are supposedly Rangers supporters need to have a hard look at themselves. Not all of our supporters are pulling in the right direction and they hand us to the media on a plate. People on the internet hide behind a *nom de plume* and all they do is play into the hands of our critics. We have to police ourselves and not give the media ammunition — Rangers chairman **Sir David Murray** addresses the club's AGM, October 2008.

I identified some of these guys, and I met them, and they were like mice — Rangers chairman **Sir David Murray** on Rangers' internet critics, November 2008.

Michael Grant is our Chief Football Writer who has a column every week. We look at the comments on his articles. One week readers call him 'a dirty Orange bastard', the next 'a dirty Fenian bastard'. Michael Grant is an Aberdeen supporter from the deepest darkest Highlands of Scotland. You will never change assumptions. People will say he is called Michael so ergo he is a Catholic and ergo he must be a Celtic fan. And that's the feedback in a quality newspaper – *Sunday Herald* sports editor **Stephen Penman**, in Andy Mitten, *Mad For It: Football's Greatest Rivalries*, 2008.

FASHION ⚽

One of the questions I had asked Timo on meeting him at Glasgow Airport was, 'What colours will the team play in?' Timo drawled, 'Bobby, we'll play in the pastel shades.' Various colours went swirling through my mind as I tried to conjure up an idea of what he might mean. When the strips eventually arrived, they consisted of red shirts with a white band across the midriff and an orange hurricane in the centre, red shorts and orange socks. It was smarter than it sounds – Former Celtic striker **Bobby Lennox** on an exchange with coach Timo Liekoski while playing for Houston Hurricane in the NASL towards the end of his career, in *Bobby Lennox: My Story*, 2007.

Somebody asked me recently, 'Why is it we don't have the spirit of the 70s anymore?' Only partially tongue in cheek, I said it's to do with the jerseys – the jerseys are not dark blue enough with the lion and nothing else on them. They've got stripes, they don't look like Scottish jerseys. A dark blue jersey with a collar and a yellow lion is a Scottish jersey – Former commentator and traditionalist **Arthur Montford**, in *Fanatical About Football*, ed. Jeff Connor, 2003.

Martin was always smart in his appearance and confident in his manner while Robbo was scruffy, wore the dirtiest pair of suede shoes I've ever seen and looked like he lived in a chip pan – Former Nottingham Forest boss **Brian Clough** on former players Martin O'Neill and John Robertson, May 2003.

In the 80s you had the wee ones that would be hitched up to your ging-gangs, and then in the early-90s you had the big ones that were so big on me that with my socks up you could see no part of my legs. I looked useless in both – Former international **Gordon Strachan** on Scotland national team shorts, February 2005.

As part of the club's strict dress code, every day we were asked to wear a shirt and tie, I was just 17 at the time and I had just two pieces of clothing. One day Paul said to me 'Rino, I've just spoken with Walter Smith and he told me to take you down the city centre to buy you five or six smart suits and their cost will be deducted week by week from your wages.' Well, that money was never deducted from my wages, it was just Paul's idea to buy me those suits, spending £2,000–3,000 out of his own pocket. How can you forget things like that? – Milan midfielder **Rino Gattuso** on Paul Gascoigne's generosity, on Italian TV show *Sfide*, March 2008.

He has improved so much as a player, maybe because he has cut off his dreadlocks. He is more aerodynamic – Former Celtic boss **Wim Jansen** on striker Henrik Larsson, January 2001.

The modern man has changed. There's a need to be recognised, a need to be known. You see that with earrings, tattoos, the way that dress sense and hairstyles change every six months – Manchester United manager **Sir Alex Ferguson**, 2002.

It's been a good week because I've got a new suit – Southampton boss **Gordon Strachan** in the build-up to the FA Cup Final, May 2003.

I had the moustache for 19 or 20 years and my theory is that ever since I shaved it off, the game in Scotland has gone downhill. I think the lack of moustaches in the game has played a big factor in the decline of it. Every player went through a phase of having one and they were better players for it, like Graeme Souness and Willie Henderson – Ayr United coach **Robert Connor**, who'd shaved his 'tache off after quitting playing in 1998, September 2004.

The worst item of clothing I've seen is Craig McEwan's tight white cords. He came round to my house and sat on my couch and my Yorkshire Terrier *Clea* jumped on him. The dog farted on him but followed through. He went home with a big brown stain on his white trousers. Personally, I think the dog did him a favour – Airdrie United's **Paul Lovering**, November 2004.

Pat Nevin was a skilful enough footballer but I didn't think we'd ever win anything with him in the side. He was a luxury player and they rarely win trophies. He was never going to mix awfully well in the dressing room either because he was a complex individual. Just after he'd signed for the club he used to come to training wearing a full-length trench coat that he must have bought 15 years earlier – Former Everton striker **Graeme Sharp** on his ex-teammate, in *Sharpy*, 2007.

Him and Brian McClair are a perfect double act because one thinks he's more intelligent than the other. They're both a pair of scruffy so-and-sos. They carry these bags about with them that you wouldn't pay two pence for, they've got all the super-duper books inside and they know all the fancy words – Former Motherwell manager **Billy Davies** on ex-Fir Park chief executive Pat Nevin, February 2008.

Everybody had to wear a costume and do you know what I wore? A f****** kilt! And a 'See-you-Jimmy' wig. Well, my name is Jimmy. Aye. Everything was done properly. I had my knife in my sock. And under my kilt? I said I did it properly. Totally! – Cardiff City striker **Jimmy Floyd Hasselbaink**, on the club's 2007 Christmas bash in Ireland, May 2008.

I consider him to be one of the two worst-dressed goalkeepers in the world, along with Oliver Kahn – Former Poland goalkeeper **Jan Tomaszewski**, on Celtic's Artur Boruc, June 2008.

FERGIE ⚽

The best British manager of all time – Celtic manager **Gordon Strachan** on Alex Ferguson, December 2007.

I grew up opposite Harland and Wolff, so I had to live through the noise of the night-shift workers banging around, the corkers' hammers going all night. But I got used to that – Manchester United manager **Sir Alex Ferguson**, May 2009.

It was necessary to quieten him down and tell him some home truths, and that he could talk when he started shaving – **Willie 'Junior' Omand**, former Queen's Park captain, on brushes with the young Alex Ferguson, in Michael Crick, *The Boss: The Many Sides of Alex Ferguson*, 2002.

He terrified us. I'd never been afraid of anyone before but he was such a frightening bastard from the start. Everything was focused towards his goals. Time didn't matter to him; he never wore a watch. If he wanted something done, he'd stay as late as it took or come in early. He always joined in with us in training and would have us playing in the dark until his five-a-side team won. He was ferocious, elbowing and kicking – Former East Stirling midfielder **Bobby McCulley** on his former Firs Park manager, in Jeff Connor, *Pointless: A Season With Britain's Worst Football Team*, 2005.

When he came in it was all, 'No, no, no. That's not how we did it at St Mirren.' I bit my tongue but then he started on at me about the set-pieces. 'At St Mirren, this is how Jackie Copland did it.' Jackie was the business according to Fergie. We all had to do it like Jackie. Eventually I told him, 'Look gaffer, I don't give a toss about St Mirren. You're in Aberdeen now.' He took it on board in fairness to him. I'll never forget Jackie Copland, though – Defender **Willie Miller** recalls early times with Alex Ferguson at Aberdeen, January 2005.

When I despatched the ball into the net – a beauty, right into the top right-hand corner – my first reaction was to stick two fingers up at him. It was just as well that I was camouflaged by half-a-dozen other Aberdeen players and Fergie did not see the gesture. As a person who abhors the yob culture in our society, I am quite embarrassed by that memory. But that's the state that Fergie could get players into – Celtic manager **Gordon Strachan**, in *Strachan: My Life In Football*, 2006. The goal was a second-half penalty for Aberdeen against Romanian club Arges Pitesti in the UEFA Cup in November 1981, following Ferguson demolishing tea-cups in the dressing room at half-time. Aberdeen had led 3–0 from the first leg, were 2–0 down at the break in the return, and Strachan's penalty helped them to a 2–2 draw to go through.

There was no pleasing Alex Ferguson and he would have ridiculous fines for players. One time he fined John Hewitt because he overtook him on the way into training – Former Aberdeen midfielder **Robert Connor** on his former Aberdeen manager, 2004.

He was from the hard school, and he'd try to break you down. It was always f******' this and f******' that, and 'call yourself a f******' footballer, do you?' He'd go on and on at you. And then he'd send them out on the field, and one or two of them would think, my God, he's right, I'm not good enough, and others would get out there and try to prove him wrong. And the first sort were out of there, fast – Coventry City manager **Gordon Strachan** on Alex Ferguson at Aberdeen, in Rick Gekoski, *Staying Up: A Fan Behind The Scenes In The Premiership*, 1998.

Alex is almost like a band leader. He's the guy who has to be the bastard because he has to give the bad news as well as the good news to his team and I can relate to that. Outside of football, he is a remarkable person – Simply Red leader and Manchester United fan **Mick Hucknall**, November 1999.

The strong impression is that Alex Ferguson cannot personally handle criticism and the club deems itself above criticism – PR guru **Max Clifford** as Manchester United fail to make new friends at the World Club Championships in Brazil, January 2000.

I will certainly not be team manager. I think I've picked the right moment to retire but equally so I would love to stay on in any capacity which does not interfere with the football – Manchester United manager **Sir Alex Ferguson**, December 2000. He said he would retire in May 2002.

I'm actually looking forward to watching the team without any managerial pressures. I'm definitely going. I won't be making comebacks like singers do. I look at Bobby Robson and think, 'Good luck to him', but it's a decison me and my family have made. I want to enjoy a lot of other things – **Sir Alex Ferguson**, December 2000.

The club are engaged in a programme of development to operate academies in places like South Africa, China and other parts of the Far East. I'll visit these places and make a contribution, but it will probably take up only about 30 days a year. That suits me, because it will leave me free to do other things – **Sir Alex Ferguson**, January 2001.

The decision has been taken. I'm going to leave the club. I had hoped there would be another role, but that's gone now – **Sir Alex Ferguson**, May 2001.

Alex (Ferguson) is still too thin-skinned, too ready to defend his players against outsiders – Former Nottingham Forest manager **Brian Clough**, July 2001.

I'm not sure that Alex has had his eye on the ball lately . . . I reckon I could wind him up on match day with a few remarks to the media if I was still in the game, and it shouldn't be happening, because he's too big to worry about it – Former Nottingham Forest manager **Brian Clough** on Ferguson, July 2001.

The way I feel just now I don't think I'll change my mind about going at the end of the season. But you never know what might happen – **Sir Alex Ferguson**, December 2001.

I'm going. That has been settled for some time now. I was asked by a reporter about my retirement and I said, as I would about anything, that you never know what might happen. That's true, but it doesn't mean I was thinking about changing my plans – **Sir Alex Ferguson**, January 2002.

I'm a fan of Alex, despite the fact that he never made me laugh or poured big enough measures of his precious whisky when I used to bump into him at Old Trafford – Former Nottingham Forest manager **Brian Clough** on Ferguson, January 2002.

I've said before that it's my intention to give up managing at the end of the season. That still goes. There are powerful reasons for the decision and those haven't changed – **Sir Alex Ferguson**, January 2002.

The Board has entered into discussions with Sir Alex and his advisers on a new contract – Manchester United club statement, February 2002.

I'm pleased to be staying but once this contract is up that will be it. I have no intention of staying on at the club in any capacity whatsoever – **Sir Alex Ferguson**, February 2002, after the club announced he would be staying until June 2005.

He's always got a smile, a laugh or a song for everyone. He sings all the time – Former Manchester United winger **Jesper Blomqvist** on Ferguson, February 2002.

I ran after him, wheeled him round and called him an ignorant bastard . . . which he is. He just turned and walked away – Former Manchester United manager **Tommy Docherty**, November 2002. He claimed Ferguson ignored his offer of congratulations after United had won the treble in 1999.

He can spot a player a mile off and motivate people well. But his tactical acumen is negligible. If you have a fantastic horse, the jockey doesn't have to be great – Former Manchester United goalkeeper **Mark Bosnich**, 2002.

He said Jacqueline Kennedy knew who did it but she would never say — **Sir Alex Ferguson** on the JFK assassination, 2002. He claimed to have met a man – at a charity dinner at Stoke City – who'd been in Dallas in 1963. (*Among the Manchester United manager's other interests is cinema trivia. In the 80s he would challenge reporters travelling with Aberdeen to name every actor in the 1957 classic, 'Twelve Angry Men'. . . then he would gleefully rhyme them off.*)

Q: Can you tell us your funniest Fergie story? — Ron Newsome, Northampton.
A: No. not really — Former Manchester United goalkeeper **Peter Schmeichel** responds to a magazine reader's query, August 2003.

I send him my best wishes, but I don't think it will stop him shouting at people. He'll never change — Real Madrid's **David Beckham**, December 2003, after Ferguson underwent treatment to correct an irregular heartbeat.

I always say Sir Alex is an Arsenal manager in a Manchester United blazer — Wycombe manager **Tony Adams**, July 2004.

Fergie gets redder and Fergier — Journalist **Hunter Davies**, *New Statesman*, August 2005.

He's a manager I played under, he taught me a lot, gave me a chance, and hopefully I repaid that with some decent performances. Then it came to an end — **Roy Keane**'s succinct view on his time with Alex Ferguson, September 2006.

We're similar in some ways — work ethic, how we treat people. I don't think I'll be throwing teacups, but that's a myth anyway. He's had his tantrums but there are managers who have done it 20 times more. He's calmed down as he's got older — Peterborough manager **Darren Ferguson** on his father, March 2007.

I've said he was a bully but I never said I didn't like it. He was a bully but he is the best sports psychologist. He was good for me, good for anyone who has worked for him. Unless you are weak-minded, because then you will have a problem. He will probably crush you and you'll have to go and find another job — Celtic manager **Gordon Strachan** on Alex Ferguson, December 2007.

I won't be manager here when I'm 70 and I won't be managing any more than another three years at the very most — Manchester United manager **Sir Alex Ferguson**, after winning the Champions League, May 2008.

There are thousands of better coaches. But management? The handling of men? There's nobody better — Former Manchester United goalkeeper **Peter Schmeichel**, May 2008.

When I've finished here I'll deserve a rest. I'll be off to my wee but'n'ben for a complete rest. After here, I'm finished – Manchester United manager **Sir Alex Ferguson**, asked if he would be interested in the Scotland manager's job when he retires, January 2009.

He's got a face like a fearless beekeeper – Former Nottingham Forest and Scotland defender **Kenny Burns** on Ferguson, May 2009.

FITNESS ⚽

A clever inside-forward who could drink like a fish, Vic hated training but loved the treatment table, where he could invariably be located all week before Friday – **Peter Marinello** on Motherwell teammate Vic Davidson, in *Fallen Idle*, 2007.

You should have seen him get on the coach. He didn't jump on or spring on with the air and surefootedness of an athlete; he waddled up to it, put his left foot first on the bottom step and was the only player to use the handrails to help himself through the door. Oh yeah, and you'd occasionally see him squash his fag under his other foot – Former Nottingham Forest manager **Brian Clough** on former winger John Robertson, in *Cloughie: Walking On Water: My Life*, 2002.

When I was a young player at Hibs, as an apprentice at 16, you were straight down the bookies and away for a pint after training. There's a lot less of that now – Everton midfielder **John Collins**, January 1999.

They did a test and the doctor told me there were three options – doing nothing, having a bypass, or having a balloon inserted through my arteries. 'In your case, I think it should be the latter,' she said. 'That would be fine,' I replied, 'because everyone's been calling me a balloon for the last 30 years.' – Former Dundee United manager **Jim McLean**, November 2001.

This voice said, 'I don't ******* believe it! There's no ****** way they've found a heart in you!' – Former Dundee United manager **Jim McLean** recalls the phone call from Manchester United manager **Sir Alex Ferguson** after news he needed a heart operation, November 2001.

These fellas (players) look after themselves. In the old days we (managers) used to be sitting outside hotel bedrooms and all that – Southampton manager **Gordon Strachan**, January 2003.

Technology has come a long way since I would have a cigarette at 2.45pm before a game. But I would go out and play 60 games a year, as opposed to these guys who fall over their laces and are out for a month — Former Rangers striker **Kevin Drinkell**, May 2009.

I'm nowhere near as fit now as I was as a footballer. I walk on to a football pitch and go, 'How did I ever run up and down this?' It seems like Arizona to me — Southampton manager **Gordon Strachan**, January 2003.

I know the guys in your (newspaper) business won't believe it, but I'm naturally fit. I'm sure I'm the sort of player who will still be playing for Scunthorpe or Doncaster when I'm 38 — Celtic's **Neil Lennon**, May 2003. He played for Wycombe Wanderers until he was 36.

When players are fit they can concentrate for longer. When they're not, they make mistakes with their mind. If your mind gets tired it sends the wrong signals to your body — Southampton manager **Gordon Strachan**, May 2003.

Just because my face goes red after five minutes out there some people think I'm knackered. I'm not. It takes a few hours for my face to go back to normal, but I do — Kilmarnock midfielder **Steve Fulton**, November 2003.

If I didn't use my home trainer before heading out, I felt like I was wearing high heels when I stepped on to the pitch. At training I thought, 'What am I doing here? I feel like an old man.' — Rangers' **Ronald de Boer**, November 2003.

I am a disgrace. I always used to train. The players drove my car back from training and I would jog back to Tannadice, and even when I was chairman I would go to the gym and train. Unfortunately, now I sit and watch bloody cricket — Former Dundee United manager and chairman **Jim McLean**, April 2004.

When I moved from Chelsea to Celtic in 1997 the pace of the game was slower; going back south to Derby two and a half years later meant I had to readjust to a faster contest once again. In my first game back for Derby against Leeds I could have done with an oxygen tank — Former Scotland midfielder **Craig Burley**, April 2004.

The thing that irritates me when people talk about it is that I didn't have a heart problem, as so many have suggested. I just got very excited, as I used to at games, shouting and hollering without breathing properly — Southampton manager **Paul Sturrock**, July 2004, on his October 1995 collapse at a game at Tannadice after hyperventilating while he was St Johnstone manager.

It's funny how he gets himself back to fitness when his contract is due to run out — Former Dundee United manager **Jim McLean** on Everton striker Duncan Ferguson, May 2005.

He played about 15 games here then discovered crisps when he was 18 – Former Celtic manager **Martin O'Neill** on former Celtic goalkeeper Stewart Kerr, who'd criticised Robert Douglas, June 2005.

That's on 40 cigarettes a day as well. I'm not joking, the guy's a genius – Falkirk manager **John Hughes** hails Russell Latapy after he helps Trinidad & Tobago to the World Cup Finals at the age of 37, 2005.

That is a blatant lie. I spoke to Craig on the morning of the game and he wasn't ill – SPFA President **Fraser Wishart** on Hearts' claim that goalkeeper Craig Gordon had been dropped from the side against Dundee United because of illness (and not because he'd faced a club disciplinary hearing the previous week), December 2006.

Football isn't just about kicking a ball. It's about lifestyle – how you live, eat, sleep, train. I've tried to make the boys here fitter and stronger. A few needed a bit of work doing on their physiques – Hibs manager **John Collins**, March 2007.

The other lads would be rubbing their hands together saying, 'Oh good, we're doing some runs.' 'F*** me,' I'd think, 'It's all right for you lightweights, but I'm carrying 16 stone here.' Honestly, I hated it – Former Celtic striker **John Hartson** on training at Parkhead, February 2008.

FOOD

He used to nick my bacon sandwiches, you know. I'd always be hungry and I was always eating garbage. He used to hijack my food. He'd sit down near the bar of our hotel and watch the room service coming. 'Where they going?' 'Mr Strachan ordered them, sir.' 'No, son, they're for me now.' I used to ring up and say, 'Where's my sandwiches?' 'Mr Stein had them.' 'Oh no,' you'd say. 'Bloody caught again.' – Celtic manager **Gordon Strachan** on Jock Stein, September 2005.

When I arrived at Pittodrie wee Gordon was what you could call a junk food junkie. It was all curries, Chinese and pizzas. He had actually slipped into a carry-out culture. Now, he was naturally endowed with stamina and it's true that junk food can give you a certain amount of energy, but it's short-lived and damaging in the long term. After about a year, Gordon began to suffer from stomach cramps and the problem was obviously being caused by his diet. I took him aside and said to him, 'Why don't you take a leaf out of Alex McLeish's book?' At that time, big Alex was already aware of the benefits of a healthy, nutritious diet. He was ahead of most people that way. He had a blender and he would use it to mix fresh fruit into healthy drinks – something that would become common practice much later — Former Aberdeen manager **Sir Alex Ferguson** on former player Gordon Strachan, December 2006.

At West Ham, I threw a plate of sandwiches at Don Hutchison. He sat there, still arguing with me, with cheese and tomato running down his face — West Ham manager **Harry Redknapp**, 1999.

The only Baxter they've got up there now is a range of soups — Pundit **Jimmy Greaves** on Scotland's lack of talent, 1999.

Unlike at Celtic Park, the terraces are very close to the pitch and, as I warmed up, I felt the burning hostility, especially when a pie hit me on the chest — Former Celtic striker **Tony Cascarino** recalls Old Firm life at Ibrox, October 2002.

Friday night was fish and chips when my dad brought the money back. 'There you are, mother,' woosh, I was away for the suppers — Southampton manager **Gordon Strachan**, January 2003.

Funniest moment of last season: Craig Easton going home to make cakes rather than buying them after being named the worst player that week in training. He's renowned for being tight — Dundee United's **Stuart Duff**, August 2003.

Cider vinegar, honey and garlic kills off viruses, keeps everything away. The acid in it cleanses your bowels, too. A herbalist I was seeing for my pigeons put me on to it — Partick Thistle manager **John Lambie**, in *Fanatical About Football*, ed. Jeff Connor, 2003.

We're given a sheet with a mixture of carbohydrates and proteins, labelled green, red and yellow, that we have to get through. They get you to write down your intake in a week and I did and he wasn't too pleased. I like a wee chip shop on a Wednesday night. It's never done me any harm — Blackburn Rovers midfielder **Barry Ferguson** runs into problems with the club dietician, December 2003.

I am the sole judge and I eat a pie every Saturday. It's about the crispness of the outer crust very often, it has to be heated to the proper temperature and nicely presented. That's how I judge it. It gives the club something to talk about. At half-time when I'm having my pie and my cup of tea in the club, I'm always approached by people who say, 'How is it?' — **Lord MacFarlane** of Bearsden, president of Bell's, who awarded a gallon of whisky to the club with the best pie in Scotland every season, in *Fanatical About Football*, ed. Jeff Connor, 2003.

I was restaurant critic for all of Devon and Cornwall for the local paper. Which meant when I wasn't critical, everyone gave me big portions – Southampton boss **Paul Sturrock** recalls the good life at Plymouth Argyle, March 2004.

He's in the gym for the first time in six years. With a cup of tea and a hot dog – Celtic captain **Neil Lennon** on teammate John Hartson, *Wright & Bright* radio show, April 2004.

Favourite TV show?: *Ready, Steady, Cook!* with Ainsley Harriott. No question, it's brilliant. For Christmas all my presents were cookbooks. I'm not that good but I love cooking. It's the truth. I'm not winding you up. I think it's great how they make those three meals in 20 minutes. I love it – Blackburn Rovers' **Barry Ferguson**, October 2004.

Last night I had mince and tatties and beans. I have a McDonald's on a Friday. I am just like that, it's something I have done for years. I know it's not right but I am not embarrassed to say that. By all accounts Kenny Dalglish used to have a black pudding supper and a bottle of American Cream Soda on a Friday, so if it was good enough for him – St Mirren defender **Andy Millen**, still playing in the SPL at 41, November 2006.

Our players have food there for them before and after training. In my day we'd go to Joe's Kitchen in London Road and have sausage, bacon, egg, tattie scone, and a milkshake to drink. We used to call it a DM – a Delicious Meal – Celtic coach **Tommy Burns** reminisces, July 2007.

The most disgusting thing I've eaten is probably porridge – Chelsea and France striker **Nicolas Anelka**, April 2008.

I couldn't even begin to pronounce the popular dishes, but I just judge whether I try them out on how they look. An awful lot grows here. There are three types of bananas, all sorts of beans and potatoes, and people look healthy. Very few of them are fat, so that can only be good for me – Uganda coach **Bobby Williamson** on local cuisine, October 2008.

FOREIGN ⚽

Motherwell were an extremely tough-tackling team, and the South American side's delicate, fancy-dan touches acted like a red rag to a bull. The friendly degenerated into a brawl with us leading 2–1 and was abandoned while our stopper, big Willie McVie, was chasing their centre forward around the track – Interesting times on Motherwell's 1976 South American tour in a game against Colombian side Santa Fe, in **Peter Marinello**'s *Fallen Idle*, 2007.

With all due respect to the foreigners, I don't think they knew just how big the Old Firm were – Former Celtic striker **Darren Jackson** on early-season problems in 1997–98, quoted in Mark Guidi, *The Inner Sanctum*, 2008.

I had just left Rennes and was a bit unhappy. I needed something else, something to give me my spark back again, and Celtic was the perfect fit for me. It was like falling in love again – Defender **Stephane Mahé** on signing for Celtic, in Mark Guidi, *The Inner Sanctum*, 2008.

Pierre wasn't well known before we bought him from NAC Breda. But his head got very big very soon after he arrived at Celtic. I found him difficult to deal with, and so did Tommy Burns – Former Celtic chairman and managing director **Fergus McCann** on striker Pierre van Hooijdonk, November 1998.

We called them the 'Three Amigos'. (Jorge) Cadete was a financial basket case and I felt sorry for him. He had two wives and never gave me the impression that he was mentally strong. But he was a better player than (Pierre) van Hooijdonk – Former Celtic chairman and managing director **Fergus McCann**, November 1998. Paolo di Canio was the third member of the gang.

Van Hooijdonk proved to be a nightmare to Nottingham Forest; di Canio ended up assaulting a referee at Sheffield Wednesday before going absent without leave; and Jorge Cadete continued a course of conduct which had seen him in serious dispute with Sporting Lisbon before arriving at Celtic and then continuing in a similar vein with Celta Vigo. It was always a matter of great amazement to me that Celtic appeared to carry all the blame for the difficulties with these players while they were in Glasgow, despite the evidence suggesting that the players were the problem – Former Celtic general manager **Jock Brown**, in *Celtic-Minded: 510 Days In Paradise*, 1999.

In Great Britain, they are nationalists. In general, Italians are a pain in the neck to them because they dress well, know how to eat well and drink with taste. We are the centre of their envy – Rangers defender **Lorenzo Amoruso** tells Italian newspaper *Gazzetta Dello Sport* about Scottish life, 1999.

I never imagined I would play and be so happy for four years in Scotland. When my father told me Rangers were interested, I said, 'No way, I'm not going there.' I couldn't see it being a success for anybody, but my wife, wisely, said I should at least go up, give it a try and get a feeling for it – Former Rangers striker **Brian Laudrup**, December 1999.

It is my way of expressing myself, my passion. Football is a kind of art in that way. There is so much emotion. If you are losing, you are unhappy. Then if it is going well, I see faces in the crowd and they are smiling, they are joyful. I have made their day, I have made their week even – Celtic defender **Ramon Vega**, May 2001.

Rossi's buggering us about. He's a fine player who obviously feels he should be playing somewhere else – Dunfermline chairman **John Yorkston** on Moroccan defender Youssef Rossi, August 2001.

I knew it hurt him when I took away his armband but after that moment Lorenzo became better and better – Rangers director of football **Dick Advocaat** on stripping Lorenzo Amoruso of the club captaincy, September 2002.

Before, I was journeying along playing football for fun. Once I got to Dortmund, it was a job – Celtic's **Paul Lambert**, September 2002.

Clubs need to spend money more wisely, not spend money for fun just because some player has got a foreign name – Rangers' **Lorenzo Amoruso**, November 2002.

When I signed Sergei Baltacha for St Johnstone we had agreed the terms and everything when he announced that he wanted a car as part of the deal and I thought, 'Oh no, he's going to want a Jag or a BMW or something like that.' But he wanted a Skoda. There's big Sergei, driving around Perth in his Skoda – Former Saints manager **Alex Totten**, in *Fanatical About Football*, ed. Jeff Connor, 2003.

Few foreigners can manage a good display in their first Glasgow derby. They just are not properly prepared. They can't be – Referee **Hugh Dallas**, March 2003.

I never said I didn't want to play in defence, and I never found out why he didn't want me to play in midfield. Perhaps he wanted another Dutch player in there. It's not right if someone says to you, 'Do this or nothing,' and that's how it ended up with (Dick) Advocaat – Milan's **Rino Gattuso**, March 2003, on problems between him and the Dutch coach at Ibrox.

I made sure I got my point across by saying that, if small countries could not produce good referees, that must mean that Alex Ferguson was not a good manager and Kenny Dalglish was not a good player – Referee **Hugh Dallas**, March 2003, after Real Madrid's Roberto Carlos had called him 'a joke' after Dallas disallowed a goal when Brazil lost a World Cup qualifier against Uruguay in July 2001.

If, by January 2004, Dundee are in third position with a healthy lead over the next team, it won't be so necessary to bring Mr Davids here. But if we are fourth or fifth or, God forbid, sixth, then it will be crucial, and we will recruit Mr Davids or somebody of his quality to Dens – Dundee director **Giovanni di Stefano** on plans to sign Juventus' Edgar Davids, October 2003. Dundee fans wait still.

I always had the feeling it wasn't going to work with Marcio. The fact Dom (Keane) was so keen I stayed suggests I was maybe his insurance policy –

Livingston manager **David Hay**, March 2004, on the club's ill-fated experiment with Marcio Maximo as coach. The Brazilian quit in October 2003 after four months in charge.

I felt Davie (Hay) and Jim (Leishman) had maybe relaxed a bit after finishing third in our second season in the SPL. It was a massive risk and, while we were only paying him £35,000, Jim and Davie were obviously less than happy with the situation. In fact, Marcio never had much support in there apart from me – Livingston ex-chairman **Dominic Keane** on Maximo, April 2004.

Ronaldinho had something in his hair. You could smell him before you saw him. I was going to ask him for his number after the game – Celtic's **Neil Lennon**, April 2004, after facing the Brazilian for Barcelona in the UEFA Cup.

To play 50 games, don't get suspended, don't get any red or yellow cards, win the treble and possibly get as far as possible in Europe – Rangers' **Fernando Ricksen** outlines his plans for the new season, July 2004. He played 51 games, scored nine goals, was booked five times, won the League and League Cup, and was voted both Rangers' Player of the Year and joint Scottish PFA Players' Player of the Year.

Some of the things that went on were quite amazing. The Ebbe Skovdahl era was a case in point. I've no problem with foreign coaches but we seem to accept that they are good before they've actually proven it while giving our own coaches a really hard time. There was a feeling here that, since he'd done well at Brondby, he must be good irrespective of how awful the results were. Ebbe, for some reason, had a cult following – Aberdeen chief executive **Willie Miller**, January 2005.

The Lithuanian players are his adopted sons. Whenever he's over he meets with them – they're his boys – Former Hearts director **George Foulkes** on club owner Vladimir Romanov, November 2005.

We sat and watched it in one of the stands, with 10,000 people. Then we had dinner with the president of Real Madrid. A very surreal day! It was the time of the 2006 World Cup, so Zidane was with the France squad but he sent us all a little message. I've not really had any feedback on whether he likes the music or not. I'm sure he thinks it's a pile of shite – Mogwai drummer **Martin Bulloch**, November 2008. His band provided the soundtrack to the film *Zidane: A 21st Century Portrait*. The film was shown at the St Jakob-Park Stadium in Basel on 15 June, 2006, two days after France and Switzerland had met in the World Cup in Stuttgart.

There's a player I go to training with and whenever he gets stopped in his car, he has to give the police money. And you can buy a car, in cash, and take it straight onto the road, no tax, MOT or anything. It's just the way it is here – Lokomotiv Moscow striker **Garry O'Connor**, July 2006.

Celtic couldn't have done enough for me, but it was a lonely life and I wish now I had been a bit easier on some of the foreign lads who came to United. I always thought, 'You're on the pitch now – do it.' I regret that now. I was very hard on Seba (Sebastian Veron), and I was wrong – **Roy Keane** after retiring, September 2006.

There are times when a coach really has to speak strongly and passionately to his team, and I don't think Paul will have been able to do that at Rangers. He was a civilised man, quite quiet, very likeable and a very successful coach in France, but communication is everything in the dressing room. Doing press conferences in a second language is one thing, but carrying it off in the dressing room is something else – Hibs manager (and French speaker) **John Collins** on former Rangers manager Paul le Guen, in Graham Spiers, *Paul le Guen: Enigma*, 2007.

Clare at the club has a players' list where she puts a tick beside our names every time we speak to the press. With me, Mickey (Stewart) and Robbie (Neilson), the ticks go way out. I hope by the end of the season that means we don't have to do too much talking. The Lithuanian lads all speak English quite a bit but they will try to kid on they don't if they've to speak to the press – Hearts captain **Christophe Berra** on problems for the club's press officer, Clare Cowan, November 2007.

He wasn't your usual footballer because he's intelligent. He would read all about philosophy and was writing his own book. He wore strange clothes, though – Partick Thistle's **David Rowson** on former Aberdeen teammate Arild Stavrum, April 2008.

There is no road rage here. I've had to drive myself quite a few times and it's completely different to Europe. People come out of side streets when you don't expect, they all try to nudge their way on to a roundabout. It's every man for himself, but nobody gets upset. You just accept it. I thought it would drive me mental, but I've changed my outlook – even if it takes me two hours to get across the city – Uganda manager **Bobby Williamson** on Kampala life, October 2008.

It was a total shambles in Germany. Actually, you won't believe this but there was a huge outcry when I was over there. The bloke who used to be Al Pacino's voice in all of his gangster movies died. Obviously, this was what the Germans had got used to listening to. To listen to the amount of time they spent talking about it, you'd think Pacino himself had died – Scotland and former Alemannia Aachen striker **Chris Iwelumo**, November 2008.

Hearts conned the referee. (David) Obua sat down on the pitch, took his gloves off one by one, lay back and held his hands over his face. It was comical. Big striker Adrian Mrowiec was carried off but came running back up the tunnel. Then Christos Karapidis was meant to have a serious injury. There was nothing wrong with him. That was proved when he (also) came bounding back up the tunnel – Dundee United manager **Craig Levein** after the defeat by Hearts, February 2009.

I have no problems with Craig Levein. My birthday is over but if in the future he has a birthday he can invite me and I come with flowers and maybe a bottle of whisky – Hearts manager **Csaba Laszlo**, March 2009. Levein had complained about Hearts players 'conning' referees after losing to them a few days earlier.

GIRLS ⚽

Another teammate proved very successful at getting one young player drunk, just so he could take him home . . . and make love to his colleague's wife. I must confess the temptation was always there, and the opportunity was huge for infidelity in Portsmouth, but shagging other players' wives was bang out of order, as far as I was concerned – Former Portsmouth winger **Peter Marinello**, in book, 'Fallen Idle', 2007.

It doesn't look nice. If women were meant to play football they'd have their tits somewhere else – Actor **John Gordon Sinclair** ('Gregory'), in Bill Forsyth's 1980 film, *Gregory's Girl*.

Someone came up to me and said, 'There's rumours you were chatting up birds in a club in Aberdeen.' And I've never been to a club in Aberdeen in my life! Maybe someone was pretending to be me to chat up a bird in Aberdeen. Can't imagine they'd get very far, mind – Everton midfielder **John Collins**, January 1999.

She's 17 going on 37. See all these lines I have on my face? They're not laughter lines, they've got nothing to do with football. They're all to do with Gemma – Southampton manager **Gordon Strachan** on his daughter, January 2003.

Everybody talks about male chauvinism in Scotland and that Holland is so emancipated, but if you look at the details, not at all. I have never had the status in Holland that I have here in Scotland – Scotland women's team coach **Vera Pauw**, May 2003.

We did *The Russia House* with Sean Connery and Michelle Pfeiffer and I found Michelle a very intelligent woman. I didn't particularly find her sexually attractive but she is a woman you can be friends with without having other intentions – Dundee director **Giovanni di Stefano**, September 2003. He claimed to have spent two years in Beverly Hills through his 'MGM interests'.

I knew it wasn't going to be our day when I arrived at Links Park and found that we had a woman running the line. She should be at home making the tea or the dinner for her man who comes in after he has been to the football. This is a professional man's game – Albion Rovers manager **Peter Hetherston** on Scotland's first female lineswoman, Morag Pirie, November 2003.

I think this statement says more about Peter Hetherston than Morag Pirie – SFA referees development chief **Donald McVicar** on criticism of lineswoman Morag Pirie in a game involving Hetherston's Albion Rovers side, November 2003.

Women should stick to refereeing women's football. That's their sport so they can do what the hell they like with it – Former Partick Thistle manager **John Lambie** steps into the Morag Pirie debate, November 2003.

Frank McAvennie: oh my God – this guy looks like a clown. If his catchphrase is 'Where's the burdz?' then the answer has to be 'in hiding' because he's revolting – **Jordan (Katie Price)**, model and TV 'personality', on being asked to rate various Scottish players for attractiveness, 2003.

Worst habit: It has to be dating psycho birds from Aberdeen. They're all totally off their heads. I advise anyone not to go near them because they are rockets. You get the groupies who hang around you and once you snog them they want to end up being your wife. My advice would be not to date an ex's best pal . . . I'm probably going to get chased out of Aberdeen for this – Sudden moment of realisation for Aberdeen defender **Zander Diamond**, newspaper questionnaire, 2004.

God said it's not right to have sex before marriage and you can see the proof of it in the world. That's why you see young kids, 15- or 16-year-old girls, walking around pregnant, not knowing who the father is, because of disobedience to what God says – Rangers defender **Marvin Andrews**, December 2005.

You'd never understand it unless you were me. I'm sorry about that, but that's the way it goes. If you tried to tell me about childbirth, you couldn't explain it to me, could you? – Celtic manager **Gordon Strachan**'s response to *Real Radio*'s Michelle Evans' question about his disappointment at there being no chance of the treble for Celtic following their Scottish Cup defeat against St Mirren, March 2009.

He must have been raging on Saturday but part of his job is to be able to respond to questions after the match and to turn round and say that nobody who hasn't been a manager would know what it's like – well, that's an insult. I don't know what it's like to dig coal out of a mine but I have a fairly good idea that it would be hard work. His off-the-cuff remarks are why a lot of Celtic fans are antagonistic towards him. It's because of the way he conducts himself. He lets himself and the club down – Sports psychologist **Tom Lucas** on Strachan's comments, March 2009.

When I first started at Cappielow, I went to introduce myself and when I spoke to the stadium manager at the time, he asked if I was the new cleaner – Morton chief executive **Gillian Donaldson**, April 2009.

I'm a team player. I've got a football player mentality. I'm Kenny Dalglish setting up Joe Jordan. That's who I am. I'm Gordon McQueen – Pretenders lead singer **Chrissie Hynde**, May 2009.

GOOD OLD DAYS

We were about to go off on holiday and I remember my uncle Andy always being a great lad for the DIY and saying to me, 'Get the tiles in and I'll have your bathroom tiled for you coming back.' And he did – **Bobby Auld**, nephew of Andy Auld, June 2002. Stevenston-born Andy Auld was one of five Scots who helped the United States reach the semi-finals of the first-ever World Cup in 1930. He died in December 1977.

I played against Paraguay, didn't get a game against Yugoslavia, didn't get a game against France. Now, you got £50 a match if you played, £30 if you were a reserve. When we got back and my expenses were deducted, I got a cheque off the SFA for £14 – Falkirk's **Alex Parker** on the glamour of playing for Scotland in the 1958 World Cup, in Gary Imlach, *My Father And Other Working-Class Football Heroes*, 2005.

As a child, I used to cut pictures of Billy Houliston, who was selected by Scotland while he was playing for Queen of the South, out of newspapers. I would paste them into home-made scrapbooks and, after a few days, when the glue had dried, they would appear to rise up out of the page. They were brought to life – Scots-born author **Hunter Davies**, November 2003.

People who've obviously never been to Castlemilk talk to me about rough areas – I had one pair of shoes for school and had to cut out a new insole from a cornflakes packet – Bolton Wanderers coach **Ricky Sbragia**, November 2005.

I remember buying an LP: Dean Martin, *Dino Latino*. It was lying on the kitchen table in Govan, my dad comes in and says, 'Jesus God! Who the hell is he?' – Manchester United manager **Sir Alex Ferguson**, 2002.

What has happened to diving headers these days? You know, the kind of goals Denis Law, Tommy Lawton, Nat Lofthouse, Dixie Dean and Alex Ferguson used to score? – Manchester United manager **Sir Alex Ferguson**, in Daniel Taylor, *This Is The One: The Uncut Story Of A Football Genius*, 2007.

Q:Who's your favourite player? A: Denis Law. I thought he was the bollocks – Former Wimbledon and Sheffield United manager, **Dave Bassett**, January 2003.

As good a footballer as Bestie, and a better pro – Former Chelsea manager **Tommy Docherty** on Charlie Cooke, October 2006.

The most I earned as a footballer with Rangers was £60 a week and £20 extra during the season. £80! I thought it was great – Manchester United manager **Sir Alex Ferguson**, in an interview with Sir David Frost, June 2008.

Willie McVie, our centre half at Shawfield, once saw me practising headers and said, 'Come here Ginge, I'll show you how to do it properly, you've got to use your arms.' He threw a ball up, jumped with me, and smashed my face in with his elbow. I wasn't often beaten in the air after that – Benfica executive director **Steve Archibald**, on early education at Clyde, June 1999. (*See the 'Foreign' section for more examples of McVie's forthright approach.*)

I was in the middle of my team talk, about ten minutes before the kick-off, when one of the stewards poked his head through the door and said, 'Excuse me boss – the toilets in the stand are blocked.' – **Sir Alex Ferguson** on early life as St Mirren manager, in Michael Crick, *The Boss: The Many Sides of Alex Ferguson*, 2002.

I only had two injuries and one of them I wasn't even playing. You had to get a job pre-season in those days because your wages were down by half when you weren't playing, and I got a job with the Co-operative, driving and debt collecting. I stepped off a lorry into a hole and did all my ankle ligaments – Partick Thistle manager **John Lambie** remembers the good times, in *Fanatical About Football*, ed. Jeff Connor, 2003.

Where the talent has gone I don't know. But when I go home to Sauchie, the park where I played as a kid – jackets down, 25-a-side – is empty now – Former Liverpool defender **Alan Hansen**, after Scotland had drawn 2–2 in the Faroes, 2002.

You get fed up fining footballers, so you've just got to try and show them examples of what can go wrong. You scare them with stories, with videos. Maybe even with a video of Jimmy Johnstone. You tell them, 'Watch that, son. And this player was ten times the player you are.' Come to think of it, whatever player I've got here, Jimmy Johnstone was ten times the player they are. I think it penetrates, it does go in. There's no drinking culture left in football, really. Oh, there are still a few dinosaurs lurching around, but they'll be gone within the next two or three years – Southampton manager **Gordon Strachan**, January 2003.

In 1979, when we played Stranraer in the Scottish Cup, I sold the pies. It was great that we made more than £100! – Annan Athletic chairman **Henry McClelland** as the club are voted into the SFL, July 2008.

In terms of the 'hairdryer treatment', so long as it wasn't you that was receiving it, it was always great to be there to watch. Fergie's style in haranguing a player was such that you couldn't put a beermat between his nose and the guy who was on the receiving end. It was a full-frontal verbal assault: a personal and brutal examination of your character. And while scolding you, Fergie would always exaggerate to make the point – Former Aberdeen defender **Stuart Kennedy**, November 2006, on the eve of Ferguson's 20th anniversary as Manchester United manager.

We had a wee bit of a run-in with the American Navy on a trip to Majorca with Manchester United. They were all big gorillas and Paul McGrath, who was never the most subtle guy, pushed one Yank aside and started dancing with his bird for bit of fun. Two of his mates started getting into McGrath. I was with Robbo (Bryan Robson) and we went over and I left-hooked one with a big haymaker. Then I hit another one with a right-hander. They both felt it and I thought, 'I'm going to get my head kicked in here.' Robbo thought the same. But then the military police stormed in and battered the living daylights out of the gorillas for causing problems – Manchester United stars unwind, recalled by **Gordon McQueen**, December 2006.

My 1984–85 (First Division Championship) medal went to auction to help victims of a car accident in Bellshill. It was bought for £250, while a bottle of Buckfast, signed by the local councillor, went for £500 – Former Motherwell winger **John Gahagan** on life as an after-dinner speaker, April 2005.

I remember nights at Wycombe when everyone else had gone home and it would be just his family and mine left in the boardroom. We'd order a Chinese takeaway and eat it on the boardroom table watching *Match of the Day*, drinking the bar dry, his two little girls, Aisling and Alana, falling asleep in the corner because they were really young then – Wycombe director **Alan Parry**, on Martin O'Neill's time there, in Alex Montgomery, *Martin O'Neill – The Biography*, 2003.

HIGH JINKS ⚽

And we'd be out jumping dykes. Some areas of Govan had great jumps, where you could jump from one dyke to another. The dangerous ones had names: the king, the queen, the suicide, the diamond, the spiky. You'd go to different areas of Govan to challenge each other into jumping dykes because it was very dangerous – Manchester United manager **Sir Alex Ferguson** on his Glasgow youth, May 2009.

I could have leapt it, there's no doubt about it, but we'd been watching people do that all tournament and I'd said to Charlie Nicholas, 'I know what's going to happen, one of us will do it and there'll be one of those seven-foot moats on the other side and we'll end up breaking our ankle or something.' That was me just checking there wasn't a drop on the other side – **Gordon Strachan** on his famous celebration at the advertising hoarding after scoring for Scotland against West Germany in the World Cup in June 1986, February 2005.

He was a big wind-up merchant. Whenever I played at Arsenal and the ball went out of play, he'd always throw it back so that it hit the sloping edge of the pitch then bounced back to him and I'd reach out and miss it and he'd wet himself laughing. He must have done me about ten times in my career – Former Arsenal defender **Lee Dixon**, December 2008, on ex-Liverpool manager Kenny Dalglish.

Gary Neville told me, 'Occasionally we'd have a night out and hide it from you. We'd all say, "Don't tell anybody about where, or at what time, we are meeting."' Then at training Cantona would say, 'Right! I'll see all of you later! This evening! At nine! In such and such a place.' They were all going, 'Shut up! The boss is here!' The point was that he was excited to have nights out with the boys. Even though he wasn't a big drinker, Cantona. A beer. A glass of wine. He just loved being part of that culture, which he'd never experienced in France – Manchester United manager **Sir Alex Ferguson**, October 2008.

Just as well for him, I'm not a fighting man, but I was waiting for him, and I'd have had him – Former Rangers midfielder **Ian Ferguson**, by then playing with Central Coast Mariners in the Australian 'A' League, recalling his March 1997 Old Firm Parkhead spat with Celtic's Paolo di Canio. Ferguson claimed di Canio didn't come into the players lounge after their very public disagreement.

We were on the bus when I climbed out of the skylight at the back, crawled along the roof while the bus was traveling at 30mph and jumped down on Howard Kendall from the front skylight. He absolutely s**t himself – Former Scotland midfielder **Don Hutchison** recalls fun in the play-offs while at Sheffield United, September 2008. (This entertaining incident occurred following the Championship

*semi-final second leg in May 1997 after a 2–2 draw at Ipswich took Sheffield United
to the Wembley play-off final.)*

When we went on a trip to Toronto some of the boys had a few too many
drinks and decided to have tattoos done. I said, 'No way, my wife would go
bananas.' But they kept saying, 'You need something to remember us by,'
and Coisty and Ian Durrant wrote 'Rangers FC: Nine In A Row, 1997' on
a scrap of paper. I woke up the next day with it on my shoulder – Former
Rangers goalkeeper **Andy Dibble**, then with Wrexham, September 2004.

Craig Burley was up to his usual pranks and put his false teeth in my glass.
I didn't know until I felt his falsers hit off my own teeth. It was disgusting.
I lifted his teeth out of the glass and pretended to throw them away. The
players and the bar staff spent half-an-hour looking for them. Burley was
shouting, 'I'm naked without my teeth. I'm naked. I'm away home.' I had
put them in my pocket and gave them back to him once I'd had a good laugh
watching him squirm – **Jackie McNamara** recalls team fun during Celtic's title-
winning 1997–98 season, in Mark Guidi, *The Inner Sanctum*, 2008.

I was asked THAT question (how much longer could Alex Smith expect to
keep his job) which I would never allow anyone to ask me. Anyone knows if
you've lost nine goals in two games your jacket's on a shoogly peg anyway,
so why ask? That's when I lost the place. 'Look,' I said, 'Can you ********
not honour an agreement?' I swung and I punched him. One punch then
I walked away. That's all there was. No fight, no nothing. Anyone who was
there would tell you, yet this **** (Mark) Hateley was going about shouting
'I saw it! I saw it!' – Former Dundee United manager and chairman **Jim McLean**'s
version of the October 2000 bust-up with BBC reporter John Barnes which led to him
standing down. The unpleasantness came following a 4–0 United home defeat by
Hearts.

You know what I'd love to do? I'd love to reverse it and find out where one of
these guys works and go down to his office, put my £10 on his desk and stand
there verbally abusing him in front of everyone for 90 minutes and then
we'd see how he likes it – Ayr manager **Gordon Dalziel** on supporters' criticism,
November 2001.

If Ronaldo had done something bad with the under-21s do you think Brazil
wouldn't pick him? – Scotland manager **Berti Vogts** on his decision to restore
Sunderland's Kevin Kyle to the national squad, November 2002. Kyle had been
frozen out after misbehaviour with the under-21 team in Poland 19 months earlier.

I always tell the coaches that all the guys in the technical area must be well-
behaved because bad behaviour in the technical area leads to bad behaviour
on the field and I tell them that my fourth official is crazy, really crazy, and
Kenny sits beside me looking really mean and scowling at them and the

majority look at us like we're mad – but more often than not it works. Kenny's great at acting it out – Referee **Hugh Dallas** on using fellow official Kenny Clark before matches abroad, March 2003.

What's the best practical joke you've seen played? – To be honest, I hate that kind of thing. I see stories of people s******g in shoes and I think, 'I would never do that.' So why should footballers be like that? I have no time for it – Alloa manager **Terry Christie**, newspaper questionnaire, May 2003.

If anything happens in this street I'm always the person who is getting the blame. Ronald de Boer lives close but he is too quiet so it's easier to blame Fernando – Rangers defender **Fernando Ricksen**, following claims someone had yelled through neighbour Alan Thompson's letterbox after the Celtic player had missed a penalty in a game, June 2003.

During a Gaelic football game both teams just piled into each other after a row. You had 30 players involved and then everyone on the sidelines joined in. Some women ran on to the park, I think they were the mothers of some of the opposition, and one of them hit me on the head with an umbrella – Gaelic football-playing memories of Motherwell's **Richie Foran**, December 2004.

I used to go to the Alva Supporters Club function every year. I'd go after a Saturday game, stay all day Sunday and I'd get home at some point on the Monday. We called it the equestrian because it was a three-day event – Former Rangers goalkeeper **Andy Goram**, May 2005.

Simon Stainrod was at Falkirk and he's a great guy, the most confident guy I've ever met. He's got that swagger – and when you mix that swagger from Sheffield with a guy from Leith with a crewcut there's a collision and the two of us were hammer and tongs at each other, but all in good spirits. We used to start fisticuffs, just body shots, and everybody used to stand on the benches and me and him would get battered into each other. Many a time I've come back and had a wee crack in my hand from punching him. The two of us got on like a house on fire, really – Falkirk player-manager **John Hughes**, in *Fanatical About Football*, ed. Jeff Connor, 2003.

I love James (McFadden). I could not understand after Hong Kong in 2002. That was my first fight with the SFA When we come back from Hong Kong they said, 'We have to make a press conference.' I said, 'Why? The new generation miss the bus or the plane, what's the problem?' They said he could never play again for Scotland. I said he was a teenager and the season was closed and he had a good night. I was more angry with the experienced guys because there was four experienced guys and James – Former Scotland manager **Berti Vogts**, November 2007, on the end-of-season trip to Hong Kong. McFadden missed the Scotland plane home.

Ronnie McQuilter was at Gretna and one day Rowan Alexander put his name on the bench as he wrote the team up on the board. Ronnie, in his strong Glasgow accent, said: 'Just scrub that name offa there and if you don't I'll no' play again ya ****. You couldnae manage a Subbuteo team ya ****.' Rowan didn't utter a word, but just wiped Ronnie's name off and stuck his own name on and Ronnie walked off – Gretna's **Ryan McGuffie** recalls Raydale Park dressing room fun, August 2006.

I nicked a sheep in Reading once. That was mad. We were driving along and we saw it, opened the door and it came to us like a dog and jumped in the car. But I can't say too much about it. He might still be running around – Former Celtic striker **John Hartson**, February 2007.

MIXU. Is the big man really mental?
– Absolutely. He tried to get me to steal a fire engine recently so that says it all. We were getting a photo shoot done at the training ground and someone opened the door to the steam room, which set off the alarms. When the fire brigade turned up they left one of the engines running. He said, 'Bet you don't drive that away.' I replied, 'You're f***ing right, I won't!' – Hibs midfielder **John Rankin** on manager Mixu Paatelainen, newspaper questionnaire, November 2008.

I was walking with Lesley, hand in hand. There was this guy 15 yards away walking towards us, smartly-dressed, about 25 or 26 years old. He wasn't a scruffbag. He smiles, but the closer he gets he starts smiling at Lesley. I was thinking he must know her. Then he goes right up to Lesley's face and goes 'Do you fancy a date?' She went 'No' and he goes 'What about some other time?' Then he says, 'I'd be better than the old guy!' Then he walks away and says, 'And by the way, he's f****** ginger-haired and ugly as well!' Have you ever heard anything like that in your life? It could only happen here! – Fun in the West End of Glasgow with Celtic manager **Gordon Strachan** and wife, May 2009.

HISTORY ⚽

Brissit brawnis and broken banis
Strife, discord and waisit wanis
Crookit in eild, sine halt withal
These are the bewteis of the fute-ball
– from the **Bannatyne manuscript**, 1568. Inscription is at the Stirling Smith Art Gallery, Stirling, site of the oldest football in the world.

It's claimed that football was invented in England but we now know that is not the case and the modern game definitely came from north of the border. There is historical evidence of the game being played up here as far back as 1424, but it probably goes back even further. The birth of the modern game was the Scotland-England game in 1872 – up until then, the English had played a hybrid game of rugby and football as we know it. There was no goalkeeper, no set number of players for each side, there was limited use of hands and no forward passing. It was only the Scottish game that developed these rules – Scottish Football Museum historian **Richard McBrearty**, August 2003.

Beware of the clever sharp men who are creeping into the game – Founder of the Football League **William McGregor** – born in Braco – *in League Football And The Men Who Made It*, 1909.

One of the great goalscorers in the history of Barcelona FC – **Manel Tomas**, archivist at Barcelona FC's Centre for Documentation and Studies, on Scottish striker John Patullo, who scored 43 goals in 21 games for the club in 1910–12.

Do not ask where Hearts are playing and then look at me askance. If it's football that you're wanting you must come with us to France! – Private **George Blaney**, Castle Brewery, Edinburgh, December 1914, in Jack Alexander, *McCrae's Battalion, The Story of the 16th Royal Scots*, 2003. McCrae's was known as the 'Heart of Midlothian Battalion' and fought at the Somme. Eleven Hearts players were killed in WWI and a further 14 wounded.

Playing for Scotland is fantastic. You look at your dark blue shirt and the wee lion looks up at you and says, 'Get out there after those English bastards!' – **Bill Shankly**, Scotland player of the 1930s, in John Keith, *Shanks For The Memory*, 1998.

It's disappointing, but what do you expect from Hollywood? It's not the true story, not at all – **Sheila McIlvenny**, widow of former U.S. national team captain Eddie, a Scot, on the 2005 film 'The Game of Their Lives', the story of the U.S.A.'s 1950 World Cup win over England in Brazil.

Against England, our coach Bill Jeffrey, who was also Scottish-born, thought it would be a big feather in Eddie's cap to be captain. It was an honour for him and I think that was the proper thing to do. I was then captain for the last game against Chile and for years to come. Yet in the film I'm captain, and that's wrong. I know Eddie's widow lives in East Sussex, and it is important she should know that an error has been made and Eddie really was the captain against England – Former USA player **Walter Bahr**, on the same film, 2005. In the film version, Bahr is the captain against England.

In my local area, in Wishaw, I am remembered for being part of a great forward line, and only occasionally for scoring a goal at Berwick – Former Motherwell and Berwick Rangers midfielder **Sammy Reid**, scorer of the goal which beat Rangers in the 1967 Scottish Cup, February 2000. Reid played for the Motherwell side which beat Rangers four times in one season in 1959–60 (twice in the League and twice in the League Cup sections).

It was totally disorganised, in fact, and you wouldn't be far wrong in saying it was a shambles at times. Bob Kelly was in charge and he knew nothing about football. Jimmy McGrory was the manager but the chairman made all the decisions. Tactics? There were no tactics — Former Celt **Pat Crerand**, May 2003, recalling Celtic's first-ever European tie, in the Inter-Cities Fairs Cup (later the UEFA Cup) against Valencia in September 1962. Celtic were 3–0 down after half an hour and eventually lost 4–2.

Stirling Albion's Jim Kerray gave me a harder time at Celtic Park in November 1966 than Inter Milan's Sandro Mazzola at the Estadio Nacional in May 1967. Six months before the European Cup final, Stirling, who always seemed to be battling relegation, stuck three past Ronnie Simpson in a league match. If my memory serves me correctly, Kerray got two. I mention big Jim because he gave me such a difficult 90 minutes — Former Celtic captain **Billy McNeill** looks back, *The Lisbon Lions*, May 2007. (*Celtic won the match in question 7–3, Kerray scoring once.*)

When Billy McNeill was recovering from a heart op, I rang to see how he was and his eight-year-old grandson answered. I told him who I was and he shot back, 'You're the guy that gave away the penalty in Lisbon.' — Former Celtic defender **Jim Craig**, 2003.

I was never worried. As long as you've got a pack of cards in a hotel then everything's okay — Scotland international **Willie Morgan**, prior to a second friendly against Israel being cancelled, two weeks before the Six-Day War broke out in June 1967.

For over 30 years I've been attending Arsenal functions, and all anyone wants to talk about is that miss. I wish I had a pound for every time someone has told me, 'If you had scored that goal, Peter, Arsenal could have won the European Cup in 1972.' Everyone remembers that f****** miss, it's haunted me all my life — **Peter Marinello** on a first-minute chance against Ajax Amsterdam in the European Cup quarter-final, in *Fallen Idle*, 2007.

I read the book but I will not be seeing the movie. I read the book because I thought it was about a part of my life, but the more I read the less I believed it had any real connection with my past. There were just too many inaccuracies, too many people were saying things they didn't say, and doing things they didn't do, and being in the wrong place at the wrong time, and of course you lose faith in what you are reading — Spurs coach **Joe Jordan**, March 2009, on David Peace novel *The Damned United*, about Brian Clough's 44 days in charge of Leeds United in 1974.

I haven't felt that good since Archie Gemmill scored against Holland in 1978
– **Ewan McGregor** *(Mark Renton)*, in film, *Trainspotting* (1996).

It was a waste of time voting. That's the best by far. Anybody who can go
from their own half and walk past people as though they are not even there,
and then just walk past the goalkeeper as though he's not there as well, should
win. John Barnes' goal for England against Brazil was far superior to mine
as well, but that was just a friendly – Former Scotland midfielder **Archie Gemmill**
on his goal against Holland in Argentina in 1978, June 2003, during a debate about
the World Cup's best-ever goal. He was referring to Diego Maradona's goal for
Argentina against England in 1986.

One more and we were through, but then within two minutes it was back to
reality. I went to close Johnny Rep down and it took a faint touch off the edge
of my toe. Roughie is not really that far away from it. So you wonder, 'Is that
touch the one that took it away from him?' – **Archie Gemmill** on another goal in
the 1978 World Cup game against Holland in Mendoza, June 2003.

In retrospect it would seem that the poor Scottish performance was due to
complacency and lack of professionalism on the part of all concerned with
Scottish football. They seemed provincials out of their depth in international
waters – **Hugh Carless**, *Chargé d'Affaires* at the British embassy in Buenos Aires, in
a cable to the Foreign Office in London following the 1978 World Cup. The contents
were made public by the National Archives Office in December 2008.

I was recently on a flight to South America and the flight attendant came
up to me and said, 'Thanks for your contribution to the history of Celtic.'
– Former Celtic manager **Wim Jansen** on the repercussions on stopping Rangers
winning ten in a row in 1998, in Mark Guidi, *The Inner Sanctum*, 2008.

I'm one of those who didn't think the Cup Final should take place. The
families said they wanted it, so fine. But I thought that if there was a gap in
the Cup, people would ask for ever more, 'What was that for?' – Everton's **Pat
Nevin** on playing in the 1989 FA Cup Final between Everton and Liverpool, after the
Hillsborough disaster.

It's difficult for people to appreciate in the modern day how large Queen's
Park were. You've got to imagine Manchester United, Juventus and Real
Madrid as one team, because this is a team that founded international
football, provided all the players for the world's first Scotland team in 1872,
were founders of both the English Cup and the Scottish Cup, and were
founders of the SFA It is important now to understand how one team could
have so much influence over the whole of world football as it was – Museum
of Scottish Football director **Ged O'Brien**, *BBC TV* documentary, June 2003.

I was only interested in one thing, the success of Dundee United Football Club and not one of the players was damaged by anything that I did. There's no doubt, in my opinion, that I would do it the same way again if I could – Former Dundee United manager **Jim McLean**, April 2004.

We spent three hours one night drinking, talking, singing. He said he wished the evening would never end. When we put him in a cab, I said, 'Treat this guy good, he's like Jesus Christ.' The driver said, 'He's better than that!' – Actor **Robert Duvall** on Jimmy Johnstone, in documentary, *Lord Of The Wing*, 2004.

Because we couldn't be there, we've made a little video. Robbo's there, piece to camera, saying he's sorry we can't be there, hopes they all have a good night. Then I come in and say, 'I'm not happy. How can you boys be arranging a reunion when you know full well you'll be missing one of the most influential players in Forest's history – and John Robertson?' – Celtic manager **Martin O'Neill**, on his message to Nottingham Forest's 25-year reunion, May 2004.

Let's look at this loyalty thing. Dundee sold me. I did seven years at Aberdeen, and left when my contract was up. I did five years at Manchester United, and they sold me. I didn't want to go. I did six years at Leeds before retiring as a player. I went to Coventry and they sacked me as manager. I've never walked out on anybody. You can answer that by looking at my record – Former Southampton manager **Gordon Strachan**, February 2005.

Britain was the first to develop the game and its structures, and in some cases you have kept some of the old models – UEFA chief executive **Lars-Christer Olsson**, May 2005. He had been on the SFA's Independent Review Commission – the 'Think Tank' – on the future of the game in 1995.

The truth is that, unlike Martin (O'Neill), I had nothing going for me with Celtic fans at the start. The whole Aberdeen thing was still manifesting itself, so that was a problem, and it maybe set me back a wee bit – Celtic manager **Gordon Strachan**, June 2007.

I don't feel comfortable going back to Celtic Park. The only time I've been back was when I was manager of Livingston. It's not my era any more – Former Celtic midfielder **Paul Lambert**, in Mark Guidi, *The Inner Sanctum*, 2008.

He (the goalkeeper) blamed the sheen that he said allowed the ball to slip through on the brand new jersey he was wearing and ever since it has been a superstition at Arsenal to put the goalkeeper's jersey through the wash before every game. They still do it to this day. Perhaps because of that, my grandfather never got the credit he deserved as the match-winner. But they all count. And boy did that one count – **Hugh Ferguson**, grandson of Cardiff

85

striker Hughie Ferguson, the Scot whose goal for the club won them the FA Cup in 1927, speaking before Cardiff's appearance in the 2008 Final, May 2008.

HO HO HO ⚽

One of the questioners asked me how I had felt on being named as a member of the greatest-ever Celtic team, for which the Celtic support had voted in 2002. 'Surprised and delighted,' I responded. Ronnie, in his own laconic style, piped up, 'Aye, we were all surprised.' — **Bobby Lennox** on Lisbon Lion Ronnie Simpson, in *Bobby Lennox: My Story*, 2007.

Where did you think you were — the bloody Sahara desert? — Then-Aberdeen manager **Alex Ferguson**, on being told by a player he'd been tackled because he 'didn't think there was anyone near me', quoted in Alex McLeish, *The Don of an Era*, 1988.

Taxi drivers ask me to this day if I ever bump into Alan — Former Aberdeen and Scotland defender **Willie Miller**, October 2008, recalling the collision between him and Alan Hansen in the 1982 World Cup tie against the USSR in Malaga which led to Ramaz Shengalia's decisive second goal.

I remember you staged the Finals here in 1989 and lost on penalties. But I'm not sure Scotland's opponents went to school at the same time as Scotland's did! — FIFA president **Sepp Blatter**, March 2007, on the suspiciously mature Saudi Arabia team who beat Scotland in the Under-16 World Championships in June 1989.

Gazza's message was short and to the point: 'Aye, too right you're back — back on the f****** bench!' — Former Celtic striker **Darren Jackson** remembers a phone message from former Newcastle teammate Paul Gascoigne, in Mark Guidi, *The Inner Sanctum*, 2008. Jackson had scored his first goal following his brain operation in a midweek game at Aberdeen – and while he could clearly be seen celebrating with the words 'I'm back!' after his goal, he was dropped to the bench for the next game against Hearts.

Alex (Ferguson) saw me as a bit of a joker, always laughing and joking. I think he appreciated that I could play. But I don't think he regarded me as a sensible lad — Coventry City manager **Gordon Strachan**, in Rick Gekoski, *Staying Up: A Fan Behind The Scenes In The Premiership*, 1998.

I don't want to mix up one game with another. When you go to the market, apples are apples and plums are plums — Celtic coach **Jozef Venglöš**, 1999.

In terms of a prospective challenger for honours in Europe next summer, here, as was said of the Falklands conflict, were two bald men fighting over a comb — Journalist **Danny Baker** on the Scotland v England Euro 2000 play-offs, November 1999. The original quote was by Argentinian poet and essayist Jorge Luis Borges.

There was a company on the phone selling outdoor equipment. I asked them if they had any gallows — Hamilton chief executive **Bill Sherry**, April 2000, after his side had 15 points deducted for failing to turn up for an 1 April fixture against Stenhousemuir. Unsurprisingly, this saw Hamilton finish bottom of Division Two.

I apologised to the linesman — although I did manage to get his address — Queen's Park manager **John McCormack**, called into the referee's room after kissing assistant ref Kenny Carter after Paul Walker's late winning goal against Brechin edged his side closer to the Division Three title, April 2000.

It has given me pleasure to see him getting better, bigger and stronger while I get older, fatter and balder — Kilmarnock manager **Bobby Williamson** on youngster Paul di Giacomo, May 2001.

There's Only One John Parrott — Celtic fans taunt Kilmarnock's **Ally McCoist** during his last game as a player, May 2001.

It's a blessing that there IS only one John Parrott — **McCoist**'s response, May 2001.

I can't tell you. It's a secret — Referee **Hugh Dallas'** droll response when asked about officials' views on Celtic fans hiring a private detective to prove alleged Masonic links with referees, November 2001.

A list of eight people was drawn up at Bradford, I was on it, did very well at the interview and was the only one of the eight to be asked back. I believe that it's only an Irishman who could get down to the last one and still fail — Celtic manager **Martin O'Neill**, March 2002. Caretaker manager Terry Dolan was given the Bradford job in January 1987.

Fergie, I'm afraid, doesn't have a sense of humour. He's bottom of the league when it comes to that. He doesn't have a personality, either. Will we ever be pals? Oh, I hope not — Former Manchester United manager **Tommy Docherty** on Alex Ferguson, November 2002.

B.A. got in touch with me and I asked him, 'Was it you who wrote that crappy Scotland song?' Do you know, when we were recording it, I couldnae stop laughing. I got chucked out of the recording studio — Southampton manager **Gordon Strachan** on singer-songwriter B.A. Robertson, January 2003. The song was 'We Have A Dream', for the 1982 World Cup.

I remember a Celtic defender was displeased with McCoist, and was charging up the field telling the Rangers player exactly what he wanted to do to him. I knew it was out of keeping with the player's game, and chances were he would calm down, so when Ally shouted, 'Hey ref, you hear that? What you gonnae do about it?' I said, 'Nothing, I'm okay – it's you he's after, not me!' – Referee **Hugh Dallas** recalls Old Firm fun, March 2003.

The slowest Scottish player I've ever seen – Former Borussia Dortmund teammate and friend (?) **Michael Zorc** on Paul Lambert, BBC TV programme, Footballers' Lives, March 2003.

The slowest Scottish player ever? What? Do you mean running-wise or intelligence-wise? – Celtic teammate (and, obviously, another friend) **Henrik Larsson** on Zorc's comment, BBC TV programme, Footballers' Lives, March 2003.

It will be the biggest shock ever – if we get a corner. We have asked the FA if we can use two goalkeepers but they said no. When I go up against Vieira I'll be heading his knees – Sheffield United's **Stuart McCall**, before the FA Cup semi-final against Arsenal, April 2003. Arsenal won 1–0.

It was a tough choice. Some of the players I've left out were geniuses – di Stefano, Puskas, Eusebio, Baptie. The list is endless – Stenhousemuir manager **John McVeigh** on picking his all-time world XI, May 2003. Crawford Baptie played for Falkirk and Motherwell in the late 80s.

Q: Describe manager Bobby Williamson in three words.
A: Fat, honest, baldy.
– Hibs striker **Tam McManus**, newspaper questionnaire, August 2003.

I just said to Graham, 'I didn't know you were a Tottenham supporter,' and he took exception to that. He didn't hear me first time so I repeated it and that's why he sent me off. I don't swear, but I believe communication is everything in life – Blackburn manager **Graeme Souness** after being sent to the stand against Spurs by referee Graham Poll, December 2003.

It should have been shown after the watershed – Hearts manager **Craig Levein** after a poor 0–0 draw against Motherwell had been shown live on BBC TV, December 2003.

His car number plate says CLA55 – 'class'. Have you ever seen anything less appropriate? There's no erse to his troosers – Preston manager **Craig Brown** on chairman Derek Shaw, January 2004.

Spartans would like to take this opportunity to thank all those in the press and media who gave such positive and extensive coverage of our memorable Tennents Scottish Cup run. Let's hope we can do it all over again next season!

We look forward to seeing you all at our next league game against Vale of Leithen – Waggish press release from East of Scotland League club Spartans, who'd just lost 4–0 to Livingston in the Scottish Cup Fourth round, February 2004.

I've rung the wife and told her to hide all the belts, ties and laces – Motherwell manager **Terry Butcher** after his side had been beaten at home by Inverness Caley Thistle in the Scottish Cup quarter-final, March 2004.

Just because I look like Russell Grant doesn't mean I can see into the future – Hibs manager **Bobby Williamson** when asked if his young players would succeed in the game, March 2004.

Before the last game we'd gone into administration and when we ran out before the match the United fans were waving Monopoly money at us. I thought that was really funny. I know we're in a difficult position but I think you have to retain a sense of humour about things and I think whichever United fan dreamed that one up deserves a pat on the back – Dundee manager **Jim Duffy**, before the Dundee derby in April 2004.

I know that their expenditure has been cut enormously with Fergie going to England and me retiring because they were always getting fines out of us, but I have no doubts at all that even with less income they have still not handled it well – Former Dundee United manager **Jim McLean** on the SFA, April 2004.

Bigger than Ipswich? In the number of letters, you mean? – Northampton boss **Colin Calderwood**, on learning the town is the biggest in England, May 2004.

I'm probably being too fussy. I'm holding out for one with compulsory Saturday shifts – East Stirling midfielder **Joe Robertson** on looking for a new job as an electrician, September 2004. 'Shire had finished bottom of the Third Division in the two previous seasons.

There's a great pub that I built called the Celtic Supporters Club. It's got smashed windows – Singer **Rod Stewart**, Q Magazine, February 2005, on his 'scale-model railroad' (not a train set).

I gave a penalty kick against his team one day and at half-time there was the predictable knock on my dressing-room door. There's Sandy, the manager, saying, 'Willie, what about that penalty?' I asked, 'Yes Sandy, is there a problem?' To which he answered, 'Well, it was gey soft.' I looked him in the eye and said, 'Sandy, let me tell you something. A penalty kick is like a boiled egg. Soft or hard, it's still a f****** boiled egg. Right?' – Retiring ref **Willie Young** recalls explaining the rules to Sandy Clark, May 2005.

He was in Amsterdam covering some European match and walked into a shop, and all he could hear were these wee voices going, 'Heh heh heh!'

It was a bunch of kids from Paisley on a school trip — Comedian **Jonathan Watson** on *BBC* journalist Chick Young, December 2006.

I had to find things to do on a Saturday when I wasn't playing, so I've now got the names of my two sons tattooed on my arms. Any more Saturdays off and I'd have been like the guy in *Cape Fear* — Gretna's **James Grady**, March 2007.

I looked down the list and the only name I didn't recognise was my own — SFA chief executive **Gordon Smith** on being named on UEFA's 14–man Football Committee, including famous ex-players like Michel Platini, Franz Beckanbauer and Dino Zoff, July 2007.

Scorer for Kilmarnock, number 16, Dick Turpin — Fir Park tannoy announcer after Kilmarnock striker Rhian Dodds scored a last-minute winner against Motherwell in a game which the home side had dominated, August 2007.

Thank goodness we won't meet them again until the Final — Rangers assistant manager **Ally McCoist** after his side had been comprehensively outplayed by Barcelona in the Champions League at the Nou Camp, November 2007.

I remember being told by big MacIntyre
Tae take mair time oan the ba. Listen son, he says
Ye're playin like the gress wis oan fire
Yer blindin us a' wi' the stour
– **Alistair Findlay**, 'Fitba Cliché', collected in *100 Favourite Scottish Football Poems*, edited by Alistair Findlay, 2007.

Should we really talk about Paul? The first two weeks were a tragedy, one joke after another. For example, if his socks smelled he simply took mine. If I left my toilet bag unattended I was dead, because Paul would get my toothbrush and use it for everything before leaving it in the same place. — Milan midfielder **Rino Gattuso** on former Rangers teammate Paul Gascoigne, Italian TV show *Sfide*, March 2008.

The funniest guy I've met in football — Cardiff City defender **Roger Johnson** on teammate Steven Thompson, May 2008.

Dick Campbell got sacked with his team at the top of the league, for not playing attractive enough football. Let's hope that doesn't f****** catch on — Rangers manager **Walter Smith**, Scottish Football Writers Association Annual Dinner, May 2008. Campbell was sacked as manager of Ross County when they were top of Division Two in October 2007. Although Smith's team had reached the UEFA Cup Final and he had been voted Scotland's Manager of the Year, his side's style had not always been popular.

It was the equivalent of falling out of a plane and missing the Earth – BBC *Radio Scotland* pundit **Chick Young** on Wolves' Chris Iwelumo's miss for Scotland on his international debut against Norway, October 2008.

He told me he'd have got on the end of some of my crosses. I don't know if he meant now, though – AC Milan's **David Beckham** on a touchline exchange with Rangers coach Ally McCoist during the friendly between the clubs, February 2009.

HOBBIES

I bought an old vinyl jukebox and have about 2,500 records from the Coasters back in the 50s all the way to Guns'n'Roses. I have an eclectic mix but I love my Motown. I have a big stash of old 50 pences, so I can use it – Former Hibs defender **Gordon Rae**, January 2009.

There's nothing better than a stripped, quiet room where you can hang wallpaper. It's very relaxing – Motherwell defender and DIY enthusiast **Shaun Teale**, December 1999.

Subbuteo is like real football and that is where I got my passion for the game. When I was eight I had Lazio and Celtic teams and would pretend they were playing each other in the Champions League – Table soccer fan and West Ham striker **Paolo di Canio**, January 2000.

It was the Saturday of the Grand National. I scored the goal against St Mirren and I backed the National winner, *Red Marauder*. Not a bad day, eh? – Former Celtic striker **Tommy Johnson** recalls a good afternoon's work on 7 April 2001, March 2008.

I was away on a golfing holiday recently and had to put my cheeks in the fridge when I came home after all the laughing I did – Former Dundee United manager **Jim McLean**, November 2001.

I got the piano and I started to learn myself but I found it difficult. My cousin brought out the competitive edge. I wanted to prove I could do it as well – Manchester United manager **Sir Alex Ferguson**, August 2002.

They have a reputation and I wouldn't want to put them off their 'Wonderwall' or whatever it's called – Dundee United manager **Alex Smith**, agreeing to move a game with Aberdeen because popular beat combo Oasis were playing in Aberdeen the same night, September 2002.

I've got the autopsy report – Manchester United manager **Sir Alex Ferguson** on the JFK assassination (a source of fascination to him), 2002.

I want to do the West Highland Way in the next four or five years, because I think we're knackered after that. I don't think I'd do it in Rab C. Nesbitt fashion, with two dozen lager cans strapped to my back – Southampton manager **Gordon Strachan**, January 2003.

Sometimes I play golf and shooting is something I like to do as well. But I also like to pick some mushrooms, and I go on long walks looking for mushrooms – Blackburn's former Rangers defender **Lorenzo Amoruso**, September 2003.

People don't know what Robbo is really like. He does *The Times* crossword. He used to do one every Saturday. At that time it was the *Telegraph* and no one else could get a single clue. I went into Leicester one day and he was there in the laundry room with Wally (Steve Walford) because it was warmer, doing the crossword. He's that sort of guy, a deep-thinking guy – Martin O'Neill's former teammate **Mick McGuire**, on John Robertson, in Alex Montgomery, 'Martin O'Neill – *The Biography*', 2003.

I've only ever read one book apart from football books and pigeon books and that was when I was in getting an operation on my knee and that was *Peyton Place*. I only read it because it was there – Partick Thistle manager **John Lambie**, in *Fanatical About Football*, ed. Jeff Connor, 2003.

At Rangers, the only guys who would give me a game were the backroom staff – mainly the physios and masseurs – Chess fan **Andrei Kanchelskis** on his passion, November 2003.

People say, 'Do you play golf?' and I say 'I wasn't a good enough footballer to play golf.' I never had any spare time, all mine was about practise, trying to get better – West Ham assistant manager **Peter Grant**, February 2004.

Sometimes I see people in a park or at an outdoor cafe sipping tea and watching the world go by. I can't imagine myself ever doing anything like that – Former Rangers manager **Dick Advocaat**, June 2004.

We ride a tandem, you see, like *Dumb & Dumber*. I'm at the front getting all the flies and crap in my face and she's at the back. I have to turn round to see if she's actually pedalling and every time I do that the wee legs start to go – **Gordon Strachan** on life with wife Lesley during his break away from the game, February 2005.

It all came too easily for Duncan. If he had the same love for football as his pigeons, he would have over 50 caps by now – Former Dundee United manager **Jim McLean** on Duncan Ferguson, May 2005.

I'm a massive fan. The originals are the best but it's still brilliant. Luke Skywalker was my favourite. In fact, I named my son after him – Norwich

City's **Gary Holt** on the new *Star Wars* film, *Episode III – Revenge of the Sith*, June 2005.

I am a member of the Erasure fan club and I once saw them play eight times in 28 days. I travelled the country to see them in Manchester, Milton Keynes, Whitley Bay and London. My wife thinks I have slightly gay tendencies. I like cheesy 80s music and I am always on the dancefloor with my cheesy dancing – Dundee United goalkeeper **Tony Bullock** confesses, 2005.

I'm a passionate fan who happens to have my own club. Why not? Some people pay £5m for a stamp. That Beckham fellow spends a fortune on rings for his wife. Apart from buying an Aston Martin, which was a mistake I now regret, this is the first thing I've ever done for me – Gretna owner **Brooks Mileson**, June 2005.

Before that, I was a dancer. I did Polish national dancing, you know, polka and modern dancing. I still like dancing, actually – Celtic goalkeeper **Artur Boruc**, September 2005.

David Graham is a bit of a thespian. He does a little bit of acting in his spare time. He has shown me some clips on his mobile of shows he's been in. – Gretna's **Ryan McGuffie** on his teammate, August 2006.

Martin doesn't do small talk because all he talks about is football – non-stop – Former Leeds chairman **Peter Ridsdale** on former Celtic manager Martin O'Neill, in book, *United We Fall: Boardroom Truths about the Beautiful Game*, 2007.

Lesley and I did things together, such as going round the world. We did lots, and we love zoos – zoos have become our great passion. Madrid's is the best, by the way, but we've done 'em all – Celtic manager **Gordon Strachan** on his time out of football, June 2007.

It was a fiction about a football agent and I wrote it as a bit of therapy. A literary agent, Peter Strauss, got hold of it, loved it and thought it was a certainty – but he couldn't find anyone to publish it. A couple of publishers said it was libelous because although it's fiction, maybe a few characters in it were pretty close to the mark – Motherwell manager **Mark McGhee** on the 75,000-word book he wrote during his nine months out of football, December 2007.

I saw Billy Connolly at Gatwick Airport. I shouted, 'Hey, Big Yin'. He turned round and gave me the finger. I was dead chuffed – Arbroath defender **Robbie Raeside**, May 2008.

I always joked to teammates that I would one day appear in *FourFourTwo* as a Celtic player, but hey, I'm here now, even though I'm not a footballing icon. There'll be a lot of shocked players and fans north of the border when they see this. 'Look! It's that weirdo who played for us!' – Glasvegas guitarist and singer **James Allan**, formerly with Falkirk, Gretna and Stirling Albion, July 2008.

It started when I went to Venice for a week with my wife. We loved it and did the whole thing, the gondolas, the food, the expensive coffee in St Mark's Square. And we went to an opera and it blew my mind. There's one where the singers actually walk among you, make you part of the performance – Wolves and Scotland's opera-loving striker **Chris Iwelumo**, November 2008.

They're for five, six, seven-year-old kids and they have an educational message within a football theme. My stories are about using football and the attributes that you learn in the game, to help with problems at school. So for example, a goalkeeper needs to be courageous to play that position, so you think about a problem he would have at school that would need him to be brave to overcome and you work that into the story – St Mirren defender **Jack Ross** on children's books he's written, February 2009.

INJURIES ⚽

There's a famous picture of me when I was with Spurs with Billy Bremner, who was at Leeds. That match was just after I was coming back from a leg break. Everybody said, 'You've broken your leg.' but I've never broken my legs, other people broke them, and that was the first day after two leg breaks, one after the other. Billy knew exactly which leg had been broken, and he came round behind me and the nearest leg to him was my right leg and he kicked me on the left leg. So what do you do? What would you do? – Spurs' **Dave Mackay**, in 'Fanatical About Football', ed. Jeff Connor, 2003.

To this day, I still give (Mark) McGhee stick about that. I made the challenge and Mark went down like he'd been shot. I got the red card and he gets up, plays like a demon, scores the winner and gets the Man of the Match award. What a f****** recovery – Former Celtic defender **Roy Aitken** on his 1984 Scottish Cup final red card against Aberdeen, in *Gordon Strachan: The Biography*, Leo Moynihan, 2004.

If it had been broken at 0–0, I wouldn't have been part of it, but I broke it at 5–0. The doctor (Stewart Hillis) asked me what I wanted to do and I said I just wanted to get home as quickly as possible. He didn't have any painkillers so as we sat waiting for the plane, we tanned his duty-free red wine. As far as I'm concerned, we won 2–1 and I got the winner – Rangers coach **Ally McCoist** recalls his April1993 broken leg playing for Scotland in Lisbon, March 2008.

Terry was speechless. He said that he had never known a player with less luck – Sheffield Wednesday's injury-jinxed **Phil O'Donnell** on manager Terry Yorath's reaction to his latest injury, June 2003.

He's not happy unless he's been kicked in the bollocks three times during training – **Graeme Le Saux** on Blackburn teammate Colin Hendry, 1997.

I was trying to give the half-time team talk and Paul is lying on the table in front of me and he's got no teeth at all, he's got a broken jaw, he's moaning and the players are trying to concentrate and I'm trying to give a team talk. That was strange – Celtic head coach **John Barnes** on Paul Lambert's injury against Rangers in November 1999, in DVD, *The Official History of Celtic*, 2008.

I could stay, earn the same money but had to train with the under-21s from the beginning of the season because he didn't need me any more. When he arrived, he needed me; I played with injections. He was begging me, nearly on his knees, 'Play please against Feyenoord, play please the final against Ayr, play against Celtic with an injection.' – Former Rangers defender **Bert Konterman** on his relationship with Ibrox manager Alex McLeish, November 2003.

A coward's tackle – Former Scotland midfielder **Craig Burley**, November 2004, on the tackle by Romania's Ioan Ganea on Scotland's John Kennedy in March 2004.

Bobo Balde is probably responsible for more injuries this season than our surface – Dunfermline chairman **John Yorkston**, in a pre-match interview before facing Celtic in a Scottish Cup-tie, February 2005. Celtic were unhappy about Dunfermline's synthetic surface and refused to play loan signing Craig Bellamy on it.

It was inflammatory and a crassly ignorant comment from someone who has made similar crassly ignorant comments in the past – Celtic manager **Martin O'Neill**'s response after the match, which Celtic won 3–0, February 2005.

There is a code in this game for certain situations and it has been broken here, badly. It is the sort of challenge you simply can't condone. He waited for our kid to play the ball and then he went over the top and stamped down on his leg. I saw it last night for the first time after the dust had settled. I sat there, shook my head and thought, 'That is f***ing horrendous.' There's no question it was intentional – Leicester City manager **Craig Levein** on the Bobo Balde tackle which broke the leg of 17-year-old debutant James Wesolowski in a pre-season friendly against Celtic, July 2005.

In American football, if someone tears knee ligaments, they're finished. Basketball's the same. It's really very rare to be able to make the comeback that John Kennedy made – in ALL of sports. But among the people I've treated I'd put him at the very top level as far as his ability to maintain his fight and focus on his goal goes – Colorado knee surgeon **Dr Richard Steadman**, who operated on the Celtic defender, July 2007.

When I left Clyde I said I'm not having any more tired old guys coming in for their last payday, limping about saying, 'No, I can't make it this week gaffer because of my ligaments,' and all that crap – Hamilton chairman **Ronnie MacDonald** on the day his side won promotion to the SPL, April 2008.

Any form of pain that I experienced here was eradicated when I won my third Michelin star. And had I not had the upset in football here at Ibrox, I don't think I'd be the chef I am today – TV chef and former Rangers youth player **Gordon Ramsay**, whose playing career was ended by injury, *The F Word* TV show, July 2008.

INTERNATIONAL FOOTBALL

I went in with Kenny Dalglish. Kenny managed to do his toilet but I struggled and struggled and the next thing I knew was that Willie (Johnston) went in and it wasn't me they wanted any more. If I had done a wee, things might have been different – Former Scotland midfielder **Archie Gemmill** on Argentina '78, June 2003.

When I first played for Scotland they used to tell us that you had to pace yourself in international games, so I would take it a little easy – not chase a ball here, not make a run there – and then I found I could never catch up with the game and I'd end up getting taken off. I finally decided I had to go out and give it 100 per cent and if after 70 minutes I was knackered I'd go off anyway – Coventry manager **Gordon Strachan**, in Rick Gekoski, 'Staying Up, A Fan Behind The Scenes In The Premiership', 1998.

When I came back from Argentina to play for Rangers, I saw more Argentina tops in Scotland than I had in Mexico. I didn't realize they were held in such high esteem here – Scotland assistant manager **Terry Butcher**, November 2008, recalls domestic reaction to Argentina knocking England out of the 1986 World Cup.

Big Duncan Ferguson came on late in the game for his international debut, only to give a lacklustre performance. When Andy Roxburgh asked him later about his half-hearted effort, the big man was candid. 'Ah cannae get ma self up for these park gemmes.' – Former Scotland international **Pat Nevin**, July 2006. Ferguson had replaced Nevin in the 1–0 win over the USA in Denver in May 1992.

Everybody else was either injured or out of form and I think I was doing particularly well – Celtic's **Chris Sutton**, October 2002, on being asked to play for England's 'B' team against Chile in 1998 rather than for the full team at Wembley the following night. He declined the offer.

I was sitting one yard away from Scotland v Brazil with my kit on and didn't get to play. If I really let that get to me, I wouldn't sleep at night. I really have to work hard to forget it and I shouldn't have to forget it. It should be brilliant, shouldn't it? It should be a once-in-a-lifetime experience, but I have mixed feelings about it – Former Scotland midfielder **Scot Gemmill**, March 2003, on being a sub at the 1998 World Cup opener.

He doesn't look like an international manager but what does an international manager look like anyway? A wee baldy man with bad knees, like me? – Scotland manager **Craig Brown** on Norway manager Egil Olsen, 1998.

It was ridiculous. I said to Japan and Korea, 'I'm not coming to any more receptions, I am not accepting any more gifts.' The stuff was arriving at the door, and of course, what do you do? The postman delivers it. It's just ridiculous. The only thing that was missing was the cash in a plain brown envelope – Former FIFA vice-president **David Will**, on the summer 1996 campaign by the two countries to win the right to stage the 2002 World Cup, in *Great Balls of Fire: How Big Money Is Highjacking World Football*, John Sugden and Alan Tomlinson, 1999.

But one of Fletcher's parents is Irish, so he qualifies for both. I keep him well warned about the colour of international jersey he'll be wearing. Every time I see Roy Keane go near him, I threaten him – Manchester United manager **Sir Alex Ferguson** on midfielder Darren Fletcher, March 2002.

It is always the same for small countries. We never get any sympathy. I could write a book on the bad decisions Iceland have had in my four years in the job. It was a clear penalty, in big capital letters. When you push someone in the box, it's a penalty, but he gave an indirect free-kick. I have never seen that – Iceland coach **Atli Edvaldsson** on a Lee Wilkie tackle on Eiður Guðjohnsen, after the 2–1 defeat at Hampden, March 2003.

It only sank in a few minutes later. I'm not sure why he didn't give the penalty. Defenders try to get away with things all the time and I fouled Guðjohnsen, though he went down easily – Scotland defender **Lee Wilkie** on the same incident, March 2003.

I remember looking around and thinking, 'What are we trying to achieve here?' (Colin) Cameron was on the bench and I was playing with guys who weren't recognised midfielders. It was quite obvious that we were getting overrun in midfield, but we just carried on the way we were – Former Scotland midfielder **Craig Burley**, after Scotland's defeat by Holland in the Euro 2004 play-off, November 2003. Burley was referring to playing under Berti Vogts in his final international against Austria in April 2003.

Cheats! f****** cheats! f****** diving cheats! – A mystery Scotland player caught off-camera venting some spleen, after Scotland's defeat in Germany, September 2003.

Christian! CHRISTIAN!!! – Scotland manager **Berti Vogts**, being interviewed on-camera, helpfully identifies the culprit to the world, September 2003.

I didn't know the cameras were there. It's the kind of thing that goes on at times, but I'm a bit disappointed in myself – Scotland's **Christian Dailly** subsequently reflects on the incident, September 2003.

I've played in international games where afterwards we've thought that we took a real pummelling. But never 6–0. I'm not suggesting for a second that under (Craig) Brown we would have went to Holland and won the match, but you couldn't see one of his teams losing 6–0 – Former Scotland midfielder **Craig Burley** after the Euro 2004 play-off thrashing in Holland, November 2003.

He is not just a wood cutter but a florist as well – Dundee and Trinidad & Tobago's **Brent Sancho** on Dutch midfielder Edgar Davids, March 2004.

I don't understand why some of the Scotland players never went over to have a go at him. I would have wanted to stick one on his chin coming up the tunnel at half-time – Former Scotland midfielder **Craig Burley**, April 2005, on Romania's Ioan Ganea's March 2004 tackle on John Kennedy which led to the Celtic player's knee ligament injury.

You need two vital ingredients as an international player: quality and a thick skin. Nobody likes to be criticised, but part of being a Scotland player is dealing with the heat. It should not be overlooked that the players have been able to hide behind the manager as he has taken the brunt of the criticism. When a new manager comes in, though, if the players are still not performing there will be nowhere to hide. When (Craig) Brown was in charge he had a lot of experienced men like myself, Gary McAllister, John Collins and Jim Leighton, so our efforts were scrutinised. If a new manager comes in, the players' performances will be dissected. If you don't want criticism, don't play international football – Former Scotland midfielder **Craig Burley**, after the draw in Moldova, October 2004. It was Berti Vogts' last game in charge.

I've not got any grievances against anybody for not getting the job. That's entirely up to the people who choose and I hope they get the right guy. What I do have a grievance about was that nobody picked up the phone and talked to someone who's been there for five years and suffered a lot and hopefully contributed a lot – Celtic coach **Tommy Burns** withdrawing from the race to be Scotland manager, January 2007.

I recommended Scotland to him and asked if any of his family had been shagging north of the border. It turns out that they had so I'm delighted – Derby's **Billy Davies** recruits striker Steve Howard for Scotland, April 2007.

He (FIFA President Sepp Blatter) is a tricky customer, but I suppose anyone in that position has to be because you're dealing with people who, to put it politely, have a totally different code of ethics. By and large, the four British countries know what fair play is and we know when we're stepping out of line. We all have an understanding. But as soon as you hit Africa, it's a slightly different kettle of fish. They're poor nations and they want to grab what they can. I presume the Caribbean is much the same, they come at things in a different way – SFA president **John McBeth**, May 2007, as he prepared to take up his role as FIFA vice-president. He resigned a few days later.

I know two or three of the characters involved who are reasonable individuals and I know two or three who I'd want to count my fingers after I shook hands with them – SFA president **John McBeth** prepares to meet his new chums on the FIFA Executive Committee, May 2007. He resigned a few days later.

I would like to congratulate the courageous decision taken by the four British associations not to highlight a member who has recently attacked Caribbean and African nations in declarations which are totally negative and don't correspond to our concept of football – FIFA President **Sepp Blatter**, May 2007, as McBeth is forced to stand down from the vice-president's position, to be replaced by England's Geoff Thompson.

I went across to him before the penalty was taken and he just shrugged and said, 'That's football, that's football.' I just said back to him, 'Well, if you want to do that fine, but the next time you get the ball you're getting it.' He just looked at me and said, 'If you do that you'll get a red card,' but I replied, 'Don't worry, I'll time it right.' – Derby's **Jay McEveley** recounts an exchange with Lithuania's Saulius Mikoliunas after the Hearts player had dived to get his side a penalty in the European Championship qualifier against Scotland, September 2007. He was banned for two games by UEFA.

Gordon Brown got abuse for saying Gazza's goal against Scotland in Euro 96 was one of the best he'd ever seen. He must have known Scots would attack him for being pro-English and the English would say he was trying to pander to them – but he still said it. No one seems to believe him and think, 'What if it was one of the best goals he'd ever seen?' – Former Labour Party director of communications **Alastair Campbell**, 2007.

There are one or two people on that Executive Committee that I wouldn't trust as far as I could throw – More FIFA views from former SFA president **John McBeth**, October 2007.

We could get a draw, end up on 25 points and still not make it to Euro 2008. That could only happen to Scotland – Former Scotland boss **Walter Smith** before the final Euro 2008 qualifier against Italy, November 2007.

The Champions League's stock seems to have risen enormously and even people like Sir Alex Ferguson are saying it is bigger and better than international football. I would never agree with that because to represent your country is the highest honour you should be able to aspire to. You cherish every cap and every call-up and I see that with the Scottish players – Scotland assistant boss **Terry Butcher**, March 2008.

An Olympic football tournament will be played for gold, silver and bronze medals. It would be strange if we were not in any way part of that. But let me make one thing clear. I do not want a GB football team at the expense of the Scottish football team. No one will sell the jerseys of Scotland, England, Northern Ireland or Wales – which footballers will proudly wear for decades to come – Prime Minister **Gordon Brown** calls for a Great Britain football team for the 2012 Olympics, August 2008.

It is the quickest way for Scotland to disappear off the international stage. FIFA is comprised of 208 countries and we have had situations in the past when the privileges of the British associations, one of which is to compete separately in international football tournaments, has come under attack. People like to claim that the four home FAs are safe, but what I would say is that it's difficult to see what guarantees can be given – UEFA chief executive **David Taylor**, August 2008, on calls for a GB team at the 2012 Olympics.

The pressure that Gordon Brown and his ministers are trying to build on this issue is ridiculous – First Minister **Alex Salmond** on the GB team issue, August 2008.

He's Scottish in every respect – except for the fact Scotland didn't want him – Hamilton chairman **Ronnie MacDonald** on Glasgow-born midfielder James McCarthy, October 2008. McCarthy plays for the Republic of Ireland through his grandfather.

I don't think that playing for your country is optional. It's like conscription. You get the call, you answer. There can be no conscientious objection – Motherwell manager **Mark McGhee** on Rangers' Kris Boyd's decision to refuse to play for Scotland under George Burley, October 2008.

JOBS

The fact that Ricky McFarlane is not mentioned is a significant thing. Very Fergie. There's no doubt: once you cross him, that's it – Former St Mirren striker **Jimmy Bone** on McFarlane's omission from Ferguson's autobiography, in Michael Crick, *The Boss: The Many Sides of Alex Ferguson*, 2002. Physiotherapist McFarlane had turned down the chance to join Ferguson at Aberdeen.

People think there are degrees of loyalty. There's no degrees of loyalty. If someone lets me down once there's no way back – Manchester United manager **Sir Alex Ferguson**, 2002.

If it's your job to scout for players for a football club, then you have to be decisive. That's why I always had a 'Yes' or 'No' answer for managers when it came to players. If I believed in a player, I would say, 'Sign him,' whereas some chief scouts would protect themselves and say to the manager, 'Aye, the player is worth you taking a look at.' For me, that's a total cop-out – Former Celtic scout **Davie Hay**, in Mark Guidi, *The Inner Sanctum*, 2008.

He saw me as no different from the groundsman or the head chef – Former Celtic manager **Lou Macari**, February 2004, on his relationship with managing director Fergus McCann.

I get to come in at 10 in the morning, have a laugh with my mates, go out in the fresh air to keep fit. I could be away home at 12 if I wanted. I get to play football in front of thousands every week. And I get paid for it. Of course it's the best job in the world – Dunfermline striker **Gerry Britton**, in Bill Leckie, *Penthouse & Pavement*, 1999.

Q: What would you have done if you hadn't been a footballer?
A: A funeral director. I like looking at dead bodies.
– Chelsea striker **Chris Sutton**, in club magazine, *Onside*, 1999.

It's an unusual role, you end up feeling you have had a great game, but if you get the video and watch the game you never touch the ball. You have to concentrate and be totally negative – Aston Villa defender **Colin Calderwood**, June 1999.

No discussions have taken place with his agent, his auntie, his dog or anyone else representing him. And as the owner, I think I might have been consulted – Motherwell owner **John Boyle** amid rumours Tommy Burns was set to replace Billy Davies as manager, October 1999.

I've never taken anything for granted. You learn that when you make your living laying bricks, and you have to go battering on some folks' doors late on a Friday night in the hope of getting your wages – Dundee goalkeeper **Robert Douglas**, a former brickie, November 1999.

It was a bit surreal. Kenny's a man of few words. He phoned me up at the end of the season and said, 'I'm going to Celtic. D'you want to come as manager?' Just like that – Former Celtic head coach **John Barnes** recalls his Parkhead invite, in DVD, *The Official History of Celtic*, 2008.

When I considered the approach I thought there were hundreds of mathematics department heads in Scotland just as good as me, but I honestly didn't think there were hundreds of part-time football managers as good as me – St Mirren manager **Tom Hendrie** on taking the Love Street job, December 1999.

I have to work or I will go crackers. One and a half hours at a football match means an hour and a half I am not thinking about him – Former Celtic manager **Lou Macari**, January 2000. His son Jonathan committed suicide in April 1999.

Reporter: Welcome to Southampton Football Club. Do you think you're the right man to turn things around? Strachan: No, I think they should have got George Graham, because I'm useless – **Gordon Strachan** on his appointment, October 2001.

I applied for loads of jobs: Stockport County, Chesterfield, York City, but only once was asked for an interview and that was at Bradford City. I still have the rejection letters – Celtic manager **Martin O'Neill**, March 2002.

I've got no ambition to be Scotland manager, no ambition to be the Leeds manager, or indeed any of the teams I played for. I'm just going along and seeing where we end up. Ambitious people scare me – Southampton manager **Gordon Strachan**, January 2003.

Tom Cruise was there and so was Russell Crowe and Kylie Minogue, but as soon as my family heard the Hibs manager was there, they were like, 'Alex McLeish!' and went over towards him – he was much more important. Tom Cruise said: 'Who's that?' I said, 'Tom, that's Alex McLeish, 77 caps for Scotland. He's a hero – and he's the manager of Hibs!' – Actor **Dougray Scott** on inviting then-Hibs boss McLeish to the premiere of *Mission Impossible 2*, March 2003.

If I had been a brickie or a plumber or a journalist it would have passed by. I would have phoned in with a sickie – end of story. But this is football. I have a profile – Aberdeen manager **Steve Paterson**, May 2003. He had missed a game against Dundee two months before because of a drinking binge.

I don't want to explain how I became a lawyer because there's a lawsuit against some newspapers on that score – Dundee director **Giovanni di Stefano**, September 2003.

I'm perfectly happy in my job and I'm not interested in any job other than Celtic, and won't be for the next 34 years – Celtic manager **Martin O'Neill**, September 2003. He was being linked with the vacant Spurs job at the time.

Rumours were abounding at the time that it was time to go and, to be honest, Spurs were strongly on the case – **Martin O'Neill** after quitting Parkhead, June 2005.

You look at managers applying for jobs when they are in jobs, that's morally wrong. Totally disrespectful to your employer. That's the corruption surrounding the game now, which I don't believe in. I think it is totally out of order – Gretna manager **Rowan Alexander**, January 2005.

Livingston could be the right club at the wrong time – Former Scotland midfielder **Craig Burley** on Richard Gough's managerial prospects, soon after he was appointed manager of Livingston, January 2005. Gough quit four months later.

This was something I had to do. As a family, we agreed I had to go for it. If I didn't, I'd have to live with the regret. I went for the interview. It cost me £400 for a return on the plane and I haven't been paid yet by the SFA. I paid my own way to get a knock-back – **Gordon Strachan** on applying for the Scotland manager's job, February 2005.

People forget that football's your job, it's not fun – Livingston manager **Paul Lambert**, October 2005.

Have we seen the end of Kenny Dalglish the manager? – Paul Francis, via e-mail
I wouldn't rule out becoming a manager again, but then I wouldn't rule it in either. Until someone offers me something I don't know what the answer would be – Former Scotland striker **Kenny Dalglish**, magazine questionnaire, May 2006.

People keep asking, 'What have you been doing?' They think I'm a tourist, but I'm here to do a job. I've been to Red Square and the Kremlin, and I'd like to see the other things, but I'd rather go with my family. It would be boring by myself – Lokomotiv Moscow striker **Garry O'Connor**, July 2006.

In an ideal world – and this is a great ideal world – I would be able to manage Plymouth, St Johnstone and Dundee United again, manage Lithuania or Latvia, and finish up managing Forfar – Sheffield Wednesday manager **Paul Sturrock**, August 2006.

It's a great job, a fantastic job, but a difficult job. When you have someone who you feel undermines you it becomes harder and harder – Rangers manager **Paul le Guen**, after axing Barry Ferguson as club captain, January 2007.

Saying the SFL is not wholly suited to the modern-day business environment paints a picture of quill pens and piles of dust as elderly gentlemen move from their desks. In actual fact what they said was 'the legal structure of the SFL was not entirely suited to the modern-day business environment' – Scottish Football League secretary **Peter Donald** on the Pannell Kerr Forster report into the SFL, amid calls for an SPL2, March 2007.

Aberdeen would be a massive job to leave. Alex Smith once said to me, 'You're the second most important man in Aberdeen, after the Lord Provost.' – Aberdeen manager **Jimmy Calderwood**, April 2007.

If you hadn't become a politician, what would you be doing now? – Newspaper reader Wendy Cornish.
I'd like to think I'd be the manager of Raith Rovers, or maybe the ex-manager because they'd have sacked me for not getting promotion this year – **Gordon Brown**, on the day he became Prime Minister, June 2007.

During my 'time-out' my life just became too easy. My heart-rate was plodding along at the same rate for about 15 months, and I just thought, 'It shouldn't be like this, life should be tougher.' I needed to be stimulated again, and that's when Celtic came along – Celtic manager **Gordon Strachan**, June 2007.

When I walk into a new job, I don't nail my picture to the wall in my office, and I don't put my carpets down nice and firm. I always make sure they're ready to be uplifted – Former Motherwell and Derby boss **Billy Davies**, February 2008.

I never hide away from the fact that when Scotland got knocked out of World Cups in the past, like in 1982 and 1986 and 1990, we cheered the roof off. The English team did that, but George (Burley) has asked me to do a job for him and that's something I want to do – Scotland assistant boss **Terry Butcher**, March 2008.

I made my decision to stick with Motherwell at the eleventh hour. I had my boarding pass in hand and was standing at Gate 47 waiting to board an aircraft to Vilnius. It was then that it dawned on me that I was not ready to leave Motherwell – Fir Park manager **Mark McGhee** on his decision to turn down the Hearts manager's job, May 2008.

It's not necessarily a bad thing that we missed out on the likes of Mark McGhee. We spoke with a few candidates and we have discussed Scottish managers in the past. But they are part of the local structure – they are all part of the Scottish football mafia. It's very hard for them to rise above that level – Hearts owner **Vladimir Romanov** handles McGhee's snub well, July 2008. The club had previously been spurned by Slovakian Vladimir Weiss and German Jürgen Röber.

I was asked to go to a house in Merrylee to price a job. Resplendent on the walls were pictures of the Queen, Ibrox Stadium and that wee guy on a white horse. Thankfully, the woman didn't recognise me, and I went about my business untroubled. I told her how much the flooring would cost, and she said, 'That's great. That's the best quote I've had. I think we'll just go with you.' However, her husband came through from the kitchen, recognised me and began shouting, 'What's that bastard doing in here?' She couldn't work out what the problem was and replied, 'What's wrong? He's very nice, and he's given us the best price.' Her pleas fell on deaf ears. 'I don't care. Get him out of here,' the man shouted. He then decided to take matters into his own hands. He literally chased me out of his house – Former Celtic striker **Frank McGarvey** on working laying floorboards, in *Totally Frank*, with Ronnie Esplin, 2008.

The chairman phoned me up at Hogmanay and asked me to come down for a chat. I'd had a bit of a celebration, it was lucky he didn't ask me to come down the next morning – Swindon Town manager **Maurice Malpas**, August 2008.

What made me laugh was people questioning my ability to do the job, as if to say, 'He's never been a chief executive anywhere.' I could've been a chief executive somewhere if I'd ever wanted to be. I was a marketing development manager at 22 years of age. I decided to go and play professional football full-time then I've had my own businesses and done other things. I could easily have gone into a company and worked my way through and been a chief executive in my late 20s or early 30s, I don't think there's any doubt about that – SFA Chief Executive **Gordon Smith**, on TV programme, *From Player To Power*, September 2008.

I totally refuse to go and sit in a ground at a game and be a shadow over a manager who's in a job. It would be inevitable that I would be linked with something if I went to matches and I will not allow that to happen. It's just not fair on the guy who is down there doing his best – Manager **Billy Davies**, November 2008, on why he hadn't been to a game in the year since being sacked by Derby County.

It was nothing to do with bloody league reconstruction, or the laws of the game, or any offside shite. I don't think the world at large or the media particularly understood what it was trying to do – Former SFA secretary **Ernie Walker**, February 2009, on heading the 1995 Independent Review Commission – the 'Think Tank'.

Whatever anyone says about the economy and the recession right now, I think he (Gordon Brown) did a terrific job as Chancellor. And I know people go on about him being a dour Scot and not having Tony's charisma and so on. But I think maybe the country needs a bit of that dour Scottishness. He has had some hellish problems thrown at him, and he's handled them well – Manchester United manager **Sir Alex Ferguson**, March 2009.

LAMBIE ⚽

People have recommended players to me and they couldn't kick my a**e – Partick Thistle manager **John Lambie** after steering the club to the top of Division One and being named Manager of the Month, January 2002.

He'll be totally serious when he asks me, 'Who the f*** signed that useless bastard?' And when I tell him he did, he just grumbles, 'Well I must have been drunk at the time.' And he says that in front of the player – Lambie's Partick Thistle assistant manager **Gerry Collins**, February 2003.

'See you three, youse are a pair of lazy bastards', was a greeting administered by the gaffer to a trio he felt had been economical in their commitment during the course of a match – Partick Thistle striker **Gerry Britton** on manager Lambie, February 2003.

I did once hit a player in the jaw with a dead pigeon. His name was Declan Roche and he was talking to me, so I got these dead pigeons out of a box and slapped him round the face with one. The reasons I had the pigeons in my office was that they had died of a disease and I was going to bury them, so I put them in a box and took them to the ground. It was a bit of fun, really – Partick Thistle manager **John Lambie**, February 2003.

The last time we went, there were guys on a stag night who'd paid a fiver for their room. That's how bad it was. He just knows it's great for team-bonding. There's never anything for us to do so we have to get on – Partick Thistle defender **Alan Archibald** on Lambie's team-building trips to Blackpool, May 2003.

If the Whitburn Pigeon Club have a meeting and one of us can't or won't vote, the vote still goes ahead. What's the problem with the SPL? Why can't they do things in the same way? – Former Falkirk manager **John Lambie**, after it was ruled there could not be a vote on the club's application to ground-share with Airdrie United at an SPL General Meeting, May 2003. Despite winning Division One, Falkirk were subsequently refused permission to ground-share and were not promoted.

There's a wee disabled guy who comes to all our games and when he sees me he says, 'Hi God!' He calls my wife 'Mrs God' – Partick Thistle manager **John Lambie**, July 2003.

I've kicked hot tea in players' faces just through temper. John McNaught, God rest his soul, he was sat there one match at half-time with a cup of tea in his hand reading a programme. Reading a programme! And I just went over and wham! Nobody else ever did that again — Partick Thistle manager **John Lambie**, in *Fanatical About Football*, ed. Jeff Connor, 2003.

I don't see their cause for banning smoking. It can't harm anyone in a dugout for goodness sake. I suppose you might brush against the arm of a substitute, but that would be a good warm-up for them — Cigar-smoking former Partick manager **John Lambie** treats news of UEFA banning smoking in technical areas with scepticism, December 2003.

LIFE ⚽

It was a great upbringing. All we ever did was play football and fight. That's what you did in these areas — Manchester United manager **Sir Alex Ferguson** on his Glasgow youth, May 2009.

If I had rescued a toddler from a burning building, certain elements of the press would portray me as a child molester — Former Celtic General Manager **Jock Brown**, in *Celtic-Minded: 510 Days In Paradise*, 1999.

Nothing in life could happen to me as awful as that — Former Celtic manager **Lou Macari** on identifying his son Jonathan's body after his suicide, January 2000.

I could be gung-ho and say 'Okay boys, let's go and play anyway,' but my conscience wouldn't let me do that — Rangers chairman **David Murray**, refusing to let the club travel to play Anzhi Makhachkala in Dagestan in the Russian Caucasus, September 2001. Rangers' concern centred around a guerrilla war in nearby Chechnya threatening the country. UEFA agreed and switched the tie to a one-off game in Warsaw.

I was so consumed by football that all I used to spend with my wife and two boys was one hour a week. We used to meet at 4pm every Thursday at a steakhouse and at 5pm I returned to work — Former Dundee United manager **Jim McLean**, November 2001.

Society is now scary. Decent manners and principles have gone. In the cities, it's a mess. Sometimes you just give up on society — Southampton manager **Gordon Strachan**, January 2003.

In Leicester, he sponsored the hospice in a local hospital and would visit sick children he knew he wouldn't see in six weeks' time. I don't think I could do that. If he falls over in a nightclub, you'll certainly hear about it. You don't always hear about the other things. But I know the boy he is — **Gerry Lennon** on his son, Celtic midfielder Neil, September 2003.

There are certain things in life you shouldn't change and one of them is a football club – *Channel 4* Head of Programmes and St Johnstone fan **Stuart Cosgrove**, in *Fanatical About Football*, ed. Jeff Connor, 2003.

I went to Luton and could hardly read or write. I can honestly say now that, at 24, I've never read a book in my life. That was my attitude to school – Doncaster's **Michael McIndoe**, after being called into the Scotland Future Squad, December 2003.

I think what Gordon is doing is hugely enviable and he has his own reasons for putting his career on hold. I often think I'd love to do just that, go to places I'd always wanted to visit, go off to watch the Buffalo Bills playing in the NFL when it's minus 25 degrees and the snow's banked up on the side of the pitch, just to see how top athletes cope. Or go to Russia and spend time just wandering around that fantastically fascinating country – Celtic manager **Martin O'Neill** on Southampton manager Gordon Strachan taking a year out of football, January 2004.

When God tells you something, to the human eye it doesn't look right. It's the same story about Noah – when he built an ark there was no water in sight and everybody was laughing. But in the end everybody wanted into that same ark. God already knew that Livingston were going to be in administration before I decided to stay – Livingston defender **Marvin Andrews**, March 2004. The club had gone into administration the previous month. Andrews signed for Rangers two months later.

I started smoking at 48. Somebody had to. Everybody else was giving up. But I very rarely drink, and for days on end I forget to eat. I live on Marlboro and Lucozade – Gretna owner **Brooks Mileson**, November 2004. He died in November 2008.

When I was at Celtic, just walking along the street in Glasgow, people were wanting to see what I was wearing. They wanted to see what was in my shopping bag. They wanted to see what car I took the shopping back to and they wanted to see what house I drove back to. It's there, it's in your face every single day, but I never let it take me under – Livingston manager **Paul Lambert**, October 2005.

Here I was, a 34-year-old man going to the pictures on his own in the afternoon. It made me think about when I came to England at first, the 18-year-old in Nottingham who went to the pictures in the afternoon. Here I was, 16 years on, back at the pictures. My life had come full circle – **Roy Keane** on life with Celtic, September 2006.

Yobs are like a plague. If someone like Bono can stand up and shout and bawl about anything in the world, then my wee shout is for my streets to be safe. Some people say I should shut up about this and stop going on about it, but I can't, 'cos I'm Scottish. We have to have the last word on everything – Celtic manager **Gordon Strachan**, June 2007.

I have probably got cancer in every single bone in my body, but you have just got to get on with it – Dundee United owner **Eddie Thompson**, March 2008. He died in October 2008.

I had to do 60 hours a week and some nights I would do more hours to get it done quickly. I might finish training at 1pm and then I'd be gardening until 8pm – I was even there until 10pm one night painting a fence in the dark. How do you paint a fence in the dark? I returned the next day and realised it needed done again – Kilmarnock striker **Kevin Kyle**, February 2009, on the 120 hours of community service he was ordered to do in April 2007 following a breach of the peace charge.

LOSING ⚽

In 1976 he became a St Mirren supporter. He was at the Hammarby game. This may explain a great deal – Author **Christopher Brookmyre**, in autobiographical note to novel, *Boiling A Frog*, 2000. *(St Mirren fans will appreciate exactly what he meant. Having drawn 3–3 in Sweden against Hammarby in the UEFA Cup second round, first leg match, Saints were 1–0 up in the November 1985 return with three minutes left. Hammarby sent on a tubby substitute, one Håkan Ivarsson. Ivarsson equalised in the 87th minute, then Hammarby had a goal – which would've taken them through – disallowed in the 88th. Undeterred, Mikael Andersson scored in the 89th minute and Hammarby progressed 5–4 on aggregate.)*

Dundee had a League Cup tie against Queen of the South who were managed by my pal from Celtic, Mike Jackson. I asked him to keep an eye on Gordon for me and called him back immediately after the game. Mike's team had thrashed Dundee 6–0, which was a huge shock, and I couldn't stop him talking about his team. 'Mike, Mike, what about the lad Strachan?' I asked. 'Big man, Dundee were hopeless, absolutely bloody hopeless; but that wee bastard, he kept showing for the ball, kept working and never lay down. He was the only player they had.' – Former Aberdeen and Celtic manager **Billy McNeill** on Gordon Strachan, in *Gordon Strachan: The Biography*, Leo Moynihan, 2004.

The outcomes of Old Firm games usually have a huge bearing on the destination of the title, and you never like to lose one. Yet we only took four points from 12 in the league against Rangers that season – Former Celtic goalkeeper **Jonathan Gould** recalls the 1997–98 season, when Celtic stopped Rangers winning ten in a row, in Mark Guidi, *The Inner Sanctum*, 2008.

Martin told him, 'I want you to get it through to the lads that I will not stand for losing away games. We don't have to win, but I don't expect to lose. Always get a point and I'll tell you if we have a chance of three.' He instilled a fear in them about losing away. You couldn't perhaps get away with it these days, but if they lost there would be no beer on the bus, they couldn't play cards and there would be no music. They might get some fish and chips, but more likely not. They went away afraid to lose – Then-Wycombe manager Martin O'Neill's orders to team captain Terry Evans, quoted by Wycombe chairman **Ivor Beeks** in Alex Montgomery, *Martin O'Neill – The Biography*, 2003.

The gaffer came in and shouted, 'I'm out the f***in' European Cup now, Butty, and it's your f***in' fault! What were you f***in' doing?' But Nicky was a young lad. He was hurt. We all felt for him – Former Manchester United reserve goalkeeper **Kevin Pilkington** recalls Alex Ferguson's reaction as Monaco knocked Manchester United out of the Champions League quarter-finals in March 1998, in Michael Crick, *The Boss: The Many Sides of Alex Ferguson*, 2002.

He was always searching to see if we had the desire. You'd be playing snooker or table tennis and he'd study you to see if losing hurt enough – Former Aberdeen midfielder **John McMaster** on Manchester United manager Alex Ferguson, before the Champions League Final, May 1999.

Super Caley Go Ballistic Celtic Are Atrocious – *The Sun* newspaper headline after Celtic's defeat by Inverness Caledonian Thistle, February 2000. (*It's a little-known fact that the headline had actually been used before – in the early 70s both the* Liverpool Daily Post *and the old Manchester-based* Daily Express *used 'Super Cally Goes Ballistic, QPR Atrocious' to describe a display by Liverpool's Ian 'Cally' Callaghan.*)

The association would like to congratulate Inverness Caledonian Thistle on their display last night. It is nice to see a spirited performance from a squad of players who obviously have some pride in their team – general secretary of Celtic Supporters Association **Eddie Toner** after the defeat by Inverness, February 2000.

The association asked for the removal of John Barnes as head coach of Celtic Football Club – general secretary of Celtic Supporters Association **Eddie Toner**, after a three-hour meeting with club chief executive Allan MacDonald following the Inverness game, February 2000. The following day they got their wish.

Somebody said we were 16/1 to win, which in a 90-minute game of football is a nonsense. We are sixth in the First Division. We are not a part-time Third Division team any more – Inverness Caley Thistle midfielder (and Man of the Match) **Charlie Christie** on the Celtic win, February 2000. (You could actually get 18/1 on his team.)

I tried to provoke something in him and it didn't work in the way that I had hoped it would work, and he responded in a way that I didn't think he would – Former Celtic assistant coach **Eric Black** on the half-time bust-up with Mark Viduka which led to the Australian failing to go out for the second-half against Inverness Caledonian Thistle in February 2000, in *The Head Bhoys*, Graham McColl, 2002.

After half-time, I think, because of what had happened at half-time, the team lacked concentration and in football you have to keep your concentration. This argument made us lose concentration and we lost that game against Inverness at half-time – Celtic's **Lubomir Moravcik** on the Inverness Caledonian Thistle defeat, in Graham McColl, *The Head Bhoys*, 2002.

At half-time I still expected us to come back and win that game. I still felt we could've come back and won that game – had we been together – Former Celtic head coach **John Barnes** on the Inverness Caley Thistle Cup-tie, in DVD, *The Official History of Celtic*, 2008.

I remember back in my days as manager of Wycombe Wanderers in the Vauxhall Conference that if ever the chairman, Mr Beeks, was unhappy about what I was doing, and indeed many a time he was, I'd tell him, 'Listen, I only got this job because you couldn't beat the Metropolitan Police.' They had been beaten at home in the FA Trophy, non-League football's FA Cup, and many supporters had thrown their season tickets away. And I've sometimes used that phrase, almost jokingly, in conversation with the Celtic chairman, that I only got this job because the team wasn't good enough to beat Inverness Caledonian Thistle in the Scottish Cup – Celtic manager **Martin O'Neill**, March 2003.

You don't know who is with you when things are going well. You only know who is with you and for you and believes in you when things are going wrong – Celtic head coach **John Barnes**, 2000.

The whole thing was an embarrassment to everyone at the club, and that includes players who were not playing. If they are not good enough to get picked for that, they really must be embarrassed – Coventry manager **Gordon Strachan** after a home defeat to Everton, January 2001.

I have all the videos but I have never once looked at a cup final again. I have never looked at the Roma video. I have never looked at Gothenburg – Former Dundee United manager **Jim McLean**, October 2002.

It was an extraordinary, fantastic year, one that everybody will keep talking about, yet we ended up without a trophy – Former Celtic manager **Martin O'Neill** on 2002–03 season, June 2005.

The strangest thing about the situation was that Celtic didn't seem to know what kind of player I was. I thought when they signed me they must know my position and where best to play me, but they didn't. After the Motherwell game – where we lost 1–0 in October 1999 and I was at fault for the goal, playing at right back – I just thought, 'What am I doing here?' The people who have brought me here don't even know what I'm doing here – Celtic midfielder **Stilian Petrov** recalls early Parkhead problems, September 2003.

How can you blame strikers when you concede goals? You have to blame the defence. That's part of the game, you play a position and you have to accept what comes with that in terms of criticism. Every time we are losing late goals so, yes, we have to change something. You cannot always put these things down to luck. It can't be bad luck to lose away from home seven times in a row in the same competition. As players we have to be honest enough to accept responsibility – Celtic's **Stan Varga** on the club's Champions' League record, October 2004. A few days later Celtic lost 3–0 in Ukraine to Shakhtar Donetsk.

I remember being down at Parkhead and we were losing 4–0 but the Aberdeen fans were still chanting his name. We ended up getting beat 7–1 and even now you won't find too many supporters here that have much of a problem with him – Aberdeen chief executive **Willie Miller** on the strange grip Ebbe Skovdahl had as manager, January 2005. (Aberdeen actually lost 7–0 to Celtic twice under Skovdahl.)

My pals are Celtic fans so I'm not turning my phone on for a while. Luckily, I'm getting out of the country – Motherwell's **Scott McDonald** after his two goals had deprived Celtic of the SPL title, May 2005.

I'll never get over it – Former Celtic manager **Martin O'Neill** on losing the league on the last day of the 2004–05 season at Motherwell, in DVD, 'The Official History of Celtic', 2008.

Celtic lost the league on the last day of the season. Does that mean Sutton, Lennon and Hartson are losers? No, it doesn't. They are competitors, and unfortunately they lost. But it didn't make them losers – Celtic manager **Gordon Strachan**, July 2005.

You can change your wife your car or your job but your allegiance to a football club never alters. It's going to take me a hell of a long time to get over this – Dundee United chairman **Eddie Thompson** after watching his team go from 2–0 ahead to 2–2 and out of the UEFA Cup against Finnish team MyPa, August 2005.

We are stuck in a rut and God knows how we are going to get out of it – Rangers captain **Barry Ferguson** after losing 2–0 to Celtic, November 2005.

When Gordon Strachan joined there wasn't a lot of support for him, especially when we lost against Artmedia, drew against Motherwell and then lost against Rangers. We made a statement and we said right throughout that the first judgment of Gordon would be after the last match of the season and the fans could shout all they like but it wasn't going to change our opinion. If everybody says something is wrong, it doesn't mean it's wrong – Majority shareholder **Dermot Desmond** to the Celtic Supporters Association, December 2005.

Although shoot-outs can reduce the finest teams to the ranks of also-rans, they do test temperament. England were found wanting in that test, just as they were in every respect apart from guarding their goal. The World Cup will be no poorer without them – Former Dundee and Hibs manager **Jim Duffy** during the World Cup, July 2006.

Do you remember when Chelsea played United at Stamford Bridge, end of last season, and there's two minutes to go in injury-time, and he gets up, walks up to where the United lads are, and he's shaking Alex Ferguson's hand and the game is still going on? Two years ago no one would've done that to Alex Ferguson. The manager would not have liked it. But (Jose) Mourinho is saying, 'The game is over, the league is over, 3–0 to us.' But Alex Ferguson would have taken that on board. That's what good managers thrive on, that kind of slight – Former Manchester United captain **Roy Keane**, September 2006.

If Roy Keane had been out there in a Falkirk jersey would he have stood for it? He'd have been kicking backsides and saved me the bother. But I don't have that and that's why we're in the bottom six – Falkirk manager **John Hughes** after his side lost 2–1 to Kilmarnock, May 2008.

I'm getting sick of playing well and getting losers' medals. I'd much prefer a scrappy, shitty 1–0 – Queen of the South midfielder **Steve Tosh** after losing 3–2 to Rangers in the Scottish Cup Final, May 2008. Tosh played for Gretna when they lost the final on penalties to Hearts in 2006.

If I couldn't get a game in that Rangers team I would be hanging up my boots – Former Rangers striker **Mark Hateley** on the Rangers side which lost to FK Kaunas in the Champions League qualifiers, August 2008.

When we went away, where our record was poor to pathetic to shite, and we didn't get a chance to play, the heads went down – Swindon Town manager **Maurice Malpas**, August 2008. Swindon had won two away games in 12 following his appointment the previous January. He was sacked in November 2008.

We congratulate Walter, Kenny, Ally, Jim Stewart and we congratulate the players as well, because they went to difficult places and won this year, near the end – Celtic manager **Gordon Strachan** praises the Rangers management team after being pipped to the 2008–09 SPL title on the last day, May 2009. He quit as manager the following day.

MANAGEMENT ⚽

I had a rule, though, that after hamstring injuries, if anyone said they were fit I wouldn't pick them for another two weeks, just to be sure. 'I'm absolutely delighted for you both. You'll enjoy the match. Neither of you are playing,' I told them. They didn't even get on the bench because in those days you couldn't have five or six substitutes. It was the closest Martin ever came to taking me up on that offer of going back to university. And Archie? It hit him like a bomb and he didn't speak to me for a month – Former Nottingham Forest manager **Brian Clough**, February 2002. He'd left Archie Gemmill and Martin O'Neill – both of whom had claimed to be fit after injury – out of the team for the 1979 European Cup Final against Malmo.

Of all the footballers who have played for me, including Martin O'Neill, (Archie) Gemmill was the one whom I believed would turn out to be a successful manager – **Brian Clough**, in *Walking On Water: My Life*, 2002.

I always thought Martin O'Neill was cut out for a future in management because he was bright and sharp, a right smart-arse – **Brian Clough**, in *Walking on Water: My Life*, 2002.

The heavy-handed style, the rule by fear and aggression, it worked in that era. If you buckled under it, if you didn't have the mentality for it, you would have been an ex-Aberdeen player – Defender **Alex McLeish** on Alex Ferguson's Pittodrie reign, in Michael Crick, *The Boss: The Many Sides of Alex Ferguson*, 2002.

I am quite friendly with William Hague's father and I said, 'I thought he took the (Conservative) leadership too early,' and he said when you get offered a job like that you can't really refuse it. You know it's too early, you know it's maybe not quite right, but you get swept along in a tide of something that's not all your doing. I was a kind of victim, if victim is the right word. I was at Reading and I got offered a job in the Premiership. How could I refuse it? – Motherwell manager **Mark McGhee**, July 2007, on leaving Reading for Leicester City in December 1994.

Quite often in those circumstances, a manager won't let you near them, no matter who you are. So, it was unusual in the first place that he should make me so welcome. But he said to me, you're a football man and you know the importance of proper preparation – Manchester United manager **Sir Alex Ferguson**, March 2002, on visiting the German training camp and meeting Berti Vogts during Euro 96 in England.

My wife's recommendation was not to go. My assistant said not to go. Anybody I phoned said not to. So what happened? I went – Plymouth Argyle manager **Paul Sturrock**, February 2002, on his September 1998 decision to leave St Johnstone to take over as manager of Dundee United.

I was daft enough to bring both Tommy and Bobby in. I brought them both in and the two bandits took my job. They took it on and maybe I didn't have the ability to do that. Tommy took them into the Premier League and kept them in the Premier League. Bobby took them into Europe. Bobby should be walking on cloud nine in Kilmarnock, getting hero worship for taking that team into Europe the way that he did – Former Kilmarnock manager **Jim Fleeting** on Tommy Burns and Bobby Williamson, September 2006.

If I had to leave a player out of the team, I would tell him. But I would keep the conversation short. When you have to give someone bad news, you do not go on about it with a one-hour explanation and debate. You get it over and done with quickly – no more than two minutes – Former Celtic manager **Wim Jansen**'s managerial philosophy, in Mark Guidi, *The Inner Sanctum*, 2008.

He never, ever, swore. Come to think of it, I don't think he ever raised his voice – Former Celtic captain **Tom Boyd** on ex-boss Wim Jansen, in Mark Guidi, *The Inner Sanctum*, 2008.

You can go through a list of people who've come out of Largs and been a success, then you can get a list of failures and it's longer. Yet they still get back on the merry-go-round and get jobs – Benfica executive director **Steve Archibald** on the SFA Coaching Courses at Largs, June 1999.

I'm here as a young manager and I still want to be here as an old one – Kilmarnock manager **Bobby Williamson** after being knocked out of the Scottish Cup by Alloa, February 2000.

I know I would've got Liverpool right but, you know, it took Fergie seven years at Manchester United – Former Anfield manager **Graeme Souness**, February 2000.

The greatest moments in my career have come when we have the challenge of overcoming better teams, like Liverpool or Lazio, but I'm not sure whether I'm up to a challenge as big as going back to Glasgow – Spurs boss **George Graham**, March 2000.

If Martin O'Neill says 'jump', the players had to jump, whereas if I said 'jump', the players didn't really have to jump – Former Celtic head coach **John Barnes** reflects, in DVD, *The Official History of Celtic*, 2008.

If Louis van Gaal had come along and said the same thing they would have accepted it – Variation on a theme from former Celtic head coach **John Barnes**, May 2000.

If I said to shite on the centre spot, my players trust me enough to do so and I'm proudest of that – Scotland manager **Craig Brown**, August 2000.

A lot of people say I've got a good personality for management but what do you need to be a manager? Do you need to be a horrible bastard? – Derby County midfielder **Craig Burley**, April 2001.

I should have approached it in a far more considered way. Changes needed to be made but I tried to do it too quickly – **Graeme Souness** on being Liverpool manager, August 2001.

Sometimes I lose my temper, sometimes I don't. If someone argues with me I have to win the argument. So I start heading towards them, that's where the hairdryer comes in. I can't lose an argument – Manchester United manager **Sir Alex Ferguson**, 2002.

There was talk of me managing Scotland, then they gave it to a schoolteacher, (Andy) Roxburgh – and let me tell you, he couldn't add up two and two, let alone coach a football team – Former Nottingham Forest manager **Brian Clough**, 2002.

Will I get the dreaded vote of confidence if we don't go up this season? No, I'll get the dreaded sack – Millwall manager **Mark McGhee** after a 1–0 win over Brighton, September 2002.

I could maybe have gone once in 22 years and bought them a pint. But I never did it – Former Dundee United manager **Jim McLean** on his players, October 2002.

I knew there'd be a certain level of suspicion – that's expected. But I also thought that, so long as a team is winning, that negativity soon disappears – Former Celtic coach **John Barnes**, March 2003.

One Saturday night Sergei Baltacha was on the phone to me: 'I'm not happy with you, you swear at me.' Years later he was manager at Inverness and he rang up and told me, 'I know now why you swear at me!' – **Alex Totten**, formerly Baltacha's boss at St Johnstone, in *Fanatical About Football*, ed. Jeff Connor, 2003.

This place is an absolute disaster. It needs a complete and utter overhaul – Coventry manager **Gary McAllister** after his side avoided relegation from Division One, April 2003.

They're all so calm. Lippi, Ancelotti, Hitzfeld. They all look like they're bloody comatose. I've tried to calm down on the touchline, I even got rid of the chewing gum when I came here but some are on a different planet – Rangers manager **Alex McLeish**, 2003.

The ideal solution for Aberdeen would be a £10m investment, a better manager and a better bunch of players. But until that happens, we'll soldier on. There is a lack of money at this club, so we cannot do that – Aberdeen manager **Steve Paterson**, September 2003.

Players are always on edge with him, and that's why he gets the best out of them. Just like Cloughie. If he was so easy, you'd work him out very quickly, and then how would be motivate you? – Grantham Town chairman **Tony Balfe** on Martin O'Neill, in Alex Montgomery, *Martin O'Neill – The Biography*, 2003.

You can compare the current situation at Livingston with an aeroplane that is flying in turbulent weather. The captain of a plane will work tirelessly to try and take the plane out of the turbulence and into calmer weather. So that makes me the captain who is piloting the Livingston plane. I'm determined to take this team out of the turbulence we are experiencing – Livingston manager **Marcio Maximo**, September 2003. He quit the following month.

I can't defend the players and I can't defend myself at the moment. I came here with a good reputation but suddenly I am looking like a bad manager. I lost a lot of trust in my players today – Aberdeen manager **Steve Paterson** after a 3–0 home defeat by Motherwell, November 2003.

After Celtic, I was applying for jobs and speaking to football chairmen about my ideas, and I could see them looking at my clothes, looking at the way I speak, possibly even looking at the colour of my skin, and not really listening to what I was saying – Former Celtic coach **John Barnes**, December 2003.

You walk into a dressing room with world-class players and they want to see what you're made of. When you think of Paul Gascoigne and David Ginola, who were here when I arrived, and Duncan Ferguson and probably ten other internationals, they were wondering what I could do for them. I wondered myself at first. And then I thought the only thing I could do was what had got me there in the first place – Everton manager **David Moyes**, January 2004.

If I was at Manchester United I would be sitting back with my arms folded, watching the game and enjoying what I was watching. The reason for that is because the higher up the ladder you go, the less correction to play you've got – Stenhousemuir manager **John McVeigh**, January 2004. He was sacked a week later.

If a man can't tackle, he can't tackle. You either hide him – put someone alongside him who can – or move him on. If he hasn't a heart for it, or the attitude, if he's a bad pro – he goes. You can't change a leopard's spots. And many's the time I've tried – Plymouth manager **Paul Sturrock**, January 2004.

You can only do so much at a club and then it's like David Bowie, you have to reinvent yourself – **Gordon Strachan** on his decision to leave Manchester United, as he prepared to leave Southampton, January 2004.

I need people to listen to me in the dressing room before a game. I need silence to make my points as quickly and as urgently as possible. If anybody talks and breaks that conversation, then I'll throw them out. What else could I do? – Celtic manager **Martin O'Neill**, January 2004.

When Andy was sent off against Southampton, he was then given permission by me to go to Dubai on a five-day break with his family while the rest of us were busy training at a cold and wet training ground. And that's victimisation? – Blackburn manager **Graeme Souness** on striker Andy Cole, March 2004. Cole had complained to the PFA about the number of days off he was given at the club.

With players, it's always a one-way street. In an average week, I'll have eight players at my door, looking for something. Maybe just a day off, or advice about a problem, sometimes more serious things. I always give them a seat beside my desk, so that they can see all the paperwork. While they're talking, I'll deal with some of that work, I'll take calls, and let them see what being in this office involves. 'Is it like this every day?' they'll finally ask. 'Every day,' I tell them. It lets them know that, whatever problems they might have, the manager's are 40 times that – Manchester United manager **Sir Alex Ferguson**, March 2004.

They slaughtered us for long-term contracts, but at the end of the day I was paid by Dundee United. I most certainly wasn't out at the public parks on a Sunday morning for Ron Saunders to be a great manager with Andy Gray down at Aston Villa – Former Dundee United manager **Jim McLean**, April 2004.

Even if Brighton go up this year, Freddy Shepherd at Newcastle isn't going to be saying, 'There's the manager for us.' – Brighton manager **Mark McGhee**, May 2004.

The players need to know that I'm the one who decides whether they're good, bad or indifferent. But they don't need the whole world to know – Southampton manager **Paul Sturrock**, July 2004.

If I buy him, which I will do, then make sure the team becomes a top-six team in a year. If they don't, your neck is on the line – **Tony Cascarino**, August 2004, quotes Chelsea chairman Ken Bates' reaction to boss Ian Porterfied's request to bring striker Robert Fleck to the club.

Congratulations to Richard on his first win. I expect to see his red hair get greyer by the week – Dundee manager **Jim Duffy** after Livingston beat his side 1–0, December 2004. It was manager Richard Gough's first win.

I asked my assistant Archie Knox how he has managed to go through that for the last 20 years. I must have made 140 clearing headers from the technical area – Livingston manager **Richard Gough** on the same game, December 2004.

When you first take over as a manager you think the whole world is against you. But it's not, we are all the same – Former Southampton manager **Gordon Strachan**, January 2005.

He's the master, isn't he? He learned a lot from big Jock. Wenger is an intelligent man but there's nobody in the world better at the mind games than Alex. You might think at times that he's out of control but I know for a fact he's not. He's definitely got into Wenger's head now. It's the boy from Govan. The university of life – Former Aberdeen captain **Willie Miller** on Sir Alex Ferguson, January 2005.

It's like diving in the North Sea. I can't prepare myself because I dived in last year. I've had time to prepare myself for this cold sea again, but when I dive in, it's still freezing – **Gordon Strachan** on the prospect of returning to management, January 2005.

At this stage I'm thinking more about England. I don't know what goes on behind the scenes up there, where the kids are and what style of play you need. Maybe when Tony Mowbray's finished, and they are another six or seven managers down the line, director of football at Hibs might appeal to me. Then, it could be time to get the old guy in, and do a Bobby Robson – Former Southampton manager **Gordon Strachan** on the possibility of managing in Scotland, February 2005. Four months later he was named manager of Celtic.

I like being down there at the heart of the action. It's like being the captain on the bridge of a ship, you want to be seen to be in control – Motherwell manager **Terry Butcher** on why he watches games from the dugout, March 2005.

They would be as well having Roger de Courcey and Nookie Bear for manager, because Vladimir Romanov just wants a puppet he can work – Former Hearts player **Allan Preston** on George Burley's departure from Tynecastle, 2005.

When he speaks, he has a great natural authority. It is something that is difficult to acquire as a football manager – either you've got it or you haven't. For me, a great manager absorbs stress and gives out energy, and that applies perfectly to Paul – Paris Saint-Germain chairman **Alain Cayzac**, on former Rangers manager Paul le Guen, in Graham Spiers, *Paul le Guen: Enigma*, 2007.

When I leave Rangers in a few years' time there might be a few players who will be glad to see the back of me. That's just the way of it – Rangers manager **Walter Smith** on his predecessor's problems with players, in Graham Spiers, *Paul le Guen: Enigma*, 2007.

All you ever ask for is respect. True love, or a fanatical adoration for a manager, can be a problem as well. But respect and an understanding of how difficult the job is, that's all you ever want. At any club there will always be a few who don't care for you, and that's fine. I'm wary of blind love in football, and players kissing badges and stuff like that. I've seen players here rushing out of a side door to get away from the very people they have been kissing the badge to. Respect is all you're after – Celtic manager **Gordon Strachan**, June 2007.

When I arrived I was fitter than half the players and had to clear the training pitch of dog shit, syringes and broken bottles – Elgin City manager **Robbie Williamson**, November 2007, on taking over in January 2007.

I hope to be in this game for an awful long time. Football never changes, neither do clubs. I know there will be spies in the camp. I know there will be people watching you and reporting back to the board of directors. They can have as many spies as they like, I don't care. I've got nothing to hide – Former Motherwell and Derby manager **Billy Davies**, February 2008.

I never got on with John Collins. It was plain and simple for everyone to see. He stripped the captaincy off me. He did numerous things to try and upset me. I am not bothered because in the end I got my dream move to Rangers. However much he thought he was mucking me about and trying to psychologically muck up my brain and put me down, he actually did me a favour because I got to where I wanted to be – Rangers midfielder **Kevin Thomson** on later days at Hibs, March 2008.

I sensed that there was a problem when I first arrived. It was, now, how can I describe the atmosphere . . . it was freezing! Now I hope that it's different. This should be enjoyable. It's a football club, not a prison. People should not see me coming and think, 'Oh, here's that bastard.' – Hibs manager **Mixu Paatelainen** on the unhappy camp he inherited, March 2008.

Every ex-pro and ex-teammate I have spoken to has slaughtered me, I have betrayed my country and all that. They say it tongue-in-cheek but afterwards they always wish me good luck – Scotland assistant manager **Terry Butcher**, March 2008.

When I speak to him, he's nice to me and says all the things players want to hear about me being part of the plans but you know by his actions he's talking rubbish – Celtic striker **Derek Riordan** on manager Gordon Strachan, April 2008. He left Celtic four months later.

Mick (Wadsworth) dismantled the team. He seems to have come out of the whole thing quite well but a lot of the problems have come from what he was doing – Former Gretna manager **Davie Irons** on club director of football and interim manager Mick Wadsworth, June 2008.

I can't speak to the newspapers after we lost a match and say, 'I don't know what happened because he told me to play this guy or that guy.' The people outside will think, 'What kind of a coach is this?' No, I make the decisions – New Hearts coach **Csaba Laszlo** rejects any prospect of interference from above, July 2008.

By Friday, everyone knows exactly what they're doing so I don't even travel on the team bus. I just go directly to the game. We do our work during the week with a view to the Saturday so when we get to the game I don't do a team talk – Dundee United manager **Craig Levein**, August 2008.

I am now in my 15th house. I was in 14 houses when I was married, through football, now I am in rented accommodation, but I regret that a little bit inasmuch as your kids were always moving school and things like that. They have been in four or five different schools, and that couldn't have done them any good at all. It must have been hard for them but they have done well – Blackburn Rovers assistant manager **Archie Knox**, August 2008.

I met one Scottish guy once and he said, 'Weren't you at one time in for the job at Celtic?' And I said yes. 'And Aberdeen?' Again I said yes. Then he went through about nine different clubs in Scotland before saying, 'What the f*** is the matter with you, are you just crap at interviews?' – Finland manager **Stuart Baxter**, October 2008. Baxter had coached in Norway, Portugal, Sweden, Japan, England and South Africa before Finland.

Maybe I'm too accessible but I can very rarely say no if someone needs to speak to me. I need time for myself but I'll spend time having a cup of coffee with the ladies in the kitchen and the chefs. They have to feel important, because they are – Sunderland manager **Ricky Sbragia**, January 2009.

Life's better if you just go along enjoying yourself. I don't think I've ever enjoyed myself in management as much as I have this year. Well, over the last couple of years. It's because I'm getting used to being a manager – Celtic manager **Gordon Strachan**, May 2009. He quit two weeks later.

There's something Alex Ferguson does right and it's hard to know exactly what. He's been fantastic at ruthlessness. They come up consistently when it counts. The trait has carried on despite the personnel changing. That suggests he's providing the continuity. He's canny. It's not quite the same thing as strategy. It's just instinct – Former England cricketer turned sports analyst **Ed Smith** on Sir Alex Ferguson, May 2009.

MANAGERS

I gave Jocky (Scott) the same criteria and I also met Bernd Schuster at Barcelona via Steve Archibald and asked him also – Dundee director **Peter Marr** on interviewing the man who'd later manage Real Madrid at the time the club appointed Ivano Bonetti as manager, in Jim Wilkie, *Bonetti's Blues: Dundee FC and its Cultural Experiment*, 2001.

Fergie made a brilliant off-the-cuff speech about Labour values at one of our events recently. All Scottish managers I meet seem to be frustrated politicians – Labour spin doctor **Alastair Campbell** on Sir Alex Ferguson, 2007.

The manager has 20-20 vision on the misdemeanours of the opposition but if it's the other way round he's never seen it properly – Referee **Kenny Clark**, August 2007.

I love Ally and he was a major personality in Scottish football, but I don't think you can say in terms of achievement that he deserves to be there. If the criterion for inclusion is success in managing Scotland, then it should be Alex McLeish – Former Scotland manager **Craig Brown**, May 2008, on an attempt by the Ayr Branch of Scotland supporters to get former national team manager Ally MacLeod inducted into the Scottish Football Hall of Fame.

You would be amazed how many shite managers are out there. I've only worked with two I regard as being good. Sir Alex Ferguson is one. Tony Mowbray is the other. Now without being too disrespectful, the rest have been shite – Hearts midfielder **Michael Stewart**, July 2008.

Managers are the most insecure guys on the planet – Hamilton chairman **Ronnie MacDonald**, July 2008.

Maybe if you look at Eric Black, possibly, but Mark (McGhee) you wouldn't have said he was going to go into coaching or management. Gordon Strachan, you wouldn't have said he was, either. Big Alex (McLeish), yeah – Blackburn Rovers assistant manager **Archie Knox** on players from the Aberdeen side of the 80s going into management, August 2008.

CLAUDE ANELKA
I have no idea why Anelka brought in the players he did. When I came here I thought their lack of ability and knowledge of the game was entirely

beyond belief. They are wonderful, lovely boys. But I am looking for football players – Raith Rovers manager **Gordon Dalziel** on the signings of his predecessor as boss, January 2005.

JOHN BARNES

An experienced manager will be given a bit of leeway if things are not going well, but my inexperience will suggest I am not the right man for the job, because I have done nothing before coming to Celtic – Celtic coach **John Barnes**, November 1999.

I will tell you something about Barnes. He didn't create the system to suit the players that he had. He made the system first and thought he would get the players to fit into his system. I don't think he was right to do this – Former Celtic midfielder **Lubo Moravcik**, 2002.

GEORGE BURLEY

Had his situation remained, we might have won an extra game, but we wouldn't have had the same team. We wouldn't have had Craig Gordon, we wouldn't have had Roman Bednar. We wouldn't have had Rudi Skacel. And on top of everything, (George) Burley was a victim of agents. He was being used by agents – Hearts owner **Vladimir Romanov**, May 2006.

George is one of those ones who speaks very well and he's very polite, very nice, his whole manner is very correct. The way he goes about things is very good and his man-management skills are great, but there's a steel there and if he's not happy about something then he'll show that steel – Scotland assistant manager **Terry Butcher** on manager George Burley, March 2008.

TOMMY BURNS

I just said, 'Look Tommy, the cameras are on us, millions are watching on TV, so why don't you just turn around and go and take a seat in the stand,' and, to be fair to him, he didn't argue and did as I suggested. I knew it was out of character and a few days later I received a letter from him apologising for his behaviour. That's the kind of guy he is – Referee **Hugh Dallas** recalls sending former Celtic boss Burns to the stand in a November 1996 Old Firm game, March 2003.

When we lost a game he gave the impression he was personally responsible and owed thousands of Celtic fans an apology – Former Celtic defender **Alan Stubbs** on ex-manager Tommy Burns, in Mark Guidi, *The Inner Sanctum*, 2008.

I have never formally or informally approached Tommy – I wouldn't know him to look at if I walked past him in Buchanan Street – Motherwell owner **John Boyle** on rumours that boss Billy Davies was about to be replaced by Burns, October 1999.

I've always said that people won't just be judged as a footballer – and there weren't many better than Tommy – but as a person. He's top of the league when it comes to being a man. I think there's a difference between legendary footballers and legendary men. I know what I would like to be remembered as – Celtic manager **Gordon Strachan**, after the death of coach Burns, May 2008.

Especially now, when the focus is on trying to get the big contract, trying to get the car, trying to get the rewards before you deserve them. Football nowadays is about ego, it's about money, it's about a lot of things and not all of them good. But people like Tommy would be some days with the reserves, the next with the first-team, another day with the academy boys. I'm looking around Ipswich now and there aren't many people like Tommy Burns around, I'm afraid – Ipswich manager and ex-Celt **Roy Keane**, preparing to play in Burns' charity tribute game on the anniversary of his death, May 2009.

BRIAN CLOUGH

Meeting Brian Clough was interesting. Very interesting. I was sitting there with the big coat on because it was cold and Clough arrives and the first thing he says is, 'Get your f****** coat off in my house, son.' – Dundee defender **Tom Cowan**, October 2003, recalling going to Clough's home to discuss signing for Nottingham Forest when he was a 17-year-old at Clyde.

He is one of that rare breed of men who can cheer you up without trying. Honest, you couldn't fall out with John Robertson if he was knocking off your wife – **Brian Clough** on the former Scotland winger, in Walking On Water: My Life, 2002.

I think you're a brilliant manager, but if you walked into a pub, I'd walk straight out – Former Nottingham Forest winger **John Robertson** on Brian Clough, in The 90-Minute Manager, Lessons From The Sharp End Of Management, David Bolsover & Chris Brady, 2002.

Not my type of man. Not one I'd go out for a pint with. I don't think so. But work for him? Pfff! I'd walk across the Sahara Desert to work for him – John McGovern on **Brian Clough**, his manager at Derby and Nottingham Forest, Clough TV programme, March 2009.

When he first met me he thought I was nuts; when he left me he was absolutely certain – Former Nottingham Forest boss **Brian Clough** on Martin O'Neill, February 2002.

OWEN COYLE

When we first spoke to Owen he struck me as being like a young Bill Shankly. That's a big label to give him but there are definitely similarities. He's teetotal like Shankly was and has the same steely determination – Burnley operations director **Brendan Flood** after appointing Coyle as the club's new manager, November 2007.

TOMMY DOCHERTY

About the worst manager there has ever been – Former Manchester United winger **Willie Morgan** on former Old Trafford manager Tommy Docherty, June 1977. Docherty sued for libel, then dropped the case three days into the Old Bailey trial in November 1978.

JIM DUFFY

So many things had happened. Our goalkeeper, Aaron Flahavan, got killed in a car crash, there were a whole lot of other things that went on that I can't talk about. I asked Duff about eight months into the job how he thought I was doing. He was and is a man I could trust with my life. I knew if he thought I was doing s**t he'd have told me straight. Instead, he says, 'How the hell you're surviving I don't know.' – Hearts manager **Graham Rix** on his former Portsmouth number two, December 2003.

GEORGE GRAHAM

George, bless him, used to say, 'What's England got to do with Arsenal? You don't want to go with England, they're crap, Bobby Robson's crap.' I could have put on another 20 (caps) but there we go – Wycombe manager **Tony Adams** on ex-Arsenal boss George Graham, January 2004.

His arguments with George weren't meant to be funny, but they were, the way they went back and forth at each other. They were a fiery Jock and a fiery south Londoner, and there was plenty of half-time entertainment – Wycombe manager **Tony Adams** on former Arsenal striker Ian Wright, July 2004.

Impossible to get close to – Former Leeds chairman **Peter Ridsdale** on Graham, in *United We Fall: Boardroom Truths about the Beautiful Game*, 2007.

EDDIE GRAY

I thought I'd seen everything at Leeds until Eddie Gray took over as caretaker and decided to keep in with that lazy Australian, Viduka . . . Eddic Gray is a very nice man but he should have showed steel on behalf of his beloved club over Viduka. He ought to have told him he was going to be bounced out of the club as soon as it suited the manager and meanwhile get your backside out on the training ground, turn up on time and shut up. But Eddie's too soft, I'm afraid – Former Nottingham Forest manager **Brian Clough** on events at Leeds United, January 2004.

RUUD GULLIT

Ruud Gullit's management was atrocious. The only way of catching him was if you had a boarding pass for a flight to Amsterdam – Former Chelsea midfielder **Craig Burley**, April 2001.

WIM JANSEN

The media were in a frenzy. On the morning of the announcement no one had a clue who the new man would be. Unforgiveable. Thus when Fergus McCann, Wim Jansen and I walked into the press conference, no one had a clue who the new man was and scarcely anyone recognised him. Unforgiveable. Hence the headline in *The Sun*: 'The second worst thing to hit Hiroshima'. Welcome to Scotland, Wim – Former Celtic General Manager **Jock Brown** on Wim Jansen's arrival as manager, in, *Celtic-Minded: 510 Days In Paradise*, 1999.

He was taciturn, largely uncommunicative and clearly a victim of the constant badgering he appeared to be receiving about the modesty of Celtic's ambitions, their penny-pinching approach and their unwillingness to go into the market for big-time players – Former Celtic general manager **Jock Brown** on manager Wim Jansen, in *Celtic-Minded: 510 Days In Paradise*, 1999.

When he found out that the board was going in a different direction to him, he said, 'Well, I'm going in a different direction too. The direction of Holland. Goodbye.' – Former Celtic midfielder **Craig Burley** on ex-Parkhead manager Wim Jansen, February 2004.

ROY KEANE

I wouldn't say he was calm and considered. He's not calm at all – Sunderland goalkeeper **Craig Gordon** on manager Roy Keane, May 2008.

PAUL LE GUEN

Martin Bain and I flew to Dinard, we were on a private plane and the weather was atrocious. We were the only plane to land that day and there was nobody to take us from the airport. I had to climb on a Land Rover trailer that belonged to the fire brigade. I said to Martin, 'I hope this bastard is good!' – Rangers chairman **Sir David Murray**, November 2008, recalling starting moves to lure Paul le Guen to Ibrox in December 2005.

Of course there are things I can improve on, because every player can improve. But if he wants the perfect player, it's not going to happen overnight – Rangers striker **Kris Boyd** on boss Paul le Guen, after the striker had scored against Dunfermline in the CIS Cup in September 2006, three days after being dropped against Hibs, in Graham Spiers, *Paul le Guen: Enigma*, 2007.

I believe in Paul le Guen, and I didn't see many of you scribes complaining when we brought him in. In fact, 18 out of 24 of you said we were going to win the league – Rangers chairman **Sir David Murray** rallies to the defence of his under-fire manager, November 2006, in Graham Spiers, *Paul le Guen: Enigma*, 2007.

I wouldn't change anything about my time with Paul le Guen. I've no regrets about that period. When things aren't going right on the pitch, you try your best to fix it. If that's a crime, then the game is totally f*****. It has been said that I disobeyed instructions. I didn't − because not once was I told what to do − Rangers captain **Barry Ferguson** on le Guen, May 2007, in Graham Spiers, *Paul le Guen: Enigma*, 2007.

I still don't know why he fell out with me. One day I'd love to book a table for a £500 dinner with le Guen, pick up the tab myself and ask him what it was I did wrong. I'd love to talk to him about it − Rangers captain **Barry Ferguson**, in Graham Spiers, *Paul le Guen: Enigma*, 2007.

He is an honourable man. He met me, and there was no compensation claim whatsoever − no financial compensation. The only thing Paul asked me to pay for was his removal van − Rangers chairman **Sir David Murray** on the aftermath of le Guen's exit, in Graham Spiers, *Paul le Guen: Enigma*, 2007.

Perhaps he should have done two months earlier what he knew to be necessary for some time. By this, I mean take urgent action − Arsenal boss **Arsène Wenger** on le Guen's Ibrox difficulties, in Graham Spiers, *Paul le Guen Enigma*, 2007.

He obviously had his reasons for doing what he did with Barry (Ferguson). But he put me in the firing line then left without saying anything. I was a bit surprised. I thought he might have said something. There was no goodbye, nothing. He left on our day off. He told a few of the boys but he certainly said nothing to me − Rangers' **Gavin Rae**, April 2007, on the acrimonious exit of Paul le Guen as coach. Le Guen stripped Ferguson of the captaincy and appointed Rae as club skipper for the match against Motherwell in January 2007, then quit two days later.

Paul Le Guen was offered money and did not spend it. Any manager can blame the tools but, with the greatest of respect, he did spend a bit of money and the tools weren't the right ones for the job − Rangers chairman **Sir David Murray**, November 2008.

MARK McGHEE

Mark is as intelligent and articulate a person as one could meet in professional football, and would tend to score points off Fergie through words and explanations that went above the manager's head. During one argument with Mark, Fergie just turned to Archie Knox and said, 'Archie, Mark is in his *Scrabble* mood. Get the board out for him.' − Celtic manager **Gordon Strachan** on former Aberdeen teammate Mark McGhee, in autobiography, *Strachan: My Life In Football*, 2006.

How he kept that team at Brighton up I will never know because I used to watch them regularly. If ever anyone deserved the Queen's award for Industry for keeping a team in the Championship, it was him — Celtic manager **Gordon Strachan** on Motherwell manager Mark McGhee's achievements at Brighton, 2007.

JIM McINALLY

It is my hope that neither Jim nor Martin (Clark, assistant) will be out of football for long as they are both very professional, honest, trustworthy and honourable men. I am sure that our loss will prove to be another club's gain. I will watch their careers with great interest — Morton chairman **Douglas Rae** after accepting the resignation of manager Jim McInally 'with regret', February 2008.

JIM McLEAN

He has made me the man I am today. I remember one time when I was 16 and doing the kit, I left a sock in the dryer on the Friday and Jim phoned me and told me to come back and put it away. I had to get the train up from Edinburgh just to put the sock away, which took 30 seconds. It worked though, because I never did it again — Livingston coach **Allan Preston** on former Dundee United manager Jim McLean, April 2004.

My football answer is 100 per cent that I was crazy to stay with Dundee United — Former manager **Jim McLean** on staying at the club rather than moving elsewhere, April 2004.

A football pervert — Motherwell assistant manager **Maurice Malpas** on his former Dundee United manager Jim McLean, on TV Show, *That Was The Team That Was*, March 2006.

Is it a regret we don't get on better? Not really — Dundee United chairman **Eddie Thompson** on previous Tannadice chairman Jim McLean, February 2008.

JOHN McVEIGH

He makes Vince Lombardi look like a lamb — Actor **Robert Duvall** on former Raith Rovers manager John McVeigh, his advisor in the film, *A Shot At Glory*, December 1999. Lombardi was the legendary and ferocious coach of American Football team the Green Bay Packers.

ALLAN MOORE

He is a great motivator. There's none better, and when he's talking, there's not a hope anyone else will get a word in — Stirling Albion director **John Smith** on manager Moore, November 2007.

DAVID MOYES

We didn't think to go for a bonus if Everton got into Europe. That would have been fanciful, but they'd have agreed it. I bloody wish we'd done it now – Preston director **David Taylor**, April 2003, on the package they agreed for Moyes to go to Everton as manager in March 2002. Moyes came within a game of getting Everton into the UEFA Cup in his first season in charge, losing out to Blackburn on the final day in May 2003.

When he realised I was getting so much of the limelight, I felt he resented it – Manchester United striker **Wayne Rooney** on his former manager, in *My Story So Far*, 2006. In June 2008 Moyes won 'substantial' damages after bringing a libel case against Rooney for a statement in the book suggesting he'd leaked details of a confidential conversation with the striker.

Mr David Moyes is probably a fine example to everybody in Government of stability and making the right decisions for the long term – Everton fan **Andy Burnham**, after his appointment as Secretary of State for Culture, Media & Sport, January 2008.

Evertonians owe everything to David Moyes, he took on our club when it was on its knees. We laid out a plan and he has never come off it. I worship the man, he is the greatest manager in the world. He's my best friend in football and I'd do anything for him – Everton chairman **Bill Kenwright**, April 2009, after Moyes led Everton to the FA Cup Final.

BRUCE RIOCH

We thought Bruce Rioch would be a safe pair of hands. He was the sergeant-major type, straight as a die, but it was the wrong decision – Former Arsenal vice-chairman **David Dein** on the 1995 decision to appoint Rioch as Arsenal manager in preference to Arsène Wenger, then with Nagoya Grampus Eight, September 2007.

You can't go into training every day and dislike somebody to the point of not wanting to look at him or train. How can you play football in that state of mind? Football is meant to be enjoyed; I hated it and I hated being anywhere near the guy – Former Arsenal striker **Ian Wright** on Bruce Rioch, July 2006.

GRAEME SOUNESS

At Rangers you had to wear your socks tied up, you had to go to training in a suit and you weren't allowed any facial hair. He arrived in an open-necked shirt, sporting a moustache and with a hairdryer under his arm – Former Rangers defender **Davie MacKinnon** on Souness, November 2003.

In two years, I won one cup. And that's more than they've won since then, and a lot of money's been thrown at it – **Graeme Souness** on managing Liverpool, February 2000.

JOCK STEIN

When my mother sends the papers down to me from home, Jock's picture is on the front page and the Prime Minister Harold Wilson can't even make the back – Former Manchester United manager **Tommy Docherty**, 1960s.

He will always be a legendary figure. Nothing will ever change that. I mean, I went to see Dean Martin years ago. It can't have been very long before he died. I didn't enjoy seeing him. I don't think anybody would have enjoyed seeing Frank Sinatra in his last three or four years, that's why he hid away, really. So, that's the only kind of upside. You've still got an image of a giant man with a sarcastic comment here and a witty comment there. A gigantic man with charisma – Celtic manager **Gordon Strachan** on Jock Stein, September 2005.

JOZEF VENGLOŠ

To think that he has been subjected to criticism over his command of the English language by some journalists who are incapable of speaking their own mother tongue properly really makes my blood boil. I did my media case even more harm at one press conference when the question of his command of English was raised and I suggested that if they found any difficulty in communicating with him in English they could try one of the seven other languages he spoke fluently. I think the word was 'insular' – Former Celtic general manager **Jock Brown** on coach Jozef Vengloš, in *Celtic-Minded: 510 Days In Paradise*, 1999.

They brought in Jozef Vengloš as Wim's replacement and that was embarrassing. When they appointed him, Celtic said Jozef was ten years ahead of the rest with his ideas on football. Rubbish. He was 30 years behind. Almost every player in the dressing room was not happy with the appointment of Jozef – Former Celtic midfielder **Craig Burley** on the appointment of the then-62–year-old Vengloš in July 1998, in Mark Guidi, *The Inner Sanctum*, 2008.

MICK WADSWORTH

I sat next to Alex Ferguson last Saturday for five hours (at Wimbledon) and we watched a bit of tennis and talked football, and I think so much of Mick Wadsworth that if I had not been manager of Newcastle, I would have recommended Alex take him on board – **Sir Bobby Robson** on former Newcastle assistant manager – and later Gretna Director of Football and caretaker boss – Mick Wadsworth, July 2001. Manchester United had just lost Steve McClaren to Middlesbrough.

ARSÈNE WENGER

Intelligence? They say he's an intelligent man, right? Speaks five languages!

I've got a 15-year-old boy from the Ivory Coast speaks five languages – Manchester United manager **Sir Alex Ferguson** on Arsenal manager Arsène Wenger's reputed intellectualism, 2002.

ALEX McLEISH

How many players of his stature would have said, 'Piss off', or 'You must be joking'? But there wasn't any of that from big McLeish. Afterwards, my strong recommendation to Andy (Roxburgh, national team coach) was that we had to get him back in the full squad, that we couldn't do without somebody with that attitude – Former Scotland under-21 manager **Craig Brown** on Alex McLeish – then 28 – playing for the under-21s as an overage player against the Republic of Ireland in February 1987, January 2007. (*McLeish had 44 full international caps at the time and went on to win 33 more.*)

As an actor, he's a great football manager – Actor **Dougray Scott** on friend Alex McLeish's (small!) role as an extra in the 2003 film *The Poet* (also starring Laura '*Mulholland Drive*' Harring). McLeish has a scene as an extra in an art gallery.

Considering where Rangers were when he took over and where he has taken them to now, and with virtually the same players, I think it's fair to say he's made a silk purse out of a sow's ear – Manchester United manager **Sir Alex Ferguson** on Alex McLeish at Rangers, May 2003. The club won the treble that season.

People are always asking me if I call for coaching advice. I have asked him for administrative advice, things like what sort of rules do you have at United regarding mobile phones and such, but I have to be my own man – Rangers manager **Alex McLeish** on former manager Alex Ferguson, 2003.

Alex McLeish has shown himself to be soft, like Mickey Mouse. He is as lightweight as paper. If Alex McLeish keeps on like this the nearest he will get to a big club in Spain or Italy will be the airport. He will only be able to coach in Scotland because that is the highest level he can reach – Disgruntled striker **Claudio Caniggia** after being freed by Rangers, June 2003.

Has he always had strength of character? He was a moaning bastard, if that's what you mean – Rangers assistant manager **Andy Watson** on McLeish, July 2003.

Alex is a motivator, a talker, a hug sometimes, a tap on the shoulder. That is the strongest quality of Alex – Rangers defender **Bert Konterman**, November 2003.

They are a perfect combination – McLeish has the aura of a great manager. It is not easy when you don't have the finances to bring in the best players. But I am sure he is getting the best out of the players he has here. He has good tactical vision, a natural authority and something really Scottish about him. You need that at a big club in Glasgow – Defender **Frank de Boer** on McLeish and coach Jan Wouters, February 2004.

For four years he showed what a great manager he was, and for the last six months he's shown what a great man he is – Celtic manager **Gordon Strachan**, February 2006, the day after Rangers announced Alex McLeish would leave the club at the end of 2005–06 season.

MONEY ⚽

I thought Scotland would beat England and I had a bet of 20 Deutschmarks on them to win at 6/4, so I was pleased. It rounded off what had been a tremendous week for me – German striker **Gerd Muller**, after Bayern Munich beat St Etienne in the European Cup Final, 1976. Scotland beat England 2–1 three days later.

I managed to sell Gerry Creaney to Portsmouth for £700,000 and was allowed to use £500,000 of that to bring in three or four players. You expect that to happen at a Third, Second or possibly poor First Division club in England, but it shows you what things were like – Former manager **Lou Macari** on financial life at Celtic, in Alex Montgomery, *Martin O'Neill – The Biography*, 2003.

Gordon has no real interest in money. It isn't what motivates him, and he has simple tastes. He and the family are flying out to Arizona next month and I've seen the tickets. They're flying economy class. He doesn't like the children to get spoiled – Former Coventry chairman **Bryan Richardson** on Gordon Strachan, in Rick Gekoski, *Staying Up: A Fan Behind The Scenes In The Premiership*, 1998.

The fee Celtic paid for me wasn't a concern, but f****** up was – Former Celtic midfielder **Craig Burley**, signed for £2.5m, in Mark Guidi, *The Inner Sanctum*, 2008.

One phrase you could not associate with Fergus was 'He let his heart rule his head' – Former Celtic captain **Tom Boyd** on former club managing director Fergus McCann, in Mark Guidi, *The Inner Sanctum*, 2008.

Come June 30, when some players are out of contract, they might find themselves quoting Dionne Warwick. She sang, 'All the stars that never were are pumping gas and parking cars.' I'm just making a point, a little aside –

Celtic managing director **Fergus McCann** on Simon Donnelly, Phil O'Donnell and Mark Burchill, who were all re-negotiating their Celtic contracts, December 1998. (*Fergus also got the final couplet of Bacharach & David's 'Do You Know The Way To San Jose?' in the wrong order*)

Bonus cheque? They need a reality check – Celtic managing director **Fergus McCann** shows his customary sympathy for overpaid footballers, 1999.

You look at what doctors and firemen get and it's embarrassing at times. It's gone way out of control and there's no way anyone can justify people getting paid this much just for kicking a ball about. Having said that, you're not going to give it back when people offer it to you – Bradford's **Stuart McCall**, January 2000.

You see two nice cars sitting out there and I'm sure you're thinking they came from fitba'. Bugger all came from fitba', or almost. They came mostly from building houses and partly from fitba' – Former Dundee United manager **Jim McLean**, November 2001.

During his reign at the club, Mr. McLean received substantial remuneration for his employment both as manager and chairman. He then received a sum of money per share from our existing chairman which is not likely to ever be repeated again in Scottish football. Dundee United Football Club feel that Mr McLean has been more than well remunerated for his work at the club. Another example of this is that we agreed a consultancy agreement for a substantial sum when he left. This agreement paid him for a period of four years. We see it as no coincidence that this article appears immediately after his last consultancy payment has just been made to him by Dundee United – Dundee United statement on **Jim McLean**, October 2006, informing him he would no longer be allowed access behind the Tannadice scenes. McLean had written a piece in his *Daily Record* column criticising then-manager Craig Brewster.

Here we are with pretensions to become a major force in the Champions League and yet we have facilities that would be laughed at by most clubs in the SPL, never mind Europe – Celtic manager **Martin O'Neill**, December 2001.

I've been a manager 28 years and it hasn't been really until the last eight years that I've earned what I should have earned. I was never paid that well at Aberdeen. I know it was 20-odd years ago but my starting wage was only £12,000 – Manchester United boss **Sir Alex Ferguson**, 2002.

Being chairman of a football club can seriously damage your wealth – **David Murray** after standing down as Rangers chairman, July 2002.

If they (manager Jim Duffy and his assistants) had told me it was £1m, then we would have bid that, but I'm not going to bid £1m just to show that you've got some stupid Rockefeller in your midst – Dundee director **Giovanni di Stefano**, on his £600,000 bid for Motherwell's James McFadden, August 2003.

I had to pay my own bloody fare. Typical Scotsman, he gave me no expenses. I had a chat with him for about three hours, but he was more interested in a British coach and mentioned Steve McClaren and Mark Hughes. He said, 'We'll talk again in the future,' but we never did – Spurs manager **Martin Jol** on being interviewed (in 2003, while he was coach of RKC Waalwijk) for the job as number two to Alex Ferguson at Manchester United, January 2005.

I don't earn as much as you think, you know. Funnily enough, I earned more at Leicester – Celtic manager **Martin O'Neill**, quizzed about reports linking him with Spurs, September 2003.

Right, let's see, in 1986 I was convicted on two counts of fraudulent trading and conspiracy to defraud, involving £80,000, but the Court of Appeal quashed the conviction in 1988 – Dundee director **Giovanni di Stefano**, October 2003.

I'd always liked a bet, even when I worked in Baron's nightclub in Swansea when I was 14, collecting glasses. I worked there on Fridays and Saturdays, got £11 a night for it, then went over to Riley's snooker club and did all the glasses there, and at the end of the night I'd put £20 in the bleedin' fruit machine. Then I started earning bigger money. The tens turned into hundreds, the hundreds into grands. I arranged with my bookie to put an extra nought on, so I'd phone him up and say, 'Can I have £250,' and the wife would think, 'That's not too bad,' but it would be £2,500 – Celtic striker **John Hartson**, November 2003.

Ultimately I owed £48,000 to 32 different people – Doncaster's **Michael McIndoe** recalls gambling problems, after being called into Scotland's Future Squad, December 2003.

Fergus is the only person I've ever known who's made money out of football – Rangers chairman **David Murray** on former Celtic managing director Fergus McCann, January 2004.

I'm not doing this job to pay a mortgage or feed a family but because I was attracted by the opportunity and the set-up – **Craig Brown** on taking the job as manager of Preston, January 2004.

It's the same as telling the girlfriend's parents she is pregnant. You have to tell them one way or another. It doesn't matter if she's a month gone or six months gone – you must tell them – Dunfermline chairman **John Yorkston** on delaying telling the players about the club's financial problems, February 2004.

My wages with Dundee United were ridiculous, with the exception of one year where we sold Duncan Ferguson to Rangers and they gave me a £150,000 bonus. But over 22 years I sold £20m worth of players and bought £8m – Former Dundee United manager **Jim McLean**, April 2004.

Footballers are overpaid. Maybe they would play better if they were paid less. We should try that in Scotland – Scottish curling skip **Jackie Lockhart**, April 2004.

It's great to see Neil Lennon arrive at the stadium at 10.10am when he was due at 10 o'clock and every minute's vital – Celtic manager **Martin O'Neill** on his fines system, April 2004.

I earned £24,298 the year that we won the League and then went to the semi-final of the European Cup. Dundee United never even gave me a penny of a bonus. Or for getting to the UEFA Cup Final against Gothenburg. Every close season I went and doubled my money by buying an old cottage and building a house in the garden and doing homers – Former manager **Jim McLean** on the impoverished 1980s at Dundee United, April 2004.

There was a real stigma about administration, from stamping the words 'in interim administration' at the bottom of every letter, to having to turn players down for trials because even those costs were outwith our budget. It could have been a whole lot worse and the club could have gone out of business – Motherwell manager **Terry Butcher**, May 2004.

To call it moral bankruptcy beggars belief. He was instrumental in a lot of the decisions and then left without taking responsibility for them. He abandoned a ship he was previously steering. That is probably more morally bankrupt than sticking with it. The moral thing to do is clean up your mess – Motherwell owner **John Boyle** on former club chief executive Pat Nevin, May 2004.

We do not like being second best, but we got it wrong. We obviously spent far too much money. We can't let it happen again because that would be total mismanagement – Rangers chairman **David Murray**, September 2004.

I don't think people realise I had to underwrite everybody's salaries this year to get management of the club. You don't get any praise for that, but Livingston was literally minutes away from being another Third Lanark – Livingston's then prospective owner **Pearse Flynn**, January 2005.

My last comment to Peter (Lawwell, chief executive) was that if he offered me £30,000 a week I wouldn't turn the car around. I told him, 'I've given you every opportunity to sort it out and you've not dealt with it right.' I came down here for less money than I was eventually offered by Celtic, but it was about principles – Wolves defender **Jackie McNamara** recalls his June 2005 exit from Celtic, January 2007.

You take the equation of how much we got out of Europe and the money we spent, we overspent to get to the UEFA Cup Final. We overspent in the Martin era to get where we are today and I've had no fans ever coming up to me and saying to me, 'Thank you for overspending.' Do you know why they don't thank you for overspending? Because they have never looked at a balance sheet and a profit and loss statement – Majority shareholder **Dermot Desmond** to the Celtic Supporters Association, December 2005.

We are financially sound, even though our absence from Europe this season cost up to £9m. The reason we didn't give Martin money is because we didn't have it. If we'd borrowed it then we would have been in bother now. We'll do what we can to help, but it's too early to come up with figures – Celtic chairman **Brian Quinn**, April 2006.

The salary we agreed with him was considerably less than £40,000 a week, and even then it was dependent on the number of first-team appearances he made. Far from being Celtic's highest earner when he joined, he was no higher than eighth on the list – Celtic manager **Gordon Strachan** on signing Roy Keane, *My Life In Football*, 2006.

One top earner signed by Martin (O'Neill) was on £34,000 a week – a figure that covered the total salaries for our major foreign signings: Artur Boruc, Maciej Zurawski and Shunsuke Nakamura after he left – Celtic manager **Gordon Strachan**, *My Life In Football*, 2006.

People like me have to pinch ourselves when you hear of players earning £100,000 a week, so the man in the street must find it hard to comprehend. But in any walk of life, who says 'You don't need to pay me that?' – New Zealand Knights midfielder **Scot Gemmill**, August 2006.

It was like playing a game of chess with Garry Kasparov except I had a draughts board in front of me – **Ally McCoist** on negotiating his Rangers assistant manager's contract with chairman Sir David Murray, January 2007.

Much of this payroll cost disparity is the result of the high remuneration of the SFL secretary – Accountants **Pannell Kerr Foster**'s report on the Scottish Football League, March 2007.

I would be delighted were it otherwise, but the remuneration of the SFL secretary is not decided upon by the SFL secretary but by his employers – SFL secretary **Peter Donald**'s typically droll response, March 2007.

There are full-timers on £200 a week now. I mean, who's kidding who on? You can drive a van around the country and earn more than that – St Johnstone chairman **Geoff Brown**, April 2007.

Jack Warner came across when Trinidad & Tobago came to play Scotland at Hibernian's ground, Easter Road, and after the game he asked me to make a cheque out to his personal account for the game. I said, 'We don't do that, it should go to the association.' I then found out later that he had approached several of the other staff in my organisation to do exactly the same thing – Former SFA President **John McBeth** on FIFA vice-president Jack Warner, October 2007. The friendly game had taken place in May 2004.

I've heard it all, that all Brooks Mileson did was throw money at it and Gretna bought their success, but for me Rangers and Celtic buy the SPL title every single season. And they don't get the criticism that comes Gretna's way – Former Gretna striker **James Grady** on the day his former club applied to go into administration, March 2008.

Without being too critical of Gretna, the club's foundations have been built on sand – Former Gretna manager **Davie Irons**, March 2008.

I don't know if I'm unfashionable but when we get into the Premier League we won't owe 10, 12, 30 or 50 million. We're one of those funny clubs that try to balance the books – Hamilton Accies chairman **Ronnie MacDonald**, the day his side won promotion to the SPL, April 2008.

Let's be under no illusions, it's cost us £100m. I'll tell you this, unless you're backed by proper cash this club will have to downsize. There is an economic crisis out there – Rangers chairman **Sir David Murray**, August 2008.

I'm accountable for the fact we don't have a sponsor for the Scottish Cup, but I'm not responsible – SFA chief executive **Gordon Smith**, on TV programme, *From Player To Power*, September 2008.

It's today's yacht. Some people want to buy a football club. Roman Abramovich got western acceptability following his decision to buy Chelsea. Before that, no one knew who Abramovich was – Rangers chairman **Sir David Murray** on owning football clubs, November 2008.

A football club went under in 2008 and my honest fear is not that 2009 will bring more, but that it will bring many more, for purely financial reasons – Airdrie United chairman **Jim Ballantyne**, December 2008.

Footballers have gone away from supporters in a financial sense. When I was first at Rangers they got £17,000 a year, now they're getting paid that a week – Rangers manager **Walter Smith** after the 'Boozegate' incident, April 2009.

We will post a loss of £200,000-£300,000 this year and that's for a promotion season, with a televised Scottish Cup tie with Rangers. When we came down (in 2002) we lost £1.75m the next season, which gives you an indication of the massive impact relegation has — St Johnstone chairman **Geoff Brown** after his side won promotion, May 2009.

OBSESSION

I never took them (sons Colin and Gary) to their sports. Never once. My wife did it. Even on a Friday night I always had the excuse that I had to get to bed early before a game. Now I'm not telling you this with pride. I'm ashamed. It's an absolute, utter disgrace the way Alex Ferguson, myself and many other managers have lived during their careers in football — Former Dundee United manager **Jim McLean**, November 2001.

Conversation comes to a standstill in our house if Kenny comes on TV — Disc jockey **John Peel** on Kenny Dalglish, August 1994. The late DJ's third child is named Thomas James Dalglish.

His obsession with Grantham Town was total, even when we were going to places like Bridgnorth to play before three men and a dog. What summed him up was that he once phoned me at one o'clock in the morning after we'd lost at Spalding to ask whether I thought their third goal was offside. When I told him the time he said, 'Gerraway'. He was always saying that — **Pat Nixon**, secretary of Southern League Grantham, on former manager Martin O'Neill, 2000.

It's an excellent book, but it's about people who are obsessed by football, for anoraks. I'm not obsessed by football, but it was good, well written — **Gordon Strachan** on Nick Hornby's *Fever Pitch*, in Rick Gekoski, *Staying Up: A Fan Behind The Scenes In The Premiership*, 1998.

Taking drugs was just something that had happened once or twice. I was getting into the wrong company and ending up in places where I shouldn't have ended up, just through chasing the drink. The drugs were there and one thing led to another — Kilmarnock's **Andy McLaren**, January 2002. He tested positive for cannabis and cocaine and admitted to alcoholism during a previous spell at Reading.

I was invited to Cheltenham for the Gold Cup. It was my wedding anniversary anyway and me and Cathy really enjoyed it. I suggested to her that night when we were in a restaurant that we buy a horse. It would be nice to get another interest. 'I suppose it's not a bad idea,' she said, laughing. 'The only thing about you is that you'll want to buy all the horses, you'll get obsessed with it.' And for a while I did get obsessed — Manchester United manager **Sir Alex Ferguson**, August 2002.

In August 2001 the international premiere of *Enigma* in Edinburgh clashed with Rangers against Hibs. So I arrived at the cinema with Kate Winslet and Saffron Burrows, then slipped out after 15 minutes to watch the game in a boozer across the road. These Americans who had bought the film to distribute in the States went round saying, 'If that guy does that when he comes to the States, I'm going to have his ass.' – Actor and Hibs fan **Dougray Scott**, March 2003.

He was just like he's been at Leicester and Celtic. He'd be dancing up and down the touchline, he'd be over the dugout. He'd even argue with the crowd, because in a small crowd you can hear a lot of what is said. He would turn around and start an argument if someone had shouted something he didn't agree with. He was just enthusiasm personified – Grantham Town chairman **Tony Balfe**, who gave Martin O'Neill his first managerial job, in Alex Montgomery, *Martin O'Neill – The Biography*, 2003.

Everything from getting up in the morning to going to bed at night was Celtic, Celtic, Celtic, Celtic. Never ever did I book in advance on a Thursday or Friday and say I was going out for a meal (on a Saturday), never ever – West Ham assistant manager **Peter Grant**, February 2004.

People told me Livingston would suck me in and they've been totally right. I was pissed off when we were four down to Celtic, more than you could imagine – Livingston's then prospective owner **Pearse Flynn**, January 2005.

It's not 'Newcastle', it's 'Newcastle United'. It's not 'Hearts', it's 'Heart of Midlothian' – Rock band The Fall's leader **Mark E. Smith**, April 2008, on his quest to transform reading the football results on an appearance on BBC1's *Final Score* in 2005.

Everybody's had the heart attack scares and the palpitations and collapsing and stress and people losing hair. It happened to Wilf McGuinness at Manchester United. All his hair fell out. People turn to drink, people lose their families, people lose their wife. It's incredible what football managers have to go through. So, I've still got my hair, still got my wife, I don't drink, so I've done everything right. People say, 'Well, then, why did you take a year out?' Because I wanted to see the world. And if I never got another job, so be it. I would always get something else. Maybe not as a football manager. I'm not obsessed with football – Celtic manager **Gordon Strachan**, September 2005.

When I hear fans question my commitment to the club I'd like to tell them to go jump into the biggest river they can find, because for one they don't even know what they're talking about. It's totally ignorant for them to say that all the problems are resolved by me putting money into the club. That will never be the case. I put money into the club because I believe it's the right thing to do for the club and for the direction of the club and the way I think it should be directed – Majority shareholder **Dermot Desmond** to the Celtic Supporters Association, December 2005.

The bottom line is, he'd always look at the bigger picture. Whatever he does, and maybe he's upset a few people, he will always do what he thinks is best for the club. I'll give him that – Roy Keane on **Sir Alex Ferguson**, September 2006.

This is our hobby, there's nothing else. I work and I have Annan – Annan Athletic chairman **Henry McClelland** on the day the club were voted into the Scottish Football League, July 2008.

OLD FIRM ⚽

I played in many derbies: Arsenal v Tottenham, Luton v Watford, West Ham v Tottenham, Wimbledon v Palace, Coventry v Villa, West Brom v Wolves. I played in front of 75,000 for Wales v England. But trust me, you could add all those games together and it would be nothing like Celtic v Rangers. I mean that – Former Celtic striker **John Hartson**, in Andy Mitten, Mad For It: Football's Greatest Rivalries, 2008.

Tony didn't open his mouth until we were past Motherwell. 'Billy, I've never seen anything like that in my life.' – Former Celtic manager **Billy McNeill** recalls taking coach Tony Book to his first Old Firm game while manager of Manchester City, in Mark Guidi, The Inner Sanctum, 2008.

We went out to a restaurant and the waiter took our order, then the next minute the maître d' came over and said, 'Mr Roberts, would you mind leaving?' I said, 'Well, I've only just come in.' He said, 'Well, we've been asked if you would leave because they won't sit in the same restaurant as you.' I asked who he was talking about and there were about 20 people on this big long table. I said, 'Tough, our money is as good as theirs,' and the four of us sat down and ate. When we got out and into my friend's car, they tried to tip it over. Whilst we were in it. I told my pal just to put his foot down and they scarpered – Former Rangers defender **Graham Roberts**' memories following his first Old Firm game in January 1987, October 2007.

I had entered the boardroom babbling away in my normal fashion, only to find that when I stopped talking there was a deadly hush in the room. Nobody was speaking to each other. On one side of the room were the Rangers directors, all dressed in navy blue suits with light blue shirts and Rangers club ties, and on the other side of the table the Celtic directors, with their green jackets, white shirts and club ties. Unlike English clubs, where the bitterest rivalries are forgotten in friendly chat, not one Rangers director was speaking to a Celtic director – Former Tottenham chairman

Irving Scholar, in *Behind Closed Doors: Dreams & Nightmares At Spurs*, 1992.

As far as the coin-throwing goes, I just wish it hadn't hit my head. Around that time loads of things were being thrown onto the pitch at grounds all over the country: coins, pies, even golf balls, and I'd been hit before. Unfortunately, this time it hit my head and I started bleeding. If it had hit my shoulder, the headlines wouldn't have been the same – Referee **Hugh Dallas** on being hit by a coin during the May 1999 Old Firm game at Parkhead, March 2003.

Maybe the Milan one has better players, but I would choose the Old Firm a million times over. Players transform themselves, not just the Scots but we foreigners as well – AC Milan's **Rino Gattuso** on derby games, November 1999.

Celtic players are saying they were the better team. You see the result today? What was the score? 4–0? Who is better, Celtic or Rangers? – Rangers winger **Andrei Kanchelskis** after the game in March 2000. Pre-match Celtic comments had angered the Rangers squad.

I learned more off the field than I would have if he had kept me on it. I thought from the first minute, 'This is not my game, this is never going to be my game.' I thought it would be like a normal game and I just didn't realise how it was going to be – Rangers' **Fernando Ricksen** on his Old Firm debut in August 2000. He was substituted after 23 minutes in Rangers' 6–2 defeat.

I'd need to have shoulders six feet wide and have skin made of rhinoceros hide to deal with a move like that – Derby's ex-Celtic midfielder **Craig Burley** on rumours linking him with a move to Rangers, May 2001.

They're like two old girls in Sauchiehall Street raising their skirts to any league that walks past – Aberdeen chief executive **Keith Wyness** on the Old Firm's proposal to move out of Scotland, December 2001.

You're aware you're driving a Mini, and the Old Firm are in a juggernaut – Motherwell assistant manager **Terry Butcher**, March 2002.

I have seen some of the world's great derbies – Lazio v Roma, Milan v Inter, Juventus v Torino, and Bayern Munich v 1860 Munich – but nothing compared to the 1–1 draw I attended at Parkhead in April. The noise, the tension, the pressure that was felt by everyone there was incredible. It was the best I've ever known and I can't wait for Sunday's match – Scotland manager **Berti Vogts** before the first Old Firm game of the new season, October 2002.

We out-played, out-tackled, out-everythinged them – Celtic captain **Neil Lennon** after the 1–0 Old Firm win, March 2003.

At one match with Dunfermline, one Celtic supporter arrested was so violent it took six policemen to remove him. He hasn't been in court yet. At our last match here with Rangers, one of their fans threw a firework. The stewards and the police did a remarkable job of tracking him down. He, too, hasn't yet been tried. We have written to the Scottish Executive, but it seems to fall on deaf ears – Celtic chief executive **Ian McLeod** on the sluggish treatment of football troublemakers, March 2003.

When you win, you're great. When you lose, you're duds. That is the bottom line – Rangers manager **Alex McLeish** on Old Firm games, 15 March 2003. He'd lost his first Old Firm game in seven earlier that month. The following day his side beat Celtic 2–1 to win the CIS Cup.

I suppose I was a bit naive in that first game; I think everyone is, whether you are a player, manager, supporter or official. Nothing can prepare you for the noise, the pace, the passion – and the microscopic scrutiny – Referee **Hugh Dallas**' early Old Firm memories, March 2003.

This wouldn't have happened if Rangers had been involved in a semi-final. Absolutely no way – Celtic manager **Martin O'Neill**, April 2003, on the SPL decision to schedule the final Old Firm game of the season for April 27 – 58 hours after Celtic played their UEFA Cup semi-final second leg against Boavista in Portugal.

Cobblers, absolute cobblers – SPL chairman **Lex Gold**'s response to O'Neill's claims, April 2003. Celtic were subsequently ordered to adhere to the original 27 April date by police (and won 2–1 at Ibrox).

I can categorically state that attending a Glasgow derby is something you must do before you die. Nothing can prepare you for the passion, atmosphere, humour, hatred and complete lack of interest in the quality of football that the majority of fans display – TV presenter **Gabby Logan**, May 2003, after Celtic had beaten Rangers 2–1 at Ibrox.

Those who tell me we have to settle for the Old Firm dominating the league indefinitely are talking bollocks – Dundee director **Giovanni di Stefano**, October 2003.

If two people become engaged in violence on the night of an Old Firm match, and one is a Rangers fan and the other a Celtic fan, is it necessarily the case that the violence occurs because they are on opposite sides of a (football) divide? – Former Rangers vice-chairman **Donald Findlay**, March 2004.

When you go abroad everyone wants to find out if you've done an Old Firm game. That's the one everyone wants to talk about. It's a bit like a commando raid, I suppose – you go in and get out, hopefully without too much flak flying – Referee **Kenny Clark**, before taking charge of his ninth Old Firm game, March 2004.

Oh, I used to love going to Celtic Park. They used to have this lovely mahogany fascia at the front of the directors' box, and I'd walk in, my hands in my pockets, looking around as if to say, 'God, here we are in this place again,' and then put my feet up on the fascia. The Celtic punters in front of the box would go nuts. It was all great fun. A total wind-up – Former Rangers vice-chairman **Donald Findlay**, March 2004.

I get a little annoyed about how much we beat ourselves up here, as if being an Old Firm fan is like having rabies. I've been to Manchester United against Liverpool, I've been to Boca Juniors against River Plate, and used to schedule my work trips around derbies – Livingston's then prospective owner **Pearse Flynn**, January 2005.

I fundamentally believe the Old Firm will play somewhere else eventually. If this was to happen, I think the investment that would come to Celtic would blow your mind. Celtic and Rangers have this unbelievable draw – Livingston's then prospective owner **Pearse Flynn**, January 2005.

I refereed Croatia against Bosnia at a time when they were actually at war with each other and it was an easier game to handle than the Old Firm – Ex-referee **Hugh Dallas** reflects on some career highlights, 2005.

The Old Firm manager's job is different. It is like telling a woman as she gives birth that you know how they feel and they wail: 'You do not know how I feel.' – Celtic manager **Gordon Strachan**, *My Life In Football*, 2006. (For more on this theme, see the 'Girls' section.)

When I flew in, I took a taxi from the airport, and ended up with a driver who was a Rangers fan. The moment he learned that I had signed for Celtic, he refused to say another word for the rest of the journey – New Celtic signing **Jean-Joël Perrier-Doumbé** gets welcomed to Glasgow, January 2007.

At Motherwell, I saw our team raise itself to play the Old Firm enormously and the next week being like a wet weekend because it's not the same build-up. It's something you have to take on board when you become an Old Firm player – that you are going to have to play to your maximum every game. You can't cruise through games – Scotland assistant boss **Terry Butcher**, March 2008.

The reaction isn't as bad now as it used to be and all I can say is, thank God for Maurice Johnston. With time, the hassle I get has eased off but at one stage it was shocking. Even recently, standing outside Ibrox, a Rangers fan said to me, 'Shouldn't you be hiding in the same cave as bin Laden?' – Former striker **Alfie Conn**, on playing for both sides of the Old Firm, April 2008.

We do not want to disadvantage Rangers should they reach the UEFA Cup final, but we are extremely disappointed and concerned at the manner of the decision-making process which was done without consulting the clubs or the SPL board, and the effects on the integrity of the competition – Celtic chief executive **Peter Lawwell** as the SPL step into the end-of-season fixture row caused by Rangers' UEFA Cup run, April 2008.

Peter Lawwell appears to be the chairman of the sporting integrity committee for the SPL. Peter would be better coming out and saying he wants Rangers to play four games in a week. If it was the other way about, I would be hoping that Celtic had to play four games in a week. So he should be honest about it instead of trying to hide behind what he is calling sporting integrity – Rangers manager **Walter Smith** on Celtic chief executive Peter Lawwell during the fixture pile-up in April 2008. Rangers failing to make the UEFA Cup Final would have meant them playing four games between May 10–18.

We stood our ground firmly. We knew we had to get our point in very early because we could see what was coming. I think that was right. Walter clearly disagreed but he has to look after his own team and I can respect that. There is nothing in it personally. I've met him a couple of times since then and both of us had a smile about it. We understand the game – **Peter Lawwell** reflects, August 2008.

Boruc spends too much time trying to appeal to that element of the Celtic support who revel in the fact that he hates Rangers. Just keep the ball out the back of the net, big man. You'll get on a whole lot better – Former Celtic striker **John Hartson** gives goalkeeper Artur Boruc some advice, October 2008. Boruc had just been fined £500 by the SFA for making a gesture towards Rangers fans in the August 2008 Old Firm game.

Tom Wharton, the famous former referee, used to say that in an Old Firm game a referee needed to have sharp eyes and dull ears – Former referee **Kenny Clark**, August 2008.

You know what happened with Tommy, don't you? He split the Scottish vote. He didn't get the Scottish vote because he's Celtic not Rangers. If he'd supported a neutral side like Motherwell or something they'd have all united behind him – TV presenter **Terry Christian** to rapper Coolio after former MSP Tommy Sheridan was evicted from *Celebrity Big Brother*, January 2009.

It's the first thing everyone's said to me. Not 'What a great place Townsville looks', or 'How do you think you'll do in your first season?', but 'How can you manage a team that play in green and white?' – Australian A League new club North Queensland Fury's manager, ex-Rangers midfielder **Ian Ferguson**, April 2009.

As a football team, we are better than Rangers. We are a team who likes to play football. Rangers have something which maybe we don't have – they like to battle, to play long balls into the box and just fight – Celtic striker **Georgios Samaras**, on the eve of the last day of the season, May 2009. Three days later, Rangers won at Tannadice to clinch the league. Samaras was substituted at half-time as Celtic drew 0–0 at home to Hearts.

I am sure Celtic will be disappointed with his comments. If you are a teammate of his, you don't want to be reading things like that – Rangers captain **David Weir** on Samaras' remarks, after his side had won the title, May 2009.

O'NEILL ⚽

If there was one player I clashed with more than any other during my time in management, it was Martin O'Neill – Nottingham Forest manager **Brian Clough**, in *Walking On Water: My Life*, 1992.

If there is one person who can talk more than me in football, it's him – Former Nottingham Forest boss **Brian Clough** on Martin O'Neill, February 2002.

If you ever went into his hotel room when he was a player, oh, it looked like a tip. There were *Racing Post*s strewn all over the place, there were letters; he was in the middle of writing letters all the time. But he knew where everything was. He was disorganised in an organised way – **Gerry Armstrong**, former teammate, on Martin O'Neill, in Alex Montgomery, *Martin O'Neill – The Biography*, 2003.

Any little bit of criticism, he's very sensitive to that. But that's the case with a lot of football managers. He's just more sensitive than most – Leicester City Supporters Club Chairman **Cliff Ginnetta**, in Alex Montgomery, *Martin O'Neill – The Biography*, 2003.

Suddenly there was a bang on the door – not a tap, a bang – and in walked Martin. He spoke extremely fluently. He gave the directors some advice on the way he thought affairs should be conducted, and on how he should be remunerated in respect of his move from Norwich. He commanded a great deal of respect . . . How many players would have the courage or the ability to address a group of men off the cuff – he had no notes – and tell them exactly what he thought? And I have to say he had a jolly good argument. He spoke very, very well and had a good hearing. The chairman thanked him for his intervention, and then Sir Arthur made that classic comment about Martin. I was on the board for ten years and it was the only interruption

I witnessed. I often felt that that incident helped get him his MBE, for Sir Arthur carried a lot of influence and was able to make recommendations about such awards – Norwich director **Robert Chase** recalls boardroom discussion of Martin O'Neill's move from Norwich to Notts County, in Alex Montgomery, *Martin O'Neill – The Biography*, 2003.

If only he could still play football as well as he can talk – Norwich chairman **Sir Arthur South**, after the above exchange, in Alex Montgomery, *Martin O'Neill – The Biography*, 2003.

The phrase 'gentleman's agreement' will disappear from my vocabulary. I've been denied the opportunity to go and speak to a club and it rankles with me. Foolish me, who once studied law for a living. I should've realised an unwritten agreement is precisely that. What it has forced me to do is to get things written down and try to understand English . . . I am going to insert about 194 clauses into the new contract – Leicester manager **Martin O'Neill**, after being refused permission to speak to Leeds United, who wanted him as replacement for George Graham in 1998, in Alex Montgomery, *Martin O'Neill – The Biography*, 2003.

It seems to me that Martin O'Neill is losing his 'Mr Clean' image – Chelsea chairman **Ken Bates** responds to then-Leicester manager Martin O'Neill's suggestion he was a 'footballing cretin', February 2000.

I spent five or six hours with him. But I knew within the first two minutes that he was the man for Celtic – Celtic majority shareholder **Dermot Desmond** on Martin O'Neill, in DVD, 'The Official History of Celtic', 2008.

I ultimately had three meetings with Martin, usually held at the headquarters of Bass plc in North Audley Street, London – the offices of Richard North (Leeds United director) – and we hammered out a deal . . . he seemed spooked that Dermot (Desmond) had granted permission but added, 'He's always said that if I wanted to leave, then I could. If I can be sure he's given permission, I'll be happy to talk terms.' – Former Leeds chairman **Peter Ridsdale** on the club's attempt to lure O'Neill as manager in the summer of 2002 to replace David O'Leary, in *United We Fall: Boardroom Truths about the Beautiful Game*, 2007. Desmond talked O'Neill out of leaving Celtic.

At no stage had I anticipated him not becoming our next manager. Martin is an honourable man who loathes being perceived as someone who would dishonour an agreement, and I respect that, but I couldn't help but feel let down – Former Leeds chairman **Peter Ridsdale** on the move for O'Neill in 2002, in *United We Fall: Boardroom Truths about the Beautiful Game*, 2007.

Martin O'Neill's contractual situation has been cleared up. He has nothing further to add regarding any speculation – Celtic statement over claims O'Neill met Leeds chairman Peter Ridsdale and agreed to become Leeds manager in summer 2002 than changed his mind, contained in Tom Bower's book, *Broken Dreams: Vanity, Greed, & The Souring of English Football*, February 2003.

Martin O'Neill is a top, top manager but you can see the criticism of him starting already. That is why I think, if Martin is really clever, he will leave Celtic – Former Rangers manager **Dick Advocaat**, September 2002.

At the third attempt, the deal to bring Martin O'Neill to Leeds United was signed, sealed and waiting to be delivered to the supporters. It was 3 January 2003 – Former Leeds chairman **Peter Ridsdale** on the next bid to appoint O'Neill following a meeting at Ridsdale's house, in book, *United We Fall: Boardroom Truths about the Beautiful Game*, 2007. The two previous attempts had been when Leicester refused Leeds permission in 1998 and then when O'Neill was talked out of leaving Celtic in 2002.

I signed a three-year contract with Celtic in June 2000 and said at the time that the only way I'd leave before the contract reached its end was if the Celtic board and supporters wanted me to. That would have been, I assume, because of poor results. That is and always has been the case. The situation has never changed despite these claims that Leeds were about to make an announcement to the Stock Market and that I would be their new manager. The allegation is simply and utterly untrue. I have never had any intention of leaving Celtic before my contract expires – **Martin O'Neill**'s take on the situation, March 2003.

Peter (Ridsdale) had wanted me to be manager a couple of times. In 1998, when Mr (John) Elsom (then-Leicester City chairman) wouldn't give me permission to speak to Leeds and then again in the summer of 2002, when David (O'Leary) left. Peter felt he had Celtic's permission to speak to me, but when I spoke to Dermot Desmond (the Celtic majority shareholder) he said that wasn't the case. I'd signed a three-year contract at Celtic and into the last few months of that contract, when there had been no discussions about a new deal, I assumed Celtic wanted me to see my time through. So I was within my rights to speak to somebody and went to meet Peter – Aston Villa manager **Martin O'Neill** on the Leeds matter, November 2007, prior to the publication of Ridsdale's book. (The Ridsdale book claimed O'Neill was free to speak to other clubs from 1 January 2003, six months before the end of his Celtic contract.)

I don't even consider this an issue. An agreement was reached in January and I'm very happy with that agreement between myself and the board. I agreed a contract at my old club Leicester and didn't get round to signing it for about nine months – **Martin O'Neill** admits he hasn't signed his new Celtic contract, May 2003.

Within six or seven weeks I signed a young lad from Lincoln United who looked like he might have a bit of potential, but he was then just 23 years old. His name was Gary Crosby. I signed him and nine games later – we had eight victories with him playing for us – Brian Clough asked to take him on trial and he signed for Nottingham Forest and ended up having a really good career. So I thought to myself that if I didn't make it as a manager, at least I would be a damn good scout – **Martin O'Neill** on early days at Southern League Grantham Town, March 2003.

There's only one contender who fits the bill when Alex calls it a day. Martin O'Neill has played under a great manager – me – has represented his country in the World Cup, done his time as a non-league manager, won trophies at Wembley with Leicester and now is getting crucial European experience in the goldfish bowl with Celtic. And he's bright and stands no nonsense from his players. The rest are nowhere, believe me – Former Nottingham Forest manager **Brian Clough** tips O'Neill for the Manchester United job, May 2003.

This is the great misconception about us: that we must be close. I don't know Martin privately at all. In seven years working together I've never once been in his house. That's how it must be – Celtic captain **Neil Lennon**, May 2003. (For much of their time together in Glasgow, the pair lived about a mile away from one another in the city's West End.)

Martin used to crave appreciation from me. One day, after I'd had a go at him, he answered back, 'But I've got 15 goals already this season.' I pointed out where they'd all come from. 'A little fat guy on the other wing is setting them all up for you. He's got so much ability that he's drawing defenders to him like bees to a honeypot.' I was always particularly sweet on the fat little Glaswegian and used to say we had a genius on one wing and O'Neill on the other, although that was perhaps a little harsh on Martin – Former Nottingham Forest boss **Brian Clough** on Martin O'Neill (and John Robertson), May 2003.

Martin taught me a big lesson when the immature Sav stood over Stefan Schwartz screaming, shouting and gesticulating during a match against Sunderland. At half-time the gaffer tore into me, shouting, 'You ever do anything like that again boy, and you'll be out of this club. You'll never play for me again.' – Midfielder **Robbie Savage** on O'Neill at Leicester, June 2003.

He was a strange guy. Some days he'd come into training and would be talking away to you. The next he would walk past you as if you weren't there – Former Celtic captain **Neil Lennon** on Martin O'Neill, June 2007.

Just when you thought you were getting to know him you'd discover you didn't know him at all. One day you'd walk into the club and he'd welcome you with a smile on his face but the next day you might as well have not existed. He blanked you — Former Leicester midfielder **Robbie Savage** on O'Neill, September 2003.

Martin weighs you up and sizes you up over a period of time. You have to prove yourself to Martin more than once to be accepted as someone he can trust — Grantham Town chairman **Tony Balfe**, in Alex Montgomery, *Martin O'Neill – The Biography*, 2003.

In Britain we have a certain image of what a manager should be. You have to wear certain clothes, you have to speak a certain way, you have to say the right things. Maybe Martin, when he was starting out and got rejected for all those jobs he applied for, failed to get them because he didn't fit an image. I don't know, maybe they thought he looked too geeky — Former Celtic coach **John Barnes**, December 2003.

Straightaway, he turned to Lubo Moravcik and said, 'You, you need to lose a stone and if you don't do it then you're not playing because you're not fit enough and you don't work hard enough. You've got ability but you need to shed it.' — Former midfielder **Craig Burley** recalls the O'Neill managerial technique on his arrival at Celtic, January 2004.

They're both leaders of men. They might not take training but they'll know about the kid struggling at school. They have a single-mindedness that gets them through — Former Norwich goalkeeper **Bryan Gunn**, on his old bosses O'Neill and Alex Ferguson, January 2004.

I am reckoned to be one of the most animated of managers but from what I have seen of Martin's technical area conduct, he has sometimes made me seem as restrained as Sven-Goran Eriksson — Celtic manager **Gordon Strachan** on predecessor Martin O'Neill, in autobiography, *Strachan: My Life In Football*, 2006.

I love Celtic and I have enormous respect for this club. But there's no doubt that Martin had something going for him which I don't, which was the Irish aspect — Celtic manager **Gordon Strachan**, June 2007.

I read something in the paper today about Martin O'Neill but he's the same, an old-fashioned coach. When you watch football from Arsenal, from Liverpool, from my big friend at Manchester United, that is world-class football. Aston Villa? That's old-fashioned — Former Scotland manager **Berti Vogts**, November 2007.

In the presence of that man, you just want to get cracking and work with him — Former Leeds chairman **Peter Ridsdale** on O'Neill, in *United We Fall: Boardroom Truths about the Beautiful Game*, 2007.

OOPS ⚽

There was a moment's pause, then Robbo (Bryan Robson) said, 'Nigel? Who's Nigel?' and Fergie points at me and goes, 'Him, Nigel Davenport.' — **Peter Davenport** recalls Alex Ferguson's first team announcement as Manchester United manager, in Stephen F. Kelly, *Fergie*, 1997. (Nigel Davenport was a popular English actor of the time.)

Lou Macari tried to sign me when he was in charge. He phoned me one Sunday afternoon when I was at home, and I thought it was someone at the wind-up and told him to f*** off — Former midfielder **Craig Burley** on a previous opportunity to join Celtic, in Mark Guidi, *The Inner Sanctum*, 2008.

I dropped my guard and made the comment about Mr Dewar. I wish sincerely that I had not done so — Former SFA chief executive **Jim Farry**, July 1999, on his aside that Donald Dewar, then Secretary of State for Scotland, might be a 'rather useful centre-half' for Scotland against Belarus after the death of Princess Diana in 1997. The SFA had initially rejected calls to postpone the match after the death of the Princess, but it was eventually rescheduled.

I only swear in an Italian regional dialect — Rangers skipper **Lorenzo Amoruso**, December 1999, after being accused of calling Borussia Dortmund's Victor Ikpeba a 'black bastard' during the previous night's UEFA Cup match between the clubs.

I was involved in an incident with Victor Ikpeba and words were exchanged between the two of us. However in a highly-charged football match it is not unusual for tempers to boil over and I do not remember making the remarks attributed to me. This morning I viewed the video recording of the game and, on this evidence, I cannot dispute the fact that I made the remarks. I would like to make an unreserved apology to Victor Ikpeba — **Amoruso**'s climbdown the following day, December 1999.

I know we are a better team than Rangers, and I know we can beat them easily if our attitude is right — Celtic defender **Johann Mjallby** prior to the March 2000 Old Firm game. Rangers won 4–0.

It was like a game of roulette and Wigan were holding all the aces — Motherwell Director of Football **Pat Nevin** gets his gambling metaphors muddled before Ged Brannan's move to Wigan, February 2001.

I am not an ambitious man. I had no ambition as a player and it's the same as a manager. I don't want to be manager of Manchester United or Juventus. I'm happy here at Southampton. That is my only priority and this is going to be my last manager's job in football — Southampton manager **Gordon Strachan**, January 2002.

There isn't much loyalty in football these days but I like to think I am showing that. The easy thing for me to do would have been to go to Dundee United, take an excellent salary and take United up the league. I have no doubts that I could have done that. Staying at Falkirk was the hard decision but I am going to stick with it – Falkirk manager **Ian McCall** turns down United's approach, October 2002. He became their manager three months later.

I let Archie Gemmill go when he was around 30, because I thought his legs had gone. Yet his pride and natural fitness enabled him to carry on playing at the top level for a few more seasons . . . I dropped a clanger with little Archie – Former Nottingham Forest manager **Brian Clough**, March 2003.

I got back to the hotel and saw it on television and Alfonso had actually jumped the goalkeeper and was at least two metres by him when he went down in a definite ploy to win a penalty. That's how much of a dive it was, but from the angle which I'd had at the game, it looked a cert. I will never forget how low I felt – Referee **Hugh Dallas** recalls a vital mistake in a June 1997 World Cup qualifier between Spain and the Czech Republic, March 2003. Fernando Hierro scored from the penalty and Spain won 1–0.

I don't believe 50,000 fans will travel to Seville. That is madness, an exaggeration. I think a fair number will be around 4,000. We are talking about a final being played on a Wednesday, a day when people normally work – Seville security chief **Rafael Carmonna**, before the UEFA Cup Final between Celtic and Porto, May 2003. An estimated 70,000 Celtic supporters travelled to the game.

Rangers will be gutted that I am not playing in the final. I was their major goal threat – Dundee defender **Lee Wilkie**, who was suspended for the Scottish Cup Final, after scoring an own goal and conceding two penalties against them in the league, May 2003.

I wish it had never happened, but in other ways it means I've been there: I've seen the dark side, I know what it's like and I don't want to go back there – Celtic striker **John Hartson**, June 2003, on the September 1998 West Ham training ground incident with teammate Eyal Berkovic. He was fined £20,000 and banned for three matches for kicking the Israeli international in the head.

That doesn't mean I don't regret it. It was a horrendous thing and I'm ever so sorry for it, but it was on *News at Ten*, we had reporters coming to the house asking my missus, 'Does he beat you at home?' – Celtic striker **John Hartson** on the Berkovic incident, November 2003.

Q: What daft things have you done in your time?
A: When I went for my first driving test I had trouble reading the registration

plate of a car as my contact lenses were giving me bother. The instructor went to get a measuring tape so I went over to the car to memorise the number but when the instructor came out the owner of the car came out too and drove off. Suffice to say I failed – Stirling Albion striker **Scott McLean**, newspaper questionnaire, September 2003.

– Who's the daftest guy you know?
– It's got to be Trigger Scott McLean. There is no doubt about it. The story I love about him is the one where he memorised a car's registration plate just before he was about to sit his driving test but the car pulled away. He failed the test – Stirling Albion's **Martin Glancy**, newspaper questionnaire, September 2004. (Mind you . . .)

When Martin Glancy heard that Julie Fleeting had signed for Ross County he thought she was going to play for the actual men's first team. He was asking questions like, 'Do you think she will score goals?' and 'What is she going to do about the showers?' – Airdrie United's **Mark Roberts**, October 2003.

I had read in the papers that she (Julie Fleeting) had signed for Ross County and I genuinely thought it was for the first team and didn't realise it was for the ladies' team. When I asked the guys at Airdrie during training they fell about laughing at me. She had a good scoring record, though, and could probably have done a good job for them – Stirling Albion's **Martin Glancy** confirms Roberts' tale, September 2004.

If people remember me for only one thing then they are short-minded. Obviously I was disappointed but it did not bother me if 10 or 15 newspapers made fun of me as long as I had the support of the people around me – Former Rangers striker **Peter van Vossen** recalls his November 1996 open-goal miss against Celtic at Parkhead, November 2003.

Living in Aberdeen wouldn't be my first choice. I'm not on a great wage and it's very cold. People told me there was a beach here – Aberdeen's Australian striker **David Zdrilic**, February 2004.

I do get occasional invitations to speak but it usually turns out they want Craig Brown the Scottish football manager instead – *Private Eye* diarist **Craig Brown**, December 2005.

When Alex McLeish left Rangers I said, 'He can bow out with his head held high.' – Radio pundit **Willie Miller** recalls an unfortunate choice of phrase, October 2008.

I could understand our supporters being annoyed if they felt there wasn't a light at the end of the tunnel. But there is a massive moonbeam of success coming to us. People have just got to accept that there are certain timing issues here. It's going to happen. We've got big plans – Rangers chairman **David Murray**, February 2006, weeks before the announcement of Paul le Guen's arrival as new coach. Le Guen left Rangers by mutual consent in January 2007.

United's goalkeeper, Gary Bailey, had come over for a chat, and upon noting Fergie sitting next to me laughing and joking, thrust out his hand and said, 'Nice to meet you, Mr. Strachan.' – **Gordon Strachan** on confusion at Manchester United's 1986 FA Cup-winning banquet, to which Strachan had invited then-Aberdeen boss Ferguson, in autobiography, *Strachan: My Life In Football*, 2006.

I take it as a compliment and maybe he does see me, in the future, becoming Hearts manager. It would be a dream of mine to manage the club but I've got to make sure when I do it I'm ready and it's right. It's not just for sentimental reasons – Hearts captain **Steven Pressley**, October 2006, after owner Vladimir Romanov had said he would be a future manager of the club. Later that month he led a press conference at which he confirmed there was 'significant unrest in the Hearts dressing room' over the way the club was being run. Two months later he left Hearts by mutual consent.

People tell me it evens itself out – but if it does we must have 15 penalties to get in the next seven games – Celtic boss **Gordon Strachan** on the lack of penalties his side was being awarded, March 2007. Celtic had been awarded a penalty in their previous match, against Falkirk, which Craig Beattie missed.

Daft little ground, silly game, f*** off – *Sky TV*'s **Richard Keys**, unaware his microphone was on, introducing highlights from Scotland's game in the Faroe Islands, June 2007.

If I get a single red card for Rangers this season, I'll buy champagne for each of you. How about that? – Rangers striker **Jean-Claude Darcheville** makes a bet with the Scottish press, July 2007. Five months later, he was, inevitably, sent off against Lyon in the Champions League. (To his credit, he duly provided the champagne for delighted journalists.)

What a pair of big weans you are, you and Mr Christie – him in the huff and you getting annoyed because he disrespects you. For goodness sake, all over a game of football, or rather, a non-game of football. What a carry-on – **Sheriff Elizabeth Munro** fining Dundee Violet player-coach Andrew Heggie £500 for breaking the jaw of player Sean Christie, February 2008, after a game on 15 September, 2007. Christie had been an unused sub in the game and refused to go for an after-match drink. Dundee Violet's club nickname is The Pansies.

He's done a fantastic job and we're 100 per cent committed to him. If the worst comes to the worst and we do go down, I can't think of a better man to get us straight back up. He has passion, he's shrewd – he's a good manager – Derby County chairman **Adam Pearson** on manager Billy Davies, 30 October, 2007. Davies was sacked on 26 November.

I didn't have my glasses with me. It was a complete and utter mistake. As a life-long Stranraer fan everyone can be assured there was no ulterior motive – Holyrood presiding officer **Alex Fergusson MSP**, November 2007, after the CIS Cup semi-final draw error which had seen him misread the teams coming out of the hat, necessitating an amendment four hours later. Hearts, originally due to play Dundee United, were in fact drawn against Rangers.

It's an error, the Presiding Officer has apologised and the integrity has remained intact. It would have been more embarrassing if we had left it – Scottish League president **Brown McMaster** on the draw fiasco, November 2007.

When Ghana called me up for the under-17 World Cup, they spelt my name like that on the official documentation and even on my passport. I said to myself, 'Now even FIFA think I am Kingston,' so I didn't bother to change it – Hearts and Ghana midfielder **Laryea Kingson** on administrative problems, January 2008.

I don't have Mark McGhee's phone number. I spoke to his agent all the way through. I'm writing Mark McGhee a letter – SFA Chief Executive **Gordon Smith**, *BBC Radio Scotland*, January 2008. Motherwell manager McGhee had been in the running for the vacant Scotland manager's job.

That people I worked with for so long and considered friends could go out of their way to make me uncomfortable was a surprise – SFA chief executive **Gordon Smith** on the verbal mauling he received on *BBC Radio Scotland* after saying he hadn't had Scotland manager's job candidate Mark McGhee's telephone number, March 2008.

He is not a bad lad (the Pope). If it had said, 'God Bless Myra Hindley' we might have a problem – Celtic manager **Gordon Strachan**, dismisses controversy over goalkeeper Artur Boruc removing his jersey to reveal a 'God Bless The Pope' T-shirt at the end of the Old Firm game on 27 April, 2008.

I think if we attempted to sell Carlos Cuellar at this moment in time the fans would burn the place down . . . and I'd be one of them – Rangers assistant manager **Ally McCoist**, May 2008. Cuellar was sold to Aston Villa in August 2008.

When I was at Hibs I could walk about in Glasgow and no one would notice me – Celtic midfielder **Scott Brown**, 8 August 2008. The day the interview was published – two days later – Brown was assaulted in an incident outside a nightclub in Glasgow during which Celtic defender Darren O'Dea and two other men were arrested.

It's great to see somebody, you've got to say maybe with limited ability, who has really worked hard at his game and progressed – Scotland manager **George Burley** on Rangers defender Kirk Broadfoot, as he called him into the squad for the World Cup qualifying games against Macedonia and Iceland, September 2008. Six days later Broadfoot scored on his international debut in Iceland to help Scotland to Burley's first win in charge.

After day two I felt down because of the bad press regarding the manager's comments. To be honest, I did speak to him about it. I felt I had to. I'm glad I did because he explained what he meant and that it was intended as a compliment. If I'm being honest, better words could have been used – **Broadfoot**'s response, September 2008.

I was about to go on the Internet to refer to their manager's name. Then I stopped myself. Because of the contempt he showed us I have not remembered it and I am not going to give him the courtesy of learning it . . . when Nancy are here on Thursday we will show them respect then we will try to kick their teeth in – Motherwell manager **Mark McGhee**, before the UEFA Cup First round, second leg tie against the French club, September 2008. Motherwell, 1–0 down from the first leg when McGhee felt the French club had been disrespectful towards him and his players, lost the second leg 2–0 four days after his words.

Who's the thickest person in the dressing room? – I'm sure people won't be surprised to hear it's Colin Nish. We were standing in the toilet at Parkhead on Saturday when he said, 'Why is it you're always facing a wall when you pee? Why don't you get to look out a window?' – Hibs midfielder **John Rankin**, newspaper questionnaire, November 2008.

I look at it this way – everyone knows about Chris Iwelumo because of that miss – The Wolves striker reflects on his World Cup qualifier miss for Scotland against Norway, March 2009.

Four-in-a-row is in the bag for Celtic. It's over now. Finished – *The Sun* newspaper columnist **John Hartson**, March 2009, after Rangers lost at home to Inverness Caledonian Thistle to slip three points behind Celtic with ten games to go. Rangers won the title by four points two months later.

Rangers have not proved me wrong and made me look stupid as a result. It's Celtic who have done that – **Hartson** after Rangers' title win, May 2009.

OUCH! (KICKINGS, NOT ALL OF THEM PHYSICAL)

With about 15 minutes to go I saw this thug standing there with a big grin on his face and decided he wasn't going to get away with it. I did a tiptoe through the tulips and hit him one almighty kick in the bollocks — Celtic's **Tommy Gemmell**, July 2007, recalling the World Club Championship play-off match against Racing Club of Argentina in Montevideo, Uruguay, November 1967, when four Celtic and two Racing players were sent off. Gemmell's foul on Norberto Raffo went unnoticed and unpunished by the Paraguayan referee.

After much of the first-half had been characterised by sporadic scuffles, Rodolfo Osorio, the referee, a Paraguayan, called the two captains together and told Billy (McNeill) and his Racing Club counterpart that the next time there was an incident, number eight of the greens — that was me — and number six of the blues, Alfio Basile, would be dismissed. It had certainly become a difficult game to referee but this was an illogical reaction — to threaten with dismissal, almost as if hostages to be sacrificed, two named players even if the next incident of on-field violence had nothing to do with them — Celtic's **Bobby Lennox** on the third match in the 1967 World Club Championship against Racing Club, in *Bobby Lennox: My Story*, 2007. At the next incident, Lennox and Basile were ordered off, with the referee inviting a solider with a sword to escort them on their way.

He had the most ungainly run I've ever seen. He was never a great footballer, just a journeyman. As George McLean used to say to him, 'There's labourers and tradesmen, and you're the labourer.' — Former Ayr captain **Johnny Graham** on Alex Ferguson's short spell at the club (his last as a player), in Michael Crick, *The Boss: The Many Sides of Alex Ferguson*, 2002.

I looked upon (Martin) O'Neill as a bit of a smart-arse — Former Nottingham Forest manager **Brian Clough**, in *Clough: The Autobiography*, 1994.

You've done well for me, son. But when Kenny (Dalglish) is fit, you're sub — Scotland manager **Jock Stein** to Dundee United striker Paul Sturrock, quoted by Sturrock in February 2002.

Gordon was great in that dressing room. With his tongue he had a punch like Sonny Liston — Former Leeds boss **Howard Wilkinson** on Strachan, in *Gordon Strachan: The Biography*, Leo Moynihan, 2004.

We had a goalkeeper, Chuck Moussaddik, who was a bit of a poseur. He was posing in front of the mirror once when O'Neill walked past and spotted him. He said, 'Here, Chuck, you look just like Joe Bugner.' Chuck puffed out his chest and said that was a big compliment. Martin replied, 'You both wear gloves for no apparent reason.' One hit, that's all he needed — Wycombe's **Keith Ryan** on Martin O'Neill, in Alex Montgomery, *Martin O'Neill – The Biography*, 2003.

If I had known you were going to write this sort of book I would never have allowed you access to myself or the team. Having said that, I think it's one of the best books about football ever written – Coventry manager **Gordon Strachan** to American author Rick Gekoski, about his fly-on-the-wall overview of the club's 1997–98 season, 'Staying Up'.

I'll never forget the thud it made as his head made contact. What a noise! It would have knocked me out. But Henrik stayed on his feet. However, it helped bring us all closer together – Former Celtic defender **Jackie McNamara**'s curious assessment of the November 1997 training-ground headbutt by Tosh McKinlay on Henrik Larsson, in Mark Guidi, *The Inner Sanctum*, 2008.

Jock Brown brought out a book the following year and I'm told that in it he stated that I wanted Tosh to be sacked for headbutting Henrik. Absolute rubbish. And I phoned Tosh to tell him that – Former Celtic assistant manager **Murdo MacLeod** on the training-ground headbutt by Tosh McKinlay on Henrik Larsson, in Mark Guidi, 'The Inner Sanctum', 2008. (Jock Brown, in his book, *Celtic-Minded: 510 Days In Paradise*, did indeed write, 'Murdo thought we should sack him. Wim (Jansen, coach) didn't demur.')

Wim rarely joined in any of the banter. I do remember one of the boys tried to make a smart comment at his expense and Wim just looked at him and said something along the lines of 'I've played in two World Cup Finals. And you?' – Former Celtic midfielder **Simon Donnelly** on ex-boss Wim Jansen, in Mark Guidi, *The Inner Sanctum*, 2008.

That dream was crumbling on the surly and largely uncommunicative Wim Jansen, aided by the man whose industry and integrity, in my opinion, did not match his ambition, Murdo MacLeod – Former Celtic General Manager **Jock Brown** on the failure of the club's coaching structure, in book, *Celtic-Minded: 510 Days In Paradise*, 1999.

He simply gave further strength to my argument that those who protest most loudly against something like that are usually those who need it most. That certainly applies to Paul, in my opinion – Former Celtic general manager **Jock Brown** on midfielder Paul Lambert's resistance to Brown's suggestions that the players have media training, in book, *Celtic-Minded: 510 Days In Paradise*, 1999.

I've got a book coming out as well. He might make an appearance – Former Aberdeen and Manchester United goalkeeper **Jim Leighton** after being criticised by Alex Ferguson in his autobiography, *Managing My Life*, January 2000.

I don't mean any disrespect to my fellow footballers, but the majority are thick – Dundee United defender **Maurice Malpas**, January 2000.

Martin (O'Neill) runs up and down the touchline quicker and more often than his No. 2 John Robertson used to during his playing days – Pundit and former manager **Ron Atkinson**, 2000.

Maryhill were playing Pollok at our home park, Lochburn, in the semi-final of the Cup. Lok player John Paisley was running to catch a ball that was about to roll over the line towards our dugout. He caught the ball before it went over the line and smashed it straight into our bench. Not only that, he followed through and jumped into our subs. A full-scale melee ensured, involving players and even Pollok boss Jim O'Donnell. It was excellent. It really got the crowd going and livened up an otherwise dull game – Clyde manager **Allan Maitland** recalls junior football fun with Maryhill, February 2000.

I went to see him but he's not the player for me – Spurs boss **George Graham** on Celtic striker Mark Viduka, March 2000.

He still makes me smile. Usually with his first touch – Kilmarnock's **Ian Durrant** on teammate Ally McCoist, September 2000.

They take too much money from this club but they all have watertight contracts. Between them, I have seen the three of them play two and a half games – Sheffield Wednesday boss **Peter Shreeves** on Scots trio Simon Donnelly, Phil O'Donnell and Philip Scott, September 2001.

Agents are trying to move their players on and I can't blame them because that's their job. But some of them don't know a ball from a banana – Partick Thistle manager **John Lambie**, opting not to sign players before the transfer deadline, August 2002.

I've seen more life in a dead slug – Manchester United manager **Alex Ferguson** to players, in Michael Crick, *The Boss: The Many Sides of Alex Ferguson*, 2002.

We regard this as two points dropped as opposed to one point won – Faroe Islands manager **Henrik Larsson** after the 2–2 draw against Scotland, September 2002. The Faroes had been 2–0 up in the opening 15 minutes.

Fergie's an outstanding football manager. Yeah, an all-time great, so good in fact that I would say he's better than Sir Matt. He's a had a lot more money to spend than Busby, of course, but in terms of getting results and winning things, he's better. But as a man, he's a dickhead. A lot of the success has gone to his head, and now he thinks he's bigger than anybody or anything. He certainly couldn't get near Busby as a person – Former Manchester United manager **Tommy Docherty**, November 2002.

If I'd tried it a hundred times or a million times it wouldn't happen again. If I could I would carry on playing – Manchester United manager **Sir Alex Ferguson** attempts to laugh off the eye cut suffered when a boot he kicked after his side's 2–0 FA Cup defeat by Arsenal hit David Beckham in the face, February 2003.

What happened in the changing room has happened to me 50 times or more. I have kicked bottles of mineral water or buckets plenty of times and it is just by chance they haven't hit a player. It is a question of technique – the Scots obviously have better technique than the Italians – Juventus coach **Marcello Lippi**'s droll take on the incident, prior to the Champions League game between the clubs, February 2003. Manchester United won 2–1 with Beckham setting up both goals.

We have a lot in common. We both thought we were better players than we actually were – Former Nottingham Forest boss **Brian Clough** on Martin O'Neill, May 2003.

I get real pelters. I'm called slow, I'm called fat, I've even been called a 'cart-horse' in print. I mean, come on, a f***ing cart-horse! – Celtic skipper **Neil Lennon**, May 2003.

When I came four years ago I freed every player bar two, (Alan) Archibald and Kenny Arthur – they were the only ones who weren't c**** – **John Lambie** after his last game as Partick Thistle manager, May 2003.

If I was playing today I would probably have been suspended for a year – Scotland under-21 manager **Rainer Bonhof**, May 2003.

Then there was Ronald de Boer. In his day he was undoubtedly a world-class talent, but that day had passed and he couldn't get into the Barcelona side when Rangers signed him – Former Rangers winger **Andrei Kanchelskis**, August 2003.

He scared me shitless. The sure sign that someone was lined up for a major blast came when he'd arrive and suddenly brush or hold the back of his hand over his mouth. That was the signal and I'd sit there praying it wasn't me he was about to launch into. See his hand near his mouth and be afraid – very afraid. He knew how to embarrass and humiliate like no man I've worked for before or since – Former Leicester midfielder **Robbie Savage** on ex-manager Martin O'Neill, September 2003.

In Holland, the captain band means something but not the kind of status Lorenzo (Amoruso) had in mind. Even without the band you can take responsibility like Arthur (Numan) or Craig (Moore). They were the real captains in my opinion and they didn't need a band for that – Former Rangers defender **Bert Konterman**, November 2003.

'Premier League? You're having a laugh.' 'First Division? You're having a laugh.' 'Sunday league? You're having a laugh.' '*Subbuteo*? You're having a laugh' – Manchester United fans taunt Rangers supporters during the 3–0 Champions League win, November 2003.

Some of the other ones had hardly kicked a ball and, in a moral rather than legal context, I didn't have quite the same sympathy for them. Of the nine, a number were malingerers who the manager was having difficulty motivating – Motherwell owner **John Boyle**, May 2004, on players made redundant when the club went into interim administration in April 2002. 19 players were made redundant, 10 who were coming to the ends of their contracts and nine who had a year to go.

I wouldn't say that any of the teams have it too hard. They have charter planes from one five-star hotel to the next. It's not a dog's life – Champions World director of communications **Rich Schneider** amid reports Celtic were unhappy at their travelling schedule during their pre-season American tour, July 2004.

It was a bit high. He nearly took my willy off – Inverness defender **Ross Tokely** on a tackle by Rangers' Bob Malcolm, August 2005.

I believe the Celtic Trust people are self-serving individuals who only want to promote themselves and not promote the Club – Majority shareholder **Dermot Desmond** to the Celtic Supporters Association, December 2005.

I told him he'd had the luckiest game of his life – because it should've been 15–0. We'd taken 1,200 fans down and at 4–0 they started singing, 'Billy, Billy, get to f***'. He mentioned that to me after the game and I told him I'd started it – Hamilton chairman **Ronnie MacDonald** recalls commiserating with manager Billy Reid after losing 6–0 at Gretna on the opening day of the season in August 2006, July 2008.

(Sasa) Papac is the best of a bad bunch. (Karl) Svensson looks like a rabbit in the headlights and (Brahim) Hemdani moves like he's pulling a caravan. None of them looks good enough for Rangers – Former Scotland midfielder **Craig Burley**'s damning verdict on new Ibrox signings, November 2006.

Any Celtic player should be experienced enough to handle this. Listen, if you are scared to play in the San Siro, then you should go and work in a pub – Former Hearts defender **Pasquale Bruno**, on Celtic's Group of 16 Champions League trip to play AC Milan, March 2007.

Marek Tomana being named man of the match was a joke and disrespectful to those who had been out there for an hour. I'll be having words with the sponsors – Stirling manager **Allan Moore** after his Slovakian striker won a sponsors' award after going on as sub, 2007.

(Gary) was having a piss one day, 45 yards away by the fence, and Scholes whacked him right on the arse – Manchester United manager **Sir Alex Ferguson** on Paul Scholes' training accuracy on Gary Neville, May 2007.

He just told lies. In years gone by, if a player had been hopeless at a club and left, the last thing any newspaper would've wanted is to talk to him about it. Simon Brown wasn't good enough to do the job here. That's why he's not at the club any more – Hibs manager **John Collins** on former goalkeeper Brown, September 2007. The goalkeeper had criticised him on his Easter Road exit.

I'd been telling him he hadn't won a header against me and he said he drove a Bentley. I'm like, 'Mate, I couldn't care less what car you drive. There's only one speed limit. I don't care if you drive a rocket.' – Dundee United's **Noel Hunt** recalls an exchange with Rangers defender Alan Hutton in the October 2007 game between the clubs, April 2008.

I'll see who the next manager is before I decide. I don't want to be here and not playing but I would like to stay at Celtic if I thought I had a chance to play. I know I won't get that chance with him – Celtic striker **Derek Riordan** on manager Gordon Strachan, April 2008. He left Celtic four months later.

My main business is the world of rock 'n' roll touring. You want to make things happen quickly? Come over to where I am. I've said on many occasions that if the footballing associations were involved in my business, they'd still be trying to get Cliff Richard's first tour out the door – Football agent and former Wham! tour manager **Jake Duncan**, July 2008.

The boy David Edgar (Rangers Supporters Trust spokesman) has made it very, very personal. Six weeks ago he sat in front of me and said it wasn't personal, we're totally supportive of the club, we want to work with you and then he went and did this. It's an ego trip. The Liberal Democrats don't get as much publicity as David Edgar – Rangers chairman **Sir David Murray**, August 2008. (Edgar had accused Rangers of asset-stripping following the sale of defender Carlos Cuellar.)

Those two (SFA chief executive Gordon Smith and President George Peat) had naively organised to play Macedonia when they should have known that the temperature would be extreme to say the least. What they have done is given George (Burley) a really difficult job to start with and he's now been left holding the baby – Dundee United manager **Craig Levein** after Scotland's World Cup defeat in Macedonia, September 2008.

What's annoyed me more than anything else is that Gordon Smith and I were complimented on the way things had worked out after the dates meeting last December. Nobody said a dicky-bird, then after the first game we play, one individual is mouthing off about how stupid the draw is. If you're going to say it, say it before the first game. Because it was a defeat, no doubt – SFA president **George Peat**'s response, September 2008.

We have played straight teams, like a team of builders from Balfour Beatty, and there haven't been any problems. Even if there were, we have some pretty tasty guys in our side who are quite capable of sorting matters out — **Ross McClung**, goalkeeper of Scotland's first gay football club, HotScots FC, September 2008.

My worst miss resulted in me receiving a verbal tirade from Sir Alex Ferguson that was more of a pyroclastic wind than the infamous hairdryer — Motherwell manager **Mark McGhee** recalls missing a sitter playing for Aberdeen against Ujpest Dozsa in the European Cup-Winners' Cup quarter-final in March 1984, October 2008. (Note: the word 'pyroclastic', not one often utilised by SPL managers, means 'volcanic'. McGhee claimed he learned it while doing an Open University course when he was at Aberdeen, part of which focussed on tectonic plates.)

I think he's as good a player as Pedro Mendes — the problem is that Stephen Hughes doesn't think he's as good a player as Pedro Mendes. And until he does, he won't be — Motherwell manager **Mark McGhee** on his midfield player, November 2008.

I've watched a number of SPL games recently when I could've played in goal — and that's sad — SFA president **George Peat**, March 2009.

I was walking off the park after one game when an old fellow came over to me and said, 'Well, referee, you've done the work of two men today.' I felt quite pleased then he said, 'Laurel and f****** Hardy.' — Ex-referee **Kenny Clark** recalls life as a young referee in the juniors following a game at Auchinleck, May 2009.

See these guys, they don't know they're born. They're pansies, walking in grounds with their wee Gucci bags and wee smelly perfumes and all the different types of hair gels; they're getting out of Porsches and Range Rovers. Why kid ourselves? They're just tarts — Former Nottingham Forest and Scotland defender **Kenny Burns**, May 2009.

PHYSICAL FACTS ⚽

Gordon was the David Beckham of his time. He did this thing that every year he went abroad for his holidays and came back a bronzed hero and the women idolised him — Alloa manager **Terry Christie** on former Dundee teammate Gordon Smith, in 'Fanatical About Football', ed. Jeff Connor, 2003.

The Celtic defender, John McNamee, mainly. I phoned him up to tell him I was mentioning him in *Managing My Life* (autobiography) and he was killing himself laughing. He was a daunting figure — Manchester United manager **Sir Alex Ferguson**, asked if anyone had ever put the frighteners up him, October 2008. The pair had come face-to-face in a reserve game between St Johnstone and Celtic.

He had a prickly nature. That may have come from a bit of a Napoleon complex that some smaller guys have. They have to try that bit harder to get where they want and in that respect Gordon was no exception – **Ken MacAskill**, English teacher at Gordon Strachan's Secondary School, Craigroyston, in *Gordon Strachan: The Biography*, Leo Moynihan, 2004.

A (Dundee United) player called Andy Rolland was given it as a nickname, but he didn't like it so he fobbed it off on me. He said, 'Look, he's got bigger ears than me.' – Plymouth Argyle manager **Paul 'Luggy' Sturrock** on his nickname, February 2002.

I've met football legends and legends of the entertainment business and they've sometimes been quite disappointing in terms of personality. But Big Jock walked in the room and you knew straight away you were in the presence of somebody special – Celtic manager **Gordon Strachan** on Jock Stein, September 2005.

Billy Stark was a fantastic player at Aberdeen but people didn't identify with him because he was 6'2" and looked like John Cleese. But Billy was a fantastic player. But they like somebody who's not very good but runs about kicking people and growls and kisses the badge. Then it's, 'Oh, you're the man for me.' But they're no use to anybody – Celtic manager **Gordon Strachan**, July 2006.

A real man's man. When he shook your hand you had to untangle your mangled fingers afterwards – Manchester United winger **Ryan Giggs** on former assistant manager Archie Knox, August 2008.

I don't think they expected this skinny guy with glasses to be the new Celtic striker. I think they thought, 'This guy doesn't look like a footballer.' – Former Celtic striker **Harald Brattbakk** remembers initial scepticism following his December 1997 arrival, in Mark Guidi, *The Inner Sanctum*, 2008.

I love his stand-up comedy routines. We have a lot in common. We have the same problem. We're both neurotic about being short – **Gordon Strachan** on Woody Allen, in Rick Gekoski, *Staying Up: A Fan Behind The Scenes In The Premiership*, 1998.

Q: Most embarrassing moment?
A: Trying to follow Craig Burley's instructions on the park when he didn't have his teeth in.
– Former Celtic defender **Malky Mackay**, then with Norwich City, newspaper questionnaire, 2002.

He looks as if he should be surfing in California and if there's one thing that annoys me about him, it's that. We haven't been to Barbados lately so he must have been on *the sun*-bed. As we approach February, I like players to have that drained, pale look that I've always had at that stage of the season – Leicester manager **Martin O'Neill** on Robbie Savage, 2000.

I'm never really happy. If a player is 5′ 10″ I think he should be 5′ 11″. That's the way I am – Manchester United manager **Sir Alex Ferguson**, 2002.

I will calm down when I retire or die – Celtic manager **Martin O'Neill** on his manic touchline style, 2002.

Technically he was excellent but he wasn't a player who would win you games. He doesn't have great physical qualities; even when he goes by a man, he's quite easily caught. He never manages to be a match-winner. I had to play him further back in the midfield because of that weakness – Reggina coach **Luigi de Canio** on Shunsuke Nakamura, in Martin Greig's book, *The Zen of Nakamura*, 2008. De Canio was his coach in 2002–03 season.

When you are at a big club you have to make sure you don't make mistakes and I made one. It was crazy – over a break of 15 days I don't know how many kilos I put on. Unbelievable. A disgrace – Kilmarnock's **David Fernandez** recalling being subbed (after going on as sub) for Celtic against Aberdeen in January 2003. He didn't start another league game for Celtic.

Martin kicks every ball and his team respond to that. Robbo's not quite so athletic, so he settled for a stately waddle – Former Nottingham Forest manager **Brian Clough** on Martin O'Neill, May 2003.

Part of my body looks like the nose of Gonzo from *The Muppet Show*. Everyone in the dressing room will know what I mean – Stirling Albion striker **Scott McLean**, September 2003.

He's played 35 league games this season, he's 6′ 4″ and turned 17 last month. He must have spent the last 15 years in a greenhouse – Derby manager **George Burley** on midfielder Tom Huddlestone, March 2004.

I'd thought about cutting them off a few times and was on the point of doing it when I broke my leg. Then there seemed more important things to think about. In the end I did it on a whim. I was driving from the ground and got to a junction where I turn left to go home or right towards the hairdresser's. I stopped for a few moments and couldn't make my mind up, then just swung the car to the right. All the press then started saying I was like Samson, that I wouldn't score without the hair. I felt quite relieved when I scored in the next match against Aberdeen – with my head – Celtic's **Henrik Larsson** on getting rid of his dreadlocks, July 2004.

We're both fat and Scottish, but that's where the similarity ends — **Bobby Williamson**, after being asked if his appointment as Plymouth manager was an attempt to continue the good work of Paul Sturrock, August 2004.

My daughter Gemma was watching an old DVD of me the other day and then she watched me on telly. She says, 'Is Dad's nose getting bigger as he gets older?' The answer is, 'Naw, my head's shrinking.' — Former Southampton manager **Gordon Strachan**, February 2005.

I wish I had the linesman's eyesight, he must have Superman's x-ray vision — Dunfermline's **Lee Makel** after being sent off for handball against Rangers, February 2005.

We even competed for the acne cream when we were younger. Obviously, I won that one — Former Aberdeen midfielder **Gordon Strachan** on ex-teammate Alex McLeish, June 2005.

The fact that he's a redhead only made my decision easier. We don't have enough of the mutant gene in MLS —NY/NJ — MetroStars General manager **Alexei Lalas** on hiring Maurice Johnston as manager, December 2005.

With the ability I possessed, and still have, I'd have played for a Manchester United, a Liverpool, or a top foreign side if I'd gone through my career a stone and a half lighter — West Brom's **John Hartson**, December 2006.

Who was the grumpiest person you came across?
You really shouldn't have to ask — Willie Miller. It was just the way he was. I spoke to him the other day and he is still the same. Just with less hair — Miller's former Aberdeen teammate **Mark McGhee**, January 2007.

The trouble with Scots like me is we are smaller people and if we can't fight the bigger people then we want to have the last word — Celtic manager **Gordon Strachan**, February 2007.

It's not important at all to keep St Johnstone full-time. I don't believe all that absolute nonsense. I've got joiners working for me on roofs and their overall fitness will be better than that of a footballer — St Johnstone chairman **Geoff Brown**, April 2007.

He'll need to keep working hard because he's the type who's got a bit of an arse on him — Former Celtic striker **John Hartson** on striker Scott McDonald's physique, February 2008.

My mother isn't too happy, she says it is for the good of my health — but I think it is the shape of my legs to be brutally honest. She's trying to protect the family name – Rangers coach **Ally McCoist** on his mother's views of him continuing to wear shorts in the technical area, February 2008. McCoist claims he does it to show his willingness to kick every ball with the team.

Chinese clubs are very disciplined, athletic and hard-working. They are almost German in their approach to the game. Sadly, the approach to football in Scotland is nothing like this. Chinese players are not the kind of guys who fight on the field. If I brought them here, not only would I have to change the squad, I'd have to change the whole league. These players should be boxing, not playing football. They are more like fighters – Hearts owner **Vladimir Romanov** on the Scottish scene, July 2008.

Experience, height and hair – Swindon Town manager **Maurice Malpas** explaining what new signing Lilian Nalis will bring to the club, August 2008.

I bumped into Derek when he was at Chelsea and I was at Manchester City. While we were chatting the Chelsea player Paul Canoville walked past us and I remarked to Derek he'd a reputation for being fast. 'Oh aye,' he said, 'We call him "Carl" after the sprinter, Carl Lewis. Mind you, they call me "Welles" here.' 'What,' I said, 'After Allan Wells?' 'No,' he replied, 'Orson.' – SFA chief executive **Gordon Smith** on his former Rangers teammate Derek Johnstone as he was inducted into the Scottish Football Hall of Fame, November 2008.

We have almost made sexual violence against Eggert because we have put him in every position – here, there, and up and down. You could go to jail if you did this outside football – Hearts manager **Csaba Laszlo** on versatile Icelander Eggert Jonsson, April 2009.

I got called that from when I was very young. It used to be bigger, the heid, believe it or not, but my body's grown into it – Celtic defender **Gary Caldwell** (nicknamed 'Heid') April 2009.

PLAYERS ⚽

I sometimes wondered if they had a competition to see who could shout the loudest and piss the most teammates off – Former Celtic goalkeeper **Jonathan Gould** on moaning defenders Marc Rieper and Alan Stubbs, in Mark Guidi, 'The Inner Sanctum', 2008.

Before this, it would have required a change of manager for either of them (Marco De Marchi and Patrizio Billio) to play for Dundee again and, as far as I am concerned, that is not going to happen. Now you can add to that a change of ownership, because as long as I am here I do not want to see them in the team – Dundee chairman **Peter Marr** on the Dens pair, who were in dispute with the club at the time, July 2001.

I was one myself and we're of the simplest ilk – Scotland assistant boss **Tommy Burns** on players' appreciation of Berti Vogts' straightforward style of management, March 2002.

When I was Clyde manager I watched eleven games in one week because it takes just 20 minutes to see whether a player is for you or not. I'd watch one game for 20 minutes then leave to get to another for the second-half – Preston manager **Craig Brown**, January 2004.

Unfortunately, too many dumplings are getting thousands of pounds. How many Scottish players deserve to be earning £3,000, £4,000, £5,000 a week? Yeah, there are some at Celtic. I don't think there's that many at Rangers – Former Dundee United manager **Jim McLean**, April 2004.

A bunch of those players are all fur coat and no knickers. The mindset isn't right, the attitude isn't right – Falkirk manager **John Hughes** after his side lost to Kilmarnock, January 2007.

One thing that's been hugely refreshing is the players. A totally different breed (from England). I am not talking about effort in training. I am talking about as people. Generally when you are dealing with players, regardless of whether they are young players or not, in England they have attitude. There's almost a naivety about the Scottish players, they are so honest it is really refreshing – Motherwell manager **Mark McGhee**, July 2007.

When I was a player and went into the dressing room the decibels increased, now I go into the dressing room and it's the opposite. It suddenly goes quiet – Hibs manager **Mixu Paatelainen**, March 2008.

(Henry) Makinwa was the highest paid at the club but was never, ever going to be good enough. He never scored a goal – Former Gretna manager **Davie Irons** as the club faced extinction, June 2008. The Nigerian striker failed to score in 14 appearances for Gretna.

JORG ALBERTZ

I had nothing personally against Jorg. With the ball at his feet he was one of the best players in the country and I told him that. But when he didn't have the ball he did nothing for us – Rangers manager **Dick Advocaat** on midfielder Albertz, September 2002. Advocaat sold Albertz to Hamburg in May 2001.

LORENZO AMORUSO

You might have thought Lorenzo Amoruso was a diddy as a player but we will miss him as a talking point. Whether linking himself with Manchester United or Juventus or bringing out a cookbook, he was always up to something –

Alan Ferguson, managing director of Glasgow sports sponsorship agency The Sports Business, August 2002.

Lorenzo is a proud man and a very kind man. He has a big heart and was one of the few players who would come up to my office and say, 'Merry Christmas, gaffer' every year. He would say the same to my wife. Little things like that show you the kind of person he is – Rangers manager **Dick Advocaat** on Amoruso, September 2002.

It was hard for me to play with Lorenzo. I know he was the big star and the hero for Rangers fans but it was hard to play with him because he is so unpredictable. I had the idea that he was playing for himself, not for Rangers, and that was annoying me and irritating me. It looked like it was a mistake by you but it was already caused by the player beside you – Former Rangers defender **Bert Konterman**, November 2003.

MARVIN ANDREWS

Not in a million years did I think he'd get to where he is now. He was just a big, raw defender at the time. His use of the ball didn't have to be brilliant in the First Division, he just had to defend the way he does now and attack everything – Aberdeen assistant boss **Jimmy Nicholl** on Rangers' Marvin Andrews, January 2005. Nicholl had been Andrews' boss at Raith Rovers.

ENRICO ANNONI

Although the fans never chanted my name I felt they were warming to me. They were too busy chanting, 'Rico, Rico' after he tried one of his 40-yard overhead kicks – Former Celtic midfielder **Craig Burley**, in Mark Guidi, *The Inner Sanctum*, 2008. The Italian defender was a fans' favourite at the time.

JIM BAXTER

He was incredible. He knew he was a good player and he let everybody else know he was a good player – Former Scotland midfielder **Archie Gemmill** on Baxter, June 2003.

CRAIG BELLAMY

He was going on about how much money he was on. Then he turned and said 'You will be doing my garden in the summer.' That is why he isn't liked – he just never shuts up. Let the football do the talking and he could shut anyone up, but dearie me, he was worse than my kids – Clyde defender **Darren Sheridan** after playing against Bellamy, February 2005.

If I was doing Craig Bellamy's lawn I'd bury him in it – Clyde defender **Darren Sheridan**, March 2005.

It's true that messages were received from Bellamy's phone but he got more than he bargained for from Alan Shearer. The text he sent to Kenneth was mildly upsetting but what he said to Shearer was insulting. It was along the lines that he was past it and his legs had gone and that he was going to come back here from Celtic. I can tell you there is no chance of that. Bellamy has taken on a hero in Alan and there is only one winner of that one. And it is not Bellamy. He has since claimed that he lost his phone. I suppose it was found by someone who knew Alan and Kenneth's numbers – Newcastle chairman **Freddy Shepherd** on text messages allegedly sent to Newcastle personnel by Celtic's on-loan striker Craig Bellamy during a trip to Ireland, April 2005.

EYAL BERKOVIC

Some of the players maybe weren't happy with Eyal Berkovic as a person, so then when he lost a 50-50 challenge that became a great big deal – Former Celtic coach **John Barnes**, in Graham McColl, The Head Bhoys, 2002.

HARALD BRATTBAKK

I can think of no finer gentleman in the game of football than Harald Brattbakk. He is intelligent, committed and dedicated but, like many others to come, he had substantial difficulty in coming to terms with the size and scale of Celtic – Former Celtic general manager **Jock Brown**, in Celtic-Minded: 510 Days In Paradise, 1999.

TOM BOYD

In my professional life I have been involved in hosts of such negotiations and I would rank Tom Boyd alongside many lawyers and experienced businessmen for the manner in which he represented his teammates, remaining courteous yet extremely forceful without ever being aggressive or offensive – Former Celtic general manager **Jock Brown** on contract talks, in Celtic-Minded: 510 Days In Paradise, 1999.

KRIS BOYD

If Boyd scores 30, 40 or 50 goals and we are good, that is okay. But I don't want Boyd to be judged just by goals. That is not enough – Rangers manager **Paul le Guen**, September 2006, in Graham Spiers, Paul le Guen: Enigma, 2007.

His record is very good, but could it be better? Could he be featuring in terms of more starts? Could he be sharper? Could he be pushing Walter to say, 'He's automatically in the team'? – Scotland assistant manager **Terry Butcher** on Boyd, the subject of speculation despite 25 goals in 25 starts for Rangers, May 2008.

He hardly moves, doesn't run, doesn't like doing anything, but put the ball in the box and he will score nine times out of 10. He's one of the best finishers I've seen but in terms of enthusiasm and work-rate he's probably the worst trainer — Manchester United's **Darren Fletcher** on Scotland teammate Boyd, *Soccer AM* TV show, October 2008.

I looked at Kris but he didn't show me enough in training to suggest he was going to go on and score. He didn't show me enough in training to give me the confidence to put him on. Other players showed me more — Scotland manager **George Burley** on his decision to leave Rangers striker Kris Boyd on the bench during the goalless draw in the World Cup qualifying game against Norway, October 2008. Boyd announced after the game that he wouldn't play for Scotland again under Burley.

TOMMY BURNS

Better footballers and managers may have passed through the gates of Celtic Park but there can't be anyone more loved — Monsignor **Tom Monaghan**, priest at Tommy Burns' local church, at his funeral service, May 2008.

For a guy who had specs as big as his, boy could he pass — Former Celtic teammate **Charlie Nicholas** on Tommy Burns, after his death in May 2008.

A football club closing is very sad. But a tragedy is Tommy Burns – Former Gretna coach **Andy Smith**, as Gretna folded, June 2008.

JORGE CADETE

He really did score goals for fun. But not much about Jorge's life, apart from that, appeared to be fun — Former Celtic general manager **Jock Brown** on striker Jorge Cadete, in book, *Celtic-Minded: 510 Days In Paradise*, 1999.

DAVIE COOPER

Unbelievably skilful — Dutch legend **Ruud Gullit** on former Rangers winger Davie Cooper, who he included in a magazine all-time 'Perfect XI', November 2007. Ronaldinho and Zinedine Zidane were among his substitutes.

CARLOS CUELLAR

We sat down with the supporters' assembly and they asked me had we had an offer for Cuellar and I said no but if we do get an offer we'll spend the money on new players. On the Friday night Carlos went to a supporters' do and told them he loved being at the club and the next day we get a phone call saying his agent is coming to Glasgow and wants to see us to talk about Carlos's sale. On the Monday Carlos tells Martin (Bain, Chief Executive) he wants to go and play in the Premiership — Rangers chairman **Sir David Murray**, August 2008.

RONALD de BOER

Ronald has the qualities to be one of the best players Rangers have ever had but he's not showing it in every game. I don't know why. When I signed him I felt he would do for the club what Brian Laudrup did in the 90s. It is not too late for him but he has to show it over a long period like Laudrup did – Rangers manager **Dick Advocaat**, September 2002.

PAOLO di CANIO

I'm not surprised by what's happened to any of the Three Amigos. What does surprise me is that there is somebody willing to pay you money to take trouble off your hands – Celtic managing director **Fergus McCann**, November 1998. 'The Three Amigos' were Di Canio, Jorge Cadete and Pierre van Hooijdonk.

As for di Canio, I have only one memory of him. Celtic were playing Hearts and won a penalty. Paolo took it and scored, and then got himself sent off before the game could be restarted. It summed him up – Celtic managing director **Fergus McCann**, November 1998. (The incident concerned was in November 1996, when di Canio scored and was then sent off by referee Stuart Dougal for scuffling with Steve Fulton.)

I wish I had taken this action some years ago and exposed di Canio and Pierre van Hooijdonk for the disreputable way they abused the backing of Celtic Football Club and the Celtic support by spreading false and damaging statements – Former Celtic Managing Director, **Fergus McCann**, announcing his plans to take legal action against former Parkhead favourite di Canio, October 2000.

As soon as I saw his name on the team-sheet, I knew that I would have my work cut out getting him through the game. He wasn't singled out in a bad way, but I knew that maybe I would have to have a wee chat with him a tackle or two earlier than I would if it was Paul McStay or Henrik Larsson. I needed to keep him on a shorter lead for his own good – Referee **Hugh Dallas**, March 2003.

While most players are fine if the game is going their way and their team is winning it wouldn't have mattered if Gazza and di Canio had scored hat-tricks. It only took an opponent to tug their sleeve and they would blow up. Other times, often when they were chopped down, they would get up and hug the culprit and beg you not to book him. I could never quite figure the pair of them out. Refereeing them was like handling a dangerous chemical and not knowing when exactly it was going to ignite – Former referee **Kenny Clark** on Old Firm pair Paul Gascoigne and Paolo di Canio, June 2008.

Di Canio would have been capable of becoming a truly great player at Manchester United. I mean, he was a great player. But when you have a player like Di Canio, who expresses himself as an individual, like (George) Best and (Eric) Cantona did, and (Ryan) Giggs, (Wayne) Rooney, Ronaldo and (Dimitar) Berbatov do . . . we make heroes quickly here. Di Canio could have been in that category – Manchester United manager **Sir Alex Ferguson**, October 2008.

CHRISTIAN DAILLY

He wouldn't get in my team unless the squad was wiped out by injuries. Walter (Smith) likes him because of his physical attributes but he managed to play for 90 minutes in Kaunas without making a tackle. He should have nailed (Rafael) Ledesma and (Pascal) Mendy in the first five minutes but didn't get near them all night. Also, if you can't pass the ball you should not be playing in the centre of midfield – Former Rangers striker **Mark Hateley** on Christian Dailly after the Champions League second qualifying round defeat to FK Kaunas, August 2008.

He used to go for a swim every morning at 8am, train, then spend the afternoon in the gym. He is the most dedicated player I have ever seen – Former Scotland teammate **Don Hutchison**, September 2008.

DAVID DUNN

He's got the hump with me but I can live with that. I've fallen out with people before. If he's pulling faces behind my back I can live with that, too. As long as he does the business for me – Blackburn manager **Graeme Souness** on David Dunn after he'd scored in the 2–1 win at Chelsea, February 2003.

ALEX FERGUSON

He was very astute – a bugger, but very astute – Falkirk manager **Willie Cunningham** on Ferguson, in Michael Crick, *The Boss: The Many Sides of Alex Ferguson*, 2002.

BARRY FERGUSON

If Barry wants his talents to be recognised far and wide, he has to leave Rangers. If he's happy and he wants to stay here he will still be a great player and maybe a top, top player, but he will not get the recognition – Rangers midfielder **Ronald de Boer**'s warning to Ferguson, July 2003.

I have a lot of respect for Ferguson as a player but sometimes his mouth engages before his brain. He made several comments last week that were contradictory – Former Scotland midfielder **Craig Burley** after Scotland's draw in Moldova, October 2004. Ferguson had criticised Burley for his comments about manager Berti Vogts.

He tried to have too much influence in different parts. When you have someone who undermines you, it is harder and harder. I know that it is a difficult decision to understand and I also know that I won't become the most popular guy in Glasgow by doing this. But I am on the inside and I know the heart of the problem. When I look in the mirror, at least I will be able to say, 'I am doing my job.' – Rangers manager **Paul le Guen** on the decision to drop Barry Ferguson and strip him of the club captaincy in January 2007, in Graham Spiers, *Paul le Guen: Enigma*, 2007.

If Barry Ferguson comes back to play for me, he will need to show another (attitude) and another way of behaving – **Paul le Guen**, in Graham Spiers, *Paul le Guen: Enigma*, 2007.

Barry Ferguson was a great player who came down from Glasgow Rangers for £7m. The funny thing about Barry's move was that I think he wanted to go home from minute one. You can call it homesickness or club sickness, whatever you like, but Barry seemed to want to go home straight away. He did, eventually, for £3m. Bang went £4m – Former Blackburn Rovers goalkeeper **Brad Friedel**, in *Thinking Outside The Box*, 2009.

DUNCAN FERGUSON

My enthusiasm for the game definitely waned when I was dealing with Duncan Ferguson, Andy McLaren and people like that. I told them when they were kids at Dundee United, 'I know the game means too much to me, but unfortunately it means f*** all to you. If I sent your wages home to your hoose you wouldn't even turn up for training or games.' – Former Dundee United manager **Jim McLean**, April 2004.

It takes into account the contradictions in him. He has an aggressive side, but there is a lyrical undertone to him, as the fact that he keeps pigeons shows – Finnish composer **Osmo Tapio Everton Raihala** on his 13–minute symphony 'Barlinnie Nine', written in honour of Duncan Ferguson, June 2005.

DARREN FLETCHER

Contrary to his Scottish-Irish roots, he's calm, but very determined. He's got this cold determination about him – Manchester United manager **Sir Alex Ferguson** on Fletcher, May 2004.

Whenever we hit a sticky patch and are going into a big game, he is one of the players I turn to and he responds like the cavalry – Manchester United manager **Sir Alex Ferguson** on Fletcher, October 2008.

PAUL GASCOIGNE

I know people have all sorts of thoughts about Paul, that's he's not so clever. Yes, he did some stupid things and, at the club, every morning you could expect something different from him. Whether it was his blond hair, the glasses or some of his unbelievable suits. But inside the dressing room he was loved by everybody – Former Rangers teammate **Brian Laudrup**, December 1999.

I can tell you his spell at Rangers was the most enjoyable of his career. I've produced a chart which backs this up. I've always thought that Walter Smith and Archie Knox let him away with murder, but he was shit scared of them. He was chucked out of Ibrox – sometimes physically – five times – Gascoigne's biographer, **Hunter Davies**, January 2004.

Coisty had his license taken off him for drink-driving and I lived closest to him. No, that's not true actually – Gazza lived closer but he couldn't be trusted to look after himself – Former Rangers midfielder **Derek McInnes**, April 2004, on a spell as McCoist's driver at Ibrox.

I can remember Gazza going on the television and saying, 'I am going to live with Archie Knox for six weeks and he's going to look after me and keep me under the thumb.' Stuff like that. It was a load of nonsense but I had flipping people coming round to the door, kids and that, asking, 'Is Gazza wanting a game of fitba'?' He was a lonely lad, a troubled lad, but one of the nicest and kindest guys you could have come across. If he could have played football 18 hours a day then he would have been fine – Blackburn Rovers assistant manager **Archie Knox**, August 2008.

ANDY GORAM

A daft laddie now and again, his own worst enemy, but great fun. In hotel corridors all throughout the world players are players and some would walk past you with their heads down and just ignore you, but never Andy. If he saw you in the street he would cross the street to you. It is his personality that makes him a good guy, not being a footballer – Scottish League secretary **Peter Donald**, on Andy Goram, in *Fanatical About Football*, ed. Jeff Connor, 2003.

RICHARD GOUGH

The first thing that struck me was Richard's firm handshake. A player being transferred can often be like a virginal bride on her wedding night, shy and unsure. Instead, Richard knew exactly what he wanted and quickly spelt out his terms – Former Tottenham chairman **Irving Scholar** on Richard Gough, in book, *Behind Closed Doors: Dreams & Nightmares At Spurs*, 1992.

It's a lot easier to rip the picture up than to paint it. I've spent my career ripping the picture up. I can kick the ball high into the stand and people say, 'Oh, great defending.' – Everton captain **Richard Gough**, 1999.

Richard Gough was another who took his captain's responsibilities seriously. At the coin toss, he would always say, 'Now, Mr Dallas, just you let me know if any of the Rangers players step out of line, and I'll deal with them.' And I would always reply, 'Yes, but who do I speak to when you step out of line?' – Former referee **Hugh Dallas**, March 2003.

A true leader and real warrior, the most professional player I ever met – **Brian Laudrup** on former Rangers' captain Richard Gough, naming him in *My Perfect XI*, March 2008.

GEORGE GRAHAM

I remember George. He was a bit of a poseur at first, a bit lazy when he played up front, the last one you could imagine going into management. Different now. He has poseurs for breakfast – **Frank McLintock**, captain of Arsenal's 1971 Double side, on George Graham, 1992.

If ever there was a player I felt definitely would not have what it took to be a manager it was George Graham. Running a nightclub? Yes. A football club? Absolutely not – **Don Howe**, Arsenal coach during Graham's playing days, 1999.

THOMAS GRAVESEN

I've never seen a player as happy on the bench as Gravesen, who spent more time high-fiving teammates than he ever did on the ball – Former Celtic midfielder **Craig Burley** on Parkhead midfielder Thomas Gravesen, March 2008.

ANDY GRAY

The player I most enjoyed watching was Joe Jordan. And also Andy Gray, they were my kind of football players. Gray would go for headers 18 inches above the ground, no matter whose feet were in the way. Absolutely fearless. Sport is about pushing yourself to extremes – First Minister **Jack McConnell**, September 2002.

ALAN HANSEN

I'm going to sue him eventually because he used to make me head all the balls. I don't know if you've heard but you lose all your brain cells every time the ball hits your head. If I get Alzheimer's in about ten years, I'm going to take civil action against him – Former Liverpool defender **Mark Lawrenson** on his Anfield teammate, 1999.

We don't really relate to people like (Alan) Hansen, who could play and think. We want someone who will welly their opponent. It's madness. Hansen was one of the best defenders in the world – Celtic manager **Gordon Strachan**, February 2008.

JOHN HARTSON

Before our five-a-side in training one day, John yelled, 'Let's have Wales v The Rest.' Someone shouted, 'But you're the only Welshman here.' He said, 'Yeah, me against you f****** lot.' That's him – Hartson's former manager at Luton, **Terry Westley**, 1997.

JOHN HUGHES

I've got you guys to thank for my football career because if youse didnae boo me as a centre forward and say 'Get that big useless bastard back to centre half', I wouldn't be where I am now – Falkirk player-manager **John Hughes** to supporters, in Fanatical About Football, ed. Jeff Connor, 2003.

ALAN HUTTON

He's like a runaway truck just now. It's like the wee comic book character who used to be my hero, 'Billy's Boots', who had a pair of boots on that would take him into the right position and take him past people – Scotland manager **Alex McLeish** on defender Alan Hutton after the Rangers fullback's successful Euro 2008 qualifying campaign, November 2007.

JIMMY JOHNSTONE

It was good to be able to give him a last embrace, because he was without doubt not only one of the best players in Scotland but also in the world – Portuguese legend **Eusebio**, May 2008, recalling seeing Johnstone shortly before his death in March 2006.

ROY KEANE

Having Roy Keane at Celtic was a considerable boost to the international image of the club. It was just a shame that he had to retire at the end of the season: it was a privilege to work with him – Celtic manager **Gordon Strachan** on signing Keane for Celtic, *My Life In Football*, 2006.

Roy was probably the biggest influence on my career. He would come down hard on me if I ever did anything wrong but he made me realise what it meant to be a Manchester United player. I can remember coming in from training one day and checking my mobile phone for text messages. Well, that was it. He absolutely hammered me, all the way into the gym. He was a great influence, really. If Roy had a go at you, he did it because he cared. He was the best captain you could wish for. He would tear you to shreds on the pitch if you gave away the ball. 'Get your effing touch right, effing this, effing that,' but, as soon as you got into the dressing room, it was over. He was a winner. I've met dedicated professionals but he had something else – Manchester United midfielder **Darren Fletcher**, March 2009.

PAUL LAMBERT

The supporters still love him. If you are asking for some players from the past, Paul Lambert is one of the heroes – Borussia Dortmund general manager **Michael Meier** on Paul Lambert, March 2003.

I found Paul an immensely likeable man in most respects, although remarkably opinionated and stubborn – Former Celtic general manager **Jock Brown** on midfielder Paul Lambert, in *Celtic-Minded: 510 Days In Paradise*, 1999.

'The Kaiser', they call him, the main man. He's the one, he's in charge. The talks in the huddle make the hairs on the back of your neck stand up when he goes for it. Because you could just see it, you could see the passion. It's a time of high emotion and the guys would get it together and it's quite a privileged moment for me to have been in the Celtic huddle. The first one I was in all I can remember is that he was so passionate and he was going on and on and I was thinking, 'This is amazing, man, this is deep stuff.' – Former Celtic striker **Ian Wright**, *BBC* TV programme, *Footballer's Lives*, March 2003.

He's got great courage on the field, great moral courage. Paul doesn't hide – Celtic manager **Martin O'Neill**, *BBC* TV programme, *Footballer's Lives*, March 2003.

HENRIK LARSSON

In moments like that you don't really decide what to do. It's when all your training kicks in and you go into automatic – Barcelona's ex-Celtic striker **Henrik Larsson**, July 2004, on his goal in the 6–2 win against Rangers in August 2000.

I don't think it hit Larsson at all. I don't know how he's getting the credit. Martyn (Corrigan) thinks he touched it, but they would probably give it to Henrik here if he was standing on the halfway line – Motherwell goalkeeper **Gordon Marshall** after the Swede had a late Celtic equaliser credited to him, March 2004.

I know there'll be tributes paid, and rightly so because he's been an unbelievable player at this club. But for now all I'd like to say is that the thing I'll miss about him most is him driving me to training every morning – Celtic teammate **Paul Lambert**, March 2004.

MAURICE MALPAS

When he retires true defenders will retire with him – Dundee United manager **Paul Sturrock** on defender Maurice Malpas after his record-breaking 613th appearance for the club agaist Motherwell, April 2000.

GARY McALLISTER

I tried to get him to Forest when he was at Leicester but I don't think he liked my sense of humour or my low opinion of his agent. Pity – he remains my sort of footballer. He treats the ball like a loved one, caressing it and not wanting to waste his time with it, he respects referees, looks after himself off the field and conducts himself well in the public eye – Former Nottingham Forest manager **Brian Clough** on McAllister, November 2001.

BRIAN McCLAIR

A fantastic footballer. You could say to Choccy, 'Go and play at right back,' and he'd say, 'Nothing surprises me about you.' He was so nonchalant, so temperamentally capable, that he could go and do it – Manchester United manager **Sir Alex Ferguson**, May 2008.

ALLY McCOIST

Coisty had a BMW Z3 but one day he turned up in a Proton which was strange. He got a flat tyre outside a pub and a guy stopped to help him, gave him his Proton car to get to training and told him when he got back from training his tyre would be fixed – Queen of the South defender (and McCoist's former Kilmarnock teammate) **Jim Lauchlan**, May 2008.

SCOTT McDONALD

He turned up like Paddington Bear at the station, although he was that big when I first saw him he could've been wearing four duffle coats – Former Motherwell manager **Terry Butcher**, March 2007, on the 'podgy little Aussie' who'd arrived at the club on trial three years before, after it was announced he'd join Celtic in the summer of 2007.

JAMES McFADDEN

My hero is now James McFadden. I just love his skinny-ma-link frame, pasty face, deprived-looking eyes, a throwback to all those jinky, weedy wingers Scotland used to produce who captivated my childhood. I like Faddy's utter confidence, on his own up front, with three thugs around him, yet always willing to take them all on, take the piss, and go for goal. I also like Scott Brown for the opposite reasons, for his brute determination rather than cocky skill. I smile at his shaven Neanderthal head and his Vinnie Jones scary glare – Author **Hunter Davies**, October 2007.

ANDY McLAREN

He makes Keith Richards look like he's led the life of Aled Jones – **Ally McCoist** on former Kilmarnock teammate McLaren, in *Tormented: The Andy McLaren Story* by Andy McLaren and Mark Guidi, 2007.

KENNY MILLER

All credit to Kenny and if he comes back he is welcome to run about like a headless chicken – Scotland striker **James McFadden** after the Scotland v France Euro 2008 qualifier, October 2006. Miller was suspended for the 1–0 win.

You can have any number of things going for you as a striker, but if you can't be relied upon to find the net then you're a bit like a joiner who can't saw – Former Celtic striker (and joiner) **Frank McGarvey** on then-Celtic striker Kenny Miller, December 2006.

He plays as though someone's chasing him with an axe – Anonymous Scottish journalist on Rangers striker **Kenny Miller**, February 2009.

CRAIG MOORE

I have a lot of respect for Craig Moore that he could play with Lorenzo

(Amoruso). Craig's a fantastic player, the best defender I played with at Rangers. Very underrated – Former Rangers defender **Bert Konterman**, November 2003.

SHUNSUKE NAKAMURA

He sees things before other players. There was a game last year against Kilmarnock at home and I expected Naka to play the ball to my feet but, instead, he played the ball in behind the defender. I never even realised that the ball was on but I ended up running behind him and I scored from it. Nobody else would have seen that – Celtic teammate **Aiden McGeady** on Nakamura, in Martin Greig, *The Zen of Nakamura*, 2008.

There's times when he has not done enough in big Champions League games. I suppose the question is, 'What level could he step up to?' I don't think it's an ability thing or a physical thing but he doesn't have the pace to get the better of players and get the ball in. For me, that is the only thing which is missing. I think he would get a game for the likes of Everton or Newcastle, a team in the middle tier of the Premiership – Former Celtic midfielder **Craig Burley** on Nakamura, in Martin Greig, *The Zen of Nakamura*, 2008.

He is a flat-track bully, only performing against the weaker teams. Now and again he strikes a good free kick, but so what? – Former Celtic midfielder **Craig Burley** on Shunsuke Nakamura, November 2008.

MARCO NEGRI

His character betrayed him a bit – AC Milan midfielder **Rino Gattuso** on former Rangers striker Marco Negri, March 2003. (The mysterious Negri scored 36 goals in 39 games in 1997–98 season.)

PHIL O'DONNELL

He was the nicest boy, husband, father, and friend you could ever meet. I am genuinely proud to have been his friend – Former Celtic striker **Darren Jackson** on former teammate, the late Phil O'Donnell, in Mark Guidi, *The Inner Sanctum*, 2008.

A quiet man whose death reduced the whole of Scottish football to silence – **Michael Grant**, *Sunday Herald*, on Motherwell captain Phil O'Donnell, December 2007.

He brought pleasure to a lot of people. What a great thing to be remembered for – Motherwell manager **Mark McGhee** on the O'Donnell tragedy, January 2008.

MIXU PAATELAINEN

I'm not at all surprised at how well Mixu is playing at the moment because I don't know if he'll ever get to an age where the pace of the game gets to him – A back-handed compliment to the 37-year-old St Johnstone striker from former Hibs teammate **Stuart Lovell**, August 2004.

DADO PRSO

When I looked in his eyes I liked what I saw. There was a bit of the warrior about him – Rangers manager **Alex McLeish** on Croatian striker Prso, May 2006.

FERNANDO RICKSEN

To do that when someone is not looking is the way of the coward – Former Rangers captain **Richard Gough** on Ricksen, March 2004, after the defender was banned for four games for elbowing Hibs' Derek Riordan in the CIS Cup semi-final the previous month.

After one minute he kicks a player into the stand. Three minutes later he does it again. Maybe it is good for him to see the tape again and he will see I was right – Former Rangers manager **Dick Advocaat** on Ricksen's Old Firm debut in August 2000 when Advocaat substituted him after 23 minutes, March 2005.

I wanted the best for Fernando, and the best thing for him seemed to me to be for him to get away from Rangers. No one was closing a door on him at Ibrox and I knew that not so long ago he had been a very good player for the club. It wasn't that I was angry with him. I was genuinely trying to help him – Rangers manager **Paul le Guen** on Ricksen, who'd been sent home from pre-season training in South Africa in 2006 and who never played for Rangers again, in Graham Spiers, *Paul le Guen: Enigma*, 2007.

DEREK RIORDAN

I'm supposed to have slept with his daughter or sister or punched him on the training ground but they are all a load of rubbish. There's nothing that I can think of I've done wrong to him. There's been no bust-ups. I don't know what his problem is with me – Celtic striker **Derek Riordan** on manager Gordon Strachan, April 2008. He left Celtic four months later.

FILIP SEBO

He was very good at kissing his badge. Every time Filip scored, he kissed his jersey or even threw it into the crowd – Austria Vienna financial director **Markus Kraetschmer**, in Graham Spiers, *Paul le Guen: Enigma*, 2007.

GORDON STRACHAN

He was always underrated as a player, you know; I'd always have him in my best half-dozen. Maybe higher – Former Coventry manager **Ron Atkinson** on Gordon Strachan, April 2009.

JAN VENNEGOOR OF HESSELINK

He's the dead horse Strachan continues to flog. His hold-up play yesterday was atrocious – Former Celtic midfielder **Craig Burley** on Celtic striker Jan Vennegoor of Hesselink after the Old Firm game which Rangers won 1–0, May 2009.

DAVID WEIR

If the young players get precious or get carried away with themselves, you only have to tell them to look at the humility of Davie Weir as a guy who has every right to shout and boast from the rooftops but instead continues to be an exemplary example – Scotland manager **Alex McLeish** on Davie Weir after the 37-year-old's Euro 2008 qualifying campaign, November 2007.

PLAYING ⚽

I was praising him for how well we'd done, and I had to say that this long-ball game suited some of the players. He took the real hump about that, too, and had a real go at me, claiming that he didn't play the long-ball game. He was the only one in Leicester who thought we didn't. But that's Martin. He wasn't devoid of tactics, but I still don't think he is the greatest tactician ever. He knows how to hold a team together, though – Leicester City Supporters Club chairman **Cliff Ginnetta** on former manager Martin O'Neill, in Alex Montgomery, *Martin O'Neill – The Biography*, 2003.

Do I miss playing football? No, not one little bit. Do I miss the lads and the dressing room? Yes – Former Celtic midfielder **Craig Burley**, in Mark Guidi, 'The Inner Sanctum', 2008.

Most of the lads on Premiership teams are all right – the bad ones have been pretty much weeded by the time they get to this level – but these guys are a particularly nice lot. You have to keep them on their toes, though. It can be hard to get the balance right, because some of them – like Williams, or McAllister or Telfer – have the inner voice, and others, like Huck and Salako, you have to keep on at them – Coventry City manager **Gordon Strachan**, in Rick Gekoski, *Staying Up: A Fan Behind The Scenes In The Premiership*, 1998.

I do it to get the blood warmed up. It started one day when I felt a wee bit sleepy. It was a bit warm and I thought, 'You have to wake yourself up here' – Aston Villa defender **Colin Calderwood** on his habit of slapping his face before matches, June 1999.

He loved wingers feeding a big centre forward and a variety of strikers playing off the main man. He had powerful defenders, too – Wycombe director **Alan Parry** on Martin O'Neill, in Alex Montgomery, *Martin O'Neill – The Biography*, 2003.

Windforce 12 and playing in front of 10 spectators and two chickens against Motherwell away – that would have driven me up the wall within four weeks – Former Rangers defender **Bert Konterman** on the end of his time at Ibrox, July 2003.

I think everybody acknowledges that the pitch that QPR put in 20 years ago was a disaster. We're the first club in the world to have this new surface down, which is the first to hold the full UEFA test certificate. They say it's better than grass. We had 18 months where, apart from against the Old Firm, we were unbeaten at East End Park. We do have a good home record. If we were to repeat that record for another 18 months, there will be some folk who will point the finger, but parks we've played on around Scotland in the winter have been horrendous. Some have been like ploughed fields, others like ice rinks – Dunfermline chairman **John Yorkston**'s defence of his side's synthetic surface, September 2003.

Good luck to Dunfermline. They'll win a lot of games on that pitch – Partick Thistle manager **Gerry Collins** after his side lost 2–1 on Dunfermline's synthetic surface, September 2003.

I've never seen a good game on that pitch. All the players were slipping all over the place – Dundee United manager **Ian McCall** after his side's 1–1 draw on Dunfermline's synthetic pitch, April 2004.

It's a load of shite and you may quote me on that – Dunfermline chairman **John Yorkston** on an SPL vote on his side's controversial plastic surface, December 2004.

Toward the end I thought about bringing on my subs, Torvill and Dean – Motherwell manager **Terry Butcher** offers further views on Dunfermline's plastic pitch after a 0–0 draw, March 2005.

I had this dream when I was a kid that I was going to play football for Scotland, rugby league for Great Britain, cricket for Yorkshire and football for Burnley. I knew I never would, but I dreamt it all the same – Tony Blair's former director of communications **Alastair Campbell**, January 2004.

Two stadiums in the one street is madness. Just look at the respective balance sheets of the clubs. Dens Park is a dive and Tannadice is on a ski slope – Former Celtic midfielder **Craig Burley**, April 2004.

Reporter: So, Gordon, in what areas do you think Middlesbrough were better than you today? Strachan: What areas? Mainly that big green one out there – Southampton manager **Gordon Strachan**, quoted in *FourFourTwo* magazine, July 2004.

He was as hyped up as any player I have ever seen in the first 10 minutes of that game. He gave the impression of looking upon it as a trial game that would decide his entire career. We had to shout at him to calm down – had he not done so, he would have blown up in a cloud of smoke or got sent off – Celtic manager **Gordon Strachan** on future captain Stephen McManus' July 2005 game against Motherwell in Strachan's first SPL game in charge, in autobiography, *Strachan: My Life In Football*, 2006.

That wasn't entertaining, it was all mistakes. If you want progression and want to go to a higher level, you need to get rid of those mistakes. I'm sure Terry will say they made a lot of mistakes themselves in letting us score. But I think there was one good goal there, with the guy cutting in with his left foot for Motherwell. The rest were kind of scruffy goals, not classic by any means – Celtic manager **Gordon Strachan** recalls the 4–4 draw at Motherwell on his SPL debut match, October 2005.

There is no sign of life in the home dressing room at Tannadice – Former Celtic midfielder **Craig Burley** on Dundee United as they prepared to sack manager Craig Brewster, October 2006.

My team will play with the ball on the ground, lots of passing, lots of movement, not kicking it up the park and hoping it lands at somebody's feet. My players will be aggressive when they have to be, although it's got to be controlled. That's my belief, pretty simple and straightforward. Wherever I end up managing, they'll get something different from what they've had in the past – **John Collins** outlines his football philosophy, October 2006. He was appointed Hibs manager four weeks later.

Tell us something we don't know about you?
I used to try and make myself sick before every game just to clear my throat. I would stick my fingers as far down as I could – Former Aston Villa and Celtic striker **Alan McInally**, newspaper questionnaire, October 2007.

It was not a good surface. It was so hard, and nobody wanted to play on it. Not even us – Stirling Albion director **John Smith** recalls the club's 1980s plastic pitch at previous home Annfield, November 2007.

> Now wi' the goal-tenders poncin' about
> No-one can touch them or they're up the spout
> They'll end up wi' lipstick and vanity bag
> The excitement has gone, now it's a drag

– Former Motherwell midfielder **Billy Hunter**, 'Long Ago The Goalie's Fear', from *Look Back In Amber & Claret*, collected in *100 Favourite Scottish Football Poems*, edited by Alistair Findlay, 2007.

All the ball companies in the world seem to be competing to see who can make it the most difficult for goalkeepers – Scotland goalkeeper **Craig Gordon** after being beaten by the Diadora ball hit by Nico Kranjcar in George Burley's first international against Croatia, March 2008.

I only get chucked on if we need a goal so he must think I can get him a goal but he obviously doesn't want me to do it unless he really has to because he doesn't want me to prove him wrong. He knows I would score quite a lot if he played me as much as he has played the other strikers but I don't think he wants proved wrong – Celtic striker **Derek Riordan** on manager Gordon Strachan, April 2008. He left Celtic four months later.

We were flying in the First Division and then, suddenly, the team was dismantled halfway through the season. I thought that was absolutely bizarre. We lost guys such as Stevie Tosh and Jamie McQuilken – guys who are still showing they can play at that level – Former Gretna manager **Davie Irons** looks back on managing the club as they faced extinction, June 2008.

With players nowadays we look after them well, we do everything for them when they're staying in five-star hotels. They have massive wages and everything is done on their behalf. How much do you care? You don't need to like everybody. This is your country – Scotland manager **George Burley** on Rangers' Kris Boyd's decision not to play for Scotland while Burley is manager, October 2008.

It seems to me they're never happy. They have all the money, get all the best players and win trophies as well. Now they don't even want us to tackle them. Are we supposed to sit back and allow them to walk all over us? – Kilmarnock assistant manager **Billy Brown**, November 2008. Celtic had been unhappy at Kilmarnock's treatment of midfielder Shunsuke Nakamura in the CIS Cup match the previous week.

I always have a laugh at the philosophy of some players when they say they like to play in the hole. There were no holes when I played, except at some of the old grounds. It's an imaginary area. It's players saying they don't want to have the responsibility of scoring goals but would like to sometimes; they don't want the responsibility of winning possession but claim they will be really effective if they are allowed to do what they want to do. It's a bit of a cop-out for me – Former Rangers striker **Kevin Drinkell**, January 2009.

Every game we play, I feel confident. At the moment, every attack fears our defence, and every defence fears our midfield and attack. That gives you confidence – Manchester United manager **Sir Alex Ferguson**, March 2009.

I can barely remember a single team talk from my days as a player. By that stage, my mind was on the game. I'm going to make my runs into the box count today. I'm going to time them right and I'm going to get on the end of crosses and I'm going to head one of them in. I'm going to score today. I have no idea what that guy in the middle of the room is saying to me right now – Former Celtic midfielder **Craig Burley**, May 2009.

PRESS

People from abroad are aghast at how some sections of the press operate in this country – Former Celtic general manager (and former TV commentator) **Jock Brown**, in *Celtic-Minded: 510 Days In Paradise*, 1999.

If it's kicking off I think the safest bet is just to turn and run. 'Cos either way, the headlines will be 'John Collins In Nightclub Brawl' – Everton's **John Collins**, January 1999.

At East Fife, it was always the same stupid headline: 'From Barca to Bayview' – Benfica executive director **Steve Archibald**, June 1999. The former Spurs and Aberdeen striker played for both clubs.

It's an amazing beast, the Scottish media, far more extreme than England. As well as the tabloids you have in England, there's the *Daily Record*, all the local papers, countless radio phone-in shows, various TV programmes, and they all live off football. So God help you if you're not looking when this juggernaut hits you – Motherwell chief executive **Pat Nevin**, March 2000. He subsequently enjoyed a successful career as a TV pundit and newspaper columnist.

I don't have a problem in here. I feel very comfortable. I don't know about anybody else – Celtic caretaker manager **Kenny Dalglish**, holding Celtic's pre-match press conference prior to an Old Firm game in 'Celtic-minded' Baird's Bar, Gallowgate, Glasgow, 24 March 2000.

Dalglish Staged His Press Conference In a Bar On Friday And Turned Out A Pub Team Yesterday – *The Sun* newspaper headline, March 2000. Rangers won the Old Firm game 4–0.

Vidar Riseth came to the press conference that day and I don't think it's a bad thing for them to see how much the people that come and stand on those terraces feel for the club. I didn't think it was such a bad thing for them to realise that. Maybe it was misguided – Former Celtic caretaker manager **Kenny Dalglish** reflects on the Baird's Bar episode, in DVD, 'The Official History of Celtic', 2008.

When I read the papers today, I thought Celtic were 12 points ahead and not us. My players wanted to get this result because of that – Rangers manager **Dick Advocaat** on the same game, March 2000. Celtic defender Johann Mjallby had claimed Celtic were a better team than Rangers in an interview published on the day of the match.

I have not knowingly told a lie to a journalist. If I don't want to speak about something I say I don't want to speak about it – Kilmarnock manager **Bobby Williamson**, February 2001.

When you go into print and criticise a player, you're also risking the relationship with their family. If I criticise my players, 'That bloody Beckham, that Keane, he's a bloody idiot, been sent off, I'm fed up with his behaviour, I'll sort him out,' that type of thing, the mother's not happy with that. The father, his brothers, his pals. You make enemies of people – Manchester United manager **Sir Alex Ferguson**, 2002.

This time next year I'll be dead and none of you will be at the funeral – I've already told my wife – **Jim McLean** says hello to his old press friends on resuming control of Dundee United, January 2002.

I'm no' f****** talking to you. He's a f****** great player. Youse are all f****** idiots – Manchester United manager **Sir Alex Ferguson** has a chat with the media over their criticism of Juan Veron, May 2002. He then threw journalists out of the club's training ground.

The praise I received was too extreme and the criticism I received was too extreme – Rangers director of football **Dick Advocaat** on press reaction to him, September 2002.

Kenny (Dalglish) came up and played in my testimonial, probably putting 20,000 on the gate, and I felt very grateful for that. Years later, he comes to work at Celtic and it all goes wrong, and as a journalist I have to offer criticism where criticism is due. What could I do? I either lose my credibility or I give an honest opinion. In the end, I'm sorry to say, it caused a fair bit of rancour between us – Former Celtic winger (and later newspaper columnist) **Davie Provan**, October 2002.

When I broke up with a girlfriend maybe two years ago, I was on the front page, just beside a guy who was killing his family or kids or whatever – Rangers defender **Lorenzo Amoruso**, November 2002.

I think that's a ridiculous question for you to ask me. I don't see anyone else in Scotland being asked why they pick some players and don't pick others. I pick the team and my record is reasonably all right. Paul Lambert is a big part of the side when he plays but I don't think that becomes an issue today after the way we played. If we had played poorly you might have a point but we were astonishingly brilliant – Celtic manager **Martin O'Neill** responds frostily to a question about the exclusion of Paul Lambert after losing 3–2 to Rangers, December 2002. BBC radio reporter Charlie Mann had posed the question.

Click here to read more on the Rangers management team's astonishingly brilliant first 12 months in charge – Rangers' club website has a bit of fun four days later, December 2002.

Britain's become nastier. Twenty years ago, all the nutcases were in one corner singing and shouting, the rest of us just got on and enjoyed the game. But watch any game now and examine the evidence. Whenever the ball goes out for a throw-in, there are people telling you you are a w*****. It's everywhere, lack of respect. The phone-ins, the letters, the e-mails, they're available to every halfwit. And the bigger halfwits print it – Southampton manager **Gordon Strachan**, January 2003.

I did consider taking him here to Glasgow, but I think now that the press would have made his life unbearable, just as Neil Lennon has found out a bit himself – Celtic manager **Martin O'Neill** on Stan Collymore, March 2003.

It's a shame because Scotland and Celtic's supporters don't really see the real Martin O'Neill. He's on his guard all the time, and he has to be, because of the media. At Leicester he would crack on in print, speak his mind, be humorous or sarcastic, and everything would be fine. Up here, though, and Martin knows it, things are written in a certain way, which is something he realised and responded to very quickly. For some reason, just about everyone up here seems to want to do someone else in. To gain what? I don't understand it – Celtic captain **Neil Lennon**, May 2003.

He was translating English into Italian and German and coming back with jokes and you couldn't help but admire him and how he had developed himself as a person through football. He showed that you don't have to be outspoken or zany to be a personality, just project yourself well and lighten the mood in a room. You sometimes want to shake these young Scottish boys when you see them mumbling away to the media – **Alan Ferguson**, managing director of Glasgow sports agency The Sports Business, on hearing German striker Jurgen Klinsmann handle the press, August 2003.

Everything was so overdone and so stupid in my opinion, but that's the Italian temperament for you. He had good PR via certain papers, that was his strong point – Former Rangers defender **Bert Konterman** on fellow defender Lorenzo Amoruso, November 2003.

One thing that gets me about my treatment is that I know the press, because I've dealt with the press for 23 years – in fact for almost all of my adult life. I think I know the press as well as anyone. So believe me, given the way many people in the media behave, the hypocrisy of my treatment wasn't lost on me for a second. If anything, amid a lot of hurt, it sometimes caused me a wry smile – Former Rangers striker **Ally McCoist** on newspaper coverage of his marital problems, November 2003.

The editor of *FourFourTwo* earns more than the geezer who works as football reporter on the *Aberdeen Hornet* because he's better – Birmingham midfielder **Robbie Savage** on Premiership wage caps, April 2004. (Charlie Allan of the Aberdeen Evening Express salutes you, Robbie.)

I am not the grumpy so-and-so you guys portray me to be. I only moaned at journalists because you guys always moan about football. You didn't want to be at Hibs. You'd all rather be at Parkhead and Ibrox – it was as simple as that – New Plymouth boss **Bobby Williamson** greets his old Scottish media pals, April 2004.

The press conference of today is a total waste of time. No one asks a question of any note. There are young guys sitting there, news agency guys, I don't know who they are, what they are or how they got there. Unknown quantities. The dailies and the Sundays, they say nothing. They don't ask a question. An absolute waste of time – Manchester United manager **Sir Alex Ferguson**, May 2004.

Without the example of the rock press, I believe no-one at *The Sun*'s sports desk would have ever dared come up with what may be the greatest headline of all time following Celtic's shock defeat by minnows Inverness Caledonian Thistle, or 'Cally', in the Scottish Cup: 'Super Cally Go Ballistic, Celtic Are Atrocious' – **Stuart Maconie**, in *Cider With Roadies, 2004.* (note: see 'Losing' section for more on this headline)

I don't socialise with them. I don't go for dinner with them, I don't go for drinks with them. There is a price to be paid for that. That doesn't bother me – Manchester United manager **Sir Alex Ferguson** on press relations, May 2004.

Different Klos – Motherwell manager **Terry Butcher** writes the headline after the Rangers' goalkeeper's excellent display in the 2–0 win over his side, October 2004.

There's also a yob culture in journalism, so that's what you've got to be wary of. With me, journalists have known for years what's serious and what's tongue-in-cheek, but the ones who are more mischievous than others would use the tongue-in-cheek stuff to cause havoc – Former Southampton manager **Gordon Strachan**, February 2005.

I remember someone saying that about Lee Chapman when I was at Leeds. 'The critics think he's poor.' 'What critics?' I asked, and he couldn't give any names. Eventually he said, 'Me' and I'm like, 'Why didn't you say that in the first place?' Anyway, reporters should be reporting, not offering opinions – Former Leeds manager **Gordon Strachan**, February 2005.

I think some of the personal bile that was directed at me was over the top. It didn't worry me because I know some of the journalists had personal agendas. I know some who actually lied in their articles, sometimes just to make a point and at other times, it seemed, for no other reason than to stretch out their piece to fill the space. But that kind of unpleasantness you put up with, because it's the football club that will either make the progress or not under the manager involved, regardless of what the press may write. And those particular reporters also didn't bother me because I know that, two miles south of Carlisle, nobody has ever heard of them – Former Celtic manager **Martin O'Neill**, June 2005.

I'm certain that if it had been any other player – and I don't just mean a Rangers player, but a Scottish player – the reaction would have been nothing like as bad. I do get an unfair press up here – Celtic captain **Neil Lennon**, October 2005, after being banned for three games for 'adopting an aggressive manner' towards the officials after being sent off by ref Stuart Dougal in the Old Firm game in August 2005.

I don't really understand why Celtic people buy some of the papers in Scotland, especially the *Record*. I don't even know whether any of the papers are left-wing, right-wing, blue, green or anything else but I get copies of cuttings about Celtic here and the *Record*, to me, they print lies, and they do everything they can to create trouble and create division between Celtic and Rangers. They like to create trouble within Celtic and they like to create trouble between Celtic and Rangers. I can't understand why anybody buys them – Majority shareholder **Dermot Desmond** to the Celtic Supporters Association, December 2005.

Well if the players go into it with the same attitude as you lot we won't get very f****** far – Scotland manager **Walter Smith** surveys a downcast and pessimistic Scottish media corps after the Euro 2008 qualifying draw in Montreux, Switzerland draw paired Scotland with France, Italy and Ukraine, January 2006.

I hear you are writing a book about me. You are crazy. You shouldn't bother – **Paul le Guen** fails to greet the news that journalist Graham Spiers is writing an analysis of his time at Rangers with unbridled joy, in Graham Spiers, *Paul le Guen: Enigma*, 2007.

The worst part is probably dealing with the media. It just takes up so much time. There's press conferences before and after matches. There will be three radio stations and four TV channels all wanting separate interviews yet all asking the same questions – Hibs manager **John Collins**, March 2007.

This is Andy from *FourFourTwo*. He was in Lisbon watching Manchester United on Wednesday night and tomorrow he'll be at Old Trafford to see Chelsea. In between, he's come here to see some quality football – Elgin City manager **Robbie Williamson** introduces journalist Andy Mitten to his team, September 2007. Elgin were bottom of Division Three at the time.

189

You people are sometimes like those serial killers you see in films who send out these horrible messages. The serial killer who cuts out the words 'I am going to get you' or 'Your wife is next'. You are the very same – Celtic manager **Gordon Strachan** addresses the media, November 2007, accusing them of 'playing on players' naiveté'.

There are some excellent journalists, honest journalists, and respected journalists. But the media has become a monster. They know all the answers, right and wrong. They want exclusive stories and confidential background. They want their cards marked. They want gossip. And believe me, if they don't get it, you're in trouble – Manchester United manager **Sir Alex Ferguson**, in Daniel Taylor, *This Is The One: The Uncut Story Of A Football Genius*, 2007.

I have researched the subject and my belief is that people with low self-esteem attack those who are more confident – SFA chief executive **Gordon Smith** on his critics, March 2008.

It's come from somewhere, and it's not just going to be made up. Unless it has been – Scotland midfielder **Darren Fletcher** on suggestions members of the national squad were unhappy with manager George Burley after the defeat in Macedonia, September 2008.

I've not spoken to him. I don't think I ever will. He has wanted to be a sports journalist since he was 14 or 15. But I think he realises that even sports journalists get a bit of stick – Celtic manager **Gordon Strachan** on reports his son Gavin is training to be a football journalist, September 2008.

The papers are a nightmare. They have all this space to fill, they're under pressure from TV and the internet, the journalists are on short-term contracts and worried for their future but so much of what they write is just rubbish. I tell you, the press in our country are a real problem. They do real damage – Manchester United manager **Sir Alex Ferguson**, March 2009.

I literally don't read it. See when you actually go without papers at first it's like missing a drug, but then after a wee while it gets easier. Now it's fine. It's the same with sports programmes. I watch *Sky*, but not the Scottish sports programmes – Celtic manager **Gordon Strachan**, May 2009.

Journalists brace themselves and start slugging hi-energy drinks when Laszlo walks into the room after games, knowing that entire new species are about to form in the time it takes him to meander through all aspects of the human condition – Journalist **Graham Spiers** on loquacious Hearts manager Csaba Laszlo, May 2009.

PRESSURE ⚽

I've done things I'm not proud of but the temper is exaggerated. It's good to let the pressure out of your system. I don't believe in this English thing of not complaining – Manchester United manager **Alex Ferguson**, August 1995.

Eight new signings arrived that summer, and it was as if they'd signed on the Thursday, trained on the Friday and been told to stop 10 in a row on the Saturday. We had a Dutch manager nobody had heard of and a commentator as a general manager. And we had 50,000 unhappy fans. Stop Rangers winning the league? Yeah, no problem! – Former Celtic midfielder **Craig Burley** looks back on the 1997–98 season, in Mark Guidi, *The Inner Sanctum*, 2008.

It won't be the meaning of life, more Rab C Nesbitt, the Scottish philosopher – Coventry manager **Gordon Strachan**, May 2001, as his side faced attempting to avoid relegation on the final day for the 11th time in 33 years. They lost 3–2 at Aston Villa and went down.

Looking back, I really wish I had enjoyed those times more than I did. After a win it was always the next game. That was the pressure I put myself under – Former Dundee United manager **Jim McLean**, October 2002.

You need the skin of a rhinoceros if you're Scotland manager – Former national coach **Craig Brown**, in *Fanatical About Football*, ed. Jeff Connor, 2003.

I am proud I survived at Rangers. I coped with all kinds of criticism and it has made me stronger. If I had not been able to cope with all that, I would have been in a nuthouse now – Former Rangers defender **Bert Konterman**, July 2003.

Irritation can add up. One day you punch Alex (McLeish) maybe, or you say something bad in the papers. It is not worth it. It is time to leave – Former Rangers defender **Bert Konterman**, on his decision to quit Ibrox, November 2003.

I told him all about the pressure. He said, 'Put the blinkers on and get tunnel vision. Don't let people into your space if you don't want them there. Don't be distracted. Do your job.' From that moment on, I did. It's an obvious thing to say, but it's one of those moments when someone you respect says something which makes perfect sense – Former Labour Party director of communications **Alastair Campbell** on Sir Alex Ferguson, January 2004.

When I came to Celtic I knew there might be trouble. I said to Garry (Pendrey), my assistant, 'You know, we might take a right few good slaps on the chops before we get it right.' So I always knew at Celtic there might be a time to get the seatbelts on – Celtic manager **Gordon Strachan** after winning two SPL titles in succession, June 2007.

Sometimes when you've got people behaving like that you're better to ignore it – Celtic manager **Gordon Strachan** on striker Scott McDonald's angry reaction to being substituted during the 1–0 defeat by Motherwell at Parkhead, April 2008.

Don't give me all this living the dream rubbish. It was a nightmare for other clubs – Airdrie chairman **Jim Ballantyne** on Gretna, May 2008.

RANGERS ⚽

No other experience in nearly forty years as a professional player and manager has created a scar comparable with that left by the treatment I received at Rangers – Manchester United manager **Sir Alex Ferguson**, *Managing My Life*, 2000.

It is to these tykes, hooligans, louts and drunkards that I pinpoint my message. It is because of your gutter-rat behaviour that we are being publicly tarred and feathered – Rangers manager **Willie Waddell** addresses his club's fans, August 1972, after his side had been banned from defending the European Cup-Winners' Cup they'd won in Barcelona three months previously, in Graham Spiers, *Paul le Guen: Enigma*, 2007.

When I was playing for Rangers, before a game Graeme Souness wouldn't really give us any instructions. He would just say, 'What's the use of giving you tactics? I've bought you, you're the best players in the land. You're playing against players who aren't as good as you. All I'm asking is for you to go and play.' – Former Rangers striker **Andy Gray**, in *Flat Back Four: The Tactical Game*, by Andy Gray and Jim Drewett, 2003.

Everything around the club was so professional but not so professional, not so clinical, as say, Bayern Munich. It was more of a special atmosphere where you had older women, who had worked in the kitchen for 40 years with their daughters. It was like a family in a way and that's very unique today – **Brian Laudrup** on Rangers, December 1999.

An orange away strip? Come on. If they're really serious about trying to rid the place of sectarianism do you think they'd play in an orange strip? I can see how it makes commercial success for Rangers but at best you have to say it is insensitive – Radio Clyde pundit **Davie Provan**, October 2002.

That story was ridiculous. I was asked to open an event at my local golf club and agreed only when I knew I wasn't needed elsewhere. Yet a year and a half on some people still go on about it – Dundee United striker **Billy Dodds**,

February 2003, on stories about him playing golf while Rangers were chasing the 2001–02 title.

What do I want to sell the stadium for? That's part of the history of the club. If I was to do that, I'd be open to being criticised and I'd deserve it. I've no intention of selling anything – Rangers chairman **David Murray**, January 2004.

When and where were you happiest, as a player, as a person?
As a player I loved being at Rangers, everything to do with it – **Paul Gascoigne** answering questionnaire in *Gazza: My Story*, 2004.

I thought Rangers was about winning games, not doing Frank de Boer a favour – Rangers defender **Henning Berg** alleging he'd been dropped by Rangers to accommodate de Boer's hopes of playing in Euro 2004, March 2004.

It was a mistake to pay £12m for Tore Andre Flo although that was the going rate at that moment – Former Rangers manager **Dick Advocaat**, September 2002.

The pressure and expectation was too much for Tore Andre – Rangers chairman **David Murray** on £12m signing Tore Andre Flo, January 2004.

The best example of the wasted money, which now limits the team in terms of the debt, is obvious. Either back then or since, I never met anyone who felt that Tore Andre Flo was worth £12m – Former Rangers vice-chairman **Donald Findlay**, March 2004.

Even at the time he was purchased, I had some concerns about spending £12.2m. I felt that was, erm, really the culmination of the absurdity of the situation that Rangers got into as a club in trying to compete on a European stage. Yes, I think there was a level of absurdity which I think has been recognised within the club. I think Flo really was the pinnacle of the point where people thought, 'This is daft. It's got to stop.' – Rangers backer **Dave King**, who invested £20m in the club in 2000, on the signing of Tore Andre Flo, October 2004.

When you have a price tag like that it's very difficult. I think it would have been much more enjoyable at Ibrox for me if the price tag had been a lot less. It made the pressure much, much more. The £12m was always over me – **Tore Andre Flo** reflects, January 2009. The striker, by then 35, had come out of retirement – during which he finished second in the Norwegian TV equivalent of *Strictly Come Dancing, Skal Vi Danse* (Shall We Dance) – to play for MK Dons.

I tried to emphasise to them that this is their chance to stand up and be counted and become great players for Rangers in the future if they feel they're up to the task. Because please believe me, I told them after here it's the English Championship. No disrespect, but I did say it's Bristol Rovers and places like that – Chairman **David Murray** explains future job prospects to the Rangers players after losing to St Johnstone in the CIS Cup, November 2006.

When I was leaving Rangers, what I did say to Ian about Paul le Guen coming was, 'Look, maybe you have to be careful. Maybe you can't be the big cheese around here anymore. You'll have to give Paul his place and take a step back.' But whether Ian took that advice or not, I really don't know – Former manager **Alex McLeish** on Rangers doctor Ian McGuinness, who was frozen out under le Guen, in Graham Spiers, *Paul le Guen: Enigma*, 2007.

Part of the squad turned up Thursday morning, thinking there was training, and the other half were sat comfortably at home. Clearly, half of the players knew it was cancelled, and the other half didn't. Let's just say it was a bit strange – Midfielder **Brahim Hemdani** on life at Rangers on the day after Paul le Guen quit, January 2007.

I don't want this situation to be held against him. I had my own problems at Everton and Davie Moyes came in and handled them better. If I handle this better, it should be no reflection on Paul le Guen – New Rangers manager **Walter Smith** on le Guen's time at Rangers, in Graham Spiers, *Paul le Guen: Enigma*, 2007.

This is no small minority of Rangers supporters, and nor are Greater Manchester Police renowned for their truncheon-wielding brutality. Instead, this is a football club with a poison somewhere at its core – Journalist **Graham Spiers**, *The Times*, after the UEFA Cup Final riots in Manchester, May 2008.

In Scotland I'm more fond of Glasgow Rangers – not Celtic – and there was also a great winger played for them, and who is still alive today, Willie Henderson – Portuguese legend **Eusebio**, May 2008.

We were all ready to go. Donald (Wilson, business associate) had negotiated it for months with complete confidentiality. Everything was pretty much agreed and then I said, 'Look, gentleman, before we do this, can you tell me how you're going to run this club?' I'm sitting there with all the legal documents in front of me and they outline their plans: 'We'll carve this up and we'll sell that off' and after a while I said, 'Enough, we're not doing the deal.' We got up and walked out – Rangers chairman **Sir David Murray** reveals he came close to selling the club in 2007, August 2008.

He'll know when it's right to move on. He's very much aware of the traditions of Glasgow Rangers. He will want to be certain whoever he passes it on to is the right person to maintain them, not just the one with the deepest pockets – Former Rangers manager **Graeme Souness** on Sir David Murray, November 2008, as the Ibrox chairman celebrated 20 years at the club.

Pedro Mendes isn't half the player Rangers fans think he is. Kyle Lafferty is way out of his depth. John Fleck is a child who could still be at school and can't be relied upon. Kenny Miller will never score enough goals on a regular basis to win any team a championship title. Davie Weir getting a new 12–month contract after his 39th birthday in May will sicken the club's supporters. Barry Ferguson isn't yet close to being the dominating figure he used to be. Do I really need to go on? – *The Sun* newspaper columnist **John Hartson**, after Rangers had lost at home to Inverness in the SPL, March 2009. They won the SPL two months later.

REAL LIFE ⚽

When I worked as a toolmaker in the middle of winter, I remember touching the steel first thing in the morning. It's absolutely freezing. You can burn yourself it's so bloody cold. And yet these people built the best ships in the world. You can over-romanticise these things, but they do have a real part to play in forging a person's character – Manchester United manager, and former Remington Rand typewriter factory worker, **Sir Alex Ferguson**, October 2008.

Gordon wasn't the confident character that we all perceived back then. He put up a show but deep down there was self-doubt. He could be very nervous at times and the front that he put up was just to dispel that side of him – Former Aberdeen teammate **Willie Miller** on Gordon Strachan, in *Gordon Strachan: The Biography*, Leo Moynihan, 2004.

I remember (Jock) Stein saying something I think was fantastic. We were driving to Glasgow during the miners' strike (in the mid-1980s) and they were shipping coal in from Belgium, these scab drivers. Big Jock stopped them. He looked at them, and said, 'I hope you're proud of yourselves. You're doing people out of a living.' None of them said a word. Then he said to me, 'This is an absolute bloody disgrace. You go down that pit shaft, a mile underground. You can't see a thing. The guy next to you, you don't know who he is. Yet he is the best friend you will ever have.' – Manchester United manager **Sir Alex Ferguson**, October 2008.

I phoned my then girlfriend Arlene and met her in Glasgow city centre. I broke my heart crying. We walked around for ages in a daze. I couldn't stop crying. And just to top off the worst day of my life, my car had been taken away and towed to the pound. I'd not put enough money in the meter – Former Celtic striker **Darren Jackson** recalls being told he needed a brain operation a month after signing for the club, in Mark Guidi, *The Inner Sanctum*, 2008.

After the game he went over to the disabled section, took off his jersey and gave it to one of the Celtic fans in there. I just thought, with all the emotion going on around that game, to have the presence of mind to know he was going to do that after the game – it just sums the guy up – Former Celtic assistant manager **Murdo MacLeod** on midfielder Paul Lambert giving his jersey to Celtic fan Martin Gilbride after scoring his first goal in an Old Firm game in January 1998, in *BBC* programme, *Footballer's Lives*, March 2003.

It's with me throughout my day and I go to bed thinking about it every night. I can be driving down the road, see a group of boys, recognise his swagger and feel sure it's him – Huddersfield worldwide scout **Lou Macari**, January 2000, on the suicide of his 19-year-old son Jonathan in April 1999.

I'm allowed to hang my washing on Glasgow Green, which is an interesting one. And if I ever get arrested in the city, I'm entitled to my own cell, which could come in handy at some point – Manchester United manager **Sir Alex Ferguson** on being made a Freeman of Glasgow, 1999.

In a previous life, if I did something fairly innovative, say creating 200 jobs, I'd give a press conference and maybe three people would turn up. But if you sign a player from Queen of the South, 35 appear. There's no logic – Motherwell owner **John Boyle**, October 1999.

To actually, at one point in time, find yourself seriously contemplating ending your life is a remarkable experience to go through – Former Rangers vice-chairman **Donald Findlay**, October 1999. Findlay had fallen into depression after quitting his Ibrox post when he was caught singing 'The Sash' after Rangers had beaten Celtic in the Scottish Cup Final in May 1999.

In my entire time at Celtic I never once dined at the home of any club official or employee, nor did they with me – Former Celtic General Manager **Jock Brown**, in book, *Celtic-Minded: 510 Days In Paradise*, 1999.

I couldn't take any more of Tom Hendrie. I have a lot of time for the guy but he's hard work. I mean, my dad was a schoolteacher for 40 years but not one like Mr Hendrie – Morton manager **Ian McCall** after being sent to the stand for arguing with the St Mirren boss in a stormy Renfrewshire derby (12 bookings, one sending-off), March 2000.

I've lived in about four different homes but I feel like I've spent most of my life in a car – Former Airdrie striker **Peter Duffield**, by then at his 13th club, Darlington, May 2000.

Some journalist asked me, 'Have you spoken to the Celtic lads about the Treble yet?' Well, no. One guy's had bloody cancer, another (Morten Wieghorst) almost died. There are more important things – Former Celtic midfielder **Craig Burley**, April 2001.

He was in a very, very big hole when he left Reading so to see him get a

Scotland cap a year later was incredible. If you had seen how low he was then you would realise that this is as big a fairytale as you'll get in football – Reading manager **Alan Pardew** on Andy McLaren, who'd been treated for drink and drug problems, January 2002.

Every time I dropped him or gave him a rollicking, he used to moan, 'I'm wasting my time here. I might as well go back to university.' – Former Nottingham Forest manager **Brian Clough** on Martin O'Neill, February 2002.

I've told him I'm against this war, absolutely. He told me to calm down – Manchester United manager **Sir Alex Ferguson** on exchanges with Labour Party director of communications Alastair Campbell, 2002.

I played a lot of football but never thought of being a professional. I had it more in my mind to be a carpenter or a park ranger – Rangers defender **Bert Konterman**, October 2002.

The yob culture is affecting our children. There's yob television, yob newspapers, yob radio stations, and that scares me. I'd be old-fashioned about it in a bid to stamp it out. I'd bring back the belt in schools, have national service and the rest of it. More discipline is needed in the schools and in the home – Southampton manager **Gordon Strachan**, January 2003.

There's a famous phrase. Lord Birkenhead (who was part of the British negotiating team) said to Collins, 'I may have just signed my political death warrant,' when he put pen to the agreement, to which Collins replied, 'I may have signed my actual death warrant.' In the Irish Civil War which followed, Collins was killed – Celtic manager **Martin O'Neill**, visiting Irish revolutionary leader Michael Collins' London house, March 2003.

Within a week of coming down here he took his two daughters to the cornfield where they (lovers Michael Gregsten and Valerie Storie) were in the car, and he retraced the steps and drove all the way up the A6. He was so obsessed with it he even went to see the judge who'd presided over the case. Martin probably knows as much, if not more, about the Hanratty trial than anyone. He went to the Fred West trial too, and visited many other murder scenes in the area – Wycombe director **Alan Parry** on Martin O'Neill's fascination with crime, in Alex Montgomery, 'Martin O'Neill – The Biography', 2003. (James Hanratty was hanged for the murder of Gregsten in April 1962, protesting his innocence. But DNA from his exhumed body in 2001 matched samples from the crime scene.)

When we were going for promotion from the Second Division in the spring of 1982, we were playing Barnsley in an evening game. During lunch in Sheffield, he said to me, 'Micky, come on, we're going.' 'Where?' I said. 'We're going to the Ripper's house.' 'Are we bollocks, I'm going to put my feet up.' But I'm sure he went anyway – Former Norwich teammate **Mick McGuire** on more crime drama with O'Neill, in Alex Montgomery, *Martin O'Neill – The Biography*, 2003.

It scares me to think of a time when I am not playing. I might be financially secure, have a nice family and stuff, but what am I going to do? It is very frightening. I need something to get up for in the morning. What am I going to be when I finish as a footballer? I haven't got an answer right now – Former Scotland international **Scot Gemmill**, March 2003.

If you look around my house, you willnae see mementoes of a football career, except one. I've a photograph of me scoring a goal, but it's not the fact that I scored that means so much to me as the people who are with me, friends having a great laugh together – Southampton manager **Gordon Strachan**, April 2003.

Since my time at Rangers, I have changed as a person. I don't trust everyone anymore. Even my wife says I have become harder. I am not proud to say that. As a player you have to put up an act as well. That is football. It's all about being macho, flash cars, women – Former Rangers defender **Bert Konterman**, July 2003.

He sailed through the war against Iraq on a sea of lies and the name of his ship was the HMS Mendacity – Dundee director **Giovanni di Stefano** on Tony Blair, August 2003.

Arsenal went to Iran in 1974 to play a tournament and we met the Shah of Persia. Then when I was with Rangers we got knocked out of the Cup by Dundee and the club went on a tour of Iraq in December. We stayed in Baghdad during their war with Iran and at 11 o'clock at night you'd hear the air raid sirens going off. We met Saddam Hussein and he told us that the Iranians were the aggressors and Iraqis were peace-loving. Then he gave us a gold pen to take home. But for me meeting Kenny Rogers was the ultimate – Kilmarnock general manager **Davie MacKinnon**'s meetings with remarkable men, November 2003.

I'd be proud if my kids can be brought up without knowing the word 'racism'. That would mean they had never come across it – Ayr United goalkeeper **Ludovic Roy**, who has a white mother and black father, November 2003.

I'm telling people every day they're going to jail and that there's nothing I'll be able to do to prevent that fate. If I can do that, I think I can tell a footballer to get off a park – Referee and lawyer **Kenny Clark** before his ninth Old Firm game, March 2004.

I don't like to get my car dirty, but Henrik's? I'm not kidding, there's everything in there. You have to wipe your feet getting out – Former Celtic midfielder **Paul Lambert** on former teammate Henrik Larsson, March 2004.

Most players now come into football from school and never realise what the real world is about. Then all of a sudden they get released because they are not good enough, big enough or fast enough and the real world hits them and hits them hard – Former Dundee United manager **Jim McLean**, April 2004.

Nobody died. If you want angst, go to Iraq or Africa. I'll take them to Romania and show them children I am trying to look after, children who are dying of Aids. Upsetting stuff for me is children being bundled up, and left abandoned in our orphanage in Bucharest. That is upsetting. Upsetting is not going to a football match – Motherwell owner **John Boyle**, May 2004, on the criticism of him over the club going into interim administration in April 2002.

This club is in my soul now. My specialist says this has put years on my life. I'd probably have ended up croaking if I hadn't come to Gretna – Club owner **Brooks Mileson**, February 2006. He died in November 2008.

I've been a lawyer for 22 years. A lot of my clients want to talk about football rather than their case. I went to see a client at Greenock Prison who was on an attempted murder charge and the first thing he said was that I cost him a packet of fags because of a penalty I'd given in a game – Criminal defence lawyer and ref **Kenny Clark**, March 2006.

This is easy. I'm a guy who's been to Auschwitz this morning, so don't give me any of that – Manager **Gordon Strachan** puts Celtic's 2–0 pre-season defeat to Poles Wisla Krakow in perspective, July 2006.

My daughter Amy starts her standard grades next week so when I think I am under pressure I think of her. It's all new to her and it's such a frightening experience. I remember myself thinking that those exams were all that mattered in the world – Gretna caretaker boss **Davie Irons** as his side faced the final-day game at Ross County which would decide if they reached the SPL, April 2007. Gretna won 3–2 and went up.

In my other investments I can do a business plan and take it on quite nicely, but in football, well, the ball hits the bar, that's you down the tube – St Johnstone chairman **Geoff Brown**, April 2007.

On some radio phone-in you might hear some guy shouting down the line about me, but up here it could be some ned with his tracksuit on sitting with his devil-dog and a can of lager shouting down the line. Don't get me started on yob society and manners. I hate it, it really offends me. Even little things like someone in the street shouting, 'Haw, Strachan!' I'll say, 'Excuse me, were you at school with me, were you my teacher? It's Mr Strachan, or my name is Gordon.' I hate the way yobs have taken over the country. I'll vote for anyone who can make my streets safe for me and my family. Never mind wars and all the rest of it, if any politician can answer the question, 'Can you make my street safe for me and my family without getting abused or attacked?' that'll do me — Celtic manager **Gordon Strachan**, June 2007.

I sat on my own one night and made a list of the possible ways to go. I thought about jumping off a building, but I'm scared of heights. Hanging myself was scored off because I didn't know how to tie a noose. I considered overdosing on paracetamol, but I looked into that and found out it could take five days to die and I didn't want a slow death. So having a car smash and making it look like an accident seemed the best way forward for all concerned. I thought it would be quick and painless. I dropped Claire off in Edinburgh and decided on the way back that I was going to do it. I was motoring along in auto-pilot fashion at about 80 miles per hour and had chosen my 'victim'. There was a massive lorry alongside me, the type with huge wheels and a luminous 'Long Vehicle' sign, and I thought that it would be perfect to go into. Belting along the motorway at that speed, I thought I'd have no chance of survival. I just wanted to drive under its wheels and be smashed to a pulp. I felt as though I'd had a shite life and f*** everybody else . . . Twice my legs went for it, pressing down on the accelerator to batter my car into the lorry, but my arms wouldn't turn the steering wheel — Morton striker **Andy McLaren** on thoughts of suicide in April 2006, in *Tormented: The Andy McLaren Story* by Andy McLaren and Mark Guidi, 2007.

I couldn't even tell you who scored in the game. Not for us and not for them — Motherwell defender **Stephen Craigan**, January 2008, on the 5–3 win over Dundee United on December 29, 2007. Motherwell captain Phil O'Donnell collapsed during the match and subsequently died of heart failure.

I opened the curtains and the window and I was just lying there at 3am still getting texts from people from the club who were awake too, saying they couldn't sleep, they couldn't believe what had happened — Motherwell manager **Mark McGhee** on the O'Donnell tragedy, January 2008.

I got a letter from a guy who said, 'You are the greatest thing that ever happened to Dundee United, my daughter is a United fan, she's nuts about you. She met you and it was the greatest thing in her life.' So it went on. Then, at the very bottom, 'by the way, I am a funeral director and if you need anything . . .' I am serious, that's the letter, somebody in Fife — Gallows humour from Dundee United owner **Eddie Thompson**, who was battling cancer at the time, March 2008. He died in October 2008.

It can get pretty rough in Iraq. Especially when the Old Firm is on — **Garry McNally**, Scots Guards, army recruiting poster, March 2008.

You could go from kicking lumps out of each other on the pitch to being friends, and I miss him as badly as I've ever missed anyone. I'm not thinking about football just now, it's a distant second – Celtic manager **Gordon Strachan** after the death of coach Tommy Burns, May 2008.

Jose Mourinho used to call himself the 'Special One'. If he was in the East End of Glasgow today he'd have seen who the real special one was – **Tommy Burns'** close friend Gerry Collins on the day of Burns' funeral, May 2008.

This clapped-out van was originally to take us to training but things got so bad we went to games in it. Me and a young boy put the kit in it. Against Hibs at Easter Road, the team went through with the gear in the Blue Bomber, as it was called. And it wouldn't start off the key. We went into the car park at Easter Road and we'd to park on a slope to get it to start. I'd to ask people after the game to clear the way because once we got it rolling, we couldn't stop it! Looking back it's embarrassing but it was the making of us. People are running about in Mercs and Porsches and here's a full-time club running about in the Blue Bomber – Queen of the South coach **Stevie Morrison** recalls troubled times as Clydebank coach, before the Scottish Cup Final, May 2008.

It might be the Scottish Cup Final, but you still need to get the messages – Queen of the South captain **Jim Thomson**, on going shopping in Tesco the day after scoring in the Scottish Cup Final against Rangers, May 2008.

There's too many examples of people who retire and are in their box soon after. Because you're taking away the very thing that makes you alive, that keeps you alive. I remember my dad had his 65th birthday and the Fairfields shipyard gave him a dinner in Glasgow with 400 people there. It was a big night for my dad. I was in Aberdeen and came down for it on a Friday. The next week my mother phones and said, 'Your dad's going in for an x-ray, he has pains in his chest.' I said, 'It'll be emotion'. Well, it was cancer. A week. One week – Manchester United manager **Sir Alex Ferguson** after announcing he wouldn't be staying as manager for more than another three years, May 2008.

I was handcuffed and taken to the cells at the police station at Aikenhead Road, a couple of hundred yards from Hampden. I was put into a cell with another dozen or so guys already in it. I sat with my head down, trying to make sense of it all. Another prisoner, full of drugs, lay on the floor beside me. I was the first person he saw when he opened his eyes, and the whole place echoed as he bellowed, 'Franky Boy, what a goal in the Cup Final!' – Former Celtic striker **Frank McGarvey** hits rough times, in *Totally Frank*, with Ronnie Esplin, 2008.

If I hadn't had the football, I have to say I would be toiling, and I have toiled, I must admit. I have been a wee bit better the last four or five months, but up until then, in my spell at Bolton, I was struggling – Blackburn Rovers assistant manager **Archie Knox**, August 2008, on the death of wife Janice from pancreatic cancer on Christmas Eve 2006.

My family are agricultural workers. They worked all year round, barely a week off, so I was taught to appreciate the life of a footballer, because I didn't want to end up doing what they were doing. It's all done by machinery now, there are no jobs like that any more, but in the holidays I would be sent to give my dad a hand, because they wanted me to recognise the chance I was being given. It was literally back-breaking work because you are bent over all day; I've got uncles with problems like that, from working every week in the field, picking potatoes – Manchester United midfielder **Darren Fletcher**, March 2009.

There was another thing that politicised me even more as an adult, and that was when my mother was dying in November 1986, just a couple of weeks after I took over at United. She was at the Southern General in Glasgow, and it was absolutely dreadful, cladding hanging off the pipes, doctors and nurses overworked, and so little dignity attached to it. All my life I've seen Labour as the party working to get better health care for ordinary people, and the Tories really only caring about the people at the top. The NHS is definitely better after 12 years of Labour – Manchester United manager **Sir Alex Ferguson**, March 2009.

REFEREES ⚽

The Duncan Ferguson thing rumbled on for ages. I turned to look up the field at the wrong moment and when I looked back Jock McStay was on the deck – I don't know how it happened. The best thing to do is get another game under your belt and the last one dies away but that never happened because of the court case. I haven't spoken to Duncan since. It's sad when a player gives up the opportunity to play for his country and a talented player at that. But I became much stronger coming through it – Ref **Kenny Clark**, March 2006. (Clark was referee at the April 1994 match between Rangers and Raith Rovers when Ferguson headbutted Raith's Jock McStay. Although Clark missed it, Ferguson was charged with assault and served 44 days in jail.)

Bobby now admits himself that he is a Rangers fan and that he should never have been in charge of such a game. It was a scandalous decision by the SFA I really don't know what they were thinking about – Former Celtic assistant manager **Murdo MacLeod** on ref Bobby Tait handling the vital Rangers v Kilmarnock game in May 1998 as the 1997–98 title race reached an end, in Mark Guidi, *The Inner Sanctum*, 2008. Kilmarnock scored a late goal to win 1–0, meaning Celtic could've won the title with a win at Dunfermline the next day (they drew 1–1).

This year Stuart Dougal did his first Old Firm game, next year someone else will be blooded – SFA head of referees' development **George Cumming**, 1999.

By and large, Scottish players play by the book, and there is little outright feigning or cheating – that's a Southern European thing. But I have had the pleasure of sending off Ally McCoist, although he was only playing for Kilnockie, in a Robert Duvall film – Referee **Willie Young**, in *Fanatical About Football*, ed. Jeff Connor, 2003.

It wasn't that I didn't respect referees, I just felt they needed a helping hand. And to be fair, I think they've struggled a bit without me – Former Aberdeen captain **Willie Miller**, February 2003.

No one else can really know how low referees can feel when they realise afterwards that they have blundered. At the time, they were sure of a decision or they wouldn't have given it, so it's always an honest error, but it still hurts when you realise it was wrong – Referee **Hugh Dallas**, March 2003.

He was a credit to referees everywhere. He's the only one we have actively sought to bring back. Coming into this atmosphere is so tough, but he looked after both matches almost perfectly. After every derby, players and coaches give interviews complaining about the officials but after Mr Dallas's games no one could find a bad word to say about him – Egyptian football official **Walid Darwash** after Hugh Dallas's performances in Cairo derby, Al Ahly v Zamalek, April 2003.

You just don't realise quite how big it is until you see it for yourself. I've done 14 or 15 Old Firm matches and even they don't come close to this. I genuinely believe that this is as big as it gets – **Hugh Dallas** on the Egyptian Al Ahly v Zamalek derby, in Andy Mitten, *Mad For It: Football's Greatest Rivalries*, 2008.

I wouldn't like to be a referee. I've tried to referee a game here with the first team and the second team and I felt like punching every one of them – Partick Thistle manager **John Lambie**, May 2003.

More men have been on the moon than have refereed a World Cup final, yet I was there, in Japan last year, as the fourth official when Brazil beat Germany to win the tournament. That was utopia – Referee **Hugh Dallas**, 2003. (Statistically, Dallas is slightly wrong – 17 referees had refereed World Cup finals at the time. Fourteen men have been to the moon in six Apollo landings. As Hugh would doubtless acknowledge, accuracy is everything.)

The higher you go in football, the easier it gets – Referee **Willie Young**, in *Fanatical About Football*, ed. Jeff Connor, 2003.

Personally I'd be delighted to explain my decisions after a game. The only thing I would ask is that I could see the replays on a monitor. If they prove that I've got a decision wrong, then I don't have a problem in putting my hand up and admitting I've made a mistake – Referee **Mike McCurry**, October 2003.

I could see it in his face. He knew he'd made a mistake. I said to him, 'Ref, what was that for?' and he just looked at me and I said, 'You've just got me suspended,' and I could see his face fall a bit and that's why he didn't book anyone for kicking the ball away after that – West Ham and Scotland's **Christian Dailly** on the booking by Norwegian ref Terje Hauge against Holland which ruled him out of the second leg of the Euro 2004 play-off, November 2003.

What irritates me about the Porto match and about the Champions League in general is that it is the greatest tournament in the world, but often has the worst match officials – Manchester United manager **Sir Alex Ferguson**, after Manchester United went out of the Champions League to Porto, March 2004. Russian referee Valentin Ivanov – who would later achieve notoriety by booking 16 players and sending four off in the 2006 World Cup game between Portugal and Holland – was the subject of his ire.

On the eve of each season the SFA invites representatives from all clubs to meet Grade One officials to help to explain any changes in the laws or answer any questions they might have. I would have thought it might be to the advantage of coaches to find out anything they can about the way officials are thinking, but hardly any of them turn up – Ref **Kenny Clark**, prior to his ninth Old Firm game, March 2004.

This kind of thing has been going on for more than 100 years and it's not going to stop now. The goal would have stood at the other end – Kilmarnock assistant manager **Billy Brown** on a disallowed Kris Boyd goal against Celtic, April 2004. Celtic won the game 1–0 to win the title.

All sorts of strange things were happening as my career neared an end. I even had a civilised conversation with Gordon Strachan – Former Premiership ref **Jeff Winter**, in Who's The B*****d In The Black? 2006.

I couldn't imagine such refereeing in my worst nightmares, when the referee told us openly that we didn't pay him for some game in Liepaja, so therefore he would bury us now. Our first reaction was that poor guy got too hot in the Greek sun – Hearts owner **Vladimir Romanov** on Russian referee Yuri Baskakov, after the 3–0 Champions League Third qualifying round defeat by AEK Athens the previous month, September 2006. The referee subsequently described the accusations as 'bullshit'.

I don't think he lost control. I don't think he was ever in control – Hibs defender **David Murphy** after ref Alan Freeland booked 10 and sent off four in the match between Hibs and Falkirk, September 2006.

The referee asked me the daftest question ever. He asked after I pulled back (Michael) Stewart if I'd already been booked, so of course I said no – Falkirk's **Stephen O'Donnell**, after the same match, September 2006.

Quite the opposite – in the circumstances the players showed great restraint – Hibs manager **Tony Mowbray** on suggestions that there had been a lack of discipline in the same game, September 2006.

Look how my disciplinary record improved at Celtic. One red card in five years. He's so strong on discipline. Like Brian Clough, he hated silly bookings – West Brom's **John Hartson** on Martin O'Neill, December 2006.

I live for the day a losing manager says he thought the referee was magnificent and it was quite right to send off his £8m striker because he behaved like a clown, but it's not going to happen – Referee **Kenny Clark**, August 2007.

I used to get booked all the time for dissent at Dundee United. Every week I would get yellow cards for mouthing off about decisions. Jim McLean used to tell me there was no point arguing because you'd never change the mind of a referee. Well today Hamilton have proved that's not true – Morton manager **Jim McInally** after the Hamilton players' protests to ref Craig Thomson had seen a last-minute equaliser for his team ruled out, October 2007.

Scottish referees are horrendous. There's no other word for them. Much worse than the whistlers south of the border in the Premiership. Some of the ones up here used to remind me of jumped-up security guards – Former Celtic striker **John Hartson**, February 2008.

Dallas would talk to you and treat you with respect – but only if you played for the Old Firm. Ask any lad from the lower leagues what they made of Dallas and they'd paint a very different picture of him – Former Scotland striker **Billy Dodds** on ex-referee Hugh Dallas, February 2008.

We hold our hands out but not many people seem to want to shake them – SFA head of referee development **Donald McVicar**, revealing two clubs out of 42 had responded to his department's invitation to have a referee visit them to discuss officiating, February 2008.

He bottled it. I thought Mike McCurry was one of the guys who had the balls to give these decisions. I said to him that we were as well not turning up. What was the point? We were as well going home. Mike could have phoned me this morning and said, 'Look, Rangers are going to get the three points today – just tell your lads to stay in the house.' It's impossible to win here in important games. The referee has bottled it at the penalty. He knew, if he had given the penalty, he would have had to send Davie Weir off and he didn't want to do it because the game meant so much to Rangers. Well, I don't give a toss about Rangers – Dundee United manager **Craig Levein** on referee Mike McCurry's performance at Ibrox, May 2008. McCurry disallowed a legitimate United goal and turned down a clear penalty. Although McCurry subsequently admitted his errors, Levein was fined £5,000 for his remarks by the SFA three months later.

It took us four minutes to sort it all out – wrongly – at Ibrox, yet within 30 seconds of the incident it had been shown twice on television. We can put satellites into space and we can transfer a heart from one person to another, but we won't use technology in football. It doesn't make any sense. All you would have needed that day and on others like it was a fourth official looking at a monitor. There and then he could have told me, 'Mike, that goal was good.' – Referee **Mike McCurry** on the Ibrox incident, March 2009.

The last important game to us was the (CIS) Cup Final and we got cheated in that as well – Dundee United manager **Craig Levein**, *Radio Scotland*, May 2008.

In my eyes using a word like that is criminal – SFA President **George Peat** on Dundee United boss Craig Levein's claim his side were also 'cheated' in the CIS Cup Final, May 2008. (Referee Kenny Clark had turned down United claims for a penalty when Rangers' Carlos Cuellar wrestled Christian Kalvenes to the ground in the March 2008 Final. Rangers went on to win on penalties.)

When I went to Strathclyde University I was picked for the First XI and I always remember the guy who picked me compared me to Ted McMinn. I'm not sure that he meant it as a compliment – Referee **Craig Thomson** ponders his decision to abandon playing in favour of officiating, June 2008.

I said to them that I didn't know where they'd all come from, but I know where I've come from. I started in the sixth division in juvenile football and my biggest worry on a match day wasn't not having enough players – it was that the referee wouldn't turn up. So when the ref turned the corner – even if he was the worst referee in the world – I was glad to see him. But the way it's going, we're putting people off becoming young referees at grass-roots level. They need a bit more respect and to become more esteemed figures – Hamilton chairman **Ronnie MacDonald** lectures his fellow chairmen at the SPL chairmen's meeting, July 2008.

I've had occasions in my career where a manager has spoken to me in the tunnel after a game and I've told him exactly what the situation was. Then the manager has said to the press afterwards that I wouldn't talk to him or answer him – Former referee **Kenny Clark**, August 2008.

Assistants are there to assist, not insist – Former referee **Kenny Clark**, August

2008, after a mistake by assistant referee Billy Baxter cost Rangers an injury-time winner against Aberdeen at Pittodrie.

What astounded me was the arrogance of the referee. The way he spoke to me on the sideline was absolutely disgraceful. It defies belief for a senior referee to lose his composure like that and start sticking his finger in my face and shouting when I hadn't even raised my voice. I wouldn't speak to anybody like that. If it happened in the pub on a Saturday night he would have got a punch in the face – Dundee United manager **Craig Levein** on referee Stuart Dougal, after his side's 2–1 defeat against Celtic, May 2009.

He said, quite arrogantly, that his kids had had bigger knocks than that, which was a stupid comment to make. His kids must be some size – Dundee United defender **Lee Wilkie** after referee Stuart Dougal refused to allow him to be treated following a tackle by Scott McDonald against Celtic, May 2009.

RELIGION ⚽

Allison was a religious bigot of the deepest dye. Such facts were sure to count for much in the twisted mind of Allison and, as an intriguer behind the scenes at Ibrox, he was as dangerous as he was despicable – Manchester United manager **Sir Alex Ferguson** on the former Rangers public relations man, Willie Allison, who he believed contributed to a whispering campaign about him during his playing days at Ibrox because Ferguson's wife Cathy was a Catholic, *Managing My Life*, 2000.

The only guy who was chasing that kind of story was Willie Allison, who hounded him as far as the players were concerned. The players wouldn't bother their arse – Former Rangers teammate **Davie Provan** on the matter, in Michael Crick, *The Boss: The Many Sides of Alex Ferguson*, 2002.

I never had the slightest bit of interest in the Old Firm or the religious baggage that came with it all. I never gave a shit about any of that stuff – Midfielder **Craig Burley** on signing for Celtic, in Mark Guidi, *The Inner Sanctum*, 2008.

Bigotry is defined as an excessively zealous adherence to a particular religious belief and, having no beliefs, I therefore cannot be a bigot – Former Rangers vice-chairman **Donald Findlay**, June 1999.

My dad said, 'We'd like you to stop playing. Your mother's worried sick. We don't want you to keep going through this.' They had expressed this before. When I came home after the Norway game, we'd actually had, not an argument, a difference of opinion. But this time we were of one mind
Celtic skipper **Neil Lennon**, September 2002, on his retirement from international football, after receiving a death threat prior to captaining Northern Ireland against

Cyprus the previous month. Nineteen months before, the words 'Neil Lennon RIP' were spraypainted, along with the silhouette of a hanged man, on a gable wall near his family home in Lurgan, prior to him being booed by Irish fans during a friendly against Norway.

If you take the proper words, for example, of 'The Sash', it's not hostile. It's pro a cause, whatever view you take of that cause – Former Rangers vice-chairman **Donald Findlay**, October 1999. Findlay was forced to stand down after singing 'The Sash' after Rangers' Scottish Cup win in May 1999.

To me that's the saddest thing of all . . . the intelligent bigot – Radio Clyde pundit **Davie Provan**, October 2002.

It's unbelievable to see how deep it still is. Then you look to Holland. Southern Holland is Catholic and the north is Protestant. A few centuries before this, southern Holland was part of Belgium. There were never fights about the religious aspects. When I hear songs and people swearing about Catholics, I don't understand it. Someone will have to say something because it's not for this world – Rangers defender and Christian, **Bert Konterman**, October 2002.

We went to see Jack McConnell like two schoolboys going to the headmaster's office – Celtic chief executive **Ian McLeod** recalling he and Rangers chairman John McClelland visiting the corridors of power over sectarianism, March 2003.

It was perhaps the biggest regret of my career that I was unsuccessful there. I was proud to play for them but, on reflection, I should have stayed and endeavoured to develop. But I wasn't a strong enough personality to be able to cope with the religious bigotry off the field. It was overwhelming and incessant. You couldn't escape from it – Former Celtic striker **Tony Cascarino**, May 2003.

It's too easy to say it's all about bigotry, so I don't. I mean, come on, Aberdeen? I can't believe that's the most bigoted of cities – Celtic skipper **Neil Lennon** on the widespread criticism he receives at grounds in Scotland, May 2003.

Five minutes before kick-off, I'll get myself in the toilet cubicle and say a wee prayer. Non-believers will find that odd, I suppose, but my faith dictates that God has mapped out a path for me and in good times or bad times, whether it be in football or in business or whatever, it helps me to have that balance in my life – Referee and Christian **Mike McCurry**, before taking charge of his second Old Firm game, October 2003.

There is simply no place at Ibrox any longer for the FTP brigade and those who would have us wading through Fenian blood – Rangers chairman **David Murray**, March 2005.

I would look at the bible and what is said in Mark, Chapter 16. We would cast the devil. We would lay our hands on the sick and the sick would recover. It is simply A,B,C. I mean, is Scotland a pagan nation? It is time people started believing the word of the Lord. It is there in the Bible – Faith-healing Reverend **Joe Nwokoye**, on Rangers' Marvin Andrews refusal to submit to a knee operation, March 2005. The defender placed his faith in God and played on.

The church I belong to has only two sister churches in Britain – one in Motherwell and one in Hull. That's how I know God is in control of my life. How else do you explain it? The odds are very slim – Hull's Christian striker **Stuart Elliott** (previously with Motherwell), March 2005.

The things that are impossible with men are possible with God. (Luke 18:27) – Message on T-shirt worn by Christian **Marvin Andrews** after Rangers' shock title win, May 2005.

I know some people are saying that sectarianism was the one thing I never addressed. The suggestion seems to be that I should be able to come up with a speech as moving as the Gettysburg Address that would put the whole thing right overnight. I'll tell you something now. I could come back to the west of Scotland in 500 years time in some other incarnation – even as a tree – and still find the sectarianism. It will not have changed. Now, that doesn't make it acceptable, but I'm sorry, the people who think I should be able to remedy it just aren't thinking properly – Former Celtic manager **Martin O'Neill**, June 2005.

This is not simply a Catholic issue but a human rights issue. Freedom of religion is part of the UN Declaration on Human Rights and the European Convention on Human Rights – Catholic Church spokesman after Celtic goalkeeper **Artur Boruc** was given a police caution after he'd made the sign of the cross during an Old Firm game, August 2006. The Crown Office insisted Boruc's 'behaviour as a whole' led to his caution.

Do you think it was a problem at Rangers that Paul was a Catholic? – **Paul le Guen**'s mother Marie-Francoise grills journalist Graham Spiers about her son's time in Scotland, in Graham Spiers, *Paul le Guen: Enigma*, 2007.

The club was founded to help the poor of the Irish immigrants to Scotland. Many of the supporters are descendants of these people. They may take a particular view of history, what happened in Ireland, which is different to many other people. So I don't call those pro-terrorist songs. You are talking about songs about the IRA but again, many of those songs are songs from what was essentially a war of independence going back over a hundred years – Chair of the Celtic Trust, academic **Dr Jeanette Findlay**, on BBC *Radio Five Live*, on songs sung at Celtic Park, November 2007. She had been asked by host Nicky Campbell about 'pro-terrorist' songs sung by some fans. Celtic immediately described her comments as 'totally unrepresentative of the Celtic support'.

There was a film actor, he was English, and he told me, 'You are Catholic, that was your biggest problem in Scotland.' I won't tell you his name but I said, 'No, I don't think so.' The people in Scotland are very, very open and very friendly – Former Scotland manager **Berti Vogts**, November 2007.

I would have been false if I'd changed my words and hidden from what I really meant. I wanted to retain ownership of my thoughts and beliefs. Sectarianism goes on across the board in Scotland and I was trying to add something helpful to the debate on the subject. But, contrary to public misconception, I was in no way critical of the Catholic school system and anybody who says I was clearly hasn't read my chapter in the book – SFA chief executive **Gordon Smith**, March 2008, on his contribution to book, *It's Rangers For Me?* by Ronnie Esplin and Graham Walker.

We use a puppet ministry team from England who do parodies of well-known songs. They basically turn well-known pop songs into what I call 'God songs', and one of the ones they use is the Tina Turner song – Referee and Baptist minister **Mike McCurry**, March 2009, on newspaper reports he had led the church singing to Tina Turner's 'Simply The Best', a well-known Rangers anthem.

There is nothing at all that could in any way be said to be racist or racially motivated about those words. It is, in my submission, an expression of political opinion. This is not about whether the political element is logical, rational or justified. That is neither here nor there – Former Rangers vice-chairman **Donald Findlay**, May 2009. He was defending William Walls, who was appealing against a conviction for racially and religiously aggravated breach of the peace after singing 'The Famine Song' during a Rangers game at Kilmarnock.

SCOTLAND (TEAM)

Even when I got called to go back (by Willie Ormond) I wasn't going to go back, no way, because once you have been kicked in the teeth you don't go back for more of it. Everybody told me I was daft and eventually I gave in. If I hadn't done that, there would have been no World Cup, so they were right – Former Scotland midfielder **Archie Gemmill** recalling how close he came to refusing a Scotland call-up before 1978 in an interview in June 2003. Gemmill didn't play for Scotland between May 1972 and October 1975.

I'd scored 31 goals for West Ham that season and everyone and his dog knew that it should have been myself and Charlie Nicholas as the strike partnership that summer. Just about everyone in the media said so but Fergie is his own man and I was the first to feel the force of his petted lip – Former Scotland striker **Frank McAvennie** on being left out of the 1986 World Cup squad, November 2003.

I didn't actually say what I was accused of saying. I didn't call them 'the scum of the earth'. A reporter said to me something like, 'What did you think of that match?' and I said, 'What match? There was no match played here today, what you saw was the scum of world football.' And it was. I didn't say they were the scum of the earth, which was the phrase which stuck to me. They were absolutely appalling. I had to apologise to the SFA later. It was something I shouldn't have said but I was quite emotional. It was the culmination of the whole thing – Jock (Stein's death), going out there, hoping to do better this time and then losing, not losing properly but going out to a bunch of shits. It was disgusting. Whoever put them up to it should have got the jail – Former SFA secretary **Ernie Walker** on the Uruguay team Scotland played in the 1986 World Cup, February 2009.

We were hovering over Wembley in a helicopter and when (Gary) McAllister stepped up to take his penalty I said, 'One, two, three, move!' and the ball moved. People smile at it but you can check the footage. I talked to McAllister and he said it was the most amazing thing he'd encountered. Oh, but I got so many hate letters from Scotland – Performer **Uri Geller** on events at Euro 96, March 2003.

I realise when the squad was named and they weren't in and I was, that the reaction in Scotland would have been, 'Not Gemmill again'. I'm very aware that I have never been the flavour of the month or a glamorous player in the eyes of Scotland fans. But what exactly am I supposed to do? Knowing people are indifferent towards me – at best – is really hurtful. It embarrasses me to say it in my English accent but I am a proud Scot and I really LOVE playing for my country – Everton midfielder **Scot Gemmill**, who'd played four full Scotland games after being named in 40 squads, March 2001.

It is not the strongest group of players Scotland has ever had and that is me being polite – Blackburn manager **Graeme Souness** rules himself out of the running for the Scotland manager's job, October 2001.

I've been asked to go to the Safeway in Dumfries. The manager there is a Tartan Army guy – Scotland manager **Craig Brown** on book-signing the revised version of his autobiography, *The Game Of My Life*, October 2001.

If any of them didn't like what I said then so be it, that's tough. I knew our heads were on the chopping block. The fact we were just accepting being 2–0 down is what upset me – Scotland midfielder **Paul Lambert**, September 2002, on the 2–2 European Championship qualifying draw in the Faroes earlier that month.

At half-time there was just, I don't know, this acceptance. The thought of coming home and getting absolutely slaughtered – we got it anyway, obviously – but I'd have hated to have thought what it would've been like if we'd lost 2–0 – Scotland midfielder **Paul Lambert** on the 2–2 Faroes draw, *BBC* TV programme, *Footballer's Lives*, March 2003.

Scotland manager? Oh dear, dear, dear. I don't think I could handle the phone-ins in the *Daily Record*. Just think, that unnecessary pressure of drunk people phoning in and telling you things are crap. I think I'd be tapping the phones to find out who those drunks were – Southampton manager **Gordon Strachan**, January 2003. He was interviewed for Scotland manager's job the following year.

I know that a lot of people didn't hold it in high esteem, but I actually scored my only goal for Scotland in the game against Hong Kong and I'll take it to the grave. I have to be selfish in a way and say I don't care what anybody says about that game. I lived my dream that day, I scored a goal for Scotland, and sod everybody else who didn't consider it a proper international match – Former Scotland midfielder **Scot Gemmill**, March 2003. He'd scored in a 4–0 Reunification Cup win over a Hong Kong XI in May 2002. Scotland awarded caps for the game, even though the Hong Kong side weren't recognised by FIFA.

It's a learning curve and the management probably have to answer some questions. You're entitled to ask where we are going to improve. At times, the right hand doesn't know what the left is doing. We made it far too easy for Austria. I can't think of any positives – Midfielder **Craig Burley** quits Scotland after the previous month's tame defeat to Austria, May 2003.

There was a lot of diving going on and somebody's got to clamp down on it, whether it's FIFA or the refs. It's unbelievably frustrating playing when people are diving like that but what can you do? That's international football, we're told that's what it's like and until people clamp down it's not going to change. We've got to be bigger than that, keep playing our way, the Scottish way – which is the best way – Scotland defender **Christian Dailly** after defeat by Germany, September 2003.

Berti kept asking me about Scott (Wilson). He took him to Turkey but never played him. Up at Aberdeen he brought (Dundee defender Lee) Wilkie back in whom he knew about. Scott Wilson was getting warmed up for 45 minutes but he never put him on again. Barry Nicholson was the best player on the park in Turkey for the Future squad. He comes back, gets played at Aberdeen but gets taken off in a position that he wasn't used to. (Goalkeeper Derek) Stillie never got a chance yet he (Vogts) was telling me he was going to let him play. A few people in Holland told me never to trust Germans and I just want him to explain that because these three boys came back here very, very disappointed – Dunfermline manager **Jimmy Calderwood**, January 2004, complaining about Vogts' treatment of Stillie, Nicholson and Wilson.

Jimmy is a good coach for Dunfermline, but international football is a big difference. I am very disappointed in Jimmy, as we spoke at the last managers' meeting and asked him to phone me if there is ever a problem – he does not need to wait for a meeting. His comments about Germans show he was perhaps too long in Holland. He says Barry Nicholson was the best player in Turkey, but I don't remember seeing Jimmy in the stadium. Lee Wilkie played in Aberdeen against Germany to prepare him for the play-off against Holland, in which he was outstanding in our victory – **Vogts'** reply to Calderwood's comments, January 2004.

I have been looking to strengthen my defence but did not know anything about Ritchie's qualifications or career. No one told me about him and it wasn't until his name was mentioned a few weeks ago that I even knew he had scored for Scotland against the Czech Republic in 1999. I can't understand how or why he was forgotten. Maybe it was because he was out injured for so long – Scotland manager **Berti Vogts**, January 2004, admitting he knew little of Walsall defender Paul Ritchie's background, prior to naming him in the squad for the friendly against Wales.

The Paul Ritchie case this week has been a fiasco. The last result against Holland means we are already a laughing stock on the pitch, but we can't even get the administrative side right. It just sums up the whole scenario, from the SFA suits right through to the tracksuits – Former Scotland midfielder **Craig Burley** on the Ritchie oversight, before the defeat in Wales, February 2004.

I've never heard anything so ridiculous – Former Scotland midfielder **Craig Burley** on suggestions Berti Vogts might recruit foreign-born players for Scotland, February 2004. At the time there were suggestions that foreign players with four years playing service in Scotland, no previous international caps for their own countries and who obtained a British passport, would be available for international selection.

I would rather play for a losing side full of Scottish lads than a winning team with Zinedine Zidane. I can't speak for anybody else but I've got to say I am utterly against this – Scotland defender **Christian Dailly**, February 2004, on suggestions players like Stefan Klos and Didier Agathe could play international football for Scotland if they applied for UK passports because of residency laws.

I'm all for guys getting their chance, but I look at some of the players that are getting picked and it's a wee bit depressing. People will say this is me and my old negative column again, but you have to call it like it is. You'll have Scottish fans buying papers and they haven't a clue who some of these guys are – Former Scotland midfielder **Craig Burley** on Berti Vogts' squad for the friendly against Wales, February 2004.

The national team is an absolute nightmare just now. I have slaughtered Berti Vogts and it's not easy, contrary to what people believe, to do that to a manager when you have been one yourself, but it's an absolute disgrace that George Graham is sitting analysing on television and Walter Smith is assistant at Manchester United and we've got Berti Vogts – Former Dundee United manager **Jim McLean**, April 2004.

The current Scotland regime is not exactly my cup of tea. It would have driven me to much stronger drinks – Former Scotland midfielder **Craig Burley**, May 2004.

He is my cheeky boy – Scotland manager **Berti Vogts** on striker James McFadden, 2004.

It was meant well. But it just didn't sound right – **James McFadden** on Berti Vogts' description of him, after his resignation, November 2004.

I just didn't get the job. That's it. I was interviewed, I was given a fair chance and I've no embarrassment in getting pipped to the post by Walter because he's a great friend, a great man and he'll be a good manager for Scotland. I do believe a Scotsman should be in the job. And it's the same down here where an Englishman should be capable of filling the post. It's not rocket science at international level, that's for sure – Former Southampton manager **Gordon Strachan** on being interviewed for the Scotland job, February 2005.

I remember that first day in Manchester. It was really obvious when you were sitting looking at them as a group that there was no confidence, there was nothing in them at all. You could sense everyone was down, even the younger players – **Walter Smith** recalls his first meeting with the Scotland squad in February 2005, at a get-together at the Mottram Hall Hotel in Cheshire, November 2007.

I've driven into the training ground wearing my Scotland shirt twice this season, after the draw against Italy and the defeat of Norway. It's a long time since I was able to do that – Sheffield United assistant manager **Stuart McCall**, October 2005.

– Did you never harbour ambitions to become Scotland manager given your success at club level? – Swifty, London.
– Never. It is an unequivocal 'No' – Former Scotland striker **Kenny Dalglish**, magazine interview, May 2006.

I had a few Polish guys in the back and I just started tooting the horn. I let them out at the Three Sisters and didn't even charge them. I just had to catch the last 20 minutes. It's a great night for Scotland – Edinburgh taxi driver **Billy Ramsay** after Scotland's 1–0 win over France in the European Championships, October 2006.

People should remember that I joined the SFA at a time when the president and the chief executive were being smuggled out of football grounds in the back of a car – Rangers manager **Walter Smith** on the day of his appointment, January 2007, referring to the SFA's decision to sue for breach of contract after he quit the Scotland job.

It's said I'm leaving Scotland at an awkward time. Well I joined Scotland at a diabolical time and it annoys me that they are making me out to be the baddie – New Rangers manager **Walter Smith**, January 2007. Scotland were top of qualifying Group B when he quit.

He can make something happen wherever he plays and we have to fit him in somewhere. He's never failed to deliver in a Scotland jersey – Scotland manager **Alex McLeish** on James McFadden, before the friendly against South Africa, August 2007.

I take my hat off to Scotland. It must be great to have such a great public but I am sure our method of selling tickets helped it happen – France coach **Raymond Domenech** after Scotland's win over France, September 2007. There were an estimated 25,000 Scots fans in the 48,712 crowd, many of whom had cheerfully logged on to the French FA website and bought tickets.

Quelle frappe! Quelle frappe! (What a strike!) – French TF1 TV commentator **Jean-Michel Larqué** on James McFadden's goal, France 0 Scotland 1, September 2007.

GOOOOOAAAALLLLL! I don't believe it. I, Jesus, what a goal here fae Scotland! (PRESENTER: Who scored, Gordon?) James McFadden. What a goal. Absolutely, so much under the cosh. He's picked up a ball, I don't know, 30 yards from goal, . . . by the time I've finished this report it'll be 40 yards. But I tell you, 30 yards from goal and it screamed into the top of the net. What a goal. My goodness gracious, the French are just turning round looking at themselves. What IS going on here? – Sky Sports TV pundit **Gordon McQueen** brings the news of McFadden's goal to the world, September 2007.

You forget sometimes you are in a studio with a camera on you. I just couldn't contain my joy – **Gordon McQueen** reflects after calming down, February 2008.

La Douche est glacée. Le ciel est tombe sur la tete de l'equipe de France, battue pour la deuxieme fois par l'Ecosse. ('The shower is ice-cold. The sky fell in on the French team's heads, beaten 1–0 for the second time by Scotland.') – French sports newspaper L'Équipe reports on Scotland's win in September 2007. It became a popular tee-shirt, made by philosophyfootball.com.

Gordon Smith says I pick the team, he decides the tactics and Alex McLeish sends on the substitutes – SFA President **George Peat**, October 2007.

I know exactly where all the television sets are here at Clairefontaine and I will switch them off on Saturday. It is dangerous to look for a result that will probably not come. We would be disappointed and we should not prepare after a disappointment. I would prefer them to play cards and find out the result the day after the game – France manager **Raymond Domenech**, three days before the Scotland v Italy game at Hampden, November 2007. If Scotland won or drew against Italy, France needed to draw their final game in Ukraine the following week to qualify.

Bloody hell, when I started we were challenging Burkina Faso in the FIFA rankings – Rangers manager **Walter Smith**, as Scotland prepared to face Italy for a place at Euro 2008, November 2007.

You could say that we've had a good campaign, we've beaten France twice but if France are there and we're not, it doesn't really matter, does it? – Scotland defender **Davie Weir**, preparing to face Italy for the right to go to Euro 2008, November 2007.

There is always the conspiracy theory. An Italian female journalist asked me last week, prior to the game, if I really thought UEFA would allow one of the top teams not to be at the finals? Did I believe they would allow the world champions not to be present? I said, 'We don't talk about those things in Scotland.' She said, 'Well, I can assure you we do in Italy!' When I asked another friend what she meant, a guy who works for *Sky* Calcio, he said, 'Well, I guess everybody in Italy thinks we will get the 50-50s.' – Scotland manager **Alex McLeish** after the Scotland v Italy qualifier, November 2007. A controversial late free-kick led to Christian Panucci's winning goal for Italy.

In my 30 years of refereeing I've never witnessed such a blatant, deliberate error. It was no mistake. The big team were going to get a little help. The same help as they got when the Spaniards were appointed to referee our tie and the Italians were appointed to referee the Spanish tie. The whole thing stinks – Former Scottish referee **David Syme** on the Scotland v Italy refereeing controversy. Scotland's game was handed by Spain's Manuel Mejuto González. Italian Roberto Rosetti refereed Spain's game against Sweden, which they won 3–0, the same day.

You were f***ing robbed by those Eyeties – Sex Pistols singer **John Lydon** steps into the Scotland v Italy debate, onstage at the SECC the same night, November 2007.

During the Berti Vogts era MPs and MSPs were asking why Scottish football was in such a bad state. So I wrote to both Parliaments and told them, give me a slot in your diary and I'll tell you. I went to London and Edinburgh and talked about all the things we're discussing now. That it wasn't down to a national coach or 11 men on a pitch, but to a whole generation of neglect – Rangers manager **Walter Smith**, November 2007.

I thought the appointment of the under-21 coach was morally wrong. In my opinion, irrespective of whether it was Billy Davies or not, he (the Scotland manager) should be going in there with a long-term commitment and strategy to improve and support every level. Yes we know that his main job is the national team, but in-between-times there should be a responsibility for him to turn up at schools, taking 14-year-olds in a training session, going down to Largs on a coaching course and showing his face, sitting there answering questions – Former Motherwell and Derby manager **Billy Davies** explaining why he withdrew his name from the running to be Scotland manager, February 2008.

I know Scotland haven't got the choice England have, they never will, but what they do have is players as passionate, if not more passionate, to play for their country. That's hard for me to say as an Englishman, but it's true – Scotland assistant manager **Terry Butcher**, March 2008.

There should be no inferiority complex now whatsoever about Scotland. The English have got too much confidence, while the Scottish probably haven't got enough. But they should have by now, after the last campaign, there should be a real, 'Bring them on'. Like Keanu Reeves in *The Matrix* when he goes like that with his hand, 'Bring them on'. That should be the case. 'Bring them on', that's a good line – Scotland assistant manager **Terry Butcher**, March 2008.

In a game like Saturday, when you want a goal, I could have at least given the team that threat. The manager clearly didn't think so and that's up to him. I have nothing against him or any of the players, but enough's enough – Rangers striker **Kris Boyd** announcing a refusal to play for Scotland under manager George Burley, October 2008. He'd been an unused substitute in the World Cup qualifying draw against Norway the day before.

Kris has shown a lack of respect to his country and to myself – Scotland manager **George Burley** on striker Kris Boyd's decision not to play for his country while Burley is manager, October 2008.

Robert Service wrote well of this area. His parents were from Glasgow, which makes him Scottish – or at least he can play for Scotland, which is the main thing. God knows, somebody should – Comedian **Billy Connolly** on Canadian Yukon Territory poet Service, *Journey To The Edge of the World*, March 2009. (Service was born in Preston in 1874, but his father – though not his mother – was indeed Scottish.)

SCOTLAND (PLAYING IN)

Somewhere like Ibrox appears to be a big wide open space, and it plays with your mind. Whenever I went there, because of the square shape of the stand behind the goal, I always felt it made the goals seem really small – Motherwell manager **Mark McGhee** recalls playing at Ibrox, November 2008.

Celtic holed me up in a room for two days in the Glasgow Hotel One Devonshire Gardens until they could announce my signing. I remember going out for a walk one afternoon during that time and I made my way along Great Western Road. I got to the junction at the Botanic Gardens and turned left towards Maryhill Road. There was nothing much to see, and it made me think there wasn't a lot in Glasgow and that it was quite a boring city. Of course, had I turned right that day and gone down Byres Road, my initial outlook would have been so different – Former Celtic striker **Regi Blinker** on Glasgow's West End geography, in Mark Guidi, *The Inner Sanctum*, 2008.

I was amazed when I first arrived in Scotland. All the shouting and swearing at players . . . I thought, this can't be the way to coach players. But it is part of the Scottish tradition. In my very first league game in Scotland, at Tynecastle in 1998, Jim Jefferies was shouting at everyone and I couldn't believe it. Also, we lost 2–1 – Former Rangers manager **Dick Advocaat**, September 2002.

A huge percentage of the public appears to believe that if something appears in print it must be true. There is also a common belief that there is no smoke without fire. I can assure you from my personal experiences that there is lots and lots of smoke without any fire as far as some of the media coverage of football in Glasgow is concerned – Former Celtic General Manager **Jock Brown**, in book, *Celtic-Minded: 510 Days In Paradise*, 1999.

When I go to schools they say, 'Scotland? Isn't that where Rangers win everything?' So they're not that ignorant – Australian side Carlton SC's **Davie MacPherson**, October 1999.

I'm just an honest person. Some people can't afford to say what they see, and that's their problem. I can see that the Premier League here is abysmal. Even if Rangers and Celtic break away, and it becomes more competitive, a 10 team league still gives you no room for bringing through players, because you're either at the top or the bottom, there's no middle zone in which you can find time to develop – Airdrie manager **Steve Archibald**, September 2000.

If anyone thinks the Partick Thistle team of today could hold their own in the Scottish Premier League, they have been smoking dope – SPL chief executive **Roger Mitchell**, as Thistle pushed for promotion, 2002.

A player like me isn't particularly loved by opposing fans, so when you go out here in Italy you can get problems. In Scotland that never happened: everybody treats you in a civilised way – AC Milan's **Rino Gattuso**, March 2003.

I think forwards playing in the Old Firm who are not scoring 20-plus goals are not doing their job. I really don't. With the amount of chances you get, the players you're playing with, and the opposition you're up against week in week out, you should score goals – Celtic striker **John Hartson**, June 2003.

The SFA cannot play God on one hand, handing down bans and the like, and then Pontius Pilate on the other, washing their hands when it suits them – Celtic manager **Martin O'Neill**, September 2003. A controversial sending-off for Didier Agathe against Dundee could not be overturned by video evidence, while Neil Lennon, caught on camera making a hand gesture to Dundee fans in the same game, was to be punished because of it.

My message to these men is simple: come to Dundee and experience real hospitality, haggis and hurry here. The four Hs! – Dundee director **Giovanni di Stefano** sends a message to players across Europe, October 2003.

Looking back, the problems came when I switched from the warm Spanish weather to chilly Glasgow. My body likes the sunshine – Rangers' **Ronald de Boer**, November 2003.

I feel a lot more Scottish than a lot of fans of Celtic and Rangers. When I watched the UEFA Cup Final between Celtic and Porto, okay maybe I am very strange about Scotland, but I only saw one Scottish flag in the Celtic corner. Most were Irish. It's the same at Rangers. I look around Ibrox and I see a few small Scottish flags – always it's Union flags – Scotland manager **Berti Vogts**, December 2003.

Ronald used to tell me on the phone how modern and trendy this city was. I found it hard to believe. But when I walk around the city centre, I even dare say Glasgow is an example for many other European big cities. The place is buzzing, it has everything – Rangers defender **Frank de Boer**, February 2004.

In Barcelona I never had a problem with my knee. I came here and you just feel the cold weather. I think my injury has a little bit to do with the climate. Why do people always go to warm countries in the winter? Because it feels better. It's true. Do it yourself. Test your finger in the cold. You can feel your joint stiff – Rangers' **Ronald de Boer** offers an alternative view, March 2004.

There are more agents in Scotland than there are good football players. I had one guy who passed me on Richard Gough's phone number and wanted a fee for it – Livingston's then prospective owner **Pearse Flynn**, January 2005.

During the five years we've played everyone to be perfectly honest – and many's a time we've played referees an' all – **Martin O'Neill** on his five years at Celtic, in DVD, 'The Official History of Celtic', 2008.

I have already warned him of the dangers of going out in Glasgow. I told him to go down to the Louden Tavern for a couple of nights – Celtic skipper **Neil Lennon** on welcoming loan striker Craig Bellamy to Glasgow, 2005. (The Louden is a famous Rangers bar in Glasgow's East End.)

He is a smashing fellow and we've left him at Barrowfield practising his free-kicks with Shaun Maloney in the rain. It's a small thing, but the weather here compared to what he has been used to. . . . to put up with that is hard. People talk about the Scottish winters and how he'll cope with that, but the Scottish summer is bad enough – Celtic manager **Gordon Strachan** on Shunsuke Nakamura, October 2005.

I like watching baseball – it's always nice and hot, not like watching Ayr United at Somerset Park – Belle & Sebastian singer **Stuart Murdoch**, January 2006.

My heart is in Scotland, everybody knows that. They hear it at Preston 10 times a day when my phone rings and 'Flower of Scotland' is my ringtone – Preston manager **Billy Davies**, April 2006.

I came in at pre-season and got all the bars taken off the windows at Tannadice. They were security windows but the windows are too high up for that to be an issue. And we got all the windows cleaned. I brought it on myself to change that because the place was like a prison – Dundee United manager **Craig Brewster**, September 2006.

In every changing room, players get ripped. People have taken the piss out of me; ripped me for not drinking, ripped for doing yoga, ripped for my diets, for my clothes, for my Irishness. But you give it back. When I say the Celtic dressing room was better, this is not a criticism of the United lads. I was as bad as any of them. We ripped people for the wrong things: the car, the house, the way you dressed. In Scotland it was more old-fashioned. I enjoyed that. Maybe you don't get the bull up there that you get in the Premiership – **Roy Keane** on his time at Celtic, September 2006.

We're playing in a fairly unattractive league in comparison to Europe's major championships – Celtic chief executive **Peter Lawwell**, speaking at the Soccerex conference in Dubai, November 2006.

You get marked tight and the pressure is immense, but it's easier to score goals than in the Premiership. There are good players at Hibs, Aberdeen and Hearts, they get paid good money, but they're not John Terry or Rio Ferdinand – **John Hartson** on the SPL, February 2007.

I believe a football club is as important to a town as a museum. It ought to be part of your heritage because more people go to the football than anywhere else – St Johnstone chairman **Geoff Brown**, April 2007.

He drives up beside me, rolls down the passenger window and starts giving me dog's abuse. I couldn't hear him but I could see he was screaming abuse. Then he tried to spit at my car but it caught in the wind and went back into his – Former Celtic captain **Neil Lennon** on life in Scotland, June 2007.

Everything I learned in Vienna, I've had to forget in Scotland. There it's about football, here it's about fight – Rangers and former Austria Vienna defender **Sasa Papac**, August 2007.

I've been in the Cumnock ground when they are playing arch-rivals Auchinleck Talbot with a crowd of nearly 4,000 – and about 2,000 of those were policemen on duty to keep the peace – Former Cumnock fan **Craig Burley** on the eve of three junior clubs being invited into the Scottish Cup, September 2007.

The offer from Greece landed straight from heaven. I have moved from Scotland, a rainy and gloomy dark land, to a place where the sun shines 12 months a year – Former Celtic striker **Maciej Zurawski** after his move to Greek side Larissa, February 2008.

Big Frank Worthington, who I played with at Birmingham City, was a playboy but he did about 45 minutes on free-kicks on his own every day after training. So did Eric Cantona and David Beckham, but our players have to catch a minibus home from training at Balgownie before the cold sets in – Aberdeen manager **Jimmy Calderwood**, February 2008.

Having worked north and south of the border, there is far more honesty north of the border. Far more honesty within football clubs, in terms of boards, coaches, players and also in terms of the fans. You can't short-change the Scottish fans, because they will let you know. There seems to be a code in Scotland where it is far more honest and there is far more respect. In England, it is dog-eat-dog and people are crawling over themselves and others to get where they want to go. You can't con people in Scotland. You can down here, but not up there – Scotland assistant manager **Terry Butcher**, March 2008.

It's an attitude that will always stop you getting the best people out there. Arsène Wenger wasn't Arsenal-minded when he took that job. Jose Mourinho wasn't Chelsea-minded when they got him. Somehow, both men overcame that crushing handicap to win championships for clubs they had never supported. Imagine that – Former Celtic midfielder **Craig Burley** on Celtic fans wanting a manager who's 'Celtic-minded', April 2008.

I've read the SPL is described as 'the laughing stock of Europe' and I laugh at that as it couldn't be further from the truth. I am on the board of the European leagues, made up of 27 countries, and I'm also on the four-man strategy committee. I'd love to think it was my intelligence, wit and personality that achieved that role. It isn't, I'm there because of the standing the SPL has in Europe, if not on the home front – SPL executive chairman **Lex Gold**, March 2008.

I felt comfortable playing in Scotland and I liked the league there. When I arrived people were probably expecting a different kind of player, an Italian inside-forward, quick and full of tricks. But eventually I proved on the playing field that I was much more Scottish than many of the natives – Milan midfielder **Rino Gattuso**, on Italian TV show *Sfide*, March 2008.

Of all the signings I've made, the most important thing I did when I came to Celtic was bring Tommy into the coaching team. Through his intelligence, common sense and humour, he made me understand what Glasgow was all about. Without him, I would have gone off my head. Tommy kept me sane – Celtic manager Gordon Strachan, after the death of coach **Tommy Burns**, May 2008.

I've been living in a cold country for three years so my body is surprised by the heat – Celtic's Japanese midfielder **Shunsuke Nakamura**, before a World Cup qualifier in 40°C temperatures in Oman, June 2008.

After you've signed a contract at Celtic the first thing you're told is where it's best not to go to refuel your car. You're also told the best way to drive to the stadium so you don't have typical Rangers neighbourhoods to drive through – Celtic's **Jan Vennegoor of Hesselink**, June 2008.

Myself and my wife, Simone, went to the House for an Art Lover in Bellahouston Park and it was incredible. (Charles Rennie) Mackintosh designed it a century ago. Even today it looks modern, so what must people have made of it back then? It must have been a revelation – Celtic defender **Andreas Hinkel**, January 2009.

I tell everyone, look for more youth players. Scottish youth players are important. I have seen a lot of reserve games, under-19s. In the next five years, something must happen. If you don't do this, you have the same shit that you have in Austria, Hungary. I know what I'm talking about, believe me – Hearts manager **Csaba Laszlo**, April 2009.

As for contentment, it couldn't be any better just now. I think it's great. I think Lesley's enjoyed living here more than anywhere else we've lived for a long time. The longer you go on the more you get used to the rules of Glasgow – Celtic manager **Gordon Strachan**, May 2009. He quit two weeks later.

Sometimes you go and make a fullback play the ball or whatever, but the fans don't want that. They just want you to go over there and kill him – Hearts' Ugandan midfielder **David Obua**, May 2009.

STRACHAN ⚽

What Strachan most dislikes, and least understands, is lack of commitment – Author **Rick Gekoski**, in *Staying Up: A Fan Behind The Scenes In The Premiership*, 1998.

Reporter: This might sound like a daft question, but you'll be happy to get your first win under your belt, won't you? Strachan: You're right. It is a daft question. I'm not even going to bother answering – Southampton manager **Gordon Strachan**, quoted in *FourFourTwo* magazine, July 2004.

He was a cheeky wee bastard. People see it today on television. That's Gordon, that's his character and if you took that away you wouldn't have the real Strachan – Former Aberdeen manager **Billy McNeill**, in *Gordon Strachan: The Biography*, Leo Moynihan, 2004.

I decided that this man could not be trusted an inch – Manchester United manager **Alex Ferguson** on Strachan, in *Managing My Life*, 1999. Ferguson claimed Strachan changed his mind on a new Manchester United contract in summer 1988 to sign for Lens, only for the move to fall through.

My feelings about Fergie's comments are simply that it works both ways. It boils down to the fact that, because of his attitude to me, I did not trust him either – Celtic manager **Gordon Strachan**'s response to Ferguson's remark, in autobiography, *Strachan: My Life In Football*, 2006.

When I see Alex I'm always civil but there's no exchange of Christmas cards. His book should have been a celebration of his achievements, something positive, but he chose to use it as something else. He had a different agenda – **Gordon Strachan** on Ferguson's criticism of him in his autobiography, 2000.

He used to play tapes of a singer he liked – I don't know who it was but it was crap. All the boys hated it, until one night it got chucked away. If he's still wondering who threw it off the bus, it was me. So maybe he's right and I'm not to be trusted – **Gordon Strachan** on Sir Alex Ferguson.

I still cringe about what I said to Arsenal's captain, Tony Adams – **Gordon Strachan**, in autobiography, *Gordon Strachan: My Life In Football*, 2007. The then-Coventry player-manager had told Adams – who'd battled alcohol problems – 'Why don't you just **** off and go for a drink' in a game in April 1997.

To be fair to Gordon, he apologised straight after the game, realising he had gone over the line. I went to see him after the game and before I could even get my arm up or words out he said he was sorry. I have a lot of time for the man – Wycombe manager **Tony Adams**, July 2004, on the incident.

I told him I was tired once and he said, 'I tell you when you're tired.' He was very British and was one for rolling up his sleeves and working hard. When he took part in five-a-sides you could never get close enough to kick him. He's the best footballer I've played with in my career – Former Coventry midfielder **George Boateng** on Strachan, February 2002.

I'd watch *Countdown*. Hey, there's nothing worse than being in the room on your own and getting the conundrum. There are no witnesses – Southampton manager **Gordon Strachan** on what he would do if he wasn't involved in football, January 2003.

Once the humour goes, the imagination goes and the life goes. That's when I'll start to panic, I think, because I know fine well I'll be on the receiving end from my grandchildren and not be able to answer them back – Southampton manager **Gordon Strachan**, January 2003.

It couldn't have been that bad. He spent the second-half smoking fags in my office – Southampton manager **Gordon Strachan** on Manchester United goalkeeper Fabien Barthez, who was carried off on a stretcher in a game against his side, February 2003.

If the league was counted on guts they'd be top of it. I told Gary he couldn't ask any more of his team. And if they do get relegated they can go back with absolutely no regrets – Southampton manager **Gordon Strachan** on West Brom manager Gary Megson after Southampton had beaten them 1–0, March 2003. West Brom were relegated.

I can't defend what happened. Some people cannot see further than 20 yards but I'm not going to lie. I saw it. I've not spoken to Kevin yet, it's not the best time straight after a game, but we'll sort it out properly on Monday – **Gordon Strachan**, after the sending off of Southampton striker Kevin Phillips against Middlesbrough, September 2003.

I don't measure my best club by the number of medals I have or how many goals I scored. I can only relate to the number of times I laughed. I laughed every day at Pittodrie – Southampton manager **Gordon Strachan**, October 2003.

The better team won, the braver team and the better passing team won. The one-dimensional team, the plodding team, the lack-of-imagination team got beaten – Southampton manager **Gordon Strachan** after his side lost 2–0 to Manchester City, November 2003.

I am not going anywhere else and I am not cracking up so people can stop looking too deeply into it. It is not stress either. This is probably the least stressful time of my seven years in management. I am fit as a fiddle mentally, my heart is fine, I just have a sore hip which needs replacing – Southampton manager **Gordon Strachan** announces plans to take a break from management, January 2004. He resigned two months later.

When Gordon Strachan was involved, it seemed there were no trouble-free-games – Former Premiership ref **Jeff Winter**, in *Who's The B*****d In The Black?*, 2006.

We should all want to be the best on the park, but if we can't manage that we should be the best possible teammate. That's when you find that those around you will help you through difficult times on and off the pitch. Take that attitude into the outside world and you have a better place to live – Celtic manager **Gordon Strachan**, November 2007.

He has not done an excellent job with supporters PR-wise but he's a football manager, not Max Clifford – Former Dundee United boss **Jim McLean** on Gordon Strachan, who was being criticised by fans after being knocked out of the Scottish Cup by Aberdeen, March 2008.

I feel let down by the manager. I remember him sitting in my mum's house trying to sign me and he said I could play anywhere in his midfield or up front. It was the same in the press conferences but now I can only play left midfield for some reason and that's not even my best position – Celtic striker **Derek Riordan** on manager Gordon Strachan, April 2008. He left Celtic four months later.

Even if he won the European Cup he might never win his critics over. Maybe they've just got a bee in their bonnet about him and will never change their views on him. But I don't think he's that worried about winning over that minority – Celtic coach **Neil Lennon**, July 2008.

I'd have no hesitation in saying that Gordon was the best player I ever played with. He just loves football and was so dedicated, the way he looked after himself. Gordon took seaweed tablets and he brought them in for the players to take. Most of the players were on them. I took them for about two days, but that was me done after that because they were disgusting. I told everyone I was taking them, but I wasn't – Former Leeds and Rangers midfielder **Mel Sterland** on former Leeds teammate Strachan, in *Boozing, Betting & Brawling: Mel Sterland, A Footballer's Life*, 2008.

He gives the impression of somebody who doesn't really want to be there. The criticism irks him, the spotlight irks him, and not having the money to spend that he thinks he should have irks him, too. It is only a matter of time before he goes – Former Celtic midfielder **Craig Burley** on manager Gordon Strachan, November 2008. Strachan quit six months later.

Having done pitchside interviews for *Sky* for long enough, I don't know how Stuart Lovell at *Setanta* manages to keep his temper with Gordon. He talks about respect and about people not showing him enough of it, but I think there are times when he could show respect. That's my take on it. I don't have a relationship with him as such. I don't have a working relationship with him, either, nor do I require one – Pundit **Davie Provan**, March 2009.

I pulled him up about it early on. Sometimes, he got, not so much aggressive with the players as spiteful with a player who he'd got a down on. I said, no, you've got to be a bit more flexible. I would think he's developed that through experience. His reaction to the press? Like John Docherty, my old No two at Cambridge, he's abrasive, a little bit anti them. I can see where that falls down with Gordon. But I still can't believe the reception he gets up there, considering his record's probably better than Martin O'Neill's – Former Coventry manager **Ron Atkinson**, April 2009.

It takes a special kind of man to give so many people so many reasons to love him. Yet to remain so unloved – Journalist **Bill Leckie** after Strachan quit as Celtic manager, May 2009.

THE GAME

In soccer there are two types of footballers: those who only use their legs and those who use their brains. The ones who only use their legs will never get to the top – Former Celtic manager **Wim Jansen**, in Mark Guidi, *The Inner Sanctum*, 2008.

(Peter) Ndlovu was going backwards, and (Eoin) Jess, who's a nice lad and had the best training-ground skills of the lot, didn't have the heart – and if you don't have it by his age, you're not going to get it – **Gordon Strachan**'s assessment on a couple of his Coventry City players, in Rick Gekoski, *Staying Up: A Fan Behind The Scenes In The Premiership*, 1998.

I do not think that football is the place for people who decide on some whim that it is a lucrative marketplace. First and foremost it is a game rather than a business venture. That is how it should remain – Former SFA chief executive **Jim Farry**, July 1999.

The way we defended was diabolical. When we went ahead we should at least have played with a bit more authority. The conditions weren't the best but that's no excuse for sloppiness. We were so slack I thought Queens were going to score every time they went up the park. If we defend like that again we are going to be punished and I have let them know in no uncertain terms what I thought of them. That was probably our worst performance of the season – Partick Thistle manager **John Lambie** after a 5–4 win over Queen of the South, February 2000.

I have been in football for 15 years and I have never known anything like this. To put out a reserve team when others were still trying to qualify for Europe shows a total lack of respect – Hearts striker **Stephane Adam** after Hearts failed to qualify for Europe, May 2001. Kilmarnock beat a Celtic side missing eight regulars to qualify.

If Hearts haven't got enough points over 38 games that's their fault. It's my prerogative as manager of Celtic to decide who I play – Celtic manager **Martin O'Neill**'s response.

I could write a book about what I have seen at this club – Dundee midfielder **Frank van Eijs** on his time at Dundee, in Jim Wilkie, *Bonetti's Blues: Dundee FC and its Cultural Experiment*, 2001.

Fitba might stop in one year, two years, five years but if you've not looked after your family then they're not going to be there for you. It's imperative to keep the unit. You see managers who have led separate lives from their wives, it's just fitba, fitba, fitba with them. Oh, gie me peace! There's more to life than fitba, fitba, fitba – Southampton manager **Gordon Strachan**, January 2003.

He spat on me and it landed on my shoulder. It was 100 per cent deliberate. It's a man's game for God's sake – but spitting on people isn't part of a man's game. I didn't speak to him at the end. I don't speak to people who do things like that. He ran off the pitch in a big huff – Ayr striker **James Grady** after an incident with Rangers defender Lorenzo Amoruso in the Ayr v Rangers Tennents Scottish Cup tie, February 2003.

Everybody knows this guy is a Celtic fan – a crazy Celtic fan. I have never had this problem in my life and I'm not going to start with him – Rangers defender **Lorenzo Amoruso** on the Grady incident, March 2003.

He plays a very simple, basic way: you need pace and you need strength in all areas, and you must be 100 per cent committed when they have the ball. Anyone who doesn't want to play ball will be moved on, but if you do, he will protect and support you to the death – **Mick McGuire**, former teammate at Norwich and Grantham, on Martin O'Neill, in Alex Montgomery, *Martin O'Neill – The Biography*, 2003.

That's the thing that the fans don't see; they don't see the fact that I hardly shut up during these matches, constantly running alongside players, warning them to keep it calm, or asking captains or cooler teammates to intervene. They don't see me shouting, 'Hey, number five, arms down, arms down, arms down', or 'number four, don't lunge in; stay on your feet,' umpteen times throughout the match. They just see me cautioning him eventually when he won't take a telling and seems intent on an early exit – Referee **Hugh Dallas**, March 2003.

Everyone has a grand idea of how football should be played but all these management courses? Forget it, they're a waste of time. I just like to see players enjoying themselves – Southampton manager **Gordon Strachan**, May 2003.

TV is enjoyable, but a football dressing room, now that's the place to be – TV personality and former Rangers striker **Ally McCoist**, November 2003.

When Maurice Ross knows his strong and weak points he can be a very good player for Rangers. His temper is his problem. I told him sometimes you play football with maybe 60, 70 per cent of your mind and the rest is the skill in your legs. You think forward and see situations. Remain quiet and observe your opponent sometimes when somebody is annoying you – Former Rangers defender **Bert Konterman**, November 2003.

I spoke to him just recently about Leicester and that play-off match against Crystal Palace when Stevie Claridge scored in the last minute as the game was about to go to a penalty shoot-out. His regular 'keeper had been absolutely brilliant. He'd stopped everything, yet Martin was about to substitute him for a massive Yugoslav who was on the touchline ready to come on. Martin felt that in the penalty shoot-out he would be a better bet because he was a big bloke, about six´six", and he filled the goal . . . If you look at the video, he was literally on the touchline ready to come on. He has to be on before the end of the match to take part in the shoot-out. It was then that the ball was wellied upfield and Claridge let fly – Wycombe director **Alan Parry** on Martin O'Neill's Leicester's May 1996 play-off win, in Alex Montgomery, 'Martin O'Neill – The Biography', 2003. (The sub goalkeeper concerned was giant Australian Zeljko Kalac – later to play for AC Milan – and he actually came on as a sub with a minute left, before Claridge's goal).

Not every football agent is bad and there is a definite clutch of good guys in the ranks, of which I believe I'm one. But frankly some of the behaviour I've observed from other agents is abhorrent – Agent **Jake Duncan**, February 2004.

If I remember rightly, in the Nationwide, two sets of 11 boys run out and kick a ball about. They do that in the Premiership – except slightly better – Southampton manager **Paul Sturrock**, March 2004.

I'm struggling to think of a single benefit the game has had from its formation. The rules clubs must obey – the stadium criteria, the setting-up of under-21 sides – have proved to be a hindrance rather than a help – Dundee manager **Jim Duffy** on the formation of the SPL, March 2004.

The scenario I always point out is a challenge has gone in at one end in an Old Firm game and the referee has allowed play to continue. Meanwhile play switches to the other end within five seconds and the referee awards a penalty and is on the point of showing a red card to the player who committed the foul when it comes through in his earpiece, you got the one at the other end wrong, so cancel that penalty, cancel that red card, go back to the other end and give a penalty and a red card the other way round. Can you imagine it? The police would lift me before I got across the halfway line for inciting a riot – Referee **Kenny Clark**, not a fan of video refereeing, speaking before handling his ninth Old Firm game, March 2004.

I played table tennis and I now play golf but mostly I've played team sports because they're best. You win with each other. You lose with each other. That must be so much better than to be like (Bjorn) Borg and win a tennis game and yell, 'Yeah' – Celtic's **Henrik Larsson**, March 2004.

I worked out if you have five superstars and three play well on the day, chances are you'll win. If only two play there's a good chance you'll lose. And if only one plays then you've a RIGHT good chance of losing. Individual players can win games but team formations stop you losing them. Simple as that – Former Southampton manager **Gordon Strachan**, May 2004.

You always feel with the press, they don't really want to know about the football side. They want the reasons why you didn't pick such-and-such a player – Manchester United manager **Sir Alex Ferguson**, May 2004.

At that time I got my chance, anybody could have slotted into the team, it was so well-organised and we were conceding so few goals. We were playing so well that even my mother could have got a game at the back without it damaging results – Celtic defender **Stan Varga**, October 2004.

I'm still not someone who likes to think about football. When I've finished a game, I'll give it two hours of thought. Maximum. When I get home I speak to my wife and we don't talk about football. If anybody tries to speak to me about it, I'll just ask them to change the subject – Celtic goalkeeper **Artur Boruc**, September 2005.

Listen to me, I have had it over the last few years with people telling me to put more money into Celtic and I find it most irritating. I see the same match as you do, I have no more responsibility to put money into Celtic than you or anybody else for that matter. So why should I? – Majority shareholder **Dermot Desmond** to the Celtic Supporters Association, December 2005.

I don't think Jim will ever score a better goal in his career. If we could have applauded, we would have – Celtic manager **Gordon Strachan** on Motherwell's Jim Hamilton's volley against his side at Fir Park, January 2006. The goal was voted Mitre SPL Goal of the Decade in August 2008.

Take Julien Brellier. He will play until he picks up an injury, or receives too many bookings and is suspended, and only then will another player come into the team. But we should rotate players like Brellier, Bruno Aguiar and Sammy Camazzola for maximum effect – Hearts owner **Vladimir Romanov**, May 2006.

Let's be open and honest and tell it as it is. You've got to understand what our football club is about. At this moment in our history we're not here to win the SPL. We're here to entertain our supporters – Hibs manager **Tony Mowbray**, September 2006. He moved to West Brom the following month.

I'd pay to watch Hibs, they play my kind of football. I was disappointed in the standards at the Hearts v Celtic game. I counted it – each goalkeeper threw the ball out twice in 90 minutes and kicked it up the park 30, 35 times. I wouldn't pay to watch. Everybody's got different beliefs. Hey, somebody will read this and say, 'He's talking nonsense.' But I often find players are too tense in Scotland, the last thing they need is fired up – Former Scotland midfielder **John Collins**, October 2006. Four weeks later he was appointed Hibs manager.

The ball's round. It's meant to roll – Hibs boss **John Collins**, March 2007.

A Catholic managing Rangers – Reader **Jimmy D**'s contribution to 'Tales of the Unexpected', *Word* magazine, August 2007, on things that wouldn't have been believed 20 years before.

The Champions League is the Champions League, it means much more than the UEFA Cup and winning it was probably the best day of my football career. But as a football game I must say that Celtic-Porto in Seville was the most exciting football game I have ever been in. An unbelievable game. I saw Vitor Baía say the same to Portuguese TV after the last game of his career. He said it was the most emotional game of his career and it is the same for me. Every time I see Martin O'Neill I remember I was the lucky one that day. An incredible match – Former Porto coach **Jose Mourinho** on the 2003 UEFA Cup Final in Seville, September 2007.

We needed to kill the space. A man with a white stick could've seen that – Hearts' **Michael Stewart** on his side's tactics in the 1–1 draw against Hibs, November 2007.

I think the criteria of having to have a 6,000 all-seater stadium is hindering Scottish football, I really do. It's putting a big financial burden on clubs. You just have to look at the history. It's killed Airdrie. Clyde are sitting with a stadium where one stand's open if they're lucky. Raith Rovers were virtually killed off by it and Partick Thistle are struggling. Outwith the big teams, who can afford to build all-seater stadiums? I think this policy is killing clubs – Gretna manager **Davie Irons**, November 2007.

What's surprised me is the lack of support I've had so far. Fraser Wishart didn't exactly embrace the idea when I discussed it with him on Monday. He was not positive at all. And if the players' union don't think it's a positive step forward then that's something we need to look at – SFA chief executive **Gordon Smith** on friction over his idea to punish divers retrospectively, April 2008.

How many players and managers know the laws of the game? In any line of business you've got to know what the rules are – Referee **Alan Freeland** as he prepared for retirement, May 2008.

The game in Scotland was going to hell in a handcart ten years ago and something had to be done to save it – SPL executive chairman **Lex Gold**, August 2008.

Here's his contract, look. We had to release him if a bid of €10m came in. And here's the offer from Aston Villa; €5m on registration, €5m in 12 months. I didn't want to sell him. I had to sell him. No criticism of Aston Villa, it's football. I don't suppose Portsmouth are all that happy that all of a sudden we've decided to jump on Pedro Mendes the day before the Premiership starts – Rangers chairman **Sir David Murray**, August 2008.

FIFA's view is that it would demean or reduce the importance of the referee, but I don't think that at all. But what it would do, for me, is take a lot of the pressure off the referee – SFA chief executive **Gordon Smith** on video replays for referees, August 2008.

FIFA and UEFA decreed that we'd have to stop this standing culture, all-male, swaying around, pissing where you stood, cursing and blinding – Former SFA secretary **Ernie Walker** on his role on committees on stadium safety and security, February 2009.

I hate it when managers go into a football club and all of a sudden (they say) the players aren't fit. I'd hate to go in and say about Maurice Malpas, 'His players are all crap,' because it's not right and it's not true – Swindon Town manager **Danny Wilson** on his predecessor, March 2009.

THE SACK ⚽

I had no option but to sack him in the end – Former St Mirren chairman **Willie Todd**, May 2008, on the club's decision to sack Alex Ferguson in May 1978 (for breach of contract in agreeing to move to Aberdeen). St Mirren are the only club ever to have sacked Ferguson.

Amicable solution? Certainly not. Amicable solutions are always best. 'Amicable' is a nice word and I wish it could prevail. But it's simple. I'm owed half my wages for this year and another year's wages. I've had no offers. Only a suspension and threats. What's amicable about that? I want them to honour my contract. If not, it has to be by another route. It will go to trial and there will be lots of lawyers – Former Rangers manager **Graeme Souness** after being sacked by Benfica in April 1999.

When you start as a manager, what are you thinking about? You're thinking about surviving. You don't want to be a casualty. There's that fear factor right through my life. The fear of failure. It's there, it's always there. Never leaves me – Manchester United manager **Sir Alex Ferguson**, 2002.

After the speech the next thing I knew *The Sun* were on to me. 'This isn't very funny you know, Gordon,' they said. I said, 'But it's a joke!' They said, 'Yeah, but you're criticising us.' I thought, at every dinner speech do I have to erect a sign which says, 'This Is Merely An Exploration Of Humour?' – Former Rangers striker **Gordon Smith** on being axed by *The Sun* as a columnist after referring to the newspaper in an after-dinner speech as 'written by people who aren't very good at writing and bought by people who aren't very good at reading', December 2002.

I'll be forever in debt to this club for showing me forgiveness when people were crying for my head – Aberdeen boss **Steve Paterson**, November 2003. The club had stood by him when he failed to turn up for a game in March 2003 because he was hung-over. He was sacked in May 2004.

How can you say to a girl in the office that they are losing their job because some footballer supposedly earns so much money or the club is supposedly losing tens of thousands of pounds a week? It's not right and it's sad because it's pushed into the background. The footballer's plight is getting the publicity but it's a football club, not a football team. There are so many people going to be affected by this. Unfortunately, they won't just lose their jobs, they'll lose them without anyone being aware of it because the focus is going to be on the players – Dundee manager **Jim Duffy**, as the club went into administration, November 2003.

When you appoint a manager you are likely to end up sacking him. I told Mark as much on day one – Millwall chairman **Theo Paphitis** after appointing Dennis Wise as manager, January 2004. He'd sacked Mark McGhee in October 2003.

If Richard doesn't get results, Richard will be fired – Livingston's then prospective owner **Pearse Flynn** on manager Richard Gough, January 2005. Gough resigned in May 2005 after six months in charge.

Kheredine, you're a lovely man but that's a daft question – Dundee United manager **Ian McCall** to *BBC* reporter Kheredine Idessane after being asked if he feared for his job after losing 2–0 to Motherwell, 5 March 2005. Nine days later United sacked him.

I always think that, if you're doing well, the people involved will look after you and if you're not doing well, you shouldn't be there anyway. In any case, if you outstay your welcome at a club where the fans are concerned, no length of contract is going to decide your future. It's not going to alter the climate – Former Celtic manager **Martin O'Neill**, June 2005.

I even managed to have a clash with someone who was being given a guided tour of Parkhead. He approached me to ask if he could have his photo taken with me. 'No problem,' I said. It is amazing how insensitive people can be because as he passed the camera to his female companion, and put an arm around my shoulder, he remarked to her, 'You'd better be quick. He will probably get the sack next week.' I know he meant it as a joke, but he hit such a raw nerve that I actually ejected him from the ground. He thought I was joking as well. He was laughing as I was pushing him out the door – Celtic manager **Gordon Strachan**, My Life In Football, 2006.

Something is wrong there. It's like bad karma – Kilmarnock's former Dundee United striker **David Fernandez** on his old club, the day before Craig Brewster was sacked as Tannadice manager, October 2006. It meant United had had six managers in four years.

Sometimes when you're in a hole, you stop digging – Rangers executive chairman **Sir David Murray** on the day Walter Smith returned as manager, January 2007, referring to Paul le Guen's time in charge.

Put it this way, I have been fired more often than I have left. It is a bit hypocritical – managers get sacked constantly but when one leaves people find it hard to bear – Motherwell manager **Mark McGhee**, July 2007.

THE WIFE ⚽

I was sitting in my house desperately wanting to go when I had a brainstorm. I decided to sell my house. I told my wife I was moving in with my mother and managed to get a deposit on the house and that got me to Lisbon. When I came back I had to go through with the sale and it didn't go down very well with my wife. It had been a trial separation but it looked like I'd stay on for the kids. When I broke the news of what I'd done it was goodbye to my marriage. It was worth every penny though – Celtic fan **Ernie Wilson**, then 25, recalls domestic drama pre-Lisbon 1967, May 2007.

We were both just bored with our marriages. At the start, it was a fresh face, a bit of fun and laughter, but it just grew and grew until we just didn't want to be away from each other. I know there were people hurt when we did what we did, but you only get one life – Former Manchester United manager **Tommy Docherty** on leaving wife Agnes for second wife Mary Brown in July 1977, in an interview in November 2002.

My dad is always boasting about how much better than me he was at football and my wife Michelle agrees. She came to watch me in my early days at Thistle when I was taking time to win over the fans because I was caught modelling for the Celtic catalogue and was interviewed in the *Celtic View*. She said to me at the end of the game, 'You're really not much cop at football, are you?' – Partick Thistle midfielder **Tam Callaghan**, son of former Celtic player Tom, January 2000.

I separate my emotions from football. Of course, sometimes I have to make decisions that I don't like and I find that hard, like anybody else. But I never show that. Not even to my wife – Former Rangers manager **Dick Advocaat**, September 2002.

Cathy said she'd had a chat with the boys. 'We just don't think you should be retiring – you're too young,' she said – Manchester United manager **Sir Alex Ferguson** goes back on his decision to resign, February 2002.

I've said it before – the wives make decisions, the big ones – Manchester United winger **David Beckham** on Ferguson's about-turn on quitting as United manager, February 2002.

You're joking aren't you? You want to try her out? I have to lose my temper to get anywhere here – Manchester United manager **Sir Alex Ferguson** after journalist Robert Crampton asked him who was the boss in his house, 2002.

My wife is also a Christian. We read the bible after dinner. She knows how I live and it makes it easier for me – Rangers defender and Christian, **Bert Konterman**, October 2002.

One thing is sure. If anything ever happened to Mary, I wouldn't want to carry on. Definitely not. I couldn't live without her – Former Manchester United manager **Tommy Docherty** on his wife, November 2002.

We went to Tenerife recently, then I thought, 'Oh, Christ, I've got a testimonial game for Kevin McAllister in Falkirk.' I had to break it to her gently – Southampton manager **Gordon Strachan** on wife Lesley, January 2003.

We've been together since 1975. She doesn't need to keep a firm rein on me, never needs to give me a bollocking. No chance. I like the training ground but as soon as it finishes, I'm home. We've got three kids and now we're grandparents, which adds another dimension. Here's me at 45, sleeping with a grannie. It's grab-a-grannie night every night in my house! – Southampton manager **Gordon Strachan**, January 2003.

I went for a game of snooker at his house and I was made a cup of tea by Cathy. That clinched me signing – Midfielder **Darren Fletcher** on Mrs Ferguson's role in him joining Manchester United, March 2003.

My marriage break-up I would put down a helluva lot to excessive drinking. When it starts to affect your personal life, your family and your working life, you have to hold your hands up. The worry for me is that you would think the hurt of a marriage breakdown and causing your kids a lot of hurt would have been a wake-up call. I thought that at the time and I pledged myself to getting sorted out, but I didn't. I had chances, had chances in my marriage and I always said I'd cut down. But I didn't and it cost me. Now if I can't sort myself out, it will cost me my job – Aberdeen manager **Steve Paterson**, admitting to a drink problem, March 2003. He was sacked in May 2004.

I finally got the wife in the garden last year after 40 years of marriage and it's the best move I've ever made – Partick Thistle manager **John Lambie**, in *Fanatical About Football*, ed. Jeff Connor, 2003.

I'd need him to treat me like a normal wife and he can't do that. First, I'd need him not to gamble the house from under me. Second, I'd need him to be faithful and third, he'd need not to be drunk by teatime. And would I know if he'd changed? Maybe I'd go to the bank one day and have nothing left – **Andy Goram**'s wife Miriam after splitting from the goalkeeper, October 2003.

How could I be the wee Hun bigot, don't like Catholics and all that, if my wife is a Catholic? My oldest goes to a Catholic school – Blackburn Rovers midfielder **Barry Ferguson**, December 2003.

The decision was made a month after I started the job and I was walking up the stairs in the De Vere Hotel with my wife to room 326. We were passing 323 at the time and Lesley was wearing a short skirt. That's why I was in such a hurry to get to our room. I think that's when my hip first went – Southampton boss **Gordon Strachan**, preparing for his time out of football, January 2004. He resigned two months later.

Gordon Strachan did a brilliant job at Southampton and I tried to get him to take over from me before I packed up. He's married to a Dundee girl and he swithered about it for a wee while – Former Dundee United manager **Jim McLean**, April 2004.

My wife used to watch me packing my bag on a Friday and if I was going to Old Trafford or Highbury the next day she'd take the blue shirt out and put the white one in. Hides the stains – Former Southampton manager **Gordon Strachan**, September 2004.

The reason we have such a happy marriage is that you must go out two nights a week for a candlelit dinner – she goes out on a Tuesday and I go out on a Thursday – Former Rangers midfielder **Bobby Russell**, August 2008. He and wife Kathleen had been married for over 30 years.

My wife cringes every time someone calls me Sir Alex or calls her Lady Cathy. She says to me, 'I don't know why you accepted it in the first place.' – Manchester United manager **Sir Alex Ferguson**, January 2009.

TO SEE OURSELVES

I had my session with him, and he told me I was too gentle to be a professional footballer and would be much more suitably employed in the arts world, maybe as a photographer or a poet. Ian St John didn't know whether to laugh or cry at the verdict, and said simply, 'So what you really mean to tell me, Peter, is that this club has paid £100,000 for someone who should be reciting f****** poetry!' – A 1974 trip to a psychoanalyst doesn't go as planned for Portsmouth's **Peter Marinello**, in *Fallen Idle*, 2007.

I won the treble with Rangers that year and we got married at the end of that season. This is how naive I was. I said to Marlene (wife) we might have to cancel the wedding because I expected to be going to Argentina with the Scotland team. I told Marlene to be prepared to postpone the wedding. But the wedding wasn't postponed. Ally MacLeod must have known I was getting married and spared me all the inconvenience – SFA chief executive **Gordon Smith** looks back, on TV programme, *From Player To Power*, September 2008.

I remember Archie Gemmill, who scored a great goal, and Jordan, a big striker with no teeth – Holland's **Johnny Rep** recalls the Scotland team of Argentina 78, October 2003.

Jock could condense a whole team meeting into a couple of sentences. Simple things. He said to John Wark one day, 'John, is it fair to say if you're no' scoring goals you're nae use to us?' and John just sat there and said 'Aye, have to agree.' And I got the same treatment. He took me off in one game. He says, 'You know why I'm taking you off?' I hadn't a clue. 'It's because you're not passing the ball well and if you're not passing the ball well you're not a good player.' 'Okay gaffer.' – Celtic manager **Gordon Strachan** on Jock Stein, September 2005.

As a manager it's your head on the block. You have to make cold-blooded decisions and if you can't, you shouldn't be in the job. To be honest, I found it difficult to be a bastard – Former Coventry and Sunderland manager **Terry Butcher**, 1994.

I got the impression I was viewed by some as just another foreigner who didn't give a f*** about the club. I did give a f*** – Former Celtic winger **Regi Blinker** on his time at Parkhead, in Mark Guidi, *The Inner Sanctum*, 2008.

I was portrayed as arrogant, over-confident, uncivil, rude and condescending. Further, I was supposed to be overbearing, I wanted to pick the team, I wouldn't entertain anyone who disagreed with me and I was contemptuous towards colleagues and members of the media. I was a monster, the Antichrist, a demon – Former Celtic general manager **Jock Brown**, in *Celtic-Minded: 510 Days In Paradise*, 1999.

On one occasion when a few of the players and their wives dropped in on Justin en route to a party at John Robertson's house, the female members of our party were agog that this New Town flat could belong to a footballer. A spacious, tidy house with vases of orchids in every room was not the norm for any footballer they had ever encountered – Former Hearts winger **John Colquhoun** on former teammate Justin Fashanu, after his suicide in May 1998.

It's a silly story, my one. Really stupid – **Paul Lambert**, May 1999, on moving from Motherwell to Borussia Dortmund and winning the Champions League in his first season.

I tried all my career to get away crowds to give me stick and I was never good enough. I'd have loved to have 40,000 people baying for my blood. It was my lifetime ambition to have an away crowd boo me like that, but generally they didn't even know I was playing – Leicester manager **Martin O'Neill** after his striker Emile Heskey had been booed by Leeds fans, 1999.

My lady friend said he should play Jesus Christ, he is such a good guy – Actor **Robert Duvall** on Ally McCoist, December 1999. The pair had worked together on the film, *A Shot At Glory*.

People seem to think I'm a raving lunatic and, well, maybe I am. But at least I've tried to address the problem. When you have a temper like mine, liable to explode at any time, you don't go around saying you're a reformed character – Manchester City's Inverness-born central defender and captain **Andy Morrison**, May 2000. (Morrison's adventures had included nightclub fights, a road rage case, 13 yellow cards and one red in 1998–99 season (including nine yellow and one red in a particularly demented 15–game period), being cautioned by police after squirting water at Liverpool fans after being substituted, and anger management sessions. He was also sent off in August 1999 for – according to referee Paul Rejer – sticking his tongue down Fulham's Stan Collymore's throat.)

He must have a tongue like Red Rum – Manchester City manager **Joe Royle** on the Morrison/Collymore incident, August 1999.

The catalyst for us was signing Andy Morrison. He was the man for the job and the man for the division. He dragged us up kicking and screaming. He is the kind of player that (Nottingham) Forest need – if they can find somebody like him. We only got him because of his injury record, and because he had had a major fall-out with the manager at Huddersfield. He was as strong as they come and feared nobody – Former Manchester City manager **Joe Royle**, who'd signed him, on Morrison, September 2005.

What I found hard to take was the fact that I was being reported as arrogant and aloof. Anyone who knows me knows that is far from the truth – Former Celtic head coach **John Barnes**, May 2000.

Looking back now, it's fairly obvious that no one, apart from Kenny Dalglish, had any confidence in me as head coach – Former Celtic head coach **John Barnes**, June 2000.

Tam Cowan calls me fat. I know I'm a fat bastard. But I got fat. He's always been fat – Kilmarnock manager **Bobby Williamson**, February 2001.

When I drive up the M1 I have to look the other way when I get to Junction 21. The chairman there had shown a lot of faith in me and I was totally out of order in the way I left – Millwall manager **Mark McGhee**, April 2001. Junction 21 is the cut-off for Leicester, who McGhee joined in December 1994 then left in December 1995 for Wolves.

I started at 33 and I'm still only 48 so it makes me laugh when people a couple of years younger than me are referred to as young managers while I'm the old bastard – Blackburn manager **Graeme Souness**, August 2001.

I know how people see me but all my life I've been a victim of self-doubt. There have been many times when I've felt despondent, when I think I'm useless. I felt it many times as a player and I've often experienced it as a manager – **Gordon Strachan**, shortly before leaving Coventry, 2001.

I was an alcoholic. I couldn't really see me having a life without drinking. I knew the bottle was my problem but I also thought it was my best friend – Kilmarnock winger **Andy McLaren**, January 2002.

Let me put it this way: If Scotland had qualified for this year's World Cup and England hadn't, there is no way I would support the Scots, and I would have to have gone and hidden in a cave if that had happened – Motherwell assistant manager **Terry Butcher**, March 2002. He was appointed Scotland assistant manager in February 2008.

I can honestly say that I have never seen a city throw itself into the organisation and celebration of a final with as much enthusiasm as the Scots. This may not be a huge nation nor a 'major market' but they are undoubtedly among the strongest in terms of passion for the game – UEFA president **Lennart Johansson** on Glasgow's hosting of the May 2002 Champions League Final at Hampden.

I glanced round to see Lorenzo Amoruso's tanned, shaved legs walking towards me. He said to me, 'OK, Barry. This is for me.' I turned to him and said, 'F*** off, ya fud!' I think that's where the *Only an Excuse* sketches started – Rangers' **Barry Ferguson**, *Blue*, 2006. The incident happened in the 2002 Scottish Cup Final against Celtic.

I don't drink, I never have. Also I like to keep to myself, I'm maybe a little intense that way. After games, well, I'm just tired, and I don't have your Scottish small-talk. But maybe I should have tried to adjust. I am a foreigner in this country and maybe I should have tried harder to adjust. But it is my personality, and my priority was always to do what was best for Rangers – Rangers director of football **Dick Advocaat**, September 2002.

I trusted my gut instinct – and I know I have a big gut – because it has served me well so far – Falkirk manager **Ian McCall** on turning down the chance to manage Dundee United, October 2002. He moved to Tannadice three months later.

I know that I am not quick, I am not strong, I am not very good at heading the ball and, recently, I haven't scored a lot of goals. When I was 16, I looked about 12. When I was 21, I looked about 14. I could easily not have made the grade. I probably only did because Brian Clough was a friend of my dad and he gave me an apprenticeship at Nottingham Forest and the extra time to develop a little bit – Self-assessment from Everton and Scotland's **Scot Gemmill**, March 2003.

If you ask anybody in Inverness, not that I did a lot of socialising in Inverness, they know that I made a f****** arse of myself on occasions through drink – Aberdeen manager **Steve Paterson**, confessing to a drink problem, March 2003.

I was essentially a midfielder. But I couldn't tackle, I couldn't pass and I certainly couldn't defend. So I needed to score goals – Former Dundee United manager **Jim McLean** on his playing career with Dundee, April 2003.

It's the way I play, the way I seem to stroll or strut almost, which is just the way I've been made. I've watched myself on tape and I walk funny. I also seem to have my chest puffed out, which is just the way I'm built. I'm not the most elegant of runners and never have been. I'm not a Roy Keane, a Patrick Vieira, and there's something about my persona on the pitch which gets at people – Celtic skipper **Neil Lennon**, May 2003.

I cannot understand why our team was even weaker than these footballing dwarfs. I am actually sorry for my mate Berti (Vogts), because the way his players are punishing the ball will give him a gastric ulcer. There is no technical quality in that team. But we were lucky to get away with a draw – German World Cup winner **Paul Breitner** after Scotland's draw with Germany, June 2003.

Maybe it's harsh but if I say 'Ally McCoist' in Holland, people say, 'Who?' and in Scotland, he is a legend. That gives you an indication of what it's like. I may not be as big a goalscorer as Ally but they know my name outside Scotland – Rangers' **Ronald de Boer**, July 2003.

It's only when you live abroad you realise how dumb we are as a nation. It's a real eye-opener – MSV Duisburg defender **Steven Tweed**, September 2003. Tweed had previously played in Greece and subsequently played in Japan.

My Rangers career was very unillustrious, that's the best way to describe it – Former Ibrox reserve **Craig Brown**, in *Fanatical About Football*, ed. Jeff Connor, 2003.

I was really pleased with my goal, though if I had missed the chance I would have chucked football there and then- – Scotland's **James McFadden** after scoring his first international goal against the Faroes, September 2003.

People say you shouldn't slate the guys publicly but I'm not really doing that. All I'm saying is I don't think they're playing as well as they can and the players are all agreeing with me, so it's not causing any rifts. They're big enough to pick up the paper and accept it – Aberdeen manager **Steve Paterson**, November 2003.

I've only been booked twice in the last 30 or 40 games. But I've always been an aggressive player, kicking and clattering people and being kicked myself. That's when I'm at my best. If I try to play tippy-tappy stuff I end up having a stinker. I have to hate the centre half – Celtic's **John Hartson**, November 2003.

I simply refuse to start jumping about like a neep for anyone. It's not my style – Aberdeen boss **Steve Paterson** on complaints he's too laid-back, December 2003.

People think, looking at you on the touchline, that you've lost it. That's a major mistake on their part. I am always conscious of what I'm saying, how I'm saying it, what I'm doing and I'm conscious of my body language. Anybody who thinks, 'He's lost the plot,' should think again – Stenhousemuir manager **John McVeigh**, January 2004. He left the club by mutual consent the same month.

'Peter The Pointer'? I am delighted. A lot of people say you don't want to be remembered for that, but that was part of my game – West Ham assistant manager **Peter Grant**, February 2004, on his organisational style as a player.

Knowing the person I am, I could fall out with anyone – Celtic manager **Martin O'Neill**, February 2004.

I've always been that way, but you can be laid-back and not have a clue about football. The most important ingredient, whatever nature you have, is that you've got to know about football. Without that, being laid-back would be a waste of time – Livingston manager **Davie Hay**, March 2004.

We were going well in the League that season and the manager just said, 'Do you think you could play in the Premiership?' and I told him, 'No, I don't think I can.' – Norwich's **Gary Holt**, April 2004. The conversation with manager Nigel Worthington had come during the previous season.

If you have the courtesy to ask me I must, from the way I have been brought up – my parents are gospel hall people and that – answer you honestly and, unfortunately when I answer honestly, I am definitely forceful with it – Former Dundee United manager **Jim McLean**, April 2004.

It's actually quite embarrassing to look back on some of the old pictures of me. When I was at Morton we had a black player called Mark Pickering and in the team photo I was darker than he was. It makes me cringe – Former Rangers midfielder **Derek McInnes** on his sunbed-loving past, April 2004.

I'm very conscious that I've not made the breakthrough to the top level. I'm also conscious of the reasons – Brighton manager **Mark McGhee**, May 2004.

Scotland is a very insular place. People usually choose from their own. There have been a couple of Englishmen who have come north but very few – Southampton manager **Paul Sturrock**, July 2004.

Loyalty in business is important to me. Honesty in business is important to me. I've never cheated anyone in my life in business, and not many people can say that. I know I'm able to look people in the eye and say, 'Look, I played fair by you.' – Rangers chairman **David Murray**, July 2004.

I'm not as bald as people think — it's just my fair hair — Hibs defender **Colin Murdock**, October 2004.

I think people will remember me for one of two things. It'll either be for being the bloke who played 2–4–4 or for my character on *Only An Excuse*. But at least I'll be remembered for something — Aberdeen manager **Jimmy Calderwood**, January 2005.

— Who would play you in the biopic of your life? — Layla Hall, Tottenham.
— I'd like to say Bogart but I see Woody Allen. I like Woody Allen a lot. I went to a recent film of his and there's a bit when this wee ginger-headed fella is walking around the room with just his shorts on and wee ginger legs on show. My wife turned to me and said, 'I've just had a vision of the future.' — Former Southampton manager **Gordon Strachan**, magazine questionnaire, February 2005.

What better sport to take part in than athletics, which is just you and your body? Anything else requires skills and I don't have any skills — I'm bloody hopeless at everything — Gretna owner and former long-distance runner **Brooks Mileson**, June 2005.

It's like Paul Dickov, the footballer. He just fouls everybody until he gets booked, then he stops. We just kept chipping away — **Noel Gallagher** of Oasis, June 2005.

I've never watched the game back, I couldn't do that. That would be torture. I've seen a couple of pictures and I didn't even recognise myself. I looked terrible — Motherwell goalkeeper **Gordon Marshall**, July 2005, on the CIS Cup Final defeat by Rangers four months earlier, when he was to blame for three goals in the 5–1 defeat.

Being a goalkeeper is like being the guy in the military who makes the bombs — one mistake and 'bang', everyone gets blown up — Celtic goalkeeper **Artur Boruc**, September 2005.

If the club does really well, say we won the UEFA Cup, the League and everything else it's Martin O'Neill, Martin O'Neill, Martin O'Neill or Gordon Strachan as the case may be, and then the players. It's not any of the directors. We are nobody. We didn't bring Martin or Gordon to the club, we didn't thrash out the contracts with the players. We didn't create the structures. And if the club goes wrong, if something happens and we don't win the League like last year, it's the directors' fault we didn't win the League because we didn't invest with Martin — Majority shareholder **Dermot Desmond** to the Celtic Supporters Association, December 2005.

When I was picked on by bigger lads as a kid, I found I could invariably talk my way out of trouble. I often did it by making them laugh, which is something I seem to be quite good at to this day – Celtic manager **Gordon Strachan**, in autobiography, *Strachan: My Life In Football*, 2006.

I can laugh when people call me moany but people who do not know me think that's the way I am. You cannot have that kind of personality and then be asked to try to motivate a dressing room – Former Kilmarnock and Hibs manager **Bobby Williamson** on his public image, May 2006.

– What do you think you'll be remembered for?
– I doubt I'll be remembered for much because I don't think I am the type of player fans warm to or who catches the eye. But I like to think I always gave my best. – St Mirren's **Mark Reilly**, retiring after 21 years as a player, newspaper questionnaire, May 2006.

I've never been out socially in Dundee for a long time and that's a deliberate thing. Especially when things haven't been going well, I'm not going to be prancing about town. That would send out the wrong message – Dundee United manager **Craig Brewster**, September 2006.

From a young lad, people said I spoke very slowly. I don't know why that is, but it maybe has helped me deal with things here – being able to think a little bit more – Hearts captain **Steven Pressley** as problems increase at the club, October 2006.

It was not just the SFA who thought Walter was the right man. Deep down, I thought so, too – **Gordon Strachan** on being in the running to become Scotland manager and losing out to Walter Smith in December 2004, *My Life In Football*, 2006.

I think of the last game I played for Celtic. I gave away one or two passes. Two stray, silly passes, and it eats away at me. All you need then is someone to say something – **Roy Keane**, after quitting football, September 2006.

Everyone says that. I think I need to learn how to celebrate without looking like I am going to kill somebody – Cardiff striker **Steven Thompson**, October 2006.

I'd got it because I was the least not-liked – SFA president **John McBeth**, May 2007, after his surprise victory to be the British vice-president of FIFA. It had been widely thought either England's Geoff Thompson or Northern Ireland's Jim Boyce would get the post. McBeth stood down later that month after making remarks about African and Caribbean associations and Thompson was appointed.

That line about 'Hotel California' applied to us. It was like no one ever leaves – Gretna boss **Davie Irons** on efforts to slim down their big squad, July 2007.

We weren't like Millwall, who revelled in being hated – Scottish rock star **Jackie Leven** on his 80s band, *doll by doll*, 2007.

You shouldn't think of yourself as greater than you are – I won't commit the sin of pride – Former Rangers manager **Paul le Guen**, in Graham Spiers, *Paul le Guen: Enigma*, 2007.

In this country we've got an excuse for everything. For instance, I love the Aussie attitude to sport, the way it's right out there as part of their cultural identity. But you mention this here and the reaction is, 'Aye, but they've got the weather.' So I ask you this: Can you name a Scandinavian golf course? Probably not. Do they have snow up there? Just a wee bit. Do they have rain? Loads. So how come they've got seven players in the European top 20 for Ryder Cup points and we, with the best courses in the world, have only got one? They manage that despite where they live, not because of it – Rangers manager **Walter Smith**, November 2007.

We have a world champion swimmer in David Carry yet we don't have a swimming pool for him to train in – he has to go to England. That makes life very difficult. But if you have your own facilities, it's different – Aberdeen manager **Jimmy Calderwood**, February 2008.

Am I supposed to be like the Prime Minister and never deviate from the original text? Am I supposed to ditch any sense of humour? Why would I have to do that? – SFA chief executive **Gordon Smith** on his job, March 2008.

If you are confident in Scotland then people think you are arrogant and have an ego – SFA chief executive **Gordon Smith**, April 2008.

Only one – he believes he has none – Arsenal manager **Arsène Wenger**, asked if Alex Ferguson had any weaknesses, quoted in May 2008.

Sometimes it would be premeditated to get my point across, to keep the players' feet on the ground, but I'm going back to 15 years ago. I'm a pussycat now – I'm too old to lose my temper – Manchester United manager **Sir Alex Ferguson**, in interview with Sir David Frost, June 2008.

I've got a CV that a lot of people would die for – yet, again, I'm sitting on the dole – Former Gretna manager **Rowan Alexander**, who led the club to three successive promotions, as the club folded in June 2008.

I did look up 'bully' in the dictionary once. And as I remember, it said a bully is somebody who preys on the weak, where weak is defined as somebody weaker than they (the bully) are. If you look at some of the people I have stood up to over the years, as a manager – and I have had dust-ups with all sorts of people in that dressing room – generally speaking they are much, much bigger than me. There is nothing bullying about that – Manchester United manager **Sir Alex Ferguson**, October 2008.

When I get up every morning, I have to face things that none of you have to. Never worry about my motivation and dedication – Rangers chairman **Sir David Murray**, November 2008.

People don't know me, they don't know how I behave every day. Yes, sometimes I am angry and I show my unhappiness, but inside I am always joking and always laughing. If I was a miserable bastard I don't think there would be such an enjoyable atmosphere among the players. I just have this poker look – Hibs manager **Mixu Paatelainen**, January 2009.

I couldn't be swayed by the big clubs. They would both like to run it themselves. They want everything to suit them. But there was no way they were going to get favours out of me that I wouldn't give to Forres Mechanics or whoever – Former secretary **Ernie Walker** on his 32–year spell at the SFA, February 2009.

I was brought up in a house where you were expected to support Rangers and vote Labour. I signed for Celtic and voted for Maggie three times. So I suppose I've always been a bit of a non-conformist – Pundit **Davie Provan**, March 2009.

It was about the turn of the year I thought it was time I started looking after myself, time I stopped blaming other people for the way my career had gone and looked at my part in it. Norway was good but I felt a little out of it, and did so big time at Millwall. I said to myself, there must be a reason why this keeps happening, it can't just be coincidence or bad luck – Former Rangers (and Viking Stavanger) defender **Maurice Ross**, by then with Turkish side Kocaelispor, April 2009.

I'm sarcastic at times. It's a Scottish trait. It's one of our great exports, sarcasm. So sarcasm's my only really fault really. But I live in Glasgow, where everyone enjoys sarcasm. Everybody does it. I use it sometimes in my humour. Some people think it's funny at times, some people don't. It depends on the individual – Celtic manager **Gordon Strachan**, May 2009.

TRANSFERS ⚽

Richard had made up his mind to go and launched what was the most remarkable guerrilla campaign I have ever seen in football. It seemed from his actions that if we didn't let him go he would make life impossible for the team: the great leader was threatening to become the great wrecker – Former Tottenham chairman **Irving Scholar** on Richard Gough, in book, *Behind Closed Doors: Dreams & Nightmares At Spurs*, 1992.

He phoned his mate to tell him he was moving from being third-choice 'keeper at Bradford to Celtic. His mate was happy and told him it would be good for him to play first-team football again and that a bit of form might lead to him getting a move to a bigger club within a couple of months. Gouldy's reply was, 'I won't get any bigger than Celtic. This is the best move of my career.' His mate said, 'Steady, Gouldy – Stalybridge Celtic are a decent club, but you've got to aim higher in the long run.' – Former Celtic midfielder **Craig Burley** on goalkeeper Jonathan Gould's remarkable career turnaround in the title-winning 1997–98 season, in Mark Guidi, *The Inner Sanctum*, 2008.

We'd given Martin £15m to invest. His first signing was Chris Sutton, who was with Chelsea but wasn't making it with the Chelsea first team. I asked Martin could we have a chat about this. So I met him in London, we went for lunch, and I said, 'Martin, I want to give you my views about Chris Sutton,' – and these were some of the views of a lot of Celtic supporters. 'We're paying six and a half million for a person that's scored one goal in the last 20 matches, that's going to be as highly-paid as Henrik Larsson, do you think this is the wise way to spend the money?' So he glared at me and he said, 'Am I the football manager or are you?' – Celtic majority shareholder **Dermot Desmond**, in DVD, 'The Official History of Celtic', 2008.

We all consider ourselves a really big club but we might not be everyone's cup of tea at the minute. I remember being asked at Leicester why we hadn't signed Luis Figo. No one thought that Figo might not want to sign for us – Celtic manager **Martin O'Neill**, March 2001.

If you want good players, you have to pay good money, but I'm a defender: you shouldn't be paying millions, millions, millions for a defender. Defenders are very important, but with all respect to Rio Ferdinand – I've met him, he's a good guy – I don't think he's worth £30m – Rangers defender **Lorenzo Amoruso**, November 2002.

I've never seen a manager or football director act in this way. They lied in the face of the player. Bain should go and hide under a rock. He should open a store somewhere because he sure as hell can't run a club. They have stabbed the player in the heart, made a liar out of Alex McLeish and a fool out of me. In 33 years of football I have never seen anything like this – American agent **Eric Manasse** on Rangers director of football business Martin Bain as the Ibrox club pulled out of the deal to sign Rosario striker Luciano Figueroa, July 2003.

The guy I would have liked was Lorenzo Amoruso. But I didn't get involved in time – Dundee director **Giovanni di Stefano** on transfer targets that got away, August 2003.

They will say that it's a depressed market, but we aren't that depressed. I could ring up Real Madrid and say I'll offer £100,000 for Zidane and tell everyone I'd made a bid for him. At the end of the day that wouldn't buy his big toe nail. You must be realistic – Motherwell manager **Terry Butcher** after Dundee bid £600,000 for James McFadden, August 2003.

I could very easily buy players and give them to the manager, a little bit like what's happened at Chelsea, but you cannot do that here. To do that here, I would have to change the whole team and say, 'There you are, Mr Duffy!' I think he would be entitled to give me a punch on the nose for disrespect, and I probably wouldn't even prosecute because he would be right – Dundee director **Giovanni di Stefano**, August 2003.

Probably my best signing – Portsmouth manager **Harry Redknapp**, September 2003, on signing John Hartson for West Ham in February 1997 for £3.2m.

I loved McFadden. I said to (coach) Jan Wouters, 'Buy McFadden,' and a few other players said the same. I asked him in the semi-final against Motherwell and he said, 'No problem, I am a Celtic fan but every player wants to play for a big team. If you ask me tomorrow, I will come today.' I asked him on the pitch 15 minutes before the end of time. £1.2m is no money for him – Former Rangers defender **Bert Konterman** reveals an on-field approach to the Motherwell striker during the April 2003 Scottish Cup semi-final, November 2003.

Nobody was more disappointed than I was, sitting with Barry in a room in Murray Park, when he said he wanted to try the Premiership – Rangers owner **David Murray** on Barry Ferguson's exit, January 2004.

It was disappointing not to get Ronaldinho. There was a problem with his brother, who was his agent, but Peter Kenyon, who was chief executive then, didn't get the job done. There have been others, like (Alan) Shearer and (Paul) Gascoigne – Manchester United manager **Sir Alex Ferguson**, March 2004.

It wasn't deliberate. We spoke to 15 players from all over the world. It just so happens that the financial position of Scottish clubs makes it easy for our chief executive to do business there – Plymouth Argyle manager **Bobby Williamson** after making five signings from the SPL, August 2004.

He has managed to get his 30 pieces of silver so I hope he's happy. When he phoned me to say what he was planning to do I just told him to f*** off. You can quote me on that because that's how strongly I feel about it – Dundee manager **Jim Duffy**, January 2005 after former defender Lee Mair joined rivals Dundee United after previously agreeing to rejoin Dundee. The club banned Mair's agent Paul Cherry from the ground.

(Manager) Richard (Gough) told me, 'Pearse, agents aren't going to deal with us because of Vivien.' Rather than being upset, it was the best news I'd heard in a long time – Livingston's then prospective owner **Pearse Flynn** on his Lionheart consortium's chief executive Vivien Kyles, January 2005. She subsequently became chief executive of Livingston.

It's not fair to say Jackie wasn't wanted here. He was more than wanted. Everything appeared to be progressing quite well in the discussions until, all of a sudden, we got a call on Monday to say that, if Jackie didn't get what he wanted by five o'clock, he'd be off. In the years I've had in management I can't ever remember a player setting a deadline like that. We reacted to it, even though the squeezing timescale was far from ideal, and agreed before the deadline to give him an increased offer. I thought that was it done, but then his agent came back asking for a lot more. Then we got a call at six o' clock on Monday to say Jackie would be signing for Wolves – Celtic manager **Gordon Strachan** on defender Jackie McNamara's exit from the club, June 2005.

When I read those comments from Gordon I phoned him up and told him what I thought of him. How he portrayed me was just really hurtful – Wolves' **Jackie McNamara** recalls his exit from Celtic, January 2007.

I feel my name has been dragged through the mud to spare Celtic's blushes. My move to Wolves has nothing to do with hard cash. I'm going to Molineux for the same money I got in my last season at Celtic Park. I felt I was being used when it took the club until 3 June to come up with their first formal offer – **McNamara** responds at the time of Celtic's original comments, June 2005.

I should have been man enough to say, 'This is where I belong.' If I could go back and change it now, I would have stayed because I knew within a few months that I had made a mistake. I'm just grateful Rangers wanted me back and the fans have been great to me since I came back. Graeme Souness is charismatic and was a great player, but I am a strong character as well and I disappointed myself by being persuaded – Rangers' **Barry Ferguson** on his August 2003 move to Blackburn, October 2005.

When Steven Pressley was available, I suggested we sign him to shore up the back. We didn't have that sort of centre half and I wanted to bring a Scot into the backroom staff – Rangers chairman **Sir David Murray** reveals suggesting a move for Hearts' Pressley in late 2006 to Paul le Guen, November 2008. Le Guen didn't act on the suggestion and Pressley signed for Celtic in December 2006.

There was no player that Martin (O'Neill) asked for that he was refused. At the same time we weren't going to go out there with a wad of money and buy up and say we have the divine right to get to the Champions League Final and the UEFA Cup Final again – Majority shareholder **Dermot Desmond** to the Celtic Supporters Association, December 2005.

Shunsuke's fee, quoted at £2.5m originally, was not even half that – Celtic manager **Gordon Strachan** on Nakamura, in autobiography, *Strachan: My Life In Football*, 2006.

Was Rafael Scheidt the worst player you ever signed? And was it your fault, or John Barnes?' – Jules Brandon, Glasgow
I never signed anyone at Celtic. It wasn't anyone's fault. If someone is in charge of a football team they are the one who make all the decisions, who comes and who goes, how they play, when they train. They are all the manager's decision. That player he's asking about was a Brazilian centre back, and he was a right good player. He left Celtic and went back to Corinthians and played for Brazil – Former Celtic caretaker manager **Kenny Dalglish**, *FourFourTwo* magazine questionnaire, May 2006. (Rafael Scheidt made three appearances for Brazil, all in friendlies in the summer of 1999 before he joined Celtic. He returned to Brazil, never played for the international side again and was last heard of playing in China for Shaanxi Baorong Chanba.)

Thomas has got that personality but it is not just personalities you sign – otherwise I would have signed Vinnie Jones. Vinnie is a personality but you have to be able to play – Celtic manager **Gordon Strachan** on new signing Thomas Gravesen, September 2006.

You've got to put it into the context of what Celtic did in the last week of the transfer window. The reported salary they have paid for one particular player is double the whole salaries of our football club put together. That is the power of what they can do to change the course of a season in a transfer window – Hibs manager **Tony Mowbray** on the Gravesen signing, September 2006.

– Is it true you found out you were being sold to West Brom on *Sky Sports*? – **Brian Reagan**, Aberdeen.
– Yeah but I have no grudge with Celtic. I was on holiday and I went up to the apartment to get a drink and *Sky* was on. The actual news story wasn't that I'd been sold, it was that West Brom and Celtic had agreed a fee. It wasn't very nice, though – – West Brom's **John Hartson**, magazine questionnaire, February 2007.

Steven has been the SPL Young Player of the Year two years in a row, second-top goalscorer last season, and is a full Scotland international. So why would you let a talent like that go for a lower figure when you see the likes of Kevin Thomson, Anthony Stokes, Lee McCulloch all in the £2million category – and that leaves aside Scott Brown in the £4.4million category? – Kilmarnock chairman **Michael Johnston** gets tough over Steven Naismith, July 2007. Rangers had had a series of bids rejected for the striker. He signed for them for a fee of £1.9m on deadline day, 31 August 2007.

It was a very satisfying economic deal for me. Going to Rangers happened too early for Šebo, and I knew it. Obviously, I did the best deal I could for my club – Austria Vienna financial director **Markus Kraetschmer**, in Graham Spiers, *Paul le Guen: Enigma*, 2007. (Slovakian striker Filip Šebo had scored just five goals in 32 games for Austria Vienna following a £400,000 move from Artmedia Bratislava before Rangers paid £1.8m for him in August 2006.)

The bargain-buy of my whole time at Leeds United – Former Leeds chairman **Peter Ridsdale** on the club's signing of Mark Viduka from Celtic in July 2000 (price: £6m), in *United We Fall: Boardroom Truths about the Beautiful Game*, 2007. The Australian scored 72 goals in 166 games for Leeds.

Peter Lawwell is the chief executive of Celtic. I am the chief executive of Bobo Balde – Celtic's Guinea international **Balde** as Celtic attempted to move him during the transfer window, August 2007.

Coaches Derek Collins and Iain Scott, scout Ray Farningham and I spent hours and hours and pounds and pounds travelling all over Britain looking at players but did not get a chance to bring any of them in. Instead players nobody had seen were signed – Former Gretna manager **Davie Irons** as the club faced extinction, June 2008.

People are posting these things on websites and then people are writing about them the next day. No foundation to them whatsoever. James McFadden? 32 grand and six million. Sorry, we don't do 32 grand a week and six million. Total rubbish – Rangers chairman **Sir David Murray**, August 2008.

When we sold Gabriel Heinze to Real Madrid (the previous summer), we knew it was going to happen, because Ronaldo was very close to Heinze. I knew what they were doing. I don't believe they were interested in Heinze – good player though he is. The endgame was to get Ronaldo – Manchester United manager **Sir Alex Ferguson** on Real Madrid's courtship of his star player, October 2008.

Jean-Alain Boumsong. Without any shadow of a doubt. It's the only sale when there was never an agent on the sale. Because I didn't let Willie Mackay get involved – Rangers chairman **Sir David Murray**, asked who was the best signing the club had made in his 20 years at Ibrox, November 2008.

Gianluca Vialli would be the one that got away. He wrote me a letter, I've still got it. He said he made a mistake. They (Juventus) had just won the European Cup and I went and met him in Turin. He then went to Chelsea and he wrote me a letter saying that it had been nice to meet me and he had made a mistake — Rangers chairman **Sir David Murray**, November 2008. The move came in the summer of 1996.

TV

There was a giant robotic arm with a camera attached to it whirring behind my goal; every time I moved, it moved. It was the start of what football has become — Former Norwich goalkeeper **Bryan Gunn** on playing in the Olympic Stadium in Munich against Bayern Munich in October 1993.

John, you've no right to ask that question. You're out of order. You know full well my ruling on that. Right, that's the interview finished. I don't want to f****** watch it! Cancel it! F****** make sure that does not go out! You f****** know the rules here! — Manchester United manager **Alex Ferguson** to BBC's John Motson in after-match interview, 28 October 1995, after taking exception to a question about Roy Keane's ordering-off against Middlesbrough, in Michael Crick, The Boss: The Many Sides of Alex Ferguson, 2002. (Match of the Day's producers decided not to show the interview.)

I feel sorry for people who only have council telly. I recommend they go to the pub on Sunday rather than watch us — Aberdeen's **Stevie Tosh** after scoring twice as Aberdeen lost 3–2 to Livingston in the CIS Cup quarter-final, December 2003.

I was in the dining room when I heard them mention a football question on Millionaire. I just thought, 'I'll know this' and went through to watch it. They asked what town St Mirren are from. When the options came up he said it wasn't Arbroath or Oban and ended up taking his 50-50 lifeline. It came up Fort William and Paisley — and he went for Fort William. He lost the money and it served him right — St. Mirren's unsympathetic midfielder **Ricky Gillies**, December 2003.

Andy Gray did a Liverpool v Chelsea game this season and his assessment, before the game started, was 100 per cent right. Liverpool actually won the game the way he said they would — Former Dundee United manager **Jim McLean** on the Sky pundit and former United striker, April 2004.

I wish I'd accepted one of those many offers to work for TV or radio, because I heard so much rubbish being spouted by so many big names. The best summarisers in sport tell you what to look out for and speak honestly without worrying if they're upsetting anyone. That's why (Alan) Hansen is good — Former Nottingham Forest boss **Brian Clough** on TV panellists at Euro 2004.

One thing I really missed at Celtic was commentating. It was hard for me not to do it. I remember looking up at the gantry and thinking I should be there — Setanta commentator **Jock Brown**, July 2004. Brown had been general manager at Celtic.

Ah, my favourite quiz: *Fifteen To One* — Former Manchester United striker **Brian McClair** after being called by manager Sir Alex Ferguson on TV show *Celebrity Who Wants To Be A Millionaire*, December 2004.

I talk especially quickly when (Peter) Schmeichel is on because I know it confuses him — Former Southampton manager **Gordon Strachan** on his TV pundit career, February 2005.

Q: What bores you?
A: Daft sports like cricket, golf, darts, bowls and snooker. How can anyone sit and watch snooker? It even bores me when I hear footballers going on about playing golf. It's rubbish. Sports like that shouldn't be on television. I'd much rather watch *Big Brother* — Rangers winger **Chris Burke**, newspaper questionnaire, January 2006.

Strange goings-on. It's better than *Celebrity Big Brother* — Bristol City (and former Hearts) defender **Jamie McAllister**, as upheavals at his former club — including the exit of captain Steven Pressley – coincided with allegations of racism towards Bollywood actress Shilpa Shetty on the TV programme, January 2007.

I think we can watch the news without yob culture but we get that garbage coming on — Celtic manager **Gordon Strachan** to BBC Scotland reporter David Currie, March 2007. The previous night Currie had joked about having Scotland manager Alex McLeish and assistant Andy Watson 'by the balls' as they were making the Scottish Cup semi-final draw live on TV.

Gordon says I'm like his screensaver, I'm on so often — Motherwell manager **Mark McGhee** on pal Gordon Strachan's views on his TV appearances after getting the Fir Park job, December 2007.

I have every respect for Alan Hansen, he was a million times better than me as a player but there have been occasions when he's got it wrong. With respect, he's never managed a football team — West Brom manager **Tony Mowbray**, November 2008. Hansen had said Mowbray's insistence on West Brom's footballing style would see them struggle in the Premiership. They hadn't won in seven league games at the time of Hansen's remarks and eventually finished bottom.

It was easy getting paid for talking rubbish — and I could talk quality rubbish — New Inverness Caley Thistle manager **Terry Butcher**, on giving up his Setanta pundit's role to take the job, January 2009.

US

Among much else we owe the Scots are whisky, raincoats, rubber wellies, the bicycle pedal, the telephone, tarmac, penicillin and an understanding of the active principles of cannabis, and think how insupportable life would be without those. So thank you, Scotland, and never mind that you seem quite unable to qualify for the World Cup these days – American humorist **Bill Bryson**, *Notes From A Small Island*, 1995.

Scotsman's desire to struggle is as if sucked in almost from mother's milk – **Guntis Indriksons**, Latvian FA President, in the match programme for the 1996 game between Latvia and Scotland.

I'd never describe myself as British except when I'm checking into a hotel. I'm very Scottish – Scotland manager **Craig Brown** before the Euro 2000 play-offs against England, November 1999.

Rangers' so-called global appeal is a myth. When I was there, we did an exercise which involved asking 50,000 fans on the database to recommend a friend or relative abroad. A big response was expected – some were even talking about getting 100,000 names because everybody in Scotland seems to know somebody abroad. We got back 2,800 names and three-quarters of them didn't know they had been nominated – Former Rangers director **Hugh Adam**, February 2002.

Why the surprise over Argentina's elimination? When did a team with a large Scottish following ever qualify for the second round of the World Cup? – Letter to *The Guardian* newspaper during the 2002 World Cup. Argentina had been in England's group.

I see kids of 13 and 14 standing around in the street drinking and smoking and getting fat – Rangers' **Bert Konterman** on the dearth of facilities in Scotland after the 2–2 draw in the Faroes, September 2002.

Once you can understand Paul Lambert you can most likely understand any Scottish person – Former Celtic striker **Ian Wright**, BBC TV programme, *Footballer's Lives*, March 2003.

We need a bit of stirring up after 'Flower of Scotland' because I don't particularly like that song. It's a bit of a dirge. It's an emotional song but it's not rousing – SFA chief executive **David Taylor**, April 2003.

I have a very stubborn streak in me that if anybody isn't very nice to me. I could quite easily not talk to them again for the rest of my life – Former Scotland midfielder **Archie Gemmill**, June 2003.

Take Stevie Tosh out of our side and the game would only have lasted 90 minutes. There was no threat from anyone else – Aberdeen manager **Steve Paterson** after Tosh had scored twice as Aberdeen lost 3–2 to Livingston after extra time in the CIS Cup quarter-final, December 2003.

I didn't realise that till I left at 32 and went to Norwich, a fantastic club. All of a sudden, I realised that people actually live a life. You can play the game, win, lose or draw and you can go out, and I thought, 'This is strange.' People would come up to you in the street and just say, 'Hello.' – West Ham assistant manager **Peter Grant** on how football with Celtic dictated his life, February 2004.

I was in the showers after a training session, with Maurice Ross standing next to me. He asked me the same question three times and every time I was doing my brains in, wondering what he said. I really felt stupid, but I honestly did not have a clue what he was saying. I bet he thought I was making him feel like an idiot, too. So in the end I just said, 'Yes.' – Language problems for Rangers' **Frank de Boer**, February 2004.

I am really proud of a lot of the things I have said about the way I wanted football to be going. Unfortunately it hasn't, but it should have gone the way I wanted. I stood in every boardroom and I told them, 'There are eight clubs here in the Premier League.' There were 10 at that time, with nothing between us (the eight outside the Old Firm). Supporters-wise we have 7,000–10,000 and we should all agree to have a basic wage we can afford, and if they don't sign for us on that wage then they don't sign. English clubs can't sign them all – Former Dundee United manager and chairman **Jim McLean**, April 2004.

I stay about four miles outside Dunfermline and I just couldn't understand a thing when I first arrived. 'Ken' this and 'ken' that, I thought, 'Who the f*** is this Ken?' I thought I was back in Holland – Dunfermline manager **Jimmy Calderwood** encounters the Fife accent, May 2004.

Somehow, we have to get back to playing street football. We can't use the streets, for safety reasons, but we can do it with a better coaching structure, and better facilities available to the community. There is something fundamentally wrong with Scottish sport. They say we have a darts player who does this, curlers who do that, but they're not really sports. It looks like we're good at pub games. I can't see a team, or athletic, sport that we're any good at – Former Southampton manager **Gordon Strachan**, February 2005.

If, like Craig (Reedie, chairman of British Olympic Asociation) you are talking from the persepctive of the BOA, then yes, there should be a GB football team. But if you're talking from the perspective of Scottish football, which is my interest, then I say 'why?' We're Scotland, we're not a member of the BOA – SFA chief executive **David Taylor**, October 2005, after suggestions of Scottish participation in a Great Britain football team at the 2012 Olympics.

We're like that with everything. We eat quickly and we drink quickly, that's what we are. You go to France, they take five hours to eat a meal, we take 20 minutes. We don't speak to each other, we get the head down and rattle it out. This is our culture, we do everything quickly. Go for a game of golf in America and it's five hours, here it's two and a half – Celtic manager **Gordon Strachan**, October 2005.

When Kenny (McDowall) was talking today, I had to ask one of my teammates what he'd said – Linguistic difficulties for Rangers' American winger **DaMarcus Beasley** with the Rangers coach, October 2007 (four months after he'd joined the club).

Being from a technically non-independent country myself, I was moved to find some way of making sure these teams got as much attention as the FIFA members – Essex-based Scot **Mark Cruickshank**, who runs The Roon Ba internet website dedicated to football-playing nations denied membership of FIFA, in Steve Menary, Outcasts! The Lands That FIFA Forgot, 2007.

I always felt a bit different, and I was quite proud of that. I was always playing on it. I've never once supported England in my whole life. I never felt English – Coventry-born Scotland defender **Graham Alexander**, October 2007. He plays for Scotland through father Andrew.

Say what you like about those days, but no one in my class grew up to be a mass murderer or a rapist or any kind of menace to society. Once you got the belt a couple of times, you didn't want it again – Celtic manager **Gordon Strachan**, November 2007.

German teams like Bayern play on a Saturday and, if they have a midweek game coming up, then they go into hospital and get put on vitamin drips that night. The Scottish boys might be in a disco – Aberdeen boss **Jimmy Calderwood** after his side's UEFA Cup defeat by Bayern Munich, February 2008.

You just don't get that many pats on the back at Blackburn Rovers, Nottingham Forest and Wycombe Wanderers. In Glasgow, there's always someone who'll tell you how good you are – Former Celtic midfielder **Craig Burley** on Neil Lennon and Barry Ferguson, after Lennon returned to Celtic as a coach, April 2008.

When I had my year out of football and was in West Palm Beach, I was out cycling one day and ended up in some Mexican-Colombian area where I stopped and watched some football. I was the only white person there.

People were saying, 'Who's the guy with the wee white legs?' I love watching football. I'll watch it anywhere. I'd love to stop (and watch kids' games in Scotland) but it would be about five minutes before I'd be abused, so I don't here – Celtic manager **Gordon Strachan**, October 2008.

I think people in the West of Scotland grow up in a different climate. Literally. It's wet, damp, unforgiving. Have you ever stood on the harbour front in Fraserburgh on a February morning? Beautiful! Fraserburgh is cold, but it's dry – Manchester United manager **Sir Alex Ferguson**, October 2008.

VLAD ⚽

From my first meeting with John, I noticed he is clear in his own mind about what he wants for himself, the team and Hearts as a whole. I like that certainty in a man – Hearts owner **Vladimir Romanov**, December 2004, a month after appointing John Robertson as head coach.

It was useless to co-operate with him at the end. He was saying one thing and doing another – **Vladimir Romanov**, July 2005, two months after sacking Robertson.

I am happy with the appointment of George. He came with good recommendations and we will work together to achieve the same goal of challenging for first place in the league – **Vladimir Romanov**, July 2005 (three weeks after Burley's appointment).

I've got to be comfortable with myself. At the end of the day, it is me who has got to make the decisions – Hearts manager **George Burley**, perhaps sensing impending problems, July 2005.

I want us to be (Scottish) champions in three years time. If we can do it sooner, so much the better – **Vladimir Romanov**, August 2005.

I want us to get to the stage where our goal has to be to become champions of Europe. The only question is when that will happen – **Vladimir Romanov**, October 2005.

No one could have envisaged we would be top of the league after ten games. But you never know what lies around the corner – More prophetic words from Hearts manager **George Burley**, October 2005, shortly before his sacking.

I want the team to do more than scrap. I want them to show real class and I'm not sure Burley is the man to bring this about. If I don't find the right Scot then I will take charge of the team myself – **Vladimir Romanov** gives a taste of things to come after sacking Burley, October 2005.

I gave these people full control and in one year there was no result . . . every day they turned up at the club, they were doing it harm – **Vladimir Romanov** on why he sacked chief executive Phil Anderton, 2005. He had been at the club for eight months.

I expressed my disappointment last week at Phil (Anderton, chief executive) and George (Burley) leaving the club but I honestly don't believe that will affect Mr Romanov's decision. I think if he sees me as the man to take Hearts forward, he will appoint me. If he wants a yes-man as a manager, he won't – **Bobby Robson** on his prospects of becoming Hearts' manager, November 2005.

(Vladimir) Romanov is behaving like a dictator and if he continues there will be a revolution against him. I very much regret bringing him in . . . he seems to be acting like a megalomaniac – Ex-Hearts chairman **George Foulkes** on the Hearts owner, November 2005.

I understand how the fans feel but I would ask them to look at his professional career – Hearts chairman **Roman Romanov**, defending the appointment of a convicted sex offender, Graham Rix, who had been unsuccessful in managerial posts at Portsmouth and Oxford United, as manager, November 2005.

Vladimir didn't come down to the dressing room and say, 'This is the team you must select.' But he went on and on and on about Julien Brellier. After a match he kept saying, 'Brellier – three out of 10. We need another player to play alongside him to get three out of 10, then that would be six out of 10, ha ha.' Brellier was man of the match a number of times he did that – Former Hearts director **George Foulkes**, November 2005.

We already have a director of football working incognito and hopefully we'll announce him soon. He is helping us at the moment and is well known in UK football – Chairman **Roman Romanov**, November 2005.

I said we had an incognito director of football, which was a joke. A director of football will be appointed. But the person himself said it may not be appropriate at this moment to add more disruption – Chairman **Roman Romanov**, January 2006.

If you are building a house and you want it to stand for a thousand years, it is sometimes better to build it yourself. As Tsar Peter the Great once said, half of the builders in Russia should be in jail. If it is your house, you need to maintain control over what goes on – Hearts owner **Vladimir Romanov**, February 2006.

He tried hard but maybe it was too big a job for him – **Roman Romanov** on Graham Rix after his sacking, March 2006. He'd lasted four months.

All of us would like to pick the team – but it's down to the professionals. I would love to pick the side, but would get dreadful results. Or maybe not! But I'm not going to take the risk – **Roman Romanov**, March 2006.

The manager was sacked when they were top of the league. The new guy informed them he was being told who to play. Eleven new players arrived without strengthening the starting XI. Another manager was sacked 11 days before a Scottish Cup semi-final and in the middle of a fight for a Champions League place. And the angriest the Hearts players got was, 'We need stability.' – Former Scotland midfielder **Craig Burley** on the Hearts problems, March 2006.

I thought I was coming to a football club, but I arrived at a circus at Hearts. The task for me was to turn this circus into a football club – Hearts owner **Vladimir Romanov**, May 2006.

Andy is a fine player but there is just one problem: his agent. I don't think we will be extending Webster's contract while he is being represented by this person – **Vladimir Romanov** on defender Andy Webster, May 2006.

I already have this coach at Hearts. He is in charge of everything and he is helping the players. Actually it is not just one person. I will give you one name, and another name when we become champions. Number one is Steven Pressley, the captain of the team. The other person's name I will tell you when we become champions – **Vladimir Romanov**, September 2006. Valdas Ivanauskas was team coach at the time.

The person will be of the highest possible quality and able to deliver the success that the club and fans deserve – **Vladimir Romanov**, as coach Valdas Ivanauskas went on a leave of absence for unspecified 'health reasons', October 2006.

I wanted to open a Ukio Bankas branch in Edinburgh from the time I was first looking to buy a club in Scotland – **Vladimir Romanov**, October 2006.

There's a very likeable side to him, a friendly side, then he changes. He's a Jekyll & Hyde character – Former Hearts chairman **George Foulkes**, on club owner Vladimir Romanov, October 2006.

Dear supporters, even the most sacred places on this earth, the places that house the remains of Christ, are blighted by profiteers and money-grabbers. Likewise, in the football world, which is sacred for those who love football, there are also those – be they agents, journalists, jealous hangers-on or other 'wunderkind' – who seek to ruin all that is good about the game. But it is the devil that is driving them forward, and they are not going to stop. All that will remain for me is to step aside and bid them farewell on their road to hell

– **Vladimir Romanov**'s Christmas message, in the match programme for the Boxing Day game against Hibs, 2006.

WALTER SMITH ⚽

I like Walter Smith and what he had to say. He was very honest with me. He could have come along with all this crap about, 'Oh, we're a good team with good players and we're going to be challenging for the championship next year.' But he didn't. He said the team needs a complete overhaul – Everton's **John Collins**, January 1999.

To this day, he is the best coach I have had – Former Rangers striker **Brian Laudrup** on Smith, December 1999.

Walter Smith was, and is, one of the most honest and honourable men in football. He brought a stability and dignity to Everton when we desperately needed it. The difficulty was the finality of ending a working relationship with someone who, on a level of integrity, stability and honesty, is as a high a human being as I have been associated with – Everton vice-chairman **Bill Kenwright**, sacking the former Rangers manager, March 2002.

Someone like him, who has made history in Scotland, can't be left outside. I think he deserves the chance to be the manager of the national side. When you think of a Scottish or English manager, you think of a really aggressive person. But even if there were problems with the players, he would always come out of it with dignity – AC Milan midfielder **Rino Gattuso**, March 2003.

He was a great coach at Dundee United but wee Jim had him tied down with a belt-and-braces contract: it was a playing contract, coaching contract, groundsman contract – so I couldn't get him – Manchester United manager **Sir Alex Ferguson** on getting Smith as his number two at Old Trafford, March 2004.

The best counsellor I ever had – **Paul Gascoigne** on Walter Smith, in *Gazza: My Story*, 2004.

During the week leading up to my first Old Firm game, Walter Smith told me, 'Rino, please, be careful for the first ten minutes, don't commit yourself in tackles and don't make silly challenges.' Well, after 20 seconds I was booked so when I was back in the dressing room at half-time Walter wanted to kill me. A boot flew over my head – luckily I was really quick to react or I'd have a huge scar today – Milan midfielder **Rino Gattuso** on Walter Smith, on Italian TV show *Sfide*, March 2008. (Gattuso committed the first foul of the game, in November 1997, after 20 seconds and was booked after three minutes following a scuffle with Tom Boyd.)

Walter's man-management was incredible – he was the type of manager you wanted to play for. He had several big egos, like Ally McCoist and Gazza, in one team but still managed to hold everything together – **Brian Laudrup** on former Rangers manager Walter Smith, naming him as manager of 'My Perfect XI', March 2008.

What I'd say about him is that he's a really good person. Leaving aside what he's done in football, he's just a really good man – Partick Thistle manager **Ian McCall** on Walter Smith, prior to facing Rangers in the Scottish Cup semi-finals, March 2008.

WINNING ⚽

When I was in my first cup final as manager of Aberdeen we were 1–0 up, and Rangers scored two goals in the last two minutes of injury-time . . . I had prayed as well, that day, and I thought I would never do it again. They beat us 2–1, even though I had prayed to God – Manchester United manager **Sir Alex Ferguson**, October 2008, recalling praying as Chelsea took their second-last penalty in the 2008 Champions League Final (which Chelsea scored from). (Aberdeen, who'd led, lost 2–1 to Rangers in the League Cup Final in March 1979, to late goals from Alex MacDonald and Colin Jackson.)

We just seemed to spend our lives having civic receptions and dinner dances – Former Aberdeen director **Chris Anderson**'s widow, Christine, on the Alex Ferguson era at Aberdeen, in Michael Crick, *The Boss: The Many Sides of Alex Ferguson*, 2002.

During the season Rangers were going for ten, whenever I was asked about the significance of the campaign, I used to try to play it down and say it didn't bother me. Believe me, it did – Former Celtic manager **Billy McNeill** on the 1997–98 season when Celtic prevented Rangers winning ten titles in succession, in Mark Guidi, *The Inner Sanctum*, 2008.

The priest spotted us and at the end of the mass he said that we should all pray for our loved ones and also that the two lads at the back of the chapel and their teammates get the right result that afternoon. Everyone turned to look at us. We were so embarrassed – Former Celtic defender **Malky Mackay** recalls going to mass with teammate Phil O'Donnell on the morning of the title-clinching game against St Johnstone in May 1998, in Mark Guidi, *The Inner Sanctum*, 2008.

I remember him saying, after we'd won the championship in 1980, Aberdeen's first for 25 years, 'Right, you're a one-trophy team, one-trophy wonders. How about winning two every year?' – Former Aberdeen midfielder **John McMaster** on Alex Ferguson's approach, May 1999.

I have my doubts that Aberdeen would have won the title without him –
Celtic manager **Gordon Strachan** on unsung Aberdeen teammate Andy Watson's
role in winning the league title in 1980, in autobiography, *Strachan: My Life In
Football*, 2006.

People tend to forget how the game was structured, how we approached
it. Although it went to extra time, we really battered them, attacked them.
That was the bravery of the team. We should have won by five or six – **Alex
Ferguson** on Aberdeen's 1983 Cup Winners' Cup Final win over Real Madrid, May
2003.

I have no hat but otherwise I would take my hat off – Rangers manager **Dick
Advocaat** on his team after the 4–0 win over Celtic, March 2000.

The toughest, meanest and most cussed competitor I've met in the whole of
my football life. To be any use to him, you have to win – Former Manchester
United captain **Steve Bruce** on Alex Ferguson, 2000.

After we won the double at the end of my second season I could sense
something was wrong. I almost had to push my players out the door to
celebrate with the supporters as if, after winning five trophies out of six, they
were taking it for granted. I was thinking, 'What is going on here?' – Former
Rangers manager **Dick Advocaat**, September 2002.

When critics of our game parade their theories about the attributes that
lift certain teams above others, I am always amused by their eagerness to
concentrate almost exclusively on technical and tactical comparisons.
Frequently they discuss football in abstract terms, overlooking the reality that
it is played by creatures of flesh and blood and feeling. Tactics are important,
but they don't win football matches. Men win football matches – Manchester
United manager **Sir Alex Ferguson**, in *The 90-Minute Manager, Lessons From The
Sharp End Of Management*, David Bolsover & Chris Brady, 2002.

If we don't win it, it will be because someone, somewhere decided it was
someone else's turn and maybe decided that two years ago. You don't know
what promises have been made to them over the last couple of years. You
don't know what deals have been done – First Minister **Jack McConnell** on
Austria/Switzerland's chance of beating Scotland/Ireland's hopes of hosting Euro
2008, September 2002. The Austria/Swiss bid was successful three months later.

The night before, the trainer came up to me and said, 'If you get the ball
try and hit a diagonal pass,' and funnily enough we got the corner and when
it broke to me that was the first thing in my head, to cross it diagonally
– and Karl-Heinz Riedle jumped and chested it down and scored – **Paul
Lambert** recalls his contribution to Riedle's opener for Borussia Dortmund in the 1997
Champions League Final, *BBC TV Footballer's Lives*, March 2003.

In football anything can happen. Even when you're 4–1 down with 10 minutes to go, you think, 'We could get three goals in 10 minutes.' – Actor, Hibs fan and optimist **Dougray Scott**, March 2003.

In Scotland, because of the Old Firm, it is very, very difficult to be a fan of a small team and accept that you may go the whole of your life and win nothing. That requires a level of dedication that is hard to comprehend – Channel 4 Head of Programes and St Johnstone fan **Stuart Cosgrove**, in *Fanatical About Football*, ed. Jeff Connor, 2003.

The thrill is only at the moment of achievement, then it's gone and we move on – Manchester United manager **Sir Alex Ferguson**, March 2004.

He's scored! He's scored! McDonald has scored for Motherwell. Scott McDonald has scored. The Celtic players can't believe it. They are dead on their feet. 1–1 at Fir Park. The title will be heading to Easter Road. To Rangers. The helicopter is changing direction – Radio Clyde commentator **Peter Martin** as Motherwell beat Celtic 2–1 and Rangers win the title, 22 May, 2005. The last line entered the Scottish football vocabulary and final-day finishes became known as 'Helicopter Sunday'.

People talk about winners and people who don't like losing but not liking losing isn't the point. It's about being a competitor. People can win or lose but you can still be a competitor. You don't become a winner if you beat your kids at Scrabble. 'I don't like my kids winning at Scrabble' or 'I won a League Cup medal in 1962' . . . oh, you're a real winner, you must be a right good competitor! – Celtic manager **Gordon Strachan**, July 2005.

As everyone knows, Martin (O'Neill) is a competitive man – he likes to win. Golf is one of those magical sports where you hit one or two good shots and feel you should be able to repeat it and Martin is definitely in what I would describe as the early stages of golf addiction – Celtic majority shareholder **Dermot Desmond**, November 2005.

He wanted to win so badly that when you looked in his eyes you saw a man on the verge of insanity – Former Rangers midfielder **Jorg Albertz** on new Hearts interim head first-team coach Valdas Ivanauskas, March 2006. They had been teammates at Hamburg in the 1990s.

I'm astonished anyone else is being mentioned. I've nothing against (Kilmarnock manager) Jim Jefferies or (Gretna's) Rowan Alexander but when you win your national championship and are 20 points ahead of the nearest club and have the edge over your greatest rivals that's not being anti-Kilmarnock, it's stating facts – Celtic chairman **Brian Quinn** as a debate rages over Scotland's Manager of the Year, April 2006. Gordon Strachan eventually won it.

Look at Alex (McLeish). He won the two available trophies when he joined Rangers with a team that Dick Advocaat could no longer motivate. People complain there is no challenge to the Old Firm, so Hearts come along. Alex gets Rangers to the last 16 of the Champions League, takes Hearts all the way in the race for second place and that constitutes a terrible season worthy of the sack. I don't understand what people want sometimes – Former Kilmarnock and Hibs manager **Bobby Williamson**, May 2006.

It's unconventional but I also believe it isn't good manners. I find it very unprofessional – St Johnstone chairman **Geoff Brown** on Gretna owner Brooks Mileson, after Gretna had pipped St Johnstone to the First Division title, April 2007. Mileson stands with Gretna's fans rather than going into boardrooms before games.

I sent Brooks, Davie Irons, and Andy Smith texts to congratulate them. Football is difficult enough without people in it having a go at each other – St Johnstone manager **Owen Coyle** takes his side's defeat differently, April 2007.

What is sport about? It's competition. If you achieve, you progress. No argument – Gretna caretaker manager **Davie Irons**, on criticism the club had bought their way to success after three successive promotions took them into the SPL, June 2007.

James McFadden said after the Italy game that UEFA don't want small countries in their European Championships. Well, there's a feeling the SPL don't want small clubs either. Who's going to come up from the First Division this season? If it's Hamilton will they let them in with their Astroturf pitch? The reality is they probably only want Dundee, Dunfermline, St Johnstone or Morton to go up – Gretna manager **Davie Irons**, November 2007.

When I was home I met my uncle Des and we went to George Square to meet some of my cousins. He introduced me to them and said I'd just won the league title in the USA for the second time and I could see them shrugging their shoulders and thinking, 'So what?' – MLS side Houston Dynamo's Glasgow-born coach **Dominic Kinnear**, December 2007.

If Scotland win George will get all the praise. And if Scotland lose I'll get all the blame – George Burley's new Scotland assistant manager **Terry Butcher** assesses his career prospects, February 2008.

In my finals in the European games, three of them have been pouring with rain – and when the rain came down I said, 'This is my day!' – Manchester United manager **Sir Alex Ferguson**, in interview with Sir David Frost, June 2008, on winning the Champions League Final against Chelsea in Moscow the previous month.

WISE WORDS ⚽

You show 'em, son. Is this the same Alex Ferguson that I knew as a young lad, that I presented with his first chance in management? The one that I saw running full-pelt down the track towards a linesman in a rage, the one I had to haul back from any trouble? Is this the same man who is going to give in easy now at Manchester United? – Former East Stirling chairman **Willie Muirhead** gives Alex Ferguson some advice during dark Old Trafford days, circa January 1990, in Alex Ferguson, 'Just Champion!', 1993.

On his first day as Wycombe manager, he came in, wished us all the best and made a promise. He looked us in the eye and said, 'I may not be successful here, but if I'm not, you'll all be gone before I will.' We laughed, but we realised the steely determination that under-pinned what he'd said – Former Celtic winger **Steve Guppy** on Martin O'Neill, August 2006.

If you get involved in that, then it is only natural you would look to see who liked to drink alcohol the most and how much they would take in an evening. You can guess about some things, but on certain things it is maybe better to not know the 100 per cent truth – Former Celtic manager **Wim Jansen** on his 1997–98 title-winning side's drinking habits, in Mark Guidi, *The Inner Sanctum*, 2008.

'Man of the Match' is irrelevant unless you win – Celtic midfielder **Paul Lambert**, May 1999.

If footballers think they are above the manager's control, there is only one word to say: 'Goodbye' – Manchester United manager **Alex Ferguson**, 1999.

If you live your life according to someone else's rules, what have you got? Someone else's life – Benfica executive director **Steve Archibald**, June 1999.

Referees don't pass the ball, score goals or win matches – Celtic coach **John Barnes**, January 2000, the day after chief executive Allan MacDonald announced the findings of an independent psychiatrist's report on the Old Firm game of May 1999.

This was a problem that John Barnes should have kept under control and he didn't. If you've got a situation like that, the coach must just say, 'Shut up! Nobody speak! Shut up! It is me who is speaking. If you concentrate when you go out there, you will beat them I'm sure. So relax.' Still, as they say in my country, 'Everyone is a general after the war.' – Former Celtic midfielder **Lubo Moravcik** on half-time in the February 2000 Celtic v Inverness Caledonian Thistle Scottish Cup-tie, in Graham McColl, *The Head Bhoys*, 2002. An argument between assistant coach Eric Black and striker Mark Viduka saw the Australian fail to appear for the second-half.

Sometimes you wake up and you don't feel at your best. That's something you learn to cope with over the years. But you can't use it as an excuse. You have to find ways of getting through it. There are lots of reasons why it might happen. You might not have slept well. You might be staying away in a strange bed. In a foreign country you might get crap food and you don't get the ideal preparation. But what you've got to get in your head is that the guy you're playing against might be feeling worse – Coventry midfielder **Gary McAllister**, March 2000.

Statistics are like miniskirts. They give you good ideas but hide the most important things – Wacky old Aberdeen manager **Ebbe Skovdahl** responds to the news that statistically, his Pittodrie striker Arild Stavrum was better than Celtic's Henrik Larsson, April 2001.

The operation was a success but the patient died – Aberdeen manager **Ebbe Skovdahl** after a stuffy defensive performance restricted Celtic to a 2–0 win over his side, September 2001. Aberdeen had lost their three previous games against Celtic by 5–0, 6–0 and 7–0. (The expression is a Danish proverb: 'Operationen var en succes, men patienten døde'.)

I don't think we should sell the skin before we kill the bear – The unstoppable **Ebbe Skovdahl**, after being asked if a top-six spot was secure after Aberdeen beat St Johnstone, February 2002. (Aberdeen finished fourth and qualified for the UEFA Cup.)

You're not allowed to be humorous and a gaffer now. The fans and the media won't have it. People see you as not caring enough and if you're too serious folk say you're miserable. It's impossible to be yourself – Dundee manager **Jim Duffy**, September 2002.

The guys with the shirts and ties have turned into yobs. They sit there and drink for three hours before the game, then they take their seats. They're actually the worst – Southampton manager **Gordon Strachan**, January 2003.

One time I gave some biscuits to a five or six-year-old boy and he started crying. I'd forgotten certain things – you get angry because you've been left on the bench, and there are children who cry with joy about getting a biscuit – AC Milan midfielder **Rino Gattuso**, March 2003. The thing is, the players think he's good. Therefore he is good – Everton boss **David Moyes** on a French fitness coach at the club, April 2003.

I'm in a terrific job. A difficult job at the best of times and an almost impossible job at the worst – Celtic manager **Martin O'Neill**, September 2003, after being linked with the Spurs job.

(Ally) McCoist was great with me, as long as he scored one goal more than me – Former Rangers striker **Kevin Drinkell**, December 2003.

The first call I got in hospital was from Fergie. Incredible! Manchester United played that day and an hour later he was on the phone. The first thing he said – before his name – was, 'You're trying to change players, aren't you? Trying to bend their characters?' I said, 'Who is that?' He told me, asked how I was, I said, 'Fine', and he went on, 'Never try it. Get rid of them.' It was a good rule. And I've often broken it! I've taken waifs and strays, thinking I can change them – Plymouth manager **Paul Sturrock**, January 2004, recalling Alex Ferguson's reaction to news he'd been taken to hospital with a suspected heart scare (actually caused by hyperventilating).

Always underplay your hand, that was the upbringing I had. Keep a calm sooch. The same manager who had a bad run last season is having a good one now. I'm not doing the job any differently – Preston boss **Craig Brown**, January 2004. ('Keep a calm sooch' means 'stay calm'.)

I always look at a knock-back as a kick-start for a comeback. You're always likely to get kicked in the teeth in this game and you've just got to respond to it – Forfar manager **Ray Stewart**, January 2004. He'd previously been sacked by Livingston and Stirling Albion. He quit as Forfar boss in November 2004.

I'd rather make a mistake playing for my country than I would playing for a pub team – Dundee United goalkeeper **Paul Gallacher** on his April 2003 blunder for Scotland against Austria, February 2004.

I would like to make it mandatory that anyone who plays football at any level has to referee at least one game a season. Whether it be a bounce game at training, a youth team game or whatever, why not have senior players referee a game? They would be a lot more sympathetic if they did – Referee **Kenny Clark**, March 2004, before refereeing his ninth Old Firm game.

When he took over the England job in 1996, Walter Smith said to me, 'Be careful – Hoddle will want to make a name for himself.' I didn't know at the time what he meant by that. It would be two years before I understood – **Paul Gascoigne** on England manager Glenn Hoddle, in *Gazza: My Story*, 2004.

They keep saying it is a short career. Your career as a writer is a short career if you're bloody rubbish at it. Why shouldn't football players that are rubbish have a short career too? A career is not short if you are good at it – Former Dundee United manager **Jim McLean** lectures *Sunday Times* journalist Douglas Alexander, April 2004.

You don't get paid for managing any team because that's great fun. You get paid for the stress that goes along with everything else – Former Southampton manager **Gordon Strachan**, January 2005.

It's one of the most stupid words I've ever heard, speculating on football.

Speculating is throwing money away. Football speculation is oxymoronic – Majority shareholder **Dermot Desmond** to the Celtic Supporters Association, December 2005.

I never talk about winning. I talk about playing well, believing in each other and respecting each other, passing the ball well. If we do all these things well enough the result will take care of itself – Hibs manager **Tony Mowbray**, September 2006.

The Old Firm Alliance thing that's been going for the last couple of years has been very successful, trying to educate kids to integrate with one another and not to pay any attention to who's a Catholic and who's a Protestant and all that rubbish. Just get out there and support your team and enjoy it and make good friends and get on with your lives. It's only the morons that keep this stuff going. But as long as they're there and influencing their children to be that way, then we're always going to have a problem. But with the new initiatives, hopefully children can grow up and think for themselves and get to the stage where they don't want to be tainted with bigotry and sectarianism. And please God that's something that comes quickly. Because we're all fed up talking about it, fed up listening to it, fed up living in it – Celtic coach **Tommy Burns**, before the Old Firm game, March 2007.

He will walk away from his toy when it gets rusty. If he stopped for any reason the club would plummet right down and wouldn't be in football at all – St Johnstone chairman **Geoff Brown**, on Division One title challengers Gretna's backer Brooks Mileson, April 2007. The club folded in August 2008.

The American philosopher and writer Elbert Hubbard said the only way to avoid criticism was to do nothing, say nothing and be nothing. That's how you avoid criticism and certainly this job is not about avoiding criticism – New SFA chief executive **Gordon Smith**, June 2007.

Wee Jim (McLean) was unique. I think he'd admit that himself. One thing I did admire about him was that after a game he never generalised. He went through it with each player individually – otherwise they kid themselves the manager's talking about someone else. He was right about that, but not the way he said it – Morton manager **Jim McInally** on his former Tannadice boss, July 2007.

We can bring the best kids here to Rangers, but for every really good young footballer, there are 10,000 who just want to kick a ball. They're the ones we need to look after. Somehow, though, it seems that priorities are always somewhere else. Holyrood came up with the smoking ban, which is great for public health – but which costs absolutely nothing to implement. Sports projects? They're expensive so they get pushed down the list – Rangers manager **Walter Smith**, November 2007.

I spoke to (former SFA secretary) Ernie Walker before I started and he put me right about how things would be. He said, 'Don't think because you have been in both football and the media you are going to be accepted. It goes with the territory that this doesn't happen.' – SFA chief executive **Gordon Smith**, March 2008.

More worrying still are the comments of Jan Vennegoor of Hesselink, who said that Lennon could teach this team what it means to play for Celtic. No need, Neil – allow me. Jan, playing for Celtic is the same as playing for PSV Eindhoven or FC Twente. You get paid and you do your job. Nothing anyone tells you about the history of this club is going to make you a better player – Former Celtic midfielder **Craig Burley** on the arrival of Neil Lennon at Celtic as a coach, April 2008.

If you sack the manager because he's made a c*** of it, what about the p*** that appointed him? – Hamilton chairman **Ronnie MacDonald** delicately explains why he gave manager Billy Reid a three-year rolling contract after winning promotion to the SPL, July 2008.

Everyone can look good when the sun is shining. But who's going to look good in the rain? – Swindon Town manager **Maurice Malpas**, August 2008. He was sacked three months later.

I learned a vital lesson that day. I went on that day with people I considered my friends. And in this job you maybe don't have friends – SFA chief executive **Gordon Smith**, on TV programme, *From Player To Power*, September 2008. He was referring to being involved in a heated debate on *BBC Radio Scotland* – where he'd previously been a pundit – in January 2008.

You know my definition of friendship – the real friend is the one who walks through the door when the others are putting on their coats to leave – Manchester United manager **Sir Alex Ferguson**, March 2009.

Everything but everything is done for Mr Modern-Day Footballer. I was talking to the catering manager at Forest recently and he was telling me they had 15 types of bread. All I wanted when I was playing was f****** pan or plain. But that's the trouble now, there's no pan or plain – Former Nottingham Forest and Scotland defender **Kenny Burns**, May 2009.

Working hard is actually good for you. I hear that people want to retire at 50 or 55 and I can't believe that. What are they going to do with their lives? Sit in the house and read the bloody papers or twiddle their thumbs when there's a world out there that you should be working for? – Manchester United manager **Sir Alex Ferguson**, aged 67, May 2009.

YOUNG PLAYERS ⚽

A man of the world in a young man's clothes – Nottingham Forest manager **Brian Clough** on Martin O'Neill, in book 'Walking On Water: My Life', 1992.

If Kenny Dalglish didn't have any Y-fronts he would moan like f***. You had to be on your toes and it made me think about others – Derby manager **Paul Jewell** recalls being on the YTS at Liverpool, December 2007.

He was a natural athlete, but very, very competitive. From a young age when the team would be getting a hiding Gordon would never give up. He would have tears in his eyes but would keep going, always chasing lost causes – **Ken MacAskill**, English teacher at Gordon Strachan's Secondary School, Craigroyston, in *Gordon Strachan: The Biography*, Leo Moynihan, 2004.

I was his bootboy at Aberdeen but he scored a goal in the Scottish Cup final with my boots on. I'm not saying I forgot to pack his boots, but his boots weren't there and he had to wear my boots against Rangers in 1982, a 4–1 victory. It was a hell of a goal – he curled it in the top corner – Norwich manager **Bryan Gunn** on Birmingham manager Alex McLeish, March 2009.

When I had played 15 first-team games, I knocked on the gaffer's door, went in and told him I thought I deserved a club car like the other guys were getting. He just looked at me for a moment before shouting, 'Club car? Club car? Club bike more like!' I've never been in there since – Manchester United's **Ryan Giggs**, 2002.

This one kid, he was Scottish, young MacDonald, he was big. He put the ball through my legs and said, 'Nuts.' My coaching staff were like, 'Oh my God, what has he done?' I went mad, jumping up and down like Yosemite Sam. 'I've played 840-odd games, and you've played none. I've played around the world and you've played for Upty Mupty XI and you've got the cheek to shout "nuts" to me.' The colour drained from his face. Be my friend, talk to me, but I deserve respect and there has to be a line drawn – **Gordon Strachan** on a training-ground incident at Coventry, February 2005.

Having joined at 16 he became top scorer at under-18 and under-21 levels. In two top-team starts he scored three goals, had an assist and won a man of the match award. I really think the fans should draw their own conclusions from that – Former Celtic defender **Andy Lynch** on son Simon, after he left Celtic for Preston, January 2003.

With every year that passes, I keep that experience inside me as something positive. I grew up lots mentally, and I can say that what Milan are giving me now, Rangers gave me before – AC Milan's **Rino Gattuso** on early years at Ibrox, March 2003.

I remember hearing that names such as Kevin McNaughton and Stephen Crainey were the new sensations coming through. After playing a couple of times under Berti, though, they've never been seen again. I don't think they're even in the under-21 set-up – Former Scotland midfielder **Craig Burley** after the 6–0 defeat by Holland, November 2003.

I think he can be the new Barry Ferguson or maybe even a bit better. He is quite like (Darren) Fletcher in style, build and posture – **Bert Konterman**, then at Vitesse Arnhem, on ex-Rangers teammate Stephen Hughes, November 2003.

Would this be the same Philip Scott for whom I procured boots and kit? The same Philip Scott who could boast an appearance in Chris Evans' 'star-bar' on live TV as a result of my contacts? The same Philip Scott for whose sister I obtained free concert tickets? – Agent **Jake Duncan** on having his services as St Johnstone player Scott's agent terminated, February 2004.

How do you calm Scott down? Maybe with a prescription. One hundred mg of Temazepam might just do the trick – Hibs defender **Colin Murdock** on midfielder Scott Brown, February 2004. Brown had been booked, was lucky not to be sent off, and punched by Hearts' Alan Maybury in a lively Edinburgh derby.

I'm as sure about those two as any players who have come here. Absolute certainties, absolute certainties, they are. Temperament, personality, character, determination – everything's there – Manchester United manager **Sir Alex Ferguson** on Cristiano Ronaldo and Darren Fletcher, May 2004.

Where we can beat Celtic and Rangers into a cocked hat is by appreciating our smallness. We are the premier club in Scotland at attracting, retaining, training and bringing young players through to maturity. Any sensible dad wants his kid to play for Motherwell, because if he has the talent he will get his chance – Motherwell owner **John Boyle**, October 2004.

At the moment he's a bit like my teeange son in that everything he does is probably the wrong thing – 'You're not wearing that are you? You're not going out like that?' Nearly everything they do goes awry because they're trying so hard to pull it together. James tries to take people on when he should pass and he passes when he should be taking someone on – Everton manager **David Moyes** on striker James McFadden, November 2004.

Unfortunately, he has also had to deal with some of the country's most arrogant and ignorant young men, who do not see selection for their national team as an honour and a privilege. Herr Bonhof has never divulged the identity of any one of these egotistical swellheads, but his job at times was nearly made impossible by their attitude and performances – Motherwell manager **Terry Butcher** on the problems that faced Scotland under-21 manager Rainer Bonhof, December 2005, days after Bonhof resigned.

I'm conducting a sweepstake to see how many players call off from each group. Does anyone want to play for Scotland? It seems that today's players simply aren't bothered and use their clubs to make up an excuse for more time on the beach. Remember this, you ungrateful egotists – holidays can always be taken after a career has finished. The chance to pull on the Scotland jersey, at any level, should never be sacrificed for a snooze on a foreign sunbed – Motherwell manager **Terry Butcher** continues on the attitude of Scotland players, prior to the full squad's end-of-season Kirin Cup trip to Japan and the under-21s' trip to Northern Ireland, May 2006.

A lot of clubs pay lip service to the notion of community football, but we are actually making it work. We are the only club in Britain that doesn't charge schools for providing them with professional coaching staff – we have forged links with over 100 schools in the south of Scotland. I have a huge moral problem with offering youngsters an opportunity to play football then, two or three years down the line, telling them that they aren't good enough and shoving them out of the door. You wouldn't treat your own children in that fashion, would you? And once these teenagers walk into Raydale Park, we are effectively their surrogate family, so we have a responsibility to treat them as more than simply assets on a balance sheet – Gretna owner **Brooks Mileson**, July 2006.

They were late once too often for Jim's liking and he told me to get the three of them to paint the gymnasium. I gave them pots of paint and brushes and told them to whitewash the gym. They were raging. After about an hour I went to see how they were getting on. I couldn't believe it when I walked in. All they'd done was write 'Jim McLean Is A C***' in huge letters on the walls – Former Dundee United striker **Paul Sturrock** on Jim McLean's disciplinary style backfiring on young United players Andy McLaren, Duncan Ferguson and John O'Neil, in *Tormented: The Andy McLaren Story* by Andy McLaren and Mark Guidi, 2007.

At the risk of sounding like an old man, today's kids have gone soft. At eight years old they go down and expect a physio to be there for them. They should just get up and get on with it – Celtic manager **Gordon Strachan**, November 2007.

You still have to invest in the youth, you have to make a programme. The boys are coming too late to football. If they don't you will have the same problems in five years that you had when I took over. It needs money but the quality now is much higher than I had. I know that, you know that, the people on the street know that – Former Scotland manager **Berti Vogts**, November 2007.

(Assistant manager) Jimmy Nicholl has these wee games for the kids. We asked one of them who was the manger of Scotland and he didn't know. It's only been in the paper over the past eight weeks. How sad is that? We asked him again the next day and he still didn't know. If he doesn't find out quick he won't be at Aberdeen too long. You would think he would have found out but he was probably on the internet or some garbage – Aberdeen manager **Jimmy Calderwood**, February 2008.

I'm not sure I would have been out in the pouring rain kicking a ball all the time if I had a Nintendo Wii at home. It's a natural thing – Head of Manchester United's youth academy **Brian McClair**, May 2008.

I'm generalising, but I don't think some kids are as hungry or as dedicated as they used to be. There's a *laissez-faire* attitude, that it's not really 'cool' to work hard and do things. The culture is changing and I'm not saying changing for the better. It's becoming harder and harder to get kids playing football – Wigan assistant manager **Eric Black**, August 2008.

I actually wouldn't want him to turn out to be some slippery wee bastard who changes his mind and plays for someone else after he's been well looked after by the Irish. And he has been – Hamilton Accies chairman **Ronnie MacDonald** on midfielder James McCarthy's decision to keep playing for the Republic of Ireland, amid suggestions Scotland were trying to woo him, October 2008. McCarthy, then 17, was born in Glasgow but plays for Ireland through his grandfather.

I'm the only one still here from my year group. There were others who could control, pass and shoot the ball as good as me but I think football is played in your head – Manchester United midfielder **Darren Fletcher**, March 2009.

All that business of people at clubs treating young players like shite, bullying them, getting them to wash their cars – all that kind of thing belongs to another era. That's not how to treat people – Hamilton Accies chairman **Ronnie MacDonald**, May 2009.

Bibliography

David Bolsover & Chris Brady: *The 90-Minute Manager, Lessons From The Sharp End Of Management*, Prentice Hall, 2002.

Tom Bower: *Broken Dreams: Vanity, Greed, & The Souring of English Football*, Simon & Schuster, 2003.

Jock Brown: *Celtic-Minded: 510 Days In Paradise*, Mainstream, 1999.

Bill Bryson: *Notes From A Small Island*, Black Swan,1995.

Brian Clough: *Cloughie: Walking On Water – My Life*, Headline, 2002

Brian Clough: *Clough: The Autobiography*, Corgi, 1994.

Jeff Connor: *Pointless: A Season With Britain's Worst Football Team*, Headline, 2005.

Michael Crick: *The Boss: The Many Sides of Alex Ferguson*, Pocket, 2002.

Ed. Jeff Connor, *Fanatical About Football*, Mainstream, 2003.

Ronnie Esplin and Graham Walker: *It's Rangers For Me?* Fort, 2008.

Alex Ferguson and Peter Fitton: *Just Champion!*, Manchester United F.C., 1993.

Alex Ferguson: *Managing My Life*, Coronet, 1999

100 Favourite Scottish Football Poems, edited by Alistair Findlay, Luath, 2007.

Brad Friedel: *Thinking Outside The Box*, Orion, 2009.

Paul Gascoigne: *Gazza: My Story*, Headline, 2004

Rick Gekoski: *Staying Up: A Fan Behind The Scenes In The Premiership*, Little, Brown, 1998.

Andy Gray and Jim Drewett: *Flat Back Four – The Tactical Game*, Reedswain Incorporated, 2003.

Martin Greig: *The Zen of Naka*, Mainstream, 2008

Mark Guidi: *The Inner Sanctum*, Mainstream, 2008

Jimmy Hill: *My Autobiography*, Coronet, 1998.

Gary Imlach: *My Father And Other Working-Class Football Heroes*, Yellow Jersey, 2005.

John Keith: *Shanks For The Memory*, Robson, 1998.

Stephen F. Kelly: *Fergie*, Headline, 1997

Bill Leckie: *Penthouse & Pavement*, Mainstream, 1999.

Bobby Lennox: *Thirty Miles From Paradise: My Story*, Headline, 2007

Graham McColl: *The Head Bhoys*, Mainstream, 2002

Ronnie Esplin and Frank McGarvey: *Totally Frank*, Mainstream, 2008.

Andy McLaren and Mark Guidi: *Tormented: The Andy McLaren Story*, Mainstream, 2007.

Alex McLeish: *The Don of an Era*, John Donald, 1988.

Peter Marinello: *Fallen Idle: Fighting Back from the Booze, Swindles and Drugs That Ripped My Life Apart*, Headline, 2007.

Steve Menary: *Outcasts! The Lands That FIFA Forgot*, Know The Score, 2007

Andy Mitten: *Mad For It: Football's Greatest Rivalries*, HarperSport, 2008.

Leo Moynihan: *Gordon Strachan: The Biography*, Virgin, 2004.

Alex Montgomery: *Martin O'Neill – The Biography*, Virgin, 2003.

Peter Ridsdale: *United We Fall: Boardroom Truths about the Beautiful Game*, Pan, 2007.

Wayne Rooney: *My Story So Far*, HarperSport, 2006.

Irving Scholar: *Behind Closed Doors: Dreams & Nightmares At Spurs*, Andrew Deutsch, 1992.

Graeme Sharp: *Sharpy*, Mainstream, 2007.

Graham Spiers : *Paul le Guen: Enigma, A Chronicle of Trauma and Turmoil at Rangers*, Mainstream, 2007.

Mel Sterland: *Boozing, Betting & Brawling: A Footballer's Life*, Green Umbrellla, 2008.

Gordon Strachan: My Life In Football, Little, Brown, 2006.

John Sugden & Alan Tomlinson: *Great Balls of Fire: How Big Money Is Highjacking World Football*, Mainstream, 1999.

Daniel Taylor: *This Is The One: The Uncut Story Of A Football Genius*, Aurum, 2007.

Jim Wilkie: *Bonetti's Blues: Dundee FC and its Cultural Experiment*, Mainstream, 2001.

Jeff Winter: *Who's The B*****d In The Black? – Confessions of a Premiership Referee*, Ebury, 2006.

Index